The Characteristic Symphony in the Age of Haydn and Beethoven

Associated through descriptive texts with literature, politics, religion, and other subjects, "characteristic" symphonies offer an opportunity to study instrumental music as it engages important social and political debates of the eighteenth and early nineteenth centuries: the nature of individual and collective identity in an era of violent political transformation; the effects of a perceived acceleration of history after the French Revolution; the conflicts between "Enlightened" and "Romantic" ideals of artistic expression. This first full-length study of the genre illuminates the relationship between symphonies and these larger contexts by focusing on the musical representation of feeling, human physical movement, and the passage of time. The works discussed include Beethoven's *Pastoral* and *Eroica* Symphonies, Haydn's *Seven Last Words of our Savior on the Cross*, Carl Ditters von Dittersdorf's symphonies on Ovid's *Metamorphoses*, and orchestral battle reenactments of the Revolutionary and Napoleonic eras. A separate chapter details the aesthetic context within which characteristic symphonies were conceived, as well as their subsequent reception, and a series of appendixes summarizes bibliographic information for over 225 relevant examples.

RICHARD WILL is Associate Professor of Music at the University of Virginia. He has articles on Beethoven, Haydn, and other topics in eighteenth- and early nineteenth-century music in the *Journal of the American Musicological Society, Music and Letters,* and *Beethoven Forum.* He has also written a series of critical essays on Jimi Hendrix for the *International Dictionary of Black Composers.*

New perspectives in music history and criticism

GENERAL EDITORS

JEFFREY KALLBERG, RUTH SOLIE, AND ANTHONY NEWCOMB

This series explores the conceptual frameworks that shape or have shaped the ways in which we understand music and its history, and aims to elaborate structures of explanation, interpretation, commentary, and criticism which make music intelligible and which provide a basis for argument about judgments of value. The intellectual scope of the series is broad. Some investigations will treat, for example, historiographical topics, others will apply cross-disciplinary methods to the criticism of music, and there will also be studies which consider music in its relation to society, culture, and politics. Overall, the series hopes to create a greater presence for music in the ongoing discourse among the human sciences.

PUBLISHED TITLES

Leslie C. Dunn and Nancy A. Jones (eds.), *Embodied voices: representing female vocality in western culture*

Downing A. Thomas, *Music and the origins of language: theories from the French Enlightenment*

Thomas S. Grey, *Wagner's musical prose*

Daniel K. L. Chua, *Absolute music and the construction of meaning*

Adam Krims, *Rap music and the poetics of identity*

Annette Richards, *The free fantasia and the musical picturesque*

Richard Will, *The characteristic symphony in the age of Haydn and Beethoven*

Christopher Morris, *Reading opera between the lines: orchestral interludes and cultural meaning from Wanger to Berg*

Emma Dillon, *Medieval Music-Making and the 'Roman de Fauvel'*

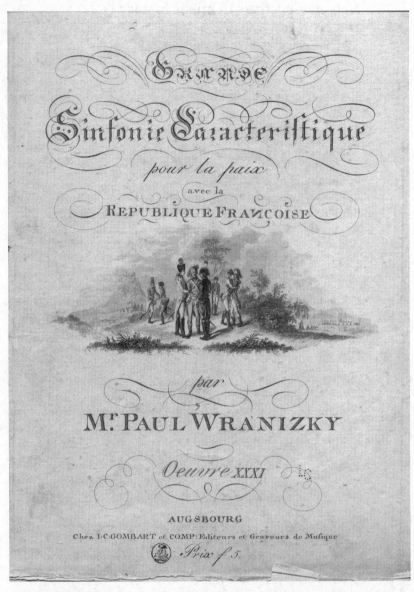

Title page of Paul Wranitzky's *Grande Sinfonie caractéristique pour la paix avec la République françoise* (1797). Library of Congress, Washington, DC

The Characteristic Symphony in the Age of Haydn and Beethoven

RICHARD WILL

CAMBRIDGE
UNIVERSITY PRESS

PUBLISHED BY THE PRESS SYNDICATE OF THE UNIVERSITY OF CAMBRIDGE
The Pitt Building, Trumpington Street, Cambridge, United Kingdom

CAMBRIDGE UNIVERSITY PRESS
The Edinburgh Building, Cambridge CB2 2RU, UK
40 West 20th Street, New York, NY 10011-4211, USA
477 Williamstown Road, Port Melbourne, VIC 3207, Australia
Ruiz de Alarcón 13, 28014 Madrid, Spain
Dock House, The Waterfront, Cape Town 8001, South Africa

http://www.cambridge.org

First published 2002

Printed in the United Kingdom at the University Press, Cambridge

Typeface Palatino 10/12 pt.   *System* LATEX 2$_\varepsilon$ [TB]

A catalogue record for this book is available from the British Library.

Library of Congress Cataloguing in Publication data

Will, Richard James.
The characteristic symphony in the age of Haydn and Beethoven / Richard Will.
      p.   cm. – (New perspectives in music history and criticism)
Includes bibliographical references and index.
ISBN 0 521 80201 6
1. Symphony – 18th century.   2. Symphony – 19th century.   3. Music – 18th
century – Philosophy and aesthetics.   4. Music – 19th century – Philosophy and
aesthetics.   5. Program music.   I. Title.   II. Series.
ML1255 .W56   2001
784.2'184 – dc21   2001035658

ISBN 0 521 80201 6 hardback

CONTENTS

ACKNOWLEDGMENTS

Research for this book was supported by grants from the German Academic Exchange Service (DAAD) and the Royalty Research Fund at the University of Washington. I am grateful to Marshall Brown, John A. Rice, and James Webster for their insightful comments on drafts of various chapters, and to the numerous scholars with whom I have had an opportunity to discuss the characteristic symphony, especially Wye Jamison Allanbrook, Berthold Hoeckner, Elaine R. Sisman, and Neal Zaslaw. John A. Rice and Mary Sue Morrow kindly shared materials from their own research on Dittersdorf's *Metamorphoses* symphonies and eighteenth-century German music criticism, respectively, and Penny Souster offered encouragement and advice throughout the entire project.

Portions of the Introduction and of Chapter 4 appeared in my article "Time, Morality, and Humanity in Beethoven's *Pastoral* Symphony," *Journal of the American Musicological Society* 50 (1997): 271–329, © 1997 by the American Musicological Society. All rights reserved. Reprinted by kind permission of the University of Chicago Press.

Illustrations are reproduced by permission of the following: frontispiece, Library of Congress, Washington, DC; Fig. 1.1, Fürst zu Bentheimschen Musikaliensammlung Burgsteinfurt.

In preparing scores and musical examples I was fortunate to have the help of several graduate student assistants at the University of Washington, including Dyne Eifertsen, Hayoung Heidi Lee, Nathan Link, George-Julius Papadopoulos, Anne Youngers, and Karla Youngers. Judy Tsou and John Gibbs of the University of Washington Music Library, as well as the staff of the U.W. Interlibrary Borrowing Service, obtained many crucial primary and secondary sources.

Special thanks to several individuals who answered numerous queries regarding manuscripts and prints, sent copies of sources, or provided assistance during visits to their institutions: Prof. Dr. Otto Biba, Archiv der Gesellschaft der Musikfreunde in Wien; Hugo Angerer, Fürst Thurn und Taxis Hofbibliothek Regensburg; Dr. Karl Wilhelm Geck, Sächsische Landesbibliothek Dresden; Dr. Bertram Haller and the late Dr. Albert Ernst, Universitäts- und Landesbibliothek, Westfälische Wilhelms-Universität Münster; Dr. Helmut Hell, Staatsbibliothek zu

Acknowledgments

Berlin – Preußischer Kulturbesitz, Musikabteilung mit Mendelssohn-Archiv; and Dr. Ernesto Milano, Biblioteca Estense, Modena. Information and sources were also graciously provided by the following librarians and institutions. *Austria*: Dr. Anna Plattner, Inge Birken-Feichtinger, and Dorothea Hunger, Österreichische Nationalbibliothek; Dr. Hildegard Herrmann-Schneider, Institut für Tiroler Musikforschung Innsbruck and RISM Westösterreich; Dr. Gregor M. Lechner, OSB, Benediktinerstift Göttweig; Dr. Norbert Müller, Diözesanarchiv, Bischöfliches Ordinariat Graz-Seckau; Regenterei, Benediktiner-Stift Kremsmünster. *Czech Republic*: Vladimír Bartošek, Státní Oblastní Archiv v Třeboni; Dr. Jana Fojtíková, Národní muzeum – České muzeum hudby, Prague; Dr. Laura De Barbieri, The Roudnice Lobkowicz Library, Nelahozeves Castle. *Denmark*: Det Kongelige Bibliotek, Copenhagen. *Finland*: Inger Jakobsson-Wärn, Sibelius Museum, Åbo Akademi University. *France*: Catherine Massip, Bibliothèque nationale de France; Joël Plassard, Bibliothèque de Versailles. *Great Britain*: Richard Andrewes, Cambridge University Library; Nicolas Bell, British Library, London; Martin Thacker, Manchester Public Library. *Germany*: Rudolf Beck, Fürstlich Waldburg-Zeil'sches Gesamtarchiv, Leutkirch; Johannes Beulertz, Hamm; Dr. Rainer Birkendorf, Deutsches Musikgeschichtliches Archiv, Kassel; Sieghard Brandenburg, Beethoven-Archiv, Bonn; Dr. Frohmut Dangel-Hofmann, Graf von Schönborn Hauptverwaltung, Wiesentheid; Gisela Holzhüter, Fürstlich Fürstenbergische Hofbibliothek, Donaueschingen; Hohenlohe-Zentralarchiv Neuenstein; Dr. Bernhard Moosbauer, Musikwissenschaftliches Institut, Universität Tübingen; Dr. Hartmut Schaefer, Bayerische Staatsbibliothek, Munich; Thüringische Landesbibliothek, Weimar; Thüringisches Staatsarchiv Rudolstadt. *Holland*: Dr. W. H. J. Dekker, Stichting Toonkunst-Bibliotheek, Amsterdam; Dr. Dick H. J. van Heuvel, Doetinchem. *Hungary*: Katalin Szerzö, Music Collection, National Széchényi Library, Budapest. *Italy*: Dr. Mario Armellini, Civico Museo Bibliografico Musicale, Bologna. *Slovakia*: Terézia Kaššayová, Matica Slovenská, Archív Literatúry a Umenia, Martin; Miriam Lehotská, Slovenské Národné Múzeum, Hudobné Múzeum, Bratislava. *Sweden*: Anna Lena Holm, Statens Musiksamlingar, Stockholm. *Switzerland*: Schweizerische Landesbibliothek; Zentralbibliothek Zürich. *United States*: Dr. Nola Reed Knouse, Moravian Music Foundation, Bethlehem, PA; New York Public Library; William C. Parsons, Music Division, Library of Congress; Charles Reynolds, University of Michigan Music Library.

Finally, thanks to Melanie Siobhan Lepper for her unfailing support and endless patience.

NOTE TO THE READER

The symphonies discussed in this book are referred to by their characterizing titles, such as *Eroica* Symphony or *Les Quatre Ages du monde*. Where there is no overall title, or the risk of confusing multiple works with the same title, an identifying number along with an author is cited from the most authoritative catalogue or index of the composer's works or symphonies: e.g., Gossec, Symphony in D (Saceanu 23). All references to catalogues and indexes as well as to manuscript locations, editions, movement or work orders, alternate titles, and other matters related to the musical sources are based on the information presented in Appendixes 1 and 2 (pp. 249–98 below).

Translations are mine unless otherwise indicated. Musical examples are provided for all works discussed in detail except the *Eroica* and *Pastoral* Symphonies of Beethoven and the *Military* Symphony of Haydn, for which scores are readily available. For pieces by lesser-known figures, the reader is also encouraged to consult the many excellent recordings being issued by, among others, Concerto Köln, the London Mozart Players, and the ensembles represented in the "18th-Century Symphony" series on the Naxos label. If historically informed performances have revolutionized our understanding of the symphonies of Haydn, Mozart, and Beethoven over the past two decades, these increasingly fine renderings of music by their contemporaries open our ears to the range of compositional voices in the later eighteenth and early nineteenth centuries. The diversity, power, and depth of expression across the whole spectrum of European musical life represented in this period have been a continuing source of inspiration for this study.

INTRODUCTION

"Characteristic" is the most common of several terms used in the eighteenth and early nineteenth centuries to indicate instrumental music in which a subject is specified, usually by a text. Over 225 orchestral works qualify, some with sentences and paragraphs describing each of several movements, or what modern listeners would call a program, and others with only a word or two characterizing a single movement or a whole work (see Appendixes 1 and 2, pp. 249–98 below). They are "symphonies" according to the way in which the word was used at the time, to encompass orchestral pieces of many shapes and sizes rather than solely the three- and four-movement examples that match later conceptions of the genre.[1] The disparity in their texts reflects varying compositional ambitions as well as chronological development, the more elaborate characterizations appearing mostly after 1770 and then with increasing frequency as the years pass.

But however long their texts and whatever their length or structure, symphonies bearing written characterizations in the years 1750–1815 are drawn together by a marked affinity for a few common subjects. Titles consisting of only one or a few words identify over 70 examples as pastoral (Appendix 2), 15 as military, 15 as hunts, 10 as storms, and more than 30 as expressions of national or regional characters – in sum, nearly 150 symphonies or movements as representations of five subject categories (Appendix 3a–d). The lengthier descriptions incorporate the same ingredients into scenarios original to the composers or adapted from literature and current events (Appendix 3e–f). Beethoven's *Pastoral* Symphony (1808) and related works combine multiple pastoral scenes with storms, and his *Wellington's Victory* (1813) belongs to a tradition (at least 16 works for orchestra and over 150 for other instrumental scorings) that absorbs the military style, pastoral interludes, storms, and all variety of national songs and dances into enactments of battles. In the *Werther* of Gaetano Pugnani (1795), the *Télémaques* of

---

[1] Neal Zaslaw, "Mozart, Haydn, and the *Sinfonia da chiesa*," *Journal of Musicology* 1 (1982): 106–07; see also pp. 5–8 below. Throughout this book I use "symphony" in this broad sense and indicate when the reference is specifically to three- and four-movement works.

Ignazio Raimondi (1777) and Antonio Rosetti (1791?), and the twelve symphonies on Ovid's *Metamorphoses* of Carl Ditters von Dittersdorf (1781–86), further pastoral settings along with storms (in Goethe and Fénélon) and hunts and battles (in Ovid) keep the focus on familiar topics. The characteristic symphony is first and foremost a genre of pastoral idylls, thunderstorms, military conflicts, hunts, and political identities.

Each of these subjects encompasses such diverse meanings that the possibilities for interpretation are inexhaustible: no two pastoral symphonies are quite the same despite their shared reliance on a single musical style. In addition, settings and events serve often as a pretext for introducing a second set of subjects, the human emotions, whose qualities and change over time are a preoccupation that envelops works of many kinds. In the tradition of an eighteenth-century keyboard genre known as the "character piece," some symphonies represent feelings in the abstract: Dittersdorf's *Il combattimento delle passioni umane* (no later than 1771) portrays *Il Amante, Il Contento, Il Malinconico*, and others in separate movements or sections (Appendix 3g). More commonly, composers assay the inner lives of dramatic protagonists or of communities caught up in political and natural-world events. In Haydn's *Seven Last Words of Our Savior on the Cross* (1787), the crucifixion becomes a panorama of hope, anger, love, despair, and resignation, each nuanced through the elaboration of the musical ideas, while in Dittersdorf's *Metamorphoses* gods, goddesses, and mortals bare their souls in similarly developmental "arias." In musical battles and other politically inspired works, societies dance for joy or weep for lost comrades, and in pastoral symphonies they express pleasure in idyllic settings or shudder before storms. The most "pictorial" moments – storms, battles, hunts – are overhung by affective connotations, confusing the emotional and the physical in ways that were central to the music's contemporary reception (Chapter 3). There is no subject, however "objective" it may seem, that does not also imply feeling.

Within a few richly significant contexts, then, the characteristic symphony explores the development and definition of human identities by representing the unfolding of emotions through time. To do so using only an orchestra and an unsung, unacted text seems an undertaking more typical of Hector Berlioz and the generations following, but it was no less timely in an age when discussion about music focused on its expressive potential, and when instrumental works with text, as is argued below, encapsulated a paradox whereby music was considered to be at once meaningful and indefinite. In addition, tracing the development of human identities engaged the social and political concerns of a milieu beset by sweeping change. Like the eighteenth- and early nineteenth-century symphony as a whole, the characteristic symphony was the product largely of central Europe and especially of the cities, courts, and religious principalities presided over from Vienna by the Habsburgs. The histories of the genre and the empire are closely entwined, beginning with the two most compelling (and, in their own time, most famous) examples from before the French Revolution, Dittersdorf's *Metamorphoses* and Haydn's *Seven Last Words*. Both treat their subjects so as to reflect on the Enlightenment as it was being imposed on Austria during the 1780s by Emperor Joseph II, Dittersdorf by interpreting Ovid's tales as allegories of an idyllic court society undermined by violent change, and Haydn by writing a Passion that underscores both the "rational" morality of Joseph's reformed church and the "irrational" faith of a more traditional theology (Chapters 1–2). After the Revolution, concerns about a perceived acceleration of history and the emergence of new political forces find echo in Beethoven's *Pastoral* and *Eroica* Symphonies and in a subgenre of works marking the battles, treaties, and deaths of the Revolutionary and Napoleonic Wars. The *Pastoral* revisits an idyllic setting to suggest how it might be rescued from the onslaught of time, and the politically inspired symphonies weigh the competing claims of individual heroes and newly recognized "nations" in the assigning of responsibility for military success (Chapters 4–5). Reflecting a culture in flux, identities both rational and unfathomable, empowered and passive, individual and collective jostle against one another in a discourse in which the emotions, not surprisingly, run high: if some characteristic symphonies exhibit the comic flair of *opera buffa*, the prevailing affinity is for *opera seria* or Revolutionary drama with their grand tableaux, overwhelming passions, paradises and hells and protagonists pushed to the limits of tolerance. The immediacy of the topics requires that feelings be intense, and often ordered so as to juxtapose the extreme states of courage and terror, joy and sorrow, hope and foreboding.

Composers did not see the symphony with text as the ideal medium for exploring aesthetic paradox or social transformation; if they had, there would be more than 225 examples from a period that produced several thousand symphonies (in the broad sense of the term) according to the most comprehensive listing to date.[2] On the other hand, just as symphonies with more and less detailed texts have elements in common, so too do symphonies with and without text, particularly where generalized subjects like the pastoral or the military are concerned. In such contexts many characteristic symphonies do little more than write out the associations that other instrumental works trigger with evocative rhythms, textures, harmonies, or melodic gestures; it might have been impossible to suggest a specific classical myth or historical battle without

---

[2] Jan LaRue, *A Catalogue of Eighteenth-Century Symphonies*, vol. I, *Thematic Identifier* (Bloomington: Indiana University Press, 1988), xii.

verbal prompting, but the idyllic, or violent, or emotive scenes that made up such plots belong to an expressive dialect shared by all music of the time. What the characteristic repertory offers is the opportunity to observe familiar subjects linked explicitly to contemporary musical and social dilemmas, a connection both interesting in its own right and suggestive for instrumental music as a whole. Borrowing language to demonstrate how an otherwise wordless medium might speak, these works stress the potential for symphonies to participate in the most fundamental cultural debates.

Character and characteristic

The primacy of feeling in most characteristic symphonies is implied by the label itself, whose root term, "character," was used partly as a synonym for affect in the eighteenth century.[3] It also carried strong overtones of unity: taking their cue from the "characters" of Theophrastus and La Bruyère, short essays that described a single personality type or temperament, the character pieces for keyboard by Couperin, C. P. E. Bach, and the northern German composers who kept the tradition alive into the 1770s and 80s generally limit themselves to one affect, one nation, one person or personality type of the sort known as "moral characters."[4] Johann Friedrich Reichardt recommends this narrow focus as a means of avoiding the "höchst unnatürlichen Vermischung der entgegengesetzten Leidenschaften . . . unsrer jetztigen Instrumentalmusik" (highly unnatural combination of the opposed passions . . . in our modern instrumental music), a reference to the quick changes of style, modeled on Italian comic opera, that German critics had long distrusted in symphonies and sonatas.[5] In the same paragraph Reichardt also declares it "psychologisch und physikalisch fast unmöglich" (psychologically and physically almost impossible) for a single composer to express contrasting emotions equally well, an opinion that is also found in

[3] Jacob de Ruiter, *Der Charakterbegriff in der Musik. Studien zur deutschen Ästhetik der Instrumentalmusik 1740–1850*, Beihefte zum Archiv für Musikwissenschaft 29 (Stuttgart: Steiner, 1989), 26–33; Mary Sue Morrow, *German Music Criticism in the Late Eighteenth Century: Aesthetic Issues in Instrumental Music* (Cambridge: Cambridge University Press, 1997), 77.

[4] See Ruiter, *Der Charakterbegriff*, 48–79; Darrell Berg, "C. P. E. Bach's Character Pieces and his Friendship Circle," in Stephen L. Clark, ed., *C. P. E. Bach Studies* (Oxford: Clarendon Press, 1988), 1–32; and David Fuller, "Of Portraits, 'Sapho' and Couperin: Titles and Characters in French Instrumental Music of the High Baroque," *Music & Letters* 78 (1997): 149–74.

[5] *Musikalisches Kunstmagazin* 1 (1782): 25. Cf. Ruiter, *Der Charakterbegriff*, 50–51; Morrow, *German Music Criticism*, 47–48, 139–50; and Bellamy Hosler, *Changing Aesthetic Views of Instrumental Music in 18th-Century Germany* (Ann Arbor: UMI Research Press, 1981), 6–8 *et passim*.

the influential *Allgemeine Theorie der schönen Künste* of Johann Georg Sulzer and that means, in effect, that founding a keyboard piece on one appropriate "character" ensures coherence both in the music and between the music and its creator.[6] At the end of the century Christian Gottfried Körner uses the term in a related sense, identifying character with a consistent tone or "ethos" that runs through the multiplicity or "pathos" of a given piece and is its marker of human agency: "Das erste Erforderniß eines Kunstwerkes ist unstreitig, daß es sich als ein menschliches Produkt durch Spuren einer ordnenden Kraft von den Wirkungen des blinden Zufalls unterscheide" (The first requirement of an artwork is indisputable; through signs of an ordering power, it must distinguish itself as a human product, in contrast to the outcome of blind coincidence).[7] Soon enough it would become commonplace to read musical works as instances of artistic self-expression: an important preparation is this connection of musical characters, understood as unifying essences, with the creative personas of their composers.

With the emergence of works naming multiple persons or affects as their subject, "character" and "characteristic" acquire more general meanings. Connotations of unity and human creativity remain; Beethoven's *Eroica* and *Pastoral* Symphonies focus to some degree on a single declared style or idea, and any instrumental work that announces its subject reveals something of the "ordering power" behind it.[8] But when Paul Wranitzky published his *Grande Sinfonie caractéristique pour la paix avec la République françoise* (1797), the qualifier in his title referred to the simple presence of specified subjects, or "caractères" as he calls them in the accompanying explanation, which include the French Revolution,

---

6 "Es ist sehr wichtig, daß der Künstler sich selbst kenne, und wenn es bey ihm steht, nichts unternehme, das gegen seinen Charakter streitet" (It is important that the artist know himself, and whenever possible decline undertaking anything contrary to his character): Sulzer, *Allgemeine Theorie der schönen Künste*, 2nd expanded edn., 4 vols. (Leipzig, 1792–94), I: 271; trans. in Nancy Kovaleff Baker and Thomas Christensen, eds., *Aesthetics and the Art of Musical Composition in the German Enlightenment: Selected Writings of Johann Georg Sulzer and Heinrich Christoph Koch* (Cambridge: Cambridge University Press, 1995), 51. Biographical essays called "Charakteristiken" in German musical journals sought to encapsulate composers' styles and affective leanings (e.g., in the *Musikalisches Taschenbuch* [1803]: 251–92 and [1805]: 338–78), and Muzio Clementi wrote a *Musical Characteristics ... Composed in the Style of Haydn, Kozeluch, Mozart, Sterkel, Vanhal, and the Author* (1787).

7 Körner, "Über Charakterdarstellung in der Musik," *Die Horen* 5 (1795), repr. in Wolfgang Seifert, *Christian Gottfried Körner, ein Musikästhetiker der deutschen Klassik* (Regensburg: Bosse, 1960), 147, trans. in Robert Riggs, " 'On the Representation of Character in Music': Christian Gottfried Körner's Aesthetics of Instrumental Music," *Musical Quarterly* 81 (1997): 613. See also Carl Dahlhaus, "Ethos und Pathos in Glucks *Iphigenie auf Tauris*," *Die Musikforschung* 27 (1974): 289–300.

8 The implication of unity is the focus of F. E. Kirby, "Beethoven's Pastoral Symphony as a *Sinfonia caracteristica*," *Musical Quarterly* 56 (1970): 605–23.

the execution of Louis XVI, and the "cries of joy" greeting the Treaty of Campo Formio between Austria and Napoleon. "Characteristic" applies to similarly mixed scenes and emotions on the title pages of several post-Revolutionary battle pieces for keyboard;[9] in the titles of overtures to spoken plays;[10] in a letter of Justin Heinrich Knecht about his symphony *Tod des Herzogs von Braunschweig*;[11] on the first page of the sketches for Beethoven's *Pastoral* Symphony, the title page of a first violin part for his *Leonore* Overture No. 1, and in a letter concerning the "Les Adieux" Sonata;[12] and in reviews and commentaries on *The Seven Last Words*, the *Metamorphoses* Symphonies, and other works with comparably elaborate texts.[13] Its purview spreads further in the *Essay on Practical Musical Composition* (1799) by Augustus Frederic Christopher Kollmann, which includes the orchestral interludes in Georg Benda's melodrama *Ariadne auf Naxos* under the rubric "characteristic symphony"; their meaning being "prescribed" by the surrounding dialogue, they are to his mind conceptually parallel to opera overtures or *The Seven Last Words*.[14] Defining the same term retrospectively, the music dictionary (1826) of Peter

---

[9] See the thematic index in Karin Schulin, *Musikalische Schlachtengemälde in der Zeit von 1756 bis 1815* (Tutzing: Schneider, 1986), 259–334.

[10] E.g., Georg Joseph Vogler, *Charakteristische Ouvertüre zu dem Schauspiel Die Kreuzfahrer* (1803), and Johann Anton André, *Charakteristische Ouvertüre zum Schauspiel Die Hussiten vor Naumburg*, op. 36 (c. 1818). "Charakteristische Sinfonien" is taken to mean opera overtures that represent the nature of the drama, or events preceding the rise of the curtain, in Daniel Gottlob Türk, *Klavierschule* (Leipzig and Halle, 1789), 392. Discussion of relevant examples by Gluck and Mozart is in Constantin Floros, "Das 'Programm' in Mozarts Meisterouvertüren," *Studien zur Musikwissenschaft* 26 (1964): 140–86, and Daniel Heartz, *Mozart's Operas*, ed. Thomas Bauman (Berkeley and Los Angeles: University of California Press, 1990), 318–41 (an expanded version of "The Overture to *La Clemenza di Tito* as Dramatic Argument," *Musical Quarterly* 64 [1978]: 29–49).

[11] Printed in the *Musikalische Realzeitung* (24 February 1790): cols. 59–60.

[12] *Pastoral* Symphony Sketchbook, fol. 2r (Beethoven, *Ein Skizzenbuch zur Pastoralsymphonie op. 68 und zu den Trios op. 70, 1 und 2*, ed. Dagmar Weise, 2 vols. [Bonn: Beethovenhaus, 1961], II: 5, and the first facsimile page); Gustav Nottebohm, *Beethoveniana* (Leipzig: C. F. Peters, 1872), 60–61; letter to Breitkopf und Härtel, 23 September 1810 (*Ludwig van Beethoven: Briefwechsel Gesamtausgabe*, ed. Sieghard Brandenburg, 7 vols. [Munich: Henle, 1996–98], II: 154). See also Constantin Floros, *Beethovens Eroica und Prometheus-Musik: Sujet-Studien* (Wilhelmshaven: Heinrichshofen, 1978), 116–19.

[13] E.g., *Musikalische Realzeitung* "Probeblatt" (5 March 1788): 1, and *Musikalisches Taschenbuch* (1803): 80. Dittersdorf and his apologist Johann Timotheus Hermes refer to the *Metamorphoses* Symphonies as "characterized" (charakterisierte, caractérisées) in Dittersdorf, *Lebensbeschreibung, seinem Sohne in die Feder diktiert*, ed. Karl Spazier (Leipzig, 1801; modern edn. by Norbert Miller, Munich: Kösel, 1967), 221, and Hermes, *Analyse de XII Métamorphoses tirées d'Ovide, et mises en musique par Mr. Charles Ditters de Dittersdorf* (Breslau, 1786; repr. in Carl Krebs, *Dittersdorfiana* [Berlin, 1900]), 167.

[14] Kollmann, *An Essay on Practical Musical Composition, According to the Nature of That Science and the Principles of the Greatest Musical Authors* (London, 1799), 15–16.

6

Lichtenthal shrinks its compass back to independent orchestral works but in that context still mentions the *Metamorphoses*, Haydn's Symphony No. 60 (originally written as music for Regnard's comedy *Le Distrait*), and also military, pastoral, tempest, hunting, and "fire" symphonies – in short, the whole range of orchestral pieces that are found with texts in the eighteenth and early nineteenth centuries.[15]

Alternatives were proposed but never accepted. At the premiere of his *Télémaque* symphony in Amsterdam in 1777, Ignazio Raimondi distributed what a report called "un espèce de Programme."[16] The journalist was undoubtedly thinking of ballet, where "programmes" detailing content had been used occasionally since the advent of the "ballet d'action" in the 1750s.[17] Later, in 1800, two notices from Paris refer to "Symphonies à programmes," which was subsequently the subject of entries both in Lichtenthal's *Dizionario* and in Heinrich Christoph Koch's earlier *Musikalisches Lexikon* (1802).[18] All the writers have in mind essentially the same repertory that was also called characteristic, listing the *Metamorphoses* and, in Koch as well as the reports from Paris, *The Seven Last Words* and the *Télémaque* of Rosetti.[19] The later nineteenth century would of course use "program music" to refer to the works of Berlioz and others, and in the twentieth century "programmatic" became in many contexts a generic term for all instrumental music with text or representational ambitions, one whose greater familiarity to modern readers (in comparison to characteristic) led me to adopt it in my earlier work on eighteenth- and early nineteenth-century symphonies.[20] But "Symphonie à programme" itself achieved no real currency before the 1830s,[21] and a German equivalent proposed by the editor of one of the Parisian notices, "historische [Sinfonie]," appears only there and in a few battle pieces.[22] Other possibilities were tried

---

[15] Lichtenthal, *Dizionario e bibliografia della musica*, 2nd edn., 4 vols. (Milan, 1836; 1st edn. 1826), II: 198.

[16] *L'Esprit des journaux* (March 1777): 301.

[17] Bruce Alan Brown, *Gluck and the French Theatre in Vienna* (Oxford: Clarendon Press, 1991), 171–75, 290–92.

[18] *Allgemeine musikalische Zeitung* (hereafter *AmZ*) 2 (1800): cols. 747–48n.; *Journal générale de la littérature de France* 3 (1800): 63; Koch, *Musikalisches Lexikon* (Frankfurt am Main, 1802), cols. 1384–85; Lichtenthal, *Dizionario*, II:198.

[19] See also Ruiter, *Der Charakterbegriff*, 108–13; and Roland Schmenner, *Die Pastorale: Beethoven, das Gewitter und der Blitzableiter* (Kassel: Bärenreiter, 1998), 44–45.

[20] Will, "Programmatic Symphonies of the Classical Period" (Ph.D. diss., Cornell University, 1994); and "Time, Morality, and Humanity in Beethoven's *Pastoral* Symphony," *Journal of the American Musicological Society* 50 (1997): 271–329.

[21] Albrecht von Massow, "Programmusik," in Hans Heinrich Eggebrecht and Albrecht Riethmüller, eds., *Handwörterbuch der musikalischen Terminologie* (Stuttgart: Steiner, 1992), 2–4.

[22] *AmZ* 2 (1800): cols. 747–48n.; Schulin, *Musikalische Schlachtengemälde*, 279, 305, 327.

The characteristic symphony

but once: "analoge Sinfonie," for Haydn's *Il distratto*;[23] "allegorische Symphonien," for the *Metamorphoses*;[24] and "dramatische Sonaten," for the *Metamorphoses* again along with *Le Portrait musical de la nature* (1785) of Knecht and the *Bataille à deux orchestres* (1777) of Johann Friedrich Klöffler.[25] At least one of these terms, "dramatic," might well better describe a symphony based on a classical, pastoral, or military narrative than does "characteristic," but like the others it represents not a standard usage but an isolated attempt to capture what was, thanks to its rarity, an unfamiliar musical phenomenon.

Only one term rivalled the popularity of characteristic, but it was loaded: "painting" ("Malerei," "Gemälde"; also "malend" or "malerisch," "pictorial"). Some writers employ the two words interchangeably – "Charakterstücke, oder wenn man lieber will, musikalische Malereien" (character pieces or, if one prefers, musical paintings) is how one review describes *The Seven Last Words*[26] – and others use "musical painting" as if it were just the name of a genre, among them the author of an enthusiastic early review of the *Pastoral* Symphony.[27] However, that Beethoven felt obliged to subtitle the same work *Mehr Ausdruck der Empfindung als Mahlerei* (more the expression of emotion than tone-painting) suggests that the term was not neutral, and indeed by his day it had been used for over a century to refer to the musical representation of physical objects and motion, a practice that was itself highly controversial (see Chapter 3). None of the symphonies discussed in this book is called "painting" in the musical sources, and of the related works that are, a number of battle pieces for keyboard, most have the qualifier "characteristic" as well (as in "charakteristische Tongemälde").[28] It clearly was the safer alternative, its connotations of emotion, unity, and humanity being preferable to the objectivity and crossing of artistic boundaries implied by painting.

From a modern perspective, one advantage to the widespread use of "characteristic," even where "dramatic" or "historical" might be more accurate, is that it reiterates the continuity between seemingly disparate

---

23 *Realzeitung* (Vienna, 13 January 1776), 107, cited in Carl Ferdinand Pohl, *Joseph Haydn*, 2 vols. (Leipzig: Breitkopf and Härtel, 1878–82), II: 76. See also Ruiter, *Der Charakterbegriff*, 83–89, and Elaine R. Sisman, "Haydn's Theater Symphonies," *Journal of the American Musicological Society* 43 (1990): 302, 311–20.

24 *Brünner Zeitung* (23 June 1786), cited in Dexter Edge, "Review Article: Mary Sue Morrow, *Concert Life in Haydn's Vienna*," *Haydn Yearbook* 17 (1992), 151; and Walther Brauneis, "Die Familie Ditters in Wien und Umgebung," in Hubert Unverricht, ed., *Carl Ditters von Dittersdorf: Leben, Umwelt, Werk* (Tutzing: Schneider, 1997), 56.

25 *Magazin der Musik*, ed. Carl Friedrich Cramer, 2 (1786): 1309.

26 *Musikalische Realzeitung* "Probeblatt" (5 March 1788): 1.

27 Friedrich Mosengeil, in *Zeitung für die elegante Welt* (5 July 1810): col. 1049.

28 Schulin, *Musikalische Schlachtengemälde*, 261, 276, 281, 309, 324.

examples. Like a number of other eighteenth-century "pastoral" symphonies, for instance, the *Sinfonia pastorale* (1754–57) of Johann Stamitz has no characterization beyond the single adjective in its title and no greater ambition than to evoke the general associations of the style. There is no series of countryside scenes, with storm, as in Beethoven's *Pastoral* or Knecht's *Portrait musical de la nature*. On the other hand, all the works use horn calls, drones, simple harmonies, song-like melodies, and other elements of a common musical vocabulary, and they all suggest a comparable range of sacred and secular meanings associated with the pastoral (see Chapters 2 and 4). They belong to the opposite ends of a continuum rather than in different categories altogether. The same can be said of "military" symphonies and full-blown battle enactments, which, again, are distinguished by the specificity of their semantics but linked by subject matter and musical style. Close by lies the question of whether symphonies always need text to be "characteristic," if the term is taken in Kollmann's sense to mean, in effect, any instrumental music in which a subject is specified by any means. In some cases it is not clear that titles like "pastoral" or "military" were seen by anyone other than the performers; they do appear on some concert programs, and more elaborate descriptions were declaimed out loud or made available in print,[29] but listeners familiar with contemporary opera and sacred music would hardly have needed to be told that a symphony with drones and shepherd horn imitations was "pastoral." On the contrary, there are several instances in which titles were applied after audiences, performers, copyists, or publishers recognized an association that the composer did not originally name: three Haydn symphonies became "military," in two cases with his approval,[30] and two others of a comparably martial splendor, by Mozart and Dittersdorf, acquired what

---

[29] See the reports on Raimondi's *Télémaque* (*L'Esprit des journaux* [March 1777]: 301), Klöffler's *Bataille à deux orchestres* (repr. in Ursula Götze, "Johann Friedrich Klöffler" [Diss., University of Münster, 1965], 105–18), Dittersdorf's *Metamorphoses* as performed in Naples in 1786 (John A. Rice, "New Light on Dittersdorf's Ovid Symphonies," *Studi musicali* 29 (2000): 471–73), Wranitzky's *Grande sinfonie caractéristique* (Arnold Schering, *Musikgeschichte Leipzigs*, vol. III, *Johann Sebastian Bach und das Musikleben Leipzigs im 18. Jahrhundert* [Leipzig: Fr. Kistner and C. F. W. Siegel, 1941], 612–13), Rosetti's *Télémaque* (*AmZ* 2 [1800]: col. 750); Beethoven's *Pastoral* (*AmZ* 11 [1809]: col. 267), Pugnani's *Werther* (*Souvenirs de F. Blangini [1797–1834] dédiés à ses élèves, et publiés par son ami Maxime de Villemarest* [Paris, 1834], 368–69), and Bernhard Heinrich Romberg's *Trauer-Sinfonie* (*AmZ* 14 [1812]: cols. 275–76).

[30] Symphony No. 100 in G (1793/94) was christened the "Military" by audiences, and Haydn subsequently used the title in his fourth London notebook (Georg August Griesinger, *Biographische Notizen über Joseph Haydn* [Leipzig, 1810], 53); a keyboard arrangement of No. 69 in C (mid-1770s) was named after the Austrian war hero Ernst Gideon Laudon, with Haydn's approval (letter to Artaria, 8 April 1783, in *Gesammelte Briefe und Aufzeichnungen: Unter Benützung der Quellensammlung von*

was, thanks to its connotations of power and rulership, the appropriate sobriquet "Jupiter."[31] The same might have happened to many other works, in response not only to general stylistic characters but also to quite specific references such as the hunting signal, the announcement of the kill, that Joseph Martin Kraus incorporates without written comment into the finale of his Symphony in A (van Boer 128, 1768–72).[32] Little if anything separates such a movement from one actually called "la chasse," whose title may have been mostly a courtesy, a warning about upcoming characteristic effects for players who, in eighteenth-century orchestras especially, sometimes performed with little or no rehearsal.

That subjects might be specified by sounds as well as words is further suggested by the fact that "associative listening," to use a term coined by Carl Dahlhaus, seems to have been as common as associative music in the eighteenth and early nineteenth centuries.[33] A powerful strand within contemporary aesthetics assumed that music always expressed feelings or approximated prelinguistic forms of human communication; as a consequence, listeners may have been predisposed to hear more or less concrete meaning in all musical works.[34] Conventions of performance suggest that they were in fact accustomed to making associations

H. C. Robbins Landon *herausgegeben und erläutert von Dénes Bartha* [Kassel: Bärenreiter, 1965], 127; and the first movement of No. 48 in C (c. 1768–69), also called "Laudon" in some sources, became the "Victoire" section of an inauthentic piano trio entitled "La Grande Bataille d'Haydn" (Anthony van Hoboken, *Joseph Haydn: Thematisch-bibliographisches Werkverzeichnis*, 3 vols. [Mainz: Schott, 1959–78], I: 724). The authenticity of many of the titles given to Haydn's symphonies is surveyed in James Webster, *Haydn's "Farewell" Symphony and the Idea of Classical Style* (Cambridge: Cambridge University Press, 1991), 236–38; and Horst Walter, "Über Haydns 'charakteristische' Sinfonien," in Gerhard J. Winkler, ed., *Das symphonische Werk Joseph Haydns* (Eisenstadt: Burgenländisches Landesmuseum, 2000), 65–68. Oddly, Walter denies that Symphony No. 69 has military overtones, although the march rhythms in its first movement and its use of trumpet and drums have clear parallels with No. 48, whose "latent military character" he does recognize (65, 74–76n.). It is true, as he notes, that Haydn expressed only economic motivations in approving the title Laudon (in Haydn's words, it "wird zu Beförderung des Verkaufes mehr als zehen Finale beytragen"), but it is unlikely that he or Artaria would have tried to sell the piece under that name did they not think the music was appropriate.

[31] Dittersdorf, Symphony in D (Grave D24, no later than 1772); on the naming of Mozart's "Jupiter," K. 551, see Neal Zaslaw, *Mozart's Symphonies: Context, Performance Practice, Reception* (Oxford: Clarendon Press, 1989), 441–42.

[32] In a comparable case, performers or copyists who recognized Haydn's quotation of a Gregorian melody did add a title to his Symphony No. 30 in A (1765), "Alleluia," which appears in early sources but not in the autograph (*Joseph Haydn: Werke* [Munich: Henle, 1958–], I/4: vi).

[33] Carl Dahlhaus, "Thesen über Programmusik," in Dahlhaus, ed., *Beiträge zur musikalischen Hermeneutik* (Regensburg: Bosse, 1975), 189, 195–96.

[34] See pp. 130–36 below, and Downing A. Thomas, *Music and the Origins of Language: Theories from the French Enlightenment* (Cambridge: Cambridge University Press, 1995), esp. 34–142.

with numerous instrumental genres. Opera overtures, ballet numbers, spoken play entractes, and the orchestral interludes in melodrama all brought instrumental music into connection with the characters and emotions of dramas, and still other works acquired visual and literary connotations from being played before tableaux vivants[35] or with spoken declamation; pioneered in Leipzig, where poems were read aloud between movements of symphonies during the 1780s, the latter practice became a regular feature of patriotic concerts during the Napoleonic era.[36] Instrumental works were also explained to the readers of musical journals and treatises with the help of poetic interpretations, which were published for symphonies, sonatas, and chamber works by C. P. E. Bach, Mozart, and both Joseph and Michael Haydn.[37] Significantly, the interpretations regularly invoke pastoral settings, storms, and people engaged in passionate speech,[38] standard subjects of the characteristic

---

[35] Kirsten Gram Holmström, *Monodrama, Attitudes, Tableaux vivants: Studies on Some Trends of Theatrical Fashion 1770–1815* (Stockholm, Almqvist & Wiksell, 1967), 110–233.

[36] Schering, *Bach und das Musikleben Leipzigs*, 615–16. Patriotic concerts are discussed below, pp. 191–94.

[37] *Magazin der Musik* 1 (1783), 1243–45 (on C. P. E. Bach, Sonata in G from the *Clavier-Sonaten nebst einigen Rondos ... für Kenner und Liebhaber*, vol. IV); *Musikalischer Almanach für Deutschland*, ed. Johann Nikolaus Forkel (1784), 22–38 (C. P. E. Bach, Sonata in F minor from *Kenner und Liebhaber*, vol. III); *Augsburger musikalischer Merkur auf das Jahr 1795*, 19–26 (Michael Haydn, duos for violin and viola); Jérôme-Joseph de Momigny, *Cours complet d'harmonie et de composition, d'après une théorie nouvelle et générale de la musique*, 3 vols. (Paris, 1803–05), II: 600–06 (Haydn, Symphony No. 103; trans. in Ian Bent, ed., *Music Analysis in the Nineteenth Century*, 2 vols. [Cambridge: Cambridge University Press, 1994], II: 137–40), and III: 109–56 (a score of Mozart, Quartet in D minor, K. 421/417b, underlaid with a text based on Dido's monologue from Virgil's *Aeneid* and accompanied by further analysis in vols. I–II [see Bent, *Music Analysis*, II: 127–28]); August Apel, *AmZ* 8 (1806): cols. 449–57, 465–70 (Mozart, Symphony in E♭, K. 543); Ernst Ludwig Gerber, *AmZ* 15 (1813): cols. 461–62 (Haydn, Symphony No. 104). Also relevant are the Hamlet and Socrates monologues written by Heinrich Wilhelm von Gerstenberg for C. P. E. Bach's C minor Fantasy and published in Cramer's *Flora* (Hamburg, 1787): xii–xiv and 19–27. See Eugene Helm, "The 'Hamlet' Fantasy and the Literary Element in C. P. E. Bach's Music," *Musical Quarterly* 58 (1972): 277–96; Albert Palm, "Mozarts Streichquartett D-moll, KV 421, in der Interpretation Momignys," *Mozart-Jahrbuch* (1962–63): 256–79; Palm, "Unbekannte Haydn-Analysen," *Haydn Yearbook* 4 (1968): 169–94; Malcolm Cole, "Momigny's Analysis of Haydn's Symphony No. 103," *Music Review* 30 (1969): 261–84; and Mark Evan Bonds, *Wordless Rhetoric: Musical Form and the Metaphor of the Oration* (Cambridge, MA: Harvard University Press, 1991), 169–76.

[38] This last subject echoes not only numerous characteristic texts but also Haydn's much-discussed admission that one of his symphony movements represents a dialogue between God and an unrepentant sinner (Griesinger, *Biographische Notizen*, 117; Albert Christoph Dies, *Biographische Nachrichten von Joseph Haydn nach mündlichen Erzählungen desselben entworfen und herausgegeben* [Vienna, 1810], 131). See Sisman, "Haydn's Theater Symphonies," 337–38; Webster, *Haydn's "Farewell" Symphony,*

symphony, and the preoccupations of the genre are echoed once again in the *Poétique de la musique* of the Comte de Lacépède, which divides symphonies into military, hunting, and pastoral types.[39] Symphonies with texts begin to look like the self-conscious subset of a much wider tradition in which instrumental works triggered a familiar and well defined repertoire of associations.

The presence of text assumes greater importance when viewed from another perspective of listening practice. In the eighteenth century (and well into the nineteenth, in some quarters) symphonies often played as a backdrop to other activities: socializing, or the comings and goings at the beginnings and ends of programs, where symphonies were typically scheduled.[40] At its academies even the famous Mannheim orchestra of Stamitz accompanied the quintessential concertgoer's pastime of card-playing.[41] Music was probably not ignored on such occasions so much as paid intermittent attention, much as at the opera where audiences reportedly listened to some numbers while eating or chatting through others. At concerts it was the vocal and instrumental soloists who provided the focal point, but passages from the symphonies must also have caused ears to prick up, among them various kinds of "characteristic" music; labeled or not, music of a distinctly pastoral, martial, ethnic, or other evocative quality may have served as a summons to an otherwise preoccupied listener, a call to appreciate both music and association. The effect would have been more pronounced where an event is suggested, a storm or a hunt; nearly always found in finales, the thunderclaps, horn calls, and racing scales that represent these subjects would have highlighted the virtuosity and semantic vividness of the orchestra just as its performance came to an end. Still elsewhere the alternation of more or less evocative music suggests the ebb and flow of attention. Stamitz's pastoral symphony begins with generic descending scales, then quotes a well-known Christmas carol, a key reference point throughout the

---

234–35; Hartmut Krones, "'Meine Sprache verstehet man durch die ganze Welt': Das 'redende Prinzip' in Joseph Haydns Instrumentalmusik," in Krones, ed., *Wort und Ton im Europäischen Raum: Gedenkschrift für Robert Schollum* (Vienna: Böhlau, 1989), 90–95; and Richard Will, "When God Met the Sinner, and Other Dramatic Confrontations in Eighteenth-Century Instrumental Music," *Music & Letters* 78 (1997): 175–209.

[39] Lacépède, *La Poétique de la musique* (Paris, 1785), 336–40.

[40] See Mary Sue Morrow, *Concert Life in Haydn's Vienna: Aspects of a Developing Musical and Social Institution* (Stuyvesant, NY: Pendragon, 1989), 142–44; Simon McVeigh, *Concert Life in London from Mozart to Haydn* (Cambridge: Cambridge University Press, 1993), 60–64; James H. Johnson, *Listening in Paris: A Cultural History* (Berkeley and Los Angeles: University of California Press, 1995), Pts. 1–2; and William Weber, "Did People Listen in the 18th Century?" *Early Music* 25 (1997): 678–91.

[41] Eugene K. Wolf, "The Mannheim Court," in Neal Zaslaw, ed., *The Classical Era: From the 1740s to the End of the 18th Century* (London: Macmillan, 1989), 225–27.

work; there follows a series of comparatively undistinguished sustained chords, then an assertive unison half-cadence and second quotation of the carol (see Examples 2.1 and 2.3a, pp. 85 and 88 below). It is not difficult to imagine such a movement periodically forcing itself to the forefront of consciousness, then subsiding to allow other entertainments their place.

Symphonies with lengthier characterizations, by contrast, reflect and promote the more concentrated listening habits that emerge in the second half of the century and grow along with the length and expressive ambitions of symphonies generally. By 1778 the return of a favorite passage in the first movement of Mozart's Symphony in D, K. 297, and also the unexpectedly quiet beginning of the finale drew applause from a Parisian audience that was obviously paying close attention to how the work unfolded.[42] In the subsequent transformation of concert behavior characteristic works provide some of the most striking milestones, most notably the *Metamorphoses* and *The Seven Last Words*. Premiered at a pair of concerts in 1786 in Vienna, the former works asserted the significance of symphonies to an audience much slower to adopt new habits than its counterparts in Paris or London (where Haydn's symphonies were greeted with intense concentration in the 1790s);[43] Dittersdorf confronted the Viennese with two programs of nothing but symphonies, six at a time, each one presenting itself not as one distraction among many but as the narration of a famous classical myth (see pp. 29–32). Haydn pressed the point in the following year with his unprecedented instrumental Passion, which consisted of nine movements, eight of them slow, designed for a church service but performed in concert throughout Europe, including Vienna. No work more obviously demanded the silent, quasi-devout concentration that would become the norm for listening to instrumental music.[44] If any reference to a recognizable subject matter drew attention to symphonies, the works with the most elaborate texts and thus the greatest semantic ambitions helped make the argument that every moment of an orchestral performance was significant. One could hardly treat the utterances of the crucified Christ, even intermittently, as background music.

---

[42] Letter of 3 July 1778 (*Mozart: Briefe und Aufzeichnungen. Gesamtausgabe*, 7 vols., ed. W. A. Bauer, O. E. Deutsch, and J. H. Eibl [Kassel: Bärenreiter, 1962–75], II: 388–89). See also Zaslaw, *Mozart's Symphonies*, 310–14, and, on Parisian enthusiasm for symphonic music generally, Bernard Harrison, *Haydn: Paris Symphonies*, Cambridge Music Handbook (Cambridge: Cambridge University Press, 1998), 5–44.

[43] Morrow, *Concert Life in Haydn's Vienna*, and, on Haydn in London, H. C. Robbins Landon, *Haydn: Chronicle and Works*, 5 vols. (London: Thames and Hudson, 1976–80), III: 19–320.

[44] See Johnson, *Listening in Paris*, 275–80, and Carl Dahlhaus, *The Idea of Absolute Music*, trans. Roger Lustig (Chicago: University of Chicago Press, 1989), 78–87.

Music and language

The belief expressed by many contemporary writers that all music has or should have meaning follows from a doctrine of mimesis that remained powerful throughout the eighteenth century but also shared the stage, in later years, with an interest in semantic indefiniteness sparked in no small part by the popularity of symphonies and other instrumental genres.[45] Characteristic works resemble some critical and theoretical texts in that they tend to endorse both perspectives at once, identifying meanings but leaving room for ambiguity. Before 1800, their texts could answer the not-uncommon plea that listeners be given some guide to understanding wordless music, as a reviewer of C. P. E. Bach's keyboard music requested in 1783: "Es wäre zu wünschen, daß der mit Commentarien zu sparsame Künstler uns nur mit einer kleinen Deduction darüber ... an die Hand ginge, um ihm vielleicht manches Bestimmte dabey nachempfinden zu können" (it is to be wished that the artist, who is too sparing of commentaries ... would only help us with a small clue, enabling us perhaps to enter into many definite feelings with him).[46] The stakes were high, for from the viewpoint of mimesis a definite subject, especially an emotion, could spare music from the moral vacuity laid at its door by Sulzer, Jean-Jacques Rousseau, and others.[47] At the same time, what characterizing texts most share beyond their subject affinities is brevity; even Dittersdorf's full-length pamphlet detailing his representations of Ovid passes off whole sonata-form movements with single sentences, leaving the listener to choose from a broad field of associations and even, on occasion at least, to suspend the interpretation and appreciate the music for its own sake – the value of which was also recognized. The same writer who asked for commentaries on Bach spends the preceding two pages defending an experience of the composer's keyboard fantasies divorced from any particular meaning: "Wer also nur nicht mit Rousseau ausschließend das Wesen und die ganze Kraft der Musik in Nachahmung und Leidenschaft setzt ... dem wird eine solche Sammlung von momentaneen Einfällen, Gedanken, Capriccio's, kurz solche freye Ausbrüche der musikalischen Dichterwut ... sicher die unterhaltendste Geistesbeschäftigung verleihen" (Whoever does not, like Rousseau, locate the essence and

---

[45] On the general course of eighteenth- and early nineteenth-century musical aesthetics see esp. Carl Dahlhaus, *Esthetics of Music*, trans. William Austin (Cambridge: Cambridge University Press, 1982), 16–42; Edward A. Lippman, *A History of Western Musical Aesthetics* (Lincoln: University of Nebraska Press, 1992), 83–136 and 203–38; and Daniel K. L. Chua, *Absolute Music and the Construction of Meaning* (Cambridge: Cambridge University Press, 1999).

[46] *Magazin der Musik* 1 (1783): 1252.

[47] Chua, *Absolute Music*, 98–125; Dahlhaus, *The Idea of Absolute Music*, 4–7.

entire power of music exclusively in imitation and passion ... such a collection of momentary notions, thoughts, caprices – in short, such free outbursts of musico-poetic frenzy ... will surely afford him the most entertaining occupation for the mind).[48] A decade earlier Michel Paul Gui de Chabanon had concluded that music was not, in fact, mimetic,[49] and a few years later Adam Smith, laying some important groundwork for the nineteenth-century notion of "absolute" music, would describe listening to an orchestral work as an intellectual challenge, like "the contemplation of a great system in any other science."[50] Most important for the characteristic symphony is that the two doctrines could coexist, not only in the Bach review but also in Chabanon's essay, which speaks of allemandes, dotted notes, and other conventional gestures triggering emotional associations even as it concludes that music does not imitate;[51] or in the treatise on composition by Jerôme-Joseph de Momigny, which analyzes periodicity and other aspects of musical structure but also offers hermeneutic interpretations of instrumental works by Haydn and Mozart.[52] In contemporary terms music was both song and firework,[53] mover of passions and tickler of the senses, metaphors that the characteristic symphony happily mixed. An instrumental music that aspired to sing but gave only some of the words inhabited a middle ground between semantics and ineffability.

The terms change, but the duality persists following the idealist turn in German musical aesthetics after 1790.[54] Sometimes said to have "emancipated" music from language,[55] the idealists more nearly loosened the relationship and provided a weightier metaphor,

---

[48] *Magazin der Musik* 1 (1783): 1250.

[49] Chabanon, *Observations sur la musique* (Paris, 1779); trans. in Edward A. Lippman, ed., *Musical Aesthetics: A Historical Reader*, 3 vols. (New York: Pendragon Press, 1986–90), I: 295–302.

[50] Smith, *Essays on Philosophical Subjects* (Dublin, 1795); repr. in Piero Weiss and Richard Taruskin, eds., *Music in the Western World: A History in Documents* (New York: Schirmer, 1984), 296.

[51] Lippman, *Musical Aesthetics: A Historical Reader*, I: 310–15.

[52] Momigny, *Cours complet d'harmonie*; analytical and poetic commentaries trans. in Bent, *Music Analysis in the Nineteenth Century*, I: 29–36 and II: 127–40.

[53] "A concert is to the hearing ... what fireworks are to the eyes" (Boyé, *L'Expression musicale, mise au rang des chimères* [Amsterdam, 1779], trans. in Lippman, *Musical Aesthetics: A Historical Reader*, I: 294).

[54] A concise account of German idealist thinking and its influence on early nineteenth-century music criticism is given in Bonds, "Idealism and the Aesthetics of Instrumental Music at the Turn of the Nineteenth Century," *Journal of the American Musicological Society* 50 (1997): 389–413.

[55] Dahlhaus, *Esthetics*, 24–31; John Neubauer, *The Emancipation of Music from Language: Departure from Mimesis in Eighteenth-Century Aesthetics* (New Haven: Yale University Press, 1986).

a variously defined "infinite," for the content of wordless music. According to Körner, music could represent character by evoking the infinite freedom that his friend Friedrich Schiller granted to the human self, the capacity to act unconstrained by anything other than moral ideals. But "Ein Unendliches in seiner Reinheit kann nicht erscheinen" (The infinite, in its purity, cannot appear), hence "Die Idee des Künstlers" must take on "eine körperlichen Hülle" (the artist's idea [must take on] a physical cloak), which turns out to be timbres and motions suggestive of "characters" in the original sense of the term as "affect": "Der schwebende Gang der Freude und der schwere Tritt des Kummers ... [und] eine unendliche Menge von Abstufungen beider entgegengesetzter Gefühle" (The elastic step of joy and the heavy tread of sorrow ... [and] an infinite number of gradations of these opposing feelings).[56] The *Frühromantiker* Wilhelm Heinrich Wackenroder writes similarly that "die idealische, engelreine Kunst" (the ideal, angelically pure art) of music, which does not know "den Zusammenhang ihrer Gefühle mit der wirklichen Welt" (the relationship of its emotions to the real world), nevertheless awakens the "Heerscharen der Phantasie, die die Töne mit magischen Bildern bevölkern und die formlosen Regungen in bestimmte Gestalten menschlicher Affekten verwandeln" (hosts of fantasy, which populate the musical strains with magical images and transmute the formless excitations into distinct shapes of human emotions).[57] The abrupt "und dennoch" (and yet) with which he links the two halves of this statement reappears in an essay by his collaborator Ludwig Tieck, now connecting a frequently quoted declaration of music's independence from semantics, "Symphonien ... brauchen sich an keine Geschichte und an keinen Charakter zu schließen" (symphonies do not need to attach themselves to any story or character), to its less noticed qualification, "Und dennoch schwimmen in den Tönen oft so individuell-anschauliche Bilder, so daß uns diese Kunst, möcht' ich sagen, durch Auge und Ohr zu gleicher Zeit gefangen nimmt" (And yet often such vivid and distinct images float in the tones, that this art, I might say, arrests our eye and ear at the same time).[58] In

---

[56] Körner, "Über Charakterdarstellung in der Musik," in Seifert, *Christian Gottfried Körner*, 150, 154–55; trans. adapted from Riggs, " 'On the Representation of Character in Music,' " 616, 621. Schiller's influence and the aesthetic context of Körner's essay are discussed in ibid., 599–610, and Ruiter, *Der Charakterbegriff*, 133–58.

[57] Wilhelm Heinrich Wackenroder and Ludwig Tieck, *Phantasien über die Kunst* (Hamburg, 1799); repr. Wackenroder, *Sämtliche Werke und Briefe*, ed. Silvio Vietta and Richard Littlejohns, 2 vols. (Heidelberg: Carl Winter Universitätsverlag, 1991), I: 220–21; trans. adapted from Mary Hurst Schubert, *Wilhelm Heinrich Wackenroder's Confessions and Fantasies* (University Park: Pennsylvania State University Press, 1971), 192.

[58] Wackenroder, *Werke und Briefe*, I: 244 (on Tieck's authorship of the essay "Symphonien," from which this quotation stems, see ibid., 368–72).

the conjunction lies the paradox of an art that is both meaningful and indefinite – and seems even more so when the two authors describe actual symphonies. Despite all his talk of infinity Wackenroder packs his prose with definite images, mainly pastoral,[59] and Tieck goes so far as to choose a characteristic work for his example, an overture to *Macbeth* (1787) by his Berlin colleague Johann Friedrich Reichardt.[60] The piece and its subject allow him to drift in and out of the ineffable, to hear both the "trübe nebelichte Heide" (bleak misty heath) of Shakespeare's setting and a more concrete "entsetzlichen Unhold . . . [The latter] stürzt mit wildem Sprunge in die Larven hinein, Jammergeschrei und Frohlocken durcheinander. Der Sieg ist entschieden, die Hölle triumphirt" (horrifying fiend . . . [The latter] leaps wildly in among the spectres, wailing and gloating mixed together. The victory is decided, hell triumphs).[61] Much as Jean Paul Richter saw the best Romantic literature as being rooted in realism, Tieck anchored the transcendent symphony in quantifiable emotions and actions.[62]

The critical fate of characteristic symphonies outside their own historical milieu testifies to the growing polarization of the transcendent and the definite, which gives rise to standards of judgment and interpretation that must be taken into account by any modern reading of the genre despite troubling anachronisms. E. T. A. Hoffmann still vacillates; he ridicules Dittersdorf's *Metamorphoses* as well as battle symphonies, "die der Plastik geradezu entgegengesetzte Kunst plastisch zu behandeln" (which treat sculpturally the art most utterly opposed to sculpture), but also admits that the correctly chosen "bestimmtes Bild aus dem Leben" (definite image from life), as in a famous hunting overture by Etienne Nicolas Méhul, can draw the listener "unwiderstehlich . . . in das bunte Gewühl phantastischer Erscheinungen" (irresistibly . . . into the colorful swirl of fantastic apparitions).[63] In subsequent decades both critical and performance traditions tend to support one verdict

---

[59] Ibid., 133–34, 221–22.

[60] Bonds, "Idealism and the Aesthetics of Instrumental Music," 407–08.

[61] Wackenroder, *Werke und Briefe*, I: 244–45.

[62] Jean Paul Richter, *Vorschule der Aesthetik* (Hamburg, 1804), trans. Margaret Hale as *Horn of Oberon: Jean Paul Richter's School for Aesthetics* (Detroit: Wayne State University Press, 1973), 15–18.

[63] Hoffmann, review of Beethoven's Fifth Symphony, *AmZ* 12 (1810): col. 631; review of Méhul, overture to *La Chasse du jeune Henri*, *AmZ* 14 (1812), col. 743; trans. Martyn Clarke in *E. T. A. Hoffmann's Musical Writings: "Kreisleriana," "The Poet and the Composer," Music Criticism*, ed. David Charlton (Cambridge: Cambridge University Press, 1989), 236, 297 (translation adapted). Related to the status of music as both meaningful and indefinite is Hoffmann's own mixture of metaphorical reference and technical description in his critical writings, especially the Fifth Symphony review (see Robin Wallace, *Beethoven's Critics: Aesthetic Dilemmas and Resolutions During the Composer's Lifetime* [Cambridge: Cambridge University Press, 1986], 20–26).

to the exclusion of the other, a division best seen in the case of Beethoven's *Pastoral*, subject of a more protracted debate on the mixing of instrumental music and language than any work save perhaps the *Symphonie fantastique*. The nineteenth century welcomed what it took to be a passionate and idealizing celebration of nature, and many embraced even the most material of Beethoven's representations, the paintings of birds and storm that the composer himself declared less important than the expressions of emotion. His caution notwithstanding, from as early as 1829 performers mounted stage productions in which the symphony's program was acted out amidst appropriate scenery,[64] and beginning in 1833 artists portrayed the composer writing the work while sitting next to a brook, pen and music paper in hand as if he were taking dictation.[65] Stagings and images alike suggested that the music had very concrete physical referents, an impression reinforced in 1860 when Anton Schindler claimed, supposedly on Beethoven's authority, that the work contained more tone-paintings than its texts indicated, including another bird in the second movement, the "Goldammer" (in the arpeggio figure at m. 58 and elsewhere), and an Austrian village dance band in the scherzo (mm. 87–122).[66] Some readers were skeptical – finding no evidence that "Goldammers" sang arpeggios, George Grove concluded that Beethoven had been pulling Schindler's leg[67] – but several late nineteenth- and early twentieth-century discussions of Beethoven's symphonies accepted the gist of the account and with it the semantic definiteness of the symphony as a whole.[68]

---

[64] See the reports in Otto Jahn, (new) *Allgemeine musikalische Zeitung* 1 (1863), 293–99 (repr. in Jahn, *Gesammelte Aufsätze über Musik* [Leipzig: Breitkopf und Härtel, 1866], 260–70; trans. in David Wyn Jones, *Beethoven: "Pastoral Symphony,"* Cambridge Music Handbook [Cambridge: Cambridge University Press, 1995], 85); George Grove, *Beethoven and His Nine Symphonies*, 3rd edn. (London, 1898; repr. New York: Dover, 1962), 226; and Bernard Shaw, "Music at Sydenham" (28 February 1877; repr. in *Shaw's Music: The Complete Musical Criticism of Bernard Shaw*, ed. Dan H. Laurence, 2nd rev. edn., 3 vols. [London: Bodley Head, 1989], I: 95).

[65] Alessandra Comini, *The Changing Image of Beethoven: A Study in Mythmaking* (New York: Rizzoli, 1987), 85–86 and figs. 50–51. Berlioz imagined Beethoven in the same pose in his essay on the *Pastoral*, *Gazette Musicale* (4 February 1838; repr. in Berlioz, *A travers chants*, 3rd edn. [Paris: Lévy, 1880], 38–39), and Robert Schumann critiqued the image in *Neue Zeitschrift für Musik* 2 (1835): 65.

[66] Schindler, *Biographie von Ludwig van Beethoven*, 3rd edn. (Münster: Aschendorff, 1860), 153–57.

[67] Grove, *Beethoven and His Nine Symphonies*, 211–12, and "The Birds in the Pastoral Symphony," *The Musical Times* 33 (15 December 1892): 14–15. For a convincing demonstration that Schindler probably fabricated the entire story, see Barry Cooper, "Schindler and the *Pastoral* Symphony," *Beethoven Newsletter* 8/1 (1993): 2–6.

[68] E.g., J.-G. Prod'homme, *Les Symphonies de Beethoven*, 4th edn. (Paris: Delagrave, 1906), 241–44; and the biography by Alexander Wheelock Thayer (see *Thayer's Life of Beethoven*, rev. and ed. by Elliot Forbes [Princeton: Princeton University Press, 1967], 437–39).

At the same time, however, the growing prestige of absolute music and the establishment of Beethoven as its greatest practitioner engineered a backlash: by the end of the nineteenth century, critics were complaining of his having "descended" to imitating birdcalls,[69] which were "a blot on an exquisite composition."[70] Donald Francis Tovey responded by separating the music from its text: "Not a bar of the 'Pastoral' Symphony would be otherwise if its 'programme' had never been thought of."[71] His proof depended on criteria developed in the reception of nineteenth-century program music and applied retroactively to the *Pastoral* and other characteristic works. According to Tovey, conventional forms underlie all those passages in Beethoven's symphony that most obviously refer to nature: the birdcalls are "a master-stroke of pure musical form" that fall into "perfectly normal" four-measure phrases and function formally like codas in other Beethoven slow movements,[72] and the storm is an "introduction" that differs from other symphony introductions only in that "it is in a quick tempo, whereas most introductions are slow."[73] Like many of his contemporaries, he assumes that programmatic music is based on "extramusical" considerations such as the narrative structure of programs rather than the "musical" principles that underpin absolute music,[74] whose presence in the *Pastoral*, conversely, reveals that it is not an unusual mixture of music and language but a "perfect classical symphony."[75] Similar thinking pervades the 1910 history of program music by Otto Klauwell, which associates its subject so closely with unconventional structures that any work using a sonata or other familiar form, including many of Dittersdorf's *Metamorphoses* as well as the *Pastoral*, is considered

[69] Quoted by Shaw from program notes by the influential critic Joseph Bennett, in "The Palace Theatre of Varieties" (8 February 1893; *Shaw's Music*, II: 799).

[70] H. Heathcote Statham, *My Thoughts on Music and Musicians* (London: Chapman and Hall, 1892), 280; similar complaints return later in Robert Haven Schauffler, *Beethoven: The Man Who Freed Music*, 2 vols. (Garden City, NJ and New York: Doubleday, Doran, and Co., 1929), I: 264; and Harvey Grace, *Ludwig van Beethoven* (London: Kegan Paul, Trench, and Trubner, J. Curwen, 1927), 269.

[71] Tovey, *Musical Articles from the Encyclopaedia Britannica* (London: Oxford University Press, 1944), 168.

[72] Tovey, *Essays in Musical Analysis*, 6 vols. (London: Oxford University Press, 1935–39), I: 45, 52; cf. *Musical Articles*, 168; and *Beethoven* (London: Oxford University Press, 1945), 123.

[73] Tovey, *Essays*, I: 45; cf. *Musical Articles*, 168.

[74] Cf. Frederick Niecks, *Programme Music in the Last Four Centuries: A Contribution to the History of Musical Expression* (London: Novello, 1906), iv and 4; William Wallace, "The Scope of Programme Music," *Proceedings of the Royal Musical Association*, Session 25 (1898–99): 139–56; and Ernest Newman, "Programme Music," in *Musical Studies*, 2nd edn. (London: Lane, 1910), 113. For further discussion see Dahlhaus, "Thesen über Programmusik," 187–88, and *The Idea of Absolute Music*, 128–40.

[75] Tovey, *Essays*, I: 46.

The characteristic symphony

absolute music with an irrelevant text.[76] The works are thereby defended from the accusations of formal incoherence leveled at programmatic works by writers like Eduard Hanslick, Edward Dannreuther, or Tovey[77] – Klauwell praises Dittersdorf for not allowing his Ovidian sources to exert "that kind of influence on the formal organization of his symphonies ... such that they cannot also in their programmatic parts be addressed as absolute music almost throughout"[78] – but they are also put decisively in the realm of the ineffable. Such would be the fate of the *Pastoral* Symphony for much of the twentieth century, as a reaction against hermeneutic interpretations of Beethoven's music inspired an effort to divorce all of his instrumental works from semantic associations. In the 1970s Leonard Bernstein went so far as to urge the audience at his Norton lectures to concentrate on Beethoven's motivic process and ignore the symphony's pastoral associations altogether. They had become a liability in an era of musical and music-analytical modernism, in Bernstein's words a "semi-transparent curtain ... that interposes itself between the listener and the music per se."[79]

Neither the nineteenth century's focus on tone-painting nor the twentieth century's on form is adequate for reading the *Pastoral* or any other characteristic symphony; taken together they leave too much out of account, most notably the expression of emotion, and considered separately they ignore the coexistence of meaning and structure in the musical thought contemporary with the works themselves. It is important to recognize the extent to which all instrumental works with text have been associated with "objective" representation and, in the wake of nineteenth-century program music, unconventional structure, but it will become clear that characteristic symphonies confirm these connections only some of the time. They also represent a wide variety of human identities, a point already made above but worth reiterating in light of

[76] Otto Klauwell, *Geschichte der Programmusik von ihren Anfängen bis zur Gegenwart* (Leipzig: Breitkopf und Härtel, 1910), v–vii, 76–79, 88–98.
[77] Hanslick, *Geschichte des Concertwesens in Wien*, 2 vols. (Vienna: Wilhelm Braumüller, 1869–70), II: 79–82 and 117–21; Hanslick, *Concerte, Componisten und Virtuosen der letzten fünfzehn Jahre, 1870–85* (Berlin: Allgemeiner Verein für Deutsche Literatur, 1886), 35–36; Edward Dannreuther, *Oxford History of Music*, vol. VI, *The Romantic Period* (Oxford: Clarendon Press, 1905), 113; Tovey, *Musical Articles*, 171–72.
[78] Klauwell, *Geschichte der Programmusik*, 97.
[79] Bernstein, *The Unanswered Question* (Cambridge, MA: Harvard University Press, 1976), 157. Cf. August Halm, *Von zwei Kulturen der Musik*, 3rd edn. (Stuttgart: Ernst Klett, 1947), 81–107, which uses the development of the symphony's first movement to demonstrate Beethoven's "harmonic economy" without mentioning its text; and Kurt von Fischer, *Die Beziehungen von Form und Motiv in Beethovens Instrumentalwerken*, 2nd edn. (Baden-Baden: Koerner, 1972), 246–47, which argues that "Beethoven is no program musician" on the grounds that the melodic motives of the storm resemble those found in non-programmatic Beethoven works.

20

the very different and, in comparison to the *Pastoral*, more thoroughly studied reception of Beethoven's *Eroica*.[80] The earlier work also found its semantic dimension emphasized in the nineteenth century, if not by staged performances then by published interpretations suggesting "characteristics" for each movement on at least one concert program,[81] and by the publication of programs suggesting Napoleonic or other battlefield narratives. Beethoven's own reticence about the subject matter – in comparison to the *Pastoral*'s movement-by-movement texts, the *Eroica* has only a title, a subtitle (*composta per festiggiare il souvenire di un grand Uomo* [composed to celebrate the memory of a great man]), and one movement description (*Marcia funebre*) – inspired a compensatory eloquence from writers like A. B. Marx, whose scenarios are as detailed as any that were ever proposed for the *Pastoral*. Where the two reception histories diverge is after the advent of modernism, which stimulated greater interest in the formal, thematic, and voice-leading technique of the *Eroica* but did not, surprisingly, stifle the interpretive urge. Tovey never once suggests that the music would be no different had its subject never been thought of; instead, he lards his commentary with references to the "courage of battle," "the stricken nations whose sorrow must be faced," and "the weeping of a *lacrimosa dies*."[82] Likewise, in an otherwise strictly technical analysis Heinrich Schenker connects aspects of the middleground of the first movement to "an initially careless impulse, a youthful insouciance and lack of inhibition," associations that evidently do not endanger the symphony's status as absolute music, as they might in the case of the *Pastoral*.[83] The contrast endures as recently as in the Cambridge Music Handbooks; far more sympathetic to the expressive aims of the *Pastoral* than most twentieth-century critics, David Wyn Jones nevertheless reassures readers that its references to nature occur within the context of an autonomous work, while Thomas Sipe connects the *Eroica* to texts by Homer, Schiller, and others in an unapologetically programmatic reading inspired by nineteenth-century models.[84] The significance of a fully described series of scenes is circumscribed, that of a merely implied story accepted and elaborated.

---

[80] The critical history of the *Eroica* is surveyed in Martin Geck and Peter Schleuning, *"Geschrieben auf Bonaparte." Beethovens "Eroica": Revolution, Reaktion, Rezeption* (Reinbek bei Hamburg: Rowohlt, 1989), 193–392; Scott Burnham, *Beethoven Hero* (Princeton: Princeton University Press, 1995), 3–28; and Thomas Sipe, *Beethoven: "Eroica Symphony,"* Cambridge Music Handbook (Cambridge: Cambridge University Press, 1998), 54–75.

[81] At the Leipzig premiere (*AmZ* 9 [1807]: col. 497).

[82] Tovey, *Essays*, I: 30, 32.

[83] Schenker, *The Masterwork in Music: A Yearbook*, vol. III (1930), trans. Ian Bent, Alfred Clayton, and Derrick Puffett, ed. William Drabkin (Cambridge: Cambridge University Press, 1997), 17.

[84] Jones, *Beethoven: "Pastoral Symphony,"* 24; Sipe, *Beethoven: "Eroica Symphony,"* 94–116.

The reasons are not limited to the fact that the *Eroica*, with so little text and only four relatively conventional movements as regards tempo and form (the fourth requires some explanation, but arguably less than the storm of the *Pastoral*), does not raise the spectre of program music quite so vividly as the *Pastoral*. More important is the cultural prestige of its heroic narrative, which, as Scott Burnham argues, has long allowed listeners to identify with a protagonist who seems to triumph over adversity and in so doing to achieve integrated selfhood.[85] The psychological attractions of such a journey plainly outweigh those of a visit to the countryside, suggesting why one set of semantic associations would be celebrated and the other suppressed, and also why the music of the *Pastoral* would sometimes be searched for "heroic" features: to concentrate on motivic process, as Bernstein does, is to look for what has always been taken as the index of psychological progress in the *Eroica*, differences between thematic treatment in the two works notwithstanding (see p. 210 below). Equally clear, however, are the disadvantages of associating only one kind of human identity with Beethoven's music, which discourages other meanings from being investigated even in the *Eroica* itself, and the problem only multiplies when the focus shifts to characteristic symphonies beyond those by Beethoven. Other works represent heroic adventures, especially those inspired, like the *Eroica*, by the events and ideals of the Revolutionary and Napoleonic eras, but their typically vigorous music and individual focus occupies only one part of an expressive spectrum. Keeping the power of heroic fulfillment in mind, an interpretation of the characteristic symphony must also take heed of the communal identities it constructs, the individuals and communities it destroys, and the people it suspends in pastoral timelessness, equally oblivious of both triumph and defeat. The human experiences encompassed by the genre are as varied as its scenic contexts – idyll, battlefield, hunting ground – are limited.

Representing character

How characteristic symphonies translate subjects into sound, as well as how they treat form, is examined in Chapter 1, a study of the works that represent more people, actions, and emotions than any other, Dittersdorf's twelve *Metamorphoses*. They reveal, first, the critical importance of motion and of intertextual resemblance in the communication of meaning.[86] Dittersdorf has frequent recourse to rhythms that modern readers will recognize from the "topics" identified by Leonard Ratner as constituting the shared inheritance of eighteenth- and early

[85] Burnham, *Beethoven Hero*, esp. 29–65 and 142–53.
[86] On intertextuality cf. Schmenner, *Die Pastorale*, 76–85.

nineteenth-century music: marches, dances with roots in the French court tradition, and a distinctive form of slow, even movement that occurs in scenes of pastoral stasis.[87] Each acquires semantic connotations from its uses elsewhere, in real-life marching or dancing or in stage works – particularly, in Dittersdorf's case, ballet and French-influenced "reform operas" such as Gluck's *Orfeo*. Many other symphonies rely on the same means to illustrate their texts, citing melodies as well as rhythms but most often the latter, which is significant given the close connection between motion and emotion in contemporary thought; for writers like Sulzer, for whom "jede Leidenschaft" is "eine Folge von Vorstellungen, welche mit der Bewegung etwas ähnliches hat" (every passion [is] a series of impressions that has something in common with movement), musical rhythm is a mirror of the mutating patterns of impulses that travel through the nervous system in reaction to emotional stimuli.[88] In the *Metamorphoses*, the rhythmic foundation of so many scenes highlights their expressive overtones, even where the subject seems most material, and the effect is enhanced by stark contrasts in motion between successive movements or sections. Illustrating another general practice of the genre, Dittersdorf routinely juxtaposes calm with disruption, weddings or idylls with battles or hunts, the former of which are marked by stable meters, balanced and articulated phrases, and clear rhythmic textures, and the latter by unpredictable and conflicting accents, undifferentiated streams of scales and arpeggios, and, frequently, an acceleration both in tempo and in the rate at which musical events occur. The implications are as much psychological as physical, whether for an individual or a community turning from confidence to confusion. Beginning with the first symphony, *Les Quatre Ages du monde*, the *Metamorphoses* repeatedly show a society bound together by the court dances lapsing into rhythmic irregularity, losing its cohesion in a way that references the experiences of Ditterdorf's own social group in the face of quickening historical change.

Scenes of disruption in the *Metamorphoses* and elsewhere also occasion the largest numbers of unconventional forms. These serve partly to project irregularity into a further domain; unlike the more familiar sonata, rondo, dance, or variation forms of the era, they tend to avoid repetition and to exchange the usual succession of distinct theme and key areas for a torrent of music coursing unpredictably through motivic fragments and chromatic harmonies. They also suggest a dramatic linearity seemingly impossible to capture in a form with repeat

---

[87] Ratner, *Classic Music: Expression, Form, and Style* (New York: Schirmer, 1980), 9–29.
[88] Sulzer, *Allgemeine Theorie*, I: 272; trans. adapted from Baker and Christensen, *Aesthetics and the Art of Musical Composition*, 52. See also Ruiter, *Der Charakterbegriff*, 44–46, and Chua, *Absolute Music*, 80–104.

signs or a recapitulation, such that it is in battles, hunts, and storms that characteristic symphonies come closest to the image of a "program music" governed by the narrative order of its subject rather than formal convention. Caution is required, however, in judging these seemingly one-way progressions of time. On the one hand, sometimes so few distinct moments are suggested that the impression is not of unfolding events but of a sustained affect, an expression through form of the confusion enveloping rhythm and meter. Most of Dittersdorf's examples have this effect. On the other hand, in the characteristic repertory as a whole a great many more dramatic actions are represented in sonata- or binary-form movements than in unconventional structures, including in storm and hunting movements that are discussed as a point of comparison for the *Metamorphoses*. Rather than abandon the traditional forms entirely, composers preferred to adjust them, often suggesting some narrative advancement by adding a coda or introducing new material in a recapitulation but also allowing parts of the "story" simply to repeat themselves. The temporal and expressive complexity of such instances is poorly served by a narrative conception of program music, and the action-oriented, "realistic" model of drama often used to explain sonata forms is equally problematic. The *Metamorphoses* suggest a better metaphor, the dramatic "tableau" theorized in the mid-eighteenth century by Denis Diderot and implemented in the genres to which Dittersdorf's symphonies most often refer, ballet and reformed opera. Encompassing both action and reflection, the tableau accommodates the static and repetitive elements of musical form as well as the concern for emotional response that informs even the most event-driven moments of characteristic symphonies.

Chapter 2 considers another metaphor applied to instrumental music of this era, that of the oration, and through it the paradox whereby symphonies with text can acquire meaning yet remain semantically ambiguous. Sonata-form movements in Haydn's *Seven Last Words* and in a group of central European pastoral symphonies exemplify recommendations given for writing instrumental music in many eighteenth-century composition treatises inasmuch as each takes a single theme, what the pedagogues call a "Hauptsatz," and elaborates it in both key areas of the exposition as well as in the development section and recapitulation. By contemporary standards this allows an associated emotional state to be impressed on listeners as through an oration – Haydn's themes "set" the words of the crucified Christ, and those of the pastoral symphonies invoke feelings attendant on the Nativity. The analogy is especially fitting in the religious context of eighteenth-century Austria, where church reformers called upon priests to explain the Gospels in comparably focused, single-subject sermons; based in classical rhetoric and updated to suit the needs of an "enlightened"

24

church, the ideal of a clear, persuasive lesson seems to inform musical and spoken orations alike. Since the texts of the orchestral works are not sung, however, they threaten constantly to break loose from their themes and leave behind only an ineffable sound that suggests not the clarity of enlightened religion but the opacity of a more traditional, revealed theology, or, in the case of the pastoral works, of popular superstition. The mystery is deepened in Haydn's work by abrupt moves to remote tonalities and other formal surprises, familiar signs for the sublime in eighteenth-century sacred music that stand here for a divine infinity, a limitless and sacred space that would soon be heard by Wackenroder and others – themselves enamored of traditional Catholicism – as immanent in all instrumental music.

Both the Romantics and their predecessors objected to overly material representation in music, generally termed tone-painting, whose complicated role in the reception of characteristic music is the focus of Chapter 3. Tone-painting diverted music from the infinite and from the emotions, and among German writers it had the additional reputation of perpetuating French-Italian domination of style and of failing the moral purpose of music, which was to be achieved through expression. Criticism could be harsh, and characteristic music suffered inasmuch as it was generally associated with the representation of things or events – this despite the tendency among composers to choose subjects with emotional connotations. On the other hand, reviewers of individual works such as the *Metamorphoses* or Beethoven's *Pastoral* found them to be as emotive or as infinite as they were graphic, thanks in part to their subject matter but still more to the difficulty, even where they "painted," of distinguishing different categories of imitation. Moralists like Sulzer encountered the same difficulty, so that, while they preserved the dichotomy of physical and emotional representation as a rhetorical trope, they also admitted overlap; events like storms triggered affective reactions, and those in turn had physiological dimensions. Characteristic symphonies benefited from the ambiguity and, as with the dualism of meaning and indefiniteness, they also put it into practice by illustrating the multiple dimensions of "objective" and "subjective" topics alike.

After the French Revolution the symphonies become increasingly affirmative, leading the personalities they represent through conflict or danger to safety: not the disintegration of a court society, but the thanksgiving of peasants after a storm is the emblematic closing image. Beethoven's *Pastoral* Symphony achieves an especially bright and culturally pregnant resolution through unique formal and expressive means examined in Chapter 4. Beethoven's storm movement is an example of "programmatic" linearity whose distance from formal convention is emphasized by the regularity of the sonata and rondo forms that surround it; moreover, its rhythmic and harmonic agitation stand out against the overwhelming calm and diatonicism of the other movements, and its speed against their deliberation, which has struck many commentators as the virtual inverse of Beethoven's "heroic-style" propulsiveness. Taken together the contrasts suggest a social transformation found also in pastoral literature by Goethe, Wordsworth, and others, in which the timeless certainties of pastoral existence are threatened by the incursion of history in the form of natural phenomena, wars, or personal crises. The disruption is magnified by further departures from tradition; Beethoven expands the scherzo from two to three dances while truncating each individual section, and he connects the final three movements of the symphony into a continuous stretch of music, lending new significance to a familiar technique in other characteristic and dramatic works. Subsequently he invests the restoration of the idyll with qualities of a Christian redemption: a textbook example of the musical sublime, the storm invokes a long-standing association between thunder and the wrathful voice of God, and the horn calls of the finale, which belong to the same tradition of sacred pastoral music as the symphonies discussed in Chapter 2, imbue the feelings of thanksgiving after the storm with a religious tone recognized both by Beethoven and by early commentators. The *Pastoral* delivers its characters from natural and social terror into a new, "moral" idyll marked by the awareness of grace.

Chapter 5 counterpoints similar dramas of communal crisis and restoration found in orchestral battle enactments with the more familiar individual triumphs of Beethoven's *Eroica* and related symphonies from the Revolutionary and Napoleonic eras. Both sets of works respond to a memorializing urge in contemporary politics and culture. By representing actual military engagements, battle symphonies helped audiences to make sense of recent history while also encouraging them to identify themselves with or as the victors, who are portrayed, like so many people in characteristic symphonies, with implied bodily movements. In each piece the fighting is preceded and followed by marches and powerfully rhythmic songs, which connote the armies involved as well as the communal rhythmic disciplines of military drill, social dancing, and patriotic singing. Regardless of the particulars of the conflict, battle is thus always experienced as a descent from rhythmic order into disorder and victory as a return to order, and while generals and other heroic protagonists are not entirely absent the emphasis is on soldiers or on the citizens of the newly-defined communities of nations. More clearly than any other kind of instrumental work, battle symphonies participate in a growing populist strain in contemporary political discourse.

Where the *Eroica* differs, and with it such related examples as symphonies written to mourn fallen leaders, is in individualizing not only its protagonist but also its own account of history. To some extent all memorial works reveal the agency of their creators, who must choose what is or is not to be remembered. The rhetoric of populism, however, requires an anonymity that composers find through constituting the reenactments from arrangements of songs, and from battle or celebration movements that have tremendous excitement but little nuance. In such a context suggestions of doubt, fear, sorrow, regret, and other emotions that distract from the progress to victory sound like editorial insertions, reminders of the human uncertainties and costs that play into military or personal struggles. The *Eroica* introduces such great emotional contrasts into its scenes of conflict and celebration that it was associated with the *Humor* of Jean Paul, a style of radical juxtaposition that in its sheer willfulness emphasized the actions not of the characters so much as of the authorial presence guiding their representation. While politically related symphonies thus mirror the division within European culture over the relative importance of heroes and communities in the conduct of war, they also engage the role of artists in the construction of memory. If a battle enactment casts the composer as self-effacing facilitator of joy, a work like the *Eroica* asserts the power of the individual bard to teach a society how its history feels and what it means.

A final word regarding this study of the characteristic symphony. As musical scholarship has become more congenial to investigations of meaning in many senses of the term, an old dilemma about instrumental pieces with texts has been turned on its head. Already in the eighteenth century some asked whether a subject could be detected by listeners unaware of the explanatory text, a question that would become commonplace in the reception of later nineteenth-century program music (see pp. 110–11 and 137–38 below). Its premise is misguided inasmuch as neither characteristic nor program music ever meant to communicate without the assistance of language, at least not where the subject was more specific than could be adumbrated by an evocative style.[89] Once words are accepted into the act of listening the problem in fact becomes the opposite of incomprehension; by their very brevity characterizing texts (and many nineteenth-century programs) tend to imply more than they would were they longer and more detailed, and subjects like Ovid's *Metamorphoses*, the crucifixion, a pastoral idyll threatened by history, or a society at war all pack so many possible meanings that the challenge is not divining them so much as deciding which are most relevant.

---

[89] On this point see Dahlhaus, "Thesen über Programmusik," 188–90; Walter Wiora, *Das musikalische Kunstwerk* (Tutzing: Schneider, 1983), 152; and James Hepokoski, "Fiery-Pulsed Libertine or Domestic Hero? Strauss's *Don Juan* Reinvestigated," in Bryan Gilliam, ed., *Richard Strauss: New Perspectives on the Composer and His Work* (Durham, NC, and London: Duke University Press, 1992), 136–37.

The rich hermeneutic legacy of the *Eroica* demonstrates the different nuances that can be gleaned from a single subject, and the point is being driven home in the growing literature on Beethoven's *Pastoral*, Haydn's *Farewell* Symphony, and other works.[90] With this in mind it is even more necessary than usual to emphasize that the account which follows does not exhaust its subject. It reads both famous and obscure characteristic symphonies from perspectives suggested largely by the origins and preoccupations of the whole genre, which turns most frequently to questions about human expression, time, and social transformation within contexts that have more or less explicit parallels in central European history of the same period. But no single book could do justice to the remarkable variety of subjects, styles, formal practices, and compositional voices found in this rich repertory. It is hoped that the appended indexes of characteristic works will truly stimulate further interpretations.

[90] Among many studies cited above and in the following chapters, particularly wide-ranging are Jones, *Beethoven: "Pastoral Symphony"*; Schmenner, *Die Pastorale*; Webster, *Haydn's "Farewell" Symphony*; Sisman, "Haydn's Theater Symphonies"; and Judith L. Schwartz, "Periodicity and Passion in the First Movement of Haydn's 'Farewell' Symphony," in Eugene K. Wolf and Edward H. Roesner, eds., *Studies in Musical Sources and Style: Essays in Honor of Jan LaRue* (Madison: A-R Editions, 1990), 293–338.

1

Paradise lost: Dittersdorf's *Four Ages of the World* and the crisis of Austrian enlightened despotism

A glittering audience attended the Viennese premiere of Dittersdorf's twelve symphonies on Ovid's *Metamorphoses*, given at two concerts in May 1786.[1] A hundred tickets were purchased and distributed by the city's most prominent patron of music, Baron van Swieten, and among those present may have been Austrian Emperor Joseph II, who granted Dittersdorf's request to use the site of the first concert, the Augarten, in a face-to-face interview.[2] He was in for a surprise. It was not simply that Dittersdorf brought symphonies from the periphery of concert programming to the center (see p. 13 above). An audience of aristocratic and upper-class Viennese would have known the *Metamorphoses*, whether firsthand from their study of Latin in school or through the many stage works and paintings based on Ovid's compendium of Classical mythology – but rarely would they have encountered so dark an interpretation of the tales. Dittersdorf's first symphony treats the Four Ages of the World, the classical parallel to the biblical Fall of Man, and nearly all of the remaining works relate comparable if more personal disasters: Phaethon's attempt to drive the chariot of the sun, Actaeon's encounter with Diana, Orpheus' failed rescue of Euridice. The composer declines to tack on the happy endings found in so many neoclassical operas and ballets of the eighteenth century; on the contrary, each conclusion is tragic and violent and associated with a dissolution of musical order, an abandoning of conventional symphonic style and form for a discourse

---

[1] According to the *Brünner Zeitung* (23 June 1786), the second concert took place on 20 May (Edge, "Review Article: Mary Sue Morrow, *Concert Life in Haydn's Vienna*," 151; Brauneis, "Die Familie Ditters in Wien und Umgebung," 56). Based on Dittersdorf's statement that the two concerts were separated by "acht Tage" (*Lebensbeschreibung*, 230), and the frequent German usage of eight days to refer to a week, John A. Rice reasons that the first must have occurred on 13 May ("New Light on Dittersdorf's Ovid Symphonies," 469). This chapter has benefited greatly from discussions and correspondence with Dr. Rice.

[2] Dittersdorf, *Lebensbeschreibung*, 221–23.

that barely qualifies as "music" by contemporary standards. So complete are the catastrophes that they threaten to destroy the medium of representation.

Given Dittersdorf's remarkable ambition, to set a whole series of action- and emotion-packed stories, no group of works better introduces the characteristic symphony as a whole. They pose nearly every challenge the repertory ever would: how to devise scenes that convey a plot and at the same time provide an appropriate variety of tempos and styles; how to give voice to voiceless protagonists; how to convey "timelessness" in a temporal medium and "drama" in a repetitious one. In the following Dittersdorf's solutions are examined in the order they arise in the first symphony, *Les Quatre Ages du monde*, with other symphonies in the set as well as other characteristic and dramatic works used as points of comparison. But the *Metamorphoses* add up to more than an experiment in musical representation. Their pessimism accords poorly with what ought to have been a climate of hope in 1780s Austria, caught up in a social and political transformation presided over by its "enlightened despot" Joseph: the aspirations of the day ran more to enabling self-fulfillment, chiefly by clearing out "irrational" privilege, than to reiterating ancient or biblical doubts about the fate of humankind. The *Metamorphoses* touch instead on an undercurrent of anxiety regarding the emperor's autocratic imposition of reform and especially his uses of violence, a topic of some controversy in contemporary Viennese literature and the press. Dittersdorf does not engage in explicit political critique – he was, among other things, an enthusiastic functionary of the empire – and at times he displays the same high humor as Ovid himself. Yet there is no denying the shadows looming over his works, or the similar doubts that plague their most ambitious contemporary, Haydn's *Seven Last Words* – but not, significantly, the characteristic symphonies played for the Viennese after the French Revolution such as Paul Wranitzky's *Grande sinfonie caractéristique pour la paix avec la République françoise*, his brother Anton's *Aphrodite*, or Beethoven's *Pastoral*. In the wake of real-world cataclysm it would become necessary to conclude each neoclassical or political or pastoral narrative with affirmation, but in 1786 Dittersdorf can still wonder how violence will transform the world he knows. His symphonies suggest the metamorphosis not just of Ovid's characters but of a whole social order.

Gold: paradise in music

Aurea prima sata est aetas, quae vindice nullo,
sponte sua, sine lege fidem rectumque colebat.

30

Table 1.1 *Dittersdorf, symphonies on Ovid's* Metamorphoses

Title	Source in Ovid
Surviving symphonies	
Les Quatre Ages du monde (prob. 1781)	1: 89–150
La Chute de Phaéton (prob. 1781)	2: 1–400
Actéon changé en cerf (prob. 1781)	3: 138–252
Andromède sauvée par Persée (prob. 1781)	4: 663–803
Phinée avec ses amis changés en rochers (prob. 1781)	5: 1–235
Les Paysans changés en grenouilles (prob. 1781–82)	6: 313–81
Jason qui enlève la toison d'or (prob. 1781–82)*	7: 1–158
Hercule changé en dieu (no later than 1786)*	9: 129–272
Ajax et Ulisse qui se disputent les armes d'Achille (no later than 1786)*	13: 1–398
Symphonies with no known sources	
Le Siège de Mégare (prob. 1781–82)	8: 1–151
Orphée et Euridice (no later than 1786)	10: 1–85
Midas élu pour juge entre Pan et Apollon (no later than 1786)	11: 146–79
Symphonies planned but not composed (see n. 4, p. 32)	
Histoire d'Iphigénie	12: 1–38
Enée et Didon	14: 75–81
Jules César	15: 745–851

*= survive in 4-hand keyboard arrangements only

> The Golden Age was First; when Man yet New,
> No Rule but uncorrupted Reason knew:
> And, with a Native bent, did Good pursue.
>
> (Ovid, *Metamorphoses* 1: lines 89–90; trans. by John Dryden[3])

The first movement Dittersdorf's audience heard has a five-word in-scription from Ovid: "Aurea prima sata est aetas" (literally, "Golden was that first age"). The composer heads each movement of the symphonies with a similar quotation, and he also gives each work a title, in this case *Les Quatre Ages du monde* (*The Four Ages of the World*; see Table 1.1).

---

[3] All quotations of Ovid are from *Metamorphoses*, 3rd edn., rev. G. P. Goold, Loeb Classical Library (Cambridge, MA: Harvard University Press, 1977). Translations are from *The Works of John Dryden*, vol. IV, ed. A. B. Chambers and William Frost (Berkeley: University of California Press, 1974), 379–81. See also n. 6 below.

These characterizations are communicated through the orchestral parts; and they are also printed in an explanatory pamphlet Dittersdorf wrote for the first Viennese concert, *Les Métamorphoses d'Ovide mises en musique par Mr. Charles Ditters noble de Dittersdorf*, which includes a general preface, a brief summary of each tale chosen from Ovid, and remarks on each individual movement as well.[4] The same information appears in four-hand keyboard arrangements Dittersdorf made of three symphonies from the second concert, which took place in Vienna's Kärntnerthortheater, and in a second pamphlet from 1786, this one by the novelist Johann Timotheus Hermes, an associate of Dittersdorf's in Austrian Silesia where the composer was employed. Fortuitously, Hermes' *Analyse de XII Métamorphoses tirées d'Ovide, et mises en musique par Mr. Charles Ditters de Dittersdorf* describes all six works performed on the second concert, for which Dittersdorf's keyboard reductions are the only known musical sources; Hermes' comments allow for the plots and movement structures of the remaining three to be provisionally reconstructed.[5] As one last aid to comprehension, the musical sources and both pamphlets cite book, line, and fable numbers for the Ovidian movement inscriptions (eighteenth-century editions of the *Metamorphoses* give separate numbers to the individual "fables" that make up each of Ovid's fifteen books). These quasi-footnotes invite the player or listener to consult the original poem, as befits the assumption by both Dittersdorf and Hermes that the subject of each symphony comprises the entire story in question and not merely the excerpted quotations.

Ovid describes the Golden Age as an eternal springtime in which humans lived together so peaceably that laws were unnecessary. The image was elaborated for eighteenth-century readers by John Dryden,

---

[4] Vienna, 1786 (repr. Rice, "New Light on Dittersdorf's Ovid Symphonies," 482–91; page references in this chapter are to the original). By the time of the Viennese concerts the *Metamorphoses* had occupied Dittersdorf for several years. The earliest reference, a letter from the composer to Artaria of 18 August 1781 (repr. in Rice, 474–81), projects fifteen works (one for each book of the *Metamorphoses*) and implies that he has already finished the first five listed in Table 1.1. How long before then he began writing them is unclear, but it may well have been some time given that the full symphonies were preceded by trial "fragments" performed in Silesia (Dittersdorf, *Les Métamorphoses d'Ovide*, 4). On 5 December 1782 he wrote to Artaria that he had performed eight symphonies; the letter, evidently lost, is excerpted in Georg Kinsky, ed., *Versteigerung von Musiker-Autographen aus dem Nachlaß des Herrn Kommerzienrates Wilhelm Heyer in Köln*, Pt. 1 (Berlin: Henrici & Liepmannssohn, 1926), 26–27. Provided he continued to compose in the order of Ovid's books, this would mean that the works based on books 6–8 were complete by 1782. The *terminus ante quem* for the remaining four is the Viennese performance of 1786.

[5] Breslau, 1786; repr. Krebs, *Dittersdorfiana*, 167–82. The *Brünner Zeitung* notice of the second concert (see n. 1 above) mistakenly reported that Dittersdorf simply repeated the six symphonies performed the previous week.

whose popular English translation went beyond the literal meaning of the opening lines to credit the first humans with natural rationality and goodness (see p. 31 above),[6] and by the Abbé Banier, whose equally popular commentary on the *Metamorphoses* equated the Golden Age with the Garden of Eden.[7] Dittersdorf, by his own account, reflects this "unité harmonieuse et innocente du premier âge" (harmonious and innocent unity of the first age) through resolutely diatonic harmony, and indeed the first movement of *Les Quatre Ages du monde* avoids all chromaticism except what is necessary to reach the secondary key of the dominant (Example 1.1).[8] But there is more to the representation than that. Eden and the Golden Age are the paradigmatic originary paradises in Western culture, and Dittersdorf responds in part with a moment of creation – not an explosion of light, as in Haydn's *Creation*, but something easier, less imposing. Between the first sonority and the middle of the second measure, the string texture opens out like a flower, expanding from a close-spaced major third to a tenth and then beyond as the first violins reach into a higher octave. The momentum of their sixteenth notes brings the four parts back to within a major third of one another (m. 4), then they open again, this time to a breadth of two octaves (m. 8). The subsequent addition of flute, oboes, bassoons, horns, and trumpets brings the whole field to life, projecting the theme into two higher octaves and refracting it into a kaleidoscope of new colors: a more obvious parallel for the births and re-births of an eternal springtime would be difficult to imagine.

Equally evocative, but with more far-reaching connotations, is the rhythm of the musical gestures, each of which begins on the second half

---

[6] First published in Dryden et al., *Examen Poeticum* (London, 1693), Dryden's translation (comprising book 1 of the *Metamorphoses* and excerpts from books 9 and 13) was reprinted in his collected *Poems* (1701) as well as in Samuel Garth's *Metamorphoses, in Fifteen Books, Translated by the Most Eminent Hands* (1716), the latter of which went through at least eight editions in the eighteenth century and was also used in the bilingual *Ovid's Metamorphoses in Latin and English, Translated by the Most Eminent Hands* (Amsterdam, 1732). Dryden's rendering is cited to give English-language readers a sense of how Ovid was understood in the eighteenth century. A list of books in the estate of Dittersdorf's widow includes a three-volume *Métamorphoses d'Ovide* (Petr Koukal, "Die letzten Jahre: Dittersdorf in Sudböhmen," in Hubert Unverricht, ed., *Carl Ditters von Dittersdorf 1739–1799: Sein Wirken in Österreichisch-Schlesien und seine letzten Jahre in Böhmen* [Würzburg: Korn, 1993], 23), which may have been the French translation of either the Abbé Banier or Fontanelle. Neither Dittersdorf nor Hermes, however, translate the movement inscriptions in their explanatory pamphlets, indicating that they expected listeners to recognize the quotations from Ovid in the original Latin.

[7] Banier's commentary was printed in several French and English editions, including *Ovid's Metamorphoses in Latin and English, Translated by the Most Eminent Hands*; his gloss on the Golden Age is on p. 7.

[8] Dittersdorf, *Les Métamorphoses d'Ovide*, 10. Further page references to this pamphlet are given in the text. Trans. in consultation with an unpublished English version by John A. Rice.

Example 1.1   Dittersdorf, The Golden Age (*Les Quatre Ages du monde*, i), mm. 1–12

of the 2/4 measure and leads in two steps to the downbeat. This is a gavotte, beautifully phrased in that Dittersdorf never lets the repeated downbeat emphases become deadening: appoggiaturas (e.g., mm. 2, 4, 6, 7) and first inversions in the bass (mm. 1, 5) ensure that each new measure bears a slightly different weight, and the melody and bass never arrive simultaneously except at the ends of sections (mm. 8, 16, 22). Rhythms from the French court dances frequently suggest expressive or social meanings in the *Metamorphoses*, much as they do in Mozart's contemporaneous *opere buffe*.[9] A protégé of Christoph Willibald Gluck in the 1760s, the period of the ballets *Don Juan* and *Sémiramis*, Dittersdorf had plenty of experience with their dramatic use, and the continuing presence of French musical drama in Vienna – most obviously, Gluck's French-influenced operas were revived there in the early 1780s[10] – meant that he and Mozart could both be confident that the traditional rhythms would trigger appropriate associations, even if the dances themselves were no longer part of the ballroom repertory. Regarding the symphony *Jason qui enlève la toison d'or*, Hermes notes of its concluding chaconne that the same dance furnished festive endings in the ballets of the famous French choreographer Jean-Georges Noverre – as it did, in fact, in many later eighteenth-century ballets as well as balletic *divertissements*

---

[9] See Wye Jamison Allanbrook, *Rhythmic Gesture in Mozart: "Le nozze di Figaro" and "Don Giovanni"* (Chicago: University of Chicago Press, 1983).

[10] Brown, *Gluck and the French Theatre in Vienna*, 441–42.

Example 1.2a Gluck, The Elysian Fields (*Orfeo ed Euridice*, Act 2 Scene 2), mm. 1–8

in opera.[11] He assumes that readers will understand the connection and find it useful in imagining the celebration Dittersdorf wants to conjure.

The gavotte of the Golden Age differs somewhat in that it shows Dittersdorf's tendency to adapt rather than simply imitate the conventions of ballet. Although unmistakable, the gavotte rhythm is also atypical inasmuch as its tempo is marked Larghetto rather than in the usual range from andante to allegro. Taken together with the richness and lyricism of the writing, this distinguishes the movement from, for instance, the jaunty and rhythmically incisive gavotte that opens *Phinée avec ses amis changés en rochers* (Example 1.14), which, like many operatic gavottes, is associated with a wedding.[12] The Golden Age has something of the same lively joy, but its slower, measured pace simultaneously recalls contemporary musical representations of less dynamic paradises, among them other idyllic movements in the *Metamorphoses* symphonies themselves. Perhaps most significant about the gavotte, in fact, is that it should figure at all in a context where exaggerated and orchestrally florid languor was the norm. The injection of celebratory dance into luxuriant idyll imbues Ovid's innocent springtime with an unexpected courtly sophistication.

The contrast is readily apparent when the Golden Age is measured against other musical paradises. For Dittersdorf and many in his audience, a *locus classicus* would have been the Elysian Fields scene from Act 2 of Gluck's *Orfeo*, which evinces a far more relaxed sense of time. It avoids the exchanges and developments of musical ideas that lend such propulsive force to the confrontation that precedes it between Orpheus and the Furies, whose loud fanfares climb in sequence from E♭ to G right at the beginning; when Orpheus reaches the Fields, there ensues a pastoral minuet that remains solidly in its tonic F and whose melodies mainly descend, reversing the earlier upward striving (Example 1.2a). The following "Che puro ciel" is even more placid, its oboe and vocal

---

[11] Hermes, *Analyse*, 175.

[12] For examples see Act 2 of Gluck's *Iphigénie en Aulide* (1774), or Act 3 of Antonio Salieri's *Les Danaïdes* (1784).

melodies so simple and so often lost in the surrounding orchestral texture that they barely stand out as discrete events. Nothing disturbs the unchanging, eternally running "fiumi e ruscelli" (rivers and brooks) indicated in the stage directions (Example 1.2b). Nor does the relatively wide-ranging harmony upset the sense of stasis; even when Orpheus interrupts the orchestra with recitatives, there is no struggle over tonal

Example 1.2b   Gluck, "Che puro ciel," beginning

(cont.)

Example 1.2b (*cont.*)

(*cont.*)

Example 1.2b (*cont.*)

che   pu - ro   ciel

direction as in the Furies scene but rather an orderly exchange in which each orchestral statement ends on a dominant that the following recitative resolves to the tonic.[13]

Contributing further to the seeming motionlessness is the luxuriant orchestral texture. Pulsing eighths in the violas, undulating triplet sixteenths in the first violin, and long tones in the horn, bassoon, and solo cello fill the middle register with images of running water, above and below which the remaining instruments add such diverse rhythmic emphases as to diffuse the sense of meter: basses pluck on one and three, second violins turn on two and four, flute and solo cello exchange leaping figures between the beats. The solo oboe and voice are not so much accompanied as enfolded, frequently disappearing into the texture altogether as when the oboe joins the long tones of the middle-register instruments or the sixteenth notes of the first violin (e.g., mm. 36–41), or when Orpheus sings in his lower register (as at most phrase endings). Sheer sound takes precedence over the progression of events that would be implied were the beginnings and endings of phrases more clearly articulated.

---

[13] Contrast this with the tonal wrangling between Orpheus and the Furies, esp. mm. 134–37; Daniel Heartz, *Haydn, Mozart, and the Viennese School, 1740–1780* (New York: Norton, 1995), 199–203.

Gluck's rendering captures a whole conception of Antiquity current in the eighteenth century, one only partially shared by Dittersdorf's more active Golden Age. The absence of dramatic events along with the material abundance suggested by the orchestration echo both classical and biblical descriptions of paradise: heroes go to the Elysian Fields after they have accomplished their great deeds and reside in unchanging splendor, and inhabitants of the Garden of Eden and the Golden Age do not travel, make war, or otherwise alter their relationship to the fertile and all-providing nature around them. Yet the rhythmic calm and melodic simplicity of Gluck's setting also bring to mind the descriptions of Greek and Roman art by the historian Johann Joachim Winckelmann, whose *Gedancken über die Nachahmung der Griechischen Wercke in der Mahlerey und Bildhauer-Kunst* (1755) and *Geschichte der Kunst in Altertums* (1st edn. 1764) appeared contemporaneously with *Orfeo* and exerted a profound influence on the course of neoclassicism in the later eighteenth century. Winckelmann asserted famously, "Das allgemeine vorzügliche Kennzeichen der Griechischen Meisterstücke ist endlich eine edle Einfalt, und eine stille Größe" (Finally, the universal and predominant characteristic of the Greek masterpieces is a noble simplicity and tranquil grandeur),[14] ideals echoed in the preface to Gluck's *Alceste* (1769) by Gluck and Ranieri de' Calzabigi, which promotes a "beautiful simplicity" to be achieved by stripping away vocal ornamentation and other obstacles to the expression of the text – Winckelmann likewise praised ancient art for its subordination of ornament to the depiction of character.[15] Equally important, he constructed an Antiquity that was itself a kind of Golden Age distinguished by perfect climate, physical fitness, and, in its art, an awareness that the soul "groß aber und edel ist in dem Stand der Einheit, in dem Stand der Ruhe" (is great and noble only in the state of unity, the state of rest).[16] "Stille Größe" becomes a sign for Antiquity itself, a defining quality of the physical and spiritual worlds of the Ancients, in which context the musical stasis of the Elysian Fields would have stood not just for

---

[14] Winckelmann, *Gedancken über die Nachahmung der Griechischen Wercke in der Mahlerey und Bildhauer-Kunst* (Friedrichstadt, 1755); repr. Helmut Pfotenhauer, Markus Bernauer, and Norbert Miller, eds., *Frühklassizismus: Position und Opposition: Winckelmann, Mengs, Heinse* (Frankfurt am Main: Deutscher Klassiker Verlag, 1995), 30; trans. H. B. Nisbet, ed., *German Aesthetic and Literary Criticism: Winckelmann, Lessing, Hamann, Herder, Schiller, Goethe* (Cambridge: Cambridge University Press, 1985), 42.

[15] Facsimile of the preface in *The New Grove Dictionary of Music and Musicians*, ed. Stanley Sadie (London: Macmillan, 1980), VII : 466; trans. in Weiss and Taruskin, eds., *Music in the Western World*, 301–02.

[16] Winckelmann, *Gedancken über die Nachahmung*, 31; *German Aesthetic and Literary Criticism*, 43. See also Nisbet's introduction to *German Aesthetic and Literary Criticism*, 3–7.

the repose of dead heroes but for the alleged stillness of the entire classical age.[17]

Before returning to Dittersdorf's treatment of that stillness it is worth examining its manifestations in an earlier set of neoclassical symphonies, fourteen works entitled after Roman deities composed in the late 1760s and early 1770s by the Bohemian Václav Pichl. Dittersdorf may well have inspired their composition and in turn have been inspired by them; in 1765 he left Vienna for Grosswardein (now Oradea, Romania), where in forming a *Kapelle* for the newly appointed Bishop Adam Patachich he hired Pichl as a violinist. They developed a friendship worthy of Orestes and Pylades,[18] and until Maria Theresa forced the bishop to economize in 1769 they also oversaw a musical life as elaborate as any outside a city, with singers and an orchestra of thirty-four performing at church services, balls, operas, and twice-weekly academies.[19] Dittersdorf may well have shared with Pichl his experiences of the not-too-distant premiere of *Orfeo* or his 1763 Italian journey with Gluck;[20] certainly the younger composer was immersed in Antiquity during these years, writing several dramatic texts in Latin on classical subjects for which he and Dittersdorf provided music.[21] His symphonies present a curious situation in that they did not always circulate with their names, which include *Flora* (goddess of Spring), *Saturnus* (father of Jove), and eight of the nine Muses (all but Erato) along with *Pallas*, *Diana*, *Mars*, and *Apollo* (all Olympians; the last work is a *sinfonia concertante*). All the evidence indicates that the titles were provided by Pichl and not added by others; not only was he occupied with classicism, but it is also unlikely that anyone else would have appended such similar texts to so many contemporaneous works, much less arranged for three of the "Muses" to be advertised with titles in the 1769 catalogue of the publisher Breitkopf.[22] The music is often transparently appropriate to its subject matter: *Mars* (god of war), *Pallas* (slayer of the Medusa, typically pictured with lance and shield), and *Calliope* (Muse of epic poetry) include trumpets and drums and resound with military march rhythms and fanfares; *Polymnia* (Muse of religious poetry) belongs to a tradition

[17] Simon Richter similarly connects Gluck to Winckelmann's vision of Antiquity in "Sculpture, Music, Text: Winckelmann, Herder, and Gluck's *Iphigénie en Tauride*," *Goethe Yearbook* 8 (1996): 157–71.

[18] See Dittersdorf, *Lebensbeschreibung*, 136–37, 150.

[19] Ibid., 139–55; Romeo Ghircoiaşiu, "Das Musikleben in Großwardein (Oradea) im 18. Jahrhundert," *Haydn Yearbook* 10 (1978): 49–52.

[20] Described in Dittersdorf, *Lebensbeschreibung*, 108–25.

[21] Ghircoiaşiu, "Das Musikleben in Großwardein," 50. Pichl also wrote a Latin ode praising Dittersdorf as a new Orpheus, repr. Brauneis, "Die Familie Ditters in Wien und Umgebung," 53.

[22] Johann Gottlob Immanuel Breitkopf, *The Breitkopf Thematic Catalogue: The Six Parts and Sixteen Supplements 1762–1787*, ed. Barry S. Brook (New York: Dover, 1966), 339.

of pastoral Nativity symphonies examined in Chapter 2; *Diana* concludes with a musical hunt. But the fact remains that Breitkopf does not list titles for the nine additional symphonies advertised in his catalogue between 1772 and 1775, nor do they appear in the manuscript sources other than those that might, given their provenance in Vienna or Prague, have had a direct connection to the composer. Pichl may have felt that the particulars of his classical allusions would not travel well. It is indicative that on the cover of the one work that was printed, *Apollo*, he or his publisher decided to engrave not a specific deity but a multipurpose classical figure, a woman in toga and sandals posed on a Mediterranean coastline and surrounded by symbols (books, music, maps) suggestive of several deities at once (Figure 1.1). The assumption is probably that the music will more readily evoke a generic Antiquity than any single figure.

In this connection it seems appropriate that beyond the military, pastoral, and hunting references mentioned above, Pichl's most obvious and frequent classical allusion is to the stillness of Winckelmann's Antiquity. The most beautiful example is in *Diana*, a work that departs from Pichl's otherwise invariable fast–slow–minuet–fast movement order to begin with a slow movement (Example 1.3). This unusual opening highlights what is almost certainly an effort to transport listeners into the forest grotto used as a refuge by Diana and her nymphs.[23] A mock-stern point of imitation softens immediately into a lazy, appoggiatura-laden melody that leaps upwards three times only to fall back in each case to a note of tonic triad (mm. 1–3), and it takes an exceptional burst of energy to reach the half-cadence on V at the end of the phrase (m. 4). Midway through the third measure, meanwhile, the lower strings begin to play pulsing sixteenths that continue virtually unbroken throughout the rest of the movement, like the murmuring triplet sixteenths in Gluck's "Che puro ciel" but here underlying a pastoral interlude for the oboes (mm. 5–6), then a new passage for strings that replicates on a larger scale the enervated descents of the opening melody (mm. 7–10); where one expects a continuation in the dominant, the strings instead sink slowly back to the tonic, the first violin decorating their fall with sensuous chromatic neighbors. The mood is then prolonged; although Pichl returns to the dominant eventually, even to a horn call suggestive of Diana's hunting (mm. 13–15), first he allows the second violin and oboe to hold pedal tones and the remaining instruments to oscillate between subdominant and tonic 6/4 for the duration of two exceptionally aimless measures (mm. 11–12). As the melody lags behind the bass in a chain of expressive suspensions, and each measure swells to *forte* but then

[23] See Ovid's description in *Metamorphoses* 3: lines 155–72.

Figure 1.1   Pichl, *Apollo*, title page with neoclassical figure. Fürst zu Bentheimschen Musikaliensammlung Burgsteinfurt

Example 1.3   Pichl, *Diana*, i, mm. 1–15

diminishes as the melody and bass recede downwards, motion seems to cease altogether. The music is savoring the lassitude of its preceding descent.[24]

Diana's grotto calls forth an even greater calm in the second movement of Dittersdorf's *Actéon changé en cerf* (Example 1.4). The use of both violins and viola (from m. 3) lends extra fullness to the familiar middle-register texture of the murmuring stream, and the predominantly whole and half notes of the flute solo create little momentum above it, even allowing that they are undoubtedly intended to be ornamented. The movement means to suspend time, like the trio, "Soave sia il vento," from Mozart's *Così fan tutte* (1790) that it so closely resembles, down to its quiet punctuations on every other beat in the bass. Both represent oases amidst hectic action, in the symphony between Actaeon's hunting, which occupies the first movement, and his subsequent encounter

---

[24] Related passages occur throughout Pichl's symphonies in fast as well as slow movements; the most ambitious is the lengthy central movement of *Apollo*, where rhythmic calm is coupled with a richer instrumental palette (including solo violin, viola, and cello) to create textures of Gluckian complexity.

Example 1.4   Dittersdorf, Diana's Grotto (*Actéon changé en cerf*, ii),
mm. 1–8

with the goddess, and in the opera between the lovers' departure and
the unfolding of Don Alfonso's plot. Dittersdorf's scene lacks the sorrowful overtones of the women's farewell, and, in keeping with Diana's
vaunted sexual innocence as well as the "purity" he attributes to ancient
paradises generally (as in the Golden Age), he also avoids the chromaticisms of Mozart's more erotically charged idyll.[25] His suspension of
forward movement is equally striking, however, and both composers'
characters seem simply to float on the steady, undirected motion of the
water and the underlying bass[26] – the flute, according to Dittersdorf, is
Diana herself (*Les Métamorphoses d'Ovide*, 19). She, Dorabella, Fiordiligi,
and the audience are all swept into Antiquity for a moment, and there
may also be a reference in both passages to a real site of classical culture,
Italy and specifically Naples, the setting of *Così* and, according to Daniel
Heartz, for a long tradition of similarly peaceful *Zefiro* pieces.[27]

[25] More sensuous is Dittersdorf's depiction of a summer's night at the beginning of
Andromède sauvée par Persée, whose solo oboe line and idyllic accompaniment
(similar although less luxuriant than that of *Actéon* or "Soave sia il vento") frequently
incorporate expressive chromaticisms.
[26] Cf. Scott Burnham, "Mozart's *felix culpa*: *Così fan tutte* and the Irony of Beauty," *Musical
Quarterly* 78 (1994): 83.
[27] Heartz, *Mozart's Operas*, 223–25, 230–31.

Dittersdorf's Golden Age also has thickly textured string writing and rich orchestration, but by now its departures from the more luxuriant versions of musical paradise should be evident. The gavotte rhythm along with the conclusion of the first two phrases on half-cadences, the regular changes in harmony (no drones here), and the tendency of the melody to circle around the third and fifth scale degrees rather than to fall to the tonic as in Gluck's Elysian minuet or Pichl's *Diana* – all of these move the music forward, not forcefully but enough for this idyll to seem comparatively active rather than static. There still are no significant events, which would contradict Ovid's description of the Golden Age as an era in which humans had yet to change their surroundings or themselves, but it is more form than rhythm or texture that gives this impression. In what is effectively a *gavotte en rondeau*, the opening melody returns some five times (A), first after an eight-measure gesture toward the dominant (B) and again after a longer, eighteen-measure interlude that reaches and remains in the dominant and is itself repeated (C):

A	A	B	A	C	A	C	A
I–V	I–V	I–V	I	V	I	V	I
stgs	tutti	stgs	tutti	stgs+ bsn	tutti	stgs+ bsn	tutti

Even more than the orchestral statements of "Che puro ciel," which at least change key at each recurrence, the refrain implies that the central scene remains unaffected by whatever might happen around it. And in fact the intervening episodes cause no significant disruption, retaining the gavotte rhythm and familiar melodic patterns and serving mainly to provide contrasting blocks of orchestral color against which the tutti can shine with added brilliance.

But if the form projects a necessary permanence, the Golden Age still distinguishes itself by virtue of its uniquely upper-class air, a result of the dance rhythm and instrumentation. Slowed down as it is, the duple-meter pulsing of the gavotte sounds faintly like a march, an association strengthened by the triadic opening of the melody and the use of trumpets, which, absent from the Elysian Fields and from the grottoes of Pichl and Dittersdorf, imbue the Golden Age with something of the martial pomp that expressed aristocratic power both on the stage and in real life in the eighteenth century. It is as if Dittersdorf wanted to incorporate a familiar element of symphony-opening fast movements, march rhythms reinforced by prominent brass scoring, into an opening slow movement, hence the noble step and the requisite orchestral luster in the midst of an otherwise idyllic textural lushness and harmonic purity. In considering the effect this has, it is worth remembering that Dittersdorf's Viennese listeners may not have been accustomed to giving their whole attention to symphonies, especially those placed at the beginnings of programs.

The composer might well have been better advised to begin with a fast movement, best of all one loaded with crowd-silencing marches and fan-fares, but he preferred to infuse his audience with a mood, partly through repetitions that impress the theme and its episodes on the conscious-ness, and partly through rhythms that reinforce familiar self-images. Concert-goers in the 1780s were not dancing gavottes any more, but they could still have known the dance's choreography from the stage and, more importantly, they would all have learned march-like steps either for marching itself, for dancing, or simply for walking in a society that placed a premium on bodily discipline and grace. To Dittersdorf's Golden Age as to countless other works underpinned by dance rhythms, they must have responded kinetically, moving or imagining themselves to move according to well-ingrained patterns. Their vision of paradise would have followed accordingly. Figuratively at least, they could walk in Dittersdorf's Golden Age where Gluck's "Che puro ciel" and similar passages encouraged them to hold still. The symphony invites listeners to join in a noble procession and then holds them there, as if in suspended animation, for the duration of the *rondeau*. They can still imagine Ovid's eternal springtime as an age before human action, even before history itself, but this idyll lies closer to their own experience than the Elysian Fields. The Golden Age offers paradise as aristocratic promenade.

Silver: drama as tableau

> subiit argentea proles,
> auro deterior, fulvo pretiosior aere.

> Succeeding Times a Silver Age behold,
> Excelling Brass, but more excell'd by Gold.

> (*Metamorphoses* 1: lines 114–15)

History begins in Ovid's Silver Age, when Jove divides the year into seasons and humans cultivate the land and build shelters. They do not yet begin to slaughter one another – that is reserved for the Brazen Age – but by altering their surroundings they forever abandon the time-less joys of gold. Dittersdorf responds with the kind of movement one might have expected at the beginning of the symphony, an Allegro in sonata form ushered in by a loud tutti and seemingly filled with action (Example 1.5a). A sighing melody in the strings answered by descending arpeggios in the trumpets turns the opening measures into a dialogue, after which dotted rhythms and a vigorous new syncopated theme make the implied marching of the previous movement explicit (mm. 9–16). Further, a linear progression from one stylistic and harmonic station to the next replaces the oscillation between refrain and episode, tonic and dominant: after an initial half cadence (m. 16) come three new ideas

Example 1.5a   Dittersdorf, The Silver Age (*Les Quatre Ages du monde*, ii), mm. 1–16

leading to a full cadence in the dominant, then a fourth idea in the dominant itself. And last, Dittersdorf avoids full stops at enough junctures for the movement to be a good representative of the "symphonic" style that eighteenth-century writers distinguished from "sonata" style on the basis of its greater continuity;[28] he concludes the first group on a half-cadence, elides the last measure of the main second-group theme with the following tutti cadence, and leaves the development hanging on a half-cadence in the relative minor (Example 1.5b, m. 84).

But for all its forward drive, the longer the movement unfolds the more it exhibits contrary impulses as well. A repeat of the exposition, and a recapitulation that differs from the exposition only in transposing the second group to the tonic, ensure that the movement's contrasting musical ideas follow one after the other in the same order three times – the

[28] Michael Broyles, *Beethoven: The Emergence and Evolution of Beethoven's Heroic Style* (New York: Excelsior, 1987), 9–36 (a revised version of "The Two Instrumental Styles of Classicism," *Journal of the American Musicological Society* 36 [1983]: 210–42).

Example 1.5b   Dittersdorf, The Silver Age, development section, mm. 57–87

Example 1.5c   Dittersdorf, The Silver Age, second group, mm. 35–42

form keeps circling back to places already visited, not unlike the rondeau of the Golden Age. The opening theme consists of two symmetrical four-measure phrases that never leave the tonic (Example 1.5a); the main second-group theme, of a three-fold repetition of the same motive over the same harmony, repeated in full, so that the melodic structures also never generate much momentum (Example 1.5c). Likewise the development section; at twenty-nine measures only half as long as the surrounding sections, it comprises a simple two-step sequence to V/vi (mm. 57–64, 65–72) and then a prolongation of that chord through arpeggios in the first violin, wonderfully mysterious but with the effect not so much of leading into the recapitulation as of backing away from it, as if the orchestra had lost itself in whole notes and preferred not to continue (Example 1.5b). Taken together with the tendency toward closed melodic structures and exact repetition, this less-than-propulsive development seems to contradict both Dittersdorf's subject and some basic assumptions about how sonata forms behave. English-language writers since Tovey have associated later eighteenth-century instrumental music and especially fast movements in sonata form with an action-oriented concept of "drama," a term Tovey himself never defines precisely but uses to describe the successions of different textures, ideas, and harmonic centers characteristic of Mozart's and Haydn's instrumental works, sequences of musical events that he repeatedly describes like turns in an unfolding plot.[29] Extending the analogy, Charles Rosen emphasizes the extent to which sonata-form movements engage in processes of resolution, especially at the point of recapitulation where the restoration of the tonic creates "an equivalent for dramatic action . . . [with] an identifiable climax, a point of maximum tension to which the first part of the work leads and which is symmetrically resolved . . . [as well as] a dynamic closure analogous to the denouement of eighteenth-century drama."[30] As we shall see, Dittersdorf could write movements that better fit this description, but he denies the Silver Age even such basic sources of action and tension as thematic development or harmonic exploration beyond tonic and dominant. The entrance of drama into human life produces curiously undramatic music.

The distribution of subjects in the *Metamorphoses* symphonies suggests that Dittersdorf did not, in fact, consider sonata form particularly well-suited for representing dramatic events. By allowing diverse musical ideas to be juxtaposed in a dynamic tonal structure, sonata form offered a useful context in which to suggest characters or natural phenomena in motion, but the repetitions inherent in even the most action-driven treatments of the form placed limits on the purely linear development composers could convey. Not only Dittersdorf but most composers who

[29] For characteristic statements see Tovey, "Sonata Forms" as well as "Music," § 7 (a historical account of the later eighteenth century revealingly entitled "The Rise of Dramatic Music and the Sonata Style"), in *Musical Articles from the Encyclopaedia Britannica*, 123–26, 208–32; also "Haydn's Chamber Music" and "The Main Stream of Music," in *Essays and Lectures on Music* (London: Oxford University Press, 1949), 1–64, 345–47.
[30] Rosen, *Sonata Forms*, rev. edn. (New York: Norton, 1988), 9–10.

sought to represent unfolding plots or storylines seemed to have recognized this, as evidenced by their tendency to abandon the form altogether or, more typically, to write movements that are at once active and static, linear and spatial, dramatic and lyric. The *Metamorphoses* mix the qualities in different proportions, with the Silver Age leaning heavily toward the static, spatial, and lyric: Dittersdorf writes, "Il s'agit ici en quelque façon d'une réprésentation du luxe qui, parmi les autres causes, pourroit bien aussi avoir contribué à la détérioration de l'âge précédent et à son anéantissement" (Here it is a question of representing in some way the luxury which, among other causes, may well have contributed to the deterioration of the preceding age and its destruction [*Les Métamorphoses d'Ovide*, 10–11]), defining his subject not as the incursion of historical development into human life so much as a proliferation of riches extrapolated from the invention of agriculture and housing. Hence the parts of the form are conceived less as events in a plot than as objects in a picture.

At the opposite pole stands the second, fast movement of *Andromède sauvée par Persée*, based on Ovid's description of Perseus flying over lands and peoples on his way to discovering Andromeda, chained to a rock awaiting sacrifice to a sea monster.[31] Dittersdorf imagines a hero overcoming obstacles: "Persée quoiqu'il ne voyage pas comme les autres par terre, il rencontre cependant beaucoup de rochers qui rendent son voyage fort pénible. Par les endroits plus animés de cette partie on exprime le courage héroïque" (Although he does not travel on the ground like others, Perseus encounters many cliffs that make his journey difficult. The most animated passages in this movement express his heroic courage [22]). The form abounds in headlong dashes from one musical idea to the next as well as in rhythmic and harmonic uncertainties, most notably in the second group (Example 1.6). Four measures of descending scales are repeated with the lower strings offset by a beat, disrupting the meter (Example 1.6, mm. 115–23). A four-measure pendant re-asserts both rhythmic and harmonic stability, but then its repetition goes awry, ending with a first-inversion tonic on the weakest beat of the measure and a suspenseful grand pause (m. 133). A new and mysterious chromatic scale leads to a tonic 6/4 (m. 140), but the anticipated cadence takes still another six measures to arrive – and when it does, the orchestra breaks immediately into one of Dittersdorf's "endroits plus animés" (m. 146). Similarly propulsive music is found elsewhere in the exposition and recapitulation, and the same descending scale that touches off events here serves as the basis for a long and tonally wide-ranging development section.

---

[31] *Metamorphoses* 4: lines 665–69.

Example 1.6   Dittersdorf, Perseus' flight (*Andromède sauvée par Persée*, ii), mm. 115–48

Yet even this movement cannot avoid disjunctions between the unfolding of its plot and the repetitions in its form. Dittersdorf indicates that the very opening measures represent a sunrise, a natural way to begin given that the preceding movement was his depiction of an idyllic summer's night (see p. 44 above, n. 25). As in more familiar works such as *The Creation* and *The Seasons* of Haydn, the rising of the sun is suggested by coordinated increases in the quickness of the rhythm, the height of the melodic line, and the number of instruments. Dittersdorf also omits the sunrise from the recapitulation, linking the end of the development directly to the beginning of the transition. But where that decision enhances the movement's linearity, the repeat sign at the end of the exposition means that Perseus must still watch the sun come up twice. Performers could always have gone on, and indeed in the sonata-form fast movement of *La Chute de Phaéton*, which begins with a musically similar depiction of Phaethon's approach to the palace of the sun, Dittersdorf ensures the event happens only once by segregating it

51

into a slow introduction. That he does not do so in *Andromède sauvée par Persée* indicates a willingness – surprising, if one is thinking in terms of dramatic realism – to accept contradictions between events in the story and in the music.

As similar contradictions pervade a good deal of characteristic music, it is worth considering what conception of "drama" Dittersdorf and his contemporaries really held. Conceptually and historically the best point of comparison is the theory of dramatic "tableaux" developed by Denis Diderot in his art criticism as well as the *Entretiens sur le Fils naturel* (1757) and *Sur la Poésie dramatique* (1758). Diderot shared with Winckelmann the conviction that a return to classical models could revolutionize what he saw as the corrupt aesthetic of the Rococo, and he also took simplicity and calm to be virtues, particularly in the theater where he called for clever plot twists (*coups de théâtre*) to be replaced by easily comprehended series of distinctive scenes. His recommendations for both the theater and painting revolve, however, around a combination of calm *and* action summed up in the notion of the tableau.[32] His understanding of the term in regard to visual art is relatively self-evident; he praises Jean-Baptiste Greuze and, later, Jacques-Louis David for capturing moments that allow for the greatest pictorial spectacle and expression of character while also implying the action of the story surrounding them.[33] On the stage, tableaux require the less obvious incorporation of painterly qualities into the development of the plot. Each scene must have a distinctive visual composition, "une disposition de ... personnages sur la scène, si naturelle et si vraie, que rendue fidèlement par un peintre, elle me plairait sur la toile" (an arrangement of ... characters on stage, so natural and so true that, faithfully rendered by a painter, it would please me on a canvas).[34] As the story progresses, action and stasis co-exist in the balance between the speeches and movements of the actors on the one hand, and their spatial distribution across the stage on the other.

Diderot's ideas found their way quickly into musical theater, especially ballet. In his *Lettres sur la danse* (1760), Noverre advocated a "ballet d'action" based on a series of tableaux, each of which was to have a characteristic stage set and *clair-obscur*: chiaroscuro, or distribution of

---

[32] *Entretiens sur le Fils naturel*, in Diderot, *Œuvres complètes*, vol. X, ed. Jacques Chouillet and Anne-Marie Chouillet (Paris: Hermann, 1980), 91–98. See also Michael Fried, *Absorption and Theatricality: Painting and Beholder in the Age of Diderot* (Berkeley: University of California Press, 1980), 93–96.

[33] Fried, *Absorption and Theatricality*, esp. 82–92, 96–105. Later eighteenth- and early nineteenth-century tableaux vivants and "attitudes" sought similarly to suggest the action of an entire (usually classical) story by representing an evocative moment, sometimes with music; see Holmström, *Monodrama, Attitudes, Tableaux vivants*, 110–233.

[34] *Entretiens sur le Fils naturel*, 92; trans. in Diderot, *Selected Writings on Art and Literature*, ed. Geoffrey Bremner (London: Penguin, 1994), 12.

light and shade. The genre would accommodate two kinds of dance, the traditional ballet based on the French court dances and a new style of pantomime inspired by classical models.[35] Both could depict events happening on stage, but each tableau could also incorporate dances that did little or nothing to carry the story forward, and indeed scenes whose chief purpose is to allow for spectacle, especially involving large groups of dancers, remain common in ballet scenarios of the later eighteenth century despite the intention of Noverre and others to introduce more narrative.[36] Like Diderot, the choreographers simply do not conceive of narrative in strictly linear terms, and indeed Noverre's model for the *ballet d'action* is Peter Paul Rubens' cycle of twenty-four paintings of the French queen Maria de' Medici, a chronicle of her life from birth through her regency during the minority of Louis XIII and beyond.[37] Walking through the original installation at the Palais du Luxembourg (the paintings were later exhibited out of order in the Louvre), eighteenth-century viewers could experience the queen's biography in the succession of one image to the next, and the pictures themselves treat not only decisive moments in her life (*The Proclamation of the Regency*) but also the qualities of individuals or eras (portraits of her parents and *The Felicity of the Regency*).[38] Similarly in Noverre's scenarios, the story moves forward mainly in the change from scene to scene, while the scenes themselves can contain any degree of action or none at all.

Dittersdorf's early years in Vienna would have exposed him to Diderotian tableaux in both ballet and opera. In *Don Juan* and *Sémiramis* Gluck and Gasparo Angiolini developed a *ballet d'action* very similar to Noverre's (indeed, the priority of Noverre's reforms versus those of Angiolini's mentor, Franz Hilverding, became a point of contention[39]),

---

[35] Noverre, *Lettres sur la danse, et sur les ballets* (Stuttgart, 1760). Diderot's *Entretiens* (101 *et passim*), to which Noverre refers several times, had already called for the introduction of mime to theater, and his art criticism stressed the importance of chiaroscuro as a unifying element in *tableaux* (Fried, *Absorption and Theatricality*, 87). On Noverre's and related reforms of eighteenth-century ballet see Brown, *Gluck and the French Theatre in Vienna*; Susan Leigh Foster, *Choreography & Narrative: Ballet's Staging of Story and Desire* (Bloomington and Indianapolis: Indiana University Press, 1996), chapters 1–3; and Ivor Forbes Guest, *The Ballet of the Enlightenment: The Establishment of the Ballet d'action in France 1770–1793* (London: Dance Books, 1996).

[36] The compromise between dramatic action and visual spectacle is especially well illustrated by Noverre's *Apelles et Campaspe* (premiered Vienna, 1772), whose "plot" consists mainly of the heroine striking poses of classical goddesses for her painter / lover Apelles; see Foster, *Choreography and Narrative*, 89–92.

[37] Noverre, *Lettres sur la danse*, 44–45.

[38] See Ronald Forsyth Millen and Robert Erich Wolf, *Heroic Deeds and Mystic Figures: A New Reading of Rubens' "Life of Maria de' Medici"* (Princeton: Princeton University Press, 1989). Rubens also fills even the queen's most active moments with so many ancient deities and other symbols that allegory tends to overwhelm story-telling.

[39] Brown, *Gluck and the French Theatre in Vienna*, 152–54.

and related principles underlie the dramaturgy of *Orfeo,* whose second act is a familiar example of a plot proceeding by virtue of successive distinctive scenes, from underworld *oscurità* to Elysian *chiarità.* It can be no coincidence that Dittersdorf originally conceived the *Metamorphoses* Symphonies along similar lines. In a letter of 17 August 1781 outlining the project to his prospective publisher, the Viennese firm of Artaria, the composer envisions the explanatory quotations from Ovid being printed not on the orchestral parts but on a series of engravings, one for each movement.[40] These were to depict his conception of the associated scene (as described in an attachment to the letter) and to be sold separately as well as inserted into the orchestral parts. Had this come to pass, listeners and orchestra members could have experienced each myth much as they did the plot of one of Noverre's ballets or the life of Maria de' Medici at Luxembourg; rather than continuous action, the engravings would have suggested a story taking place in discrete stages, each of which might include dramatic events but would also, like a painting, capture static or at least non-narrative qualities of a single moment in time.

Probably because of cost or the novelty of the idea, Artaria declined to publish the engravings, but Dittersdorf seems nevertheless to have carried his original conception through the composition and performance of the symphonies. The preface to his explanatory pamphlet appeals to Diderot's terminology – "l'étude ... de ses magnifiques tableaux m'avoient souvent fait venir la pensée d'exprimer quelques images de ce divin Poëte par la musique" (the study of Ovid's magnificent tableaux often led me to the idea of expressing some of the pictures of this divine poet in music [3]) – and despite differences in its interpretation of Ovid from the earlier suggestions for the engravings, the text shows an unchanged commitment to relating the myths through a series of independent distinctive scenes. *Les Quatre Ages du monde* establishes a pattern by treating a subject that Dittersdorf himself says is not a "fable formelle" (formal story [9]): instead, the masterfully painted Ages (Dittersdorf's words for Ovid) follow one after the next without any developing personalities or plot devices to connect them. The approach remains the same even as individual scenes acquire identifiable

---

[40] The letter is reprinted in Rice, "New Light on Dittersdorf's Ovid Symphonies," 474–81. Rice suggests that Artaria's activity as a print-maker and dealer may have encouraged Dittersdorf to propose the publication of music together with engravings (456). It may also be significant that the Viennese publisher Schalbacher printed an illustrated edition of the *Metamorphoses* in 1780 (Hermann Jung, "Antiker Mythos im symphonischen Gewand der Wiener Klassik: Karl Ditters von Dittersdorfs Symphonien nach Ovids Metamorphosen [1785]," in Petr Macek, ed., *Das internationale musikwissenschaftliche Kolloquium "Wenn es nicht Österreich gegeben hätte...," 30.9.–2.10.1996* [Brno: Filozofická fakulta Masarykovy univerzity Brno, 1997], 166).

characters and events. *Andromède sauvée par Persée* gets underway by presenting an idyllic nocturne and then Perseus' flight, the one seemingly static and the other active, but the repeated sunrise in the second movement shows that, in fact, they are both conceived to some extent spatially. Ovid's plot unfolds primarily in the succession of tableaux, within which the order of events counts for less than the vividness of the whole. Any single element – in this case the sunrise – may be intensified by repetition.

Dittersdorf was not alone in mixing linear and spatial elements in sonata forms; on the contrary, characteristic symphonies of the years surrounding the *Metamorphoses* do so to such varying degrees that they read like a debate on the nature of drama in instrumental music. This is particularly true of hunting symphonies, which would have led listeners to expect unfolding events inasmuch as the formalized, upper-class hunt to which they refer was divided into stages occurring in a more or less unvarying order, from the summoning of the hounds to the killing of the prey (see Appendix 3b, pp. 299–300 below). Each stage was associated with a distinctive horn signal, making it possible for composers to mark every turn in the plot if they wished.[41] Yet most did not, using only one or two calls or composing their own call-like themes, which tend to evoke hunting generally rather than specific events. Composers also incorporated the calls primarily into sonata-form movements, necessitating a variety of compromises between the narrative impetus of the subject and the repetitious structure of the form. The most spatial conception is not surprisingly Dittersdorf's, in a depiction of Actaeon hunting with his friends at the opening of *Actéon changé en cerf*. Right from its initial arpeggiation not of the tonic but of V^7, this is one of the most propulsive sonata-form movements in the *Metamorphoses* symphonies: the opening paragraph never settles in the tonic but concludes on a dominant cadence preparing a boisterous hunting signal of Dittersdorf's own invention (m. 14), which itself concludes on a half-cadence followed by a forward-driving chain of suspensions (Example 1.7). There is no rest other than at the exposition and recapitulation cadences – but on the other hand, the recapitulation reproduces the exposition with nothing more than the usual tonal adjustment, and both halves of the movement are repeated. Dittersdorf creates a headlong gallop but refrains from suggesting any beginning, middle, or end points in the hunt.

---

[41] The signals are printed and discussed in Alexander L. Ringer, "The 'Chasse': Historical and Analytical Bibliography of a Musical Genre" (Ph.D. diss., Columbia University, 1955), 7–10, 192–93, 415; J. Murray Barbour, *Trumpets, Horns and Music* (Lansing, MI: Michigan State University Press, 1964), 118–22; and Heartz, "The Hunting Chorus in Haydn's *Jahreszeiten* and the 'Airs de Chasse' in the *Encyclopédie*," *Eighteenth-Century Studies* 9 (1975–76): 523–39.

Example 1.7   Dittersdorf, Actaeon hunting with his friends (*Actéon changé en cerf*, i), mm. 1–18

The finale of Antonio Rosetti's *La Chasse* exemplifies a more typical strategy, avoiding any too complicated narrative but configuring the recapitulation so as to suggest a later state of affairs than the exposition. The opening builds up even more steam than Dittersdorf's, moving seamlessly from the first group into the transition and pausing only at a unison arpeggiation of V/V over thirty measures in. A horn signal, newly composed like Dittersdorf's and scored for clarinets and bassoons rather than the horn itself, follows in the dominant (Example 1.8a). It is elided with a *crescendo*, enhancing the sense of continuity further, and its head motive becomes the subject of transformation both later in the exposition and in the development. A *fortissimo* in the latter section has no parallel in Dittersdorf's movement and suggests some kind of event, perhaps a sighting of the prey or the kill, but it is the recapitulation that really suggests action (Example 1.8b). Rosetti rewrites his transition to incorporate the grace-note appoggiaturas that serve throughout hunting music as signs for barking hounds (mm. 134–41) and to conclude on the home dominant rather than V/V (m. 144). He then repeats his hunting call at the original pitch level but with enough alteration to ensure that it sounds as if *on* a dominant pedal rather than *in* the dominant key (mm. 144–52). The horns now reinforce the clarinets at the end of each phrase, drawing the theme into association with the traditional hunting instrument. All of this prepares a triumphant continuation of the signal in the tonic, scored for all the winds but dominated by the horns (mm. 152–57). Together with the preceding changes, the newness of this passage implies that the hunt has moved beyond whatever stage was achieved in the exposition, and the return to the tonic provides closure, halting at last the continuous forward push of the movement and marking the successful conclusion of the chase.[42]

---

[42] Rosetti's symphony along with Carl Stamitz's *Simphonie de chasse* and the works by Gossec, Haydn, Hoffmeister, and Paul Wranitzky mentioned in the following paragraphs are discussed at greater length in Ringer, "The 'Chasse,' " 273–94.

Example 1.8a   Rosetti, *La Chasse,* iv, mm. 35–44

Example 1.8b   Rosetti, *La Chasse,* iv, mm. 132–57

(cont.)

Example 1.8b (*cont.*)

Other hunts make similar efforts at suggesting plot development. In the finales of Haydn's as well as Franz Anton Hoffmeister's symphonies, a horn signal is postponed from its expected reappearance in the second group of the recapitulation into a celebratory coda; in Haydn's case there is an additional decrescendo to suggest denouement.[43] Paul Wineberger takes a step further with an original call that sounds very much like a "Halali," the signal that the hounds have caught the prey: not heard at all in the exposition, it appears briefly in the strings during the development section and then in the whole orchestra toward the end of the recapitulation, suggesting again that the hunt has reached a successful conclusion. Ignaz von Beecke uses the real "Halali" in the coda of the first movement of his work and also goes furthest in incorporating the successive events of the hunt into a form that is still recognizably a sonata. His exposition already contains two horn signals, which return in the recapitulation but lead to a third call and then to the "Halali." In

---

[43] In Hoffmeister, cf. mm. 105–20 and 257–82; in Haydn, mm. 30–36 and 219–52. See also Will, "Programmatic Symphonies of the Classical Period," 90–96. Haydn's movement was originally the overture to *La fedeltà premiata*.

place of a development section, moreover, there comes what is presumably a moment of rest, a lyrical passage for strings in a different meter from the rest of the movement (*alla breve* rather the 6/8 which governs the surrounding music and hunting music generally). This begins to approach those rare movements in which hunting plots produce a very unusual, wholly linear form. In the first and last movements of François-Joseph Gossec's *Sinfonia di caccia*, and in the finales of the *Simphonie de chasse, Le Jour variable*, and Symphony in F of Carl Stamitz, the form follows a series of anywhere from three to ten horn signals heard in the order they would be in an actual hunt, while the music in between consists chiefly of galloping orchestral passages that do not establish anything like the profile of a sonata or other familiar pattern, the occasional reprise notwithstanding. Such "realistic" equations of musical and dramatic plot would be adopted only gradually, primarily in battle pieces of the 1790s and after; the composers of Dittersdorf's generation preferred to combine linearity and circularity, line and symmetry. Stories could progress only within a context that allowed the perceiver to grasp their synchronous unity, whether through the painterly composition of a stage set or the symmetrical resolutions of a musical form.

In Dittersdorf's Silver Age, the tableau-like balancing of forward impetus by formal closure and symmetry suggests that the society transformed by history still enjoys stability: the innocence of the Golden Age may be gone, but the rush to embrace new activities and possessions is orderly. Moreover, the resulting "luxury," to recall Dittersdorf's term, brooks no challenges. To repeat: the ear accustomed to Haydn's or Mozart's sonata forms of the 1780s will find Dittersdorf's movement remarkable not merely for the regularity of its large-scale form but also for the avoidance of anomalies on the local level: beginnings that sound like endings, unusual phrase structures, chromatic notes intruding from foreign keys – in short, all those devices that disrupt the musical discourse and create the demand for resolution that Rosen describes. Even the development section generates little tension, the quick entry of the recapitulation dispelling even the faint shadow cast by the strings' atmospheric hovering on V/vi (see Example 1.5b). Despite its faster tempo and more dynamic musical structure, then, Silver resembles Gold more than one might expect. The listener remains in an Age that seems to endure without fundamental change and, significantly, to move in aristocratic steps. Already hinted at in the preceding movement and here made obvious, marching rhythms confirm that Dittersdorf sees the inhabitants of these early Ages as noble, the mirror of his audience and of the implied participants in hunting symphonies as well. Comporting themselves vigorously but with poise, the oldest residents of Antiquity retain the bearing of Europe's cultivated classes.

Brass: drama as feeling

Tertia post illam successit aenea proles,
saevior ingeniis et ad horrida promptior arma,
non scelerata tamen;

To this came next in course, the Brazen Age:
A Warlike Offspring, prompt to Bloody Rage,
Not impious yet –   *(Metamorphoses* 1: lines 125–27)

Dittersdorf had to extrapolate his program for the next movement from a mere two-and-a-half lines on the Brazen Age in Ovid, given in their entirety above. The advent of violence suggested the topic of the minuet, "le despotisme," which in turn must have triggered the idea for the trio, not found in Ovid at all: "les gémissements de ceux qui s'en trouvent les victimes" (the groans of those who find themselves victims [11]). The first dance is appropriately dark and fraught with aggression (Example 1.9a). As if triggered by the unresolved V/vi at the end of the preceding movement's development section, the orchestra takes off in the relative minor, a shift that is all the more striking given that the great majority of eighteenth-century symphony minuets are cast in the overall tonic of the work.[44] Still more ominous are the unison scoring, suggestive of a voice issuing commands, and a jagged melody composed in equal parts of the dotted rhythms of military fanfares and the wide leaps associated in contemporary vocal music with high-flown emotion. A reprise midway through the second part brings an intensification that is one of Dittersdorf's most effective passages in both musical and dramatic terms; against a chain of suspensions in the woodwinds, the two violins engage in a kind of duel over the main theme, exchanging its harsh rhythms and contours in canon (Example 1.9b). The "Alternativo" continues in the minor but shifts to a language of sighing falls suitable for the laments of a despot's victims (Example 1.9c).

Most of Dittersdorf's contemporaries omitted minuets in characteristic symphonies where all the movements were intended to take part in a story. Presumably it was too difficult to justify the dance dramatically; Gossec's *Sinfonia di caccia* does include a minuet, but the movement has no hunting signals and thus – unlike the other three – no obvious role in the plot. But Dittersdorf writes, "En composant ces Symphonies je me suis fait la loi de ne point m'écarter du style qui est en usage aujourd'hui, et c'est par cette raison-ci que dans chacune d'elles il se trouve

---

[44] Rice also hears a programmatically appropriate archaism in the cadence of the first part in the key of the fifth (E minor) rather than the relative major that would be more typical for a later eighteenth-century dance form ("New Light on Dittersdorf's Ovid Symphonies," 464).

Example 1.9a   Dittersdorf, The Brazen Age (*Les Quatre Ages du monde*, iii), mm. 1–8. Accent markings indicate choreographic emphases.

Example 1.9b   Dittersdorf, The Brazen Age, mm. 17–26

Example 1.9c   Dittersdorf, The Brazen Age, trio, mm. 27–36

un *Menuet* et un *Alternatif*, qui suivant l'exigeance des cas en font même quelques fois la clôture" (In composing these symphonies I made it a rule not to deviate at all from the style that is in use today, and it is for this reason that in each of them are found a *Menuet* and *Alternatif*, which sometimes even serve as a conclusion depending on the requirements of the case [7]). The final sentence refers to two symphonies, *Andromède sauvée par Persée* and *Phinée avec ses amis changés en rochers*, in which he not only reverses the usual fast–slow order of the first two movements (as in *Les Quatre Ages*) but also inserts a second slow movement where the minuet would normally be. The dances are not eliminated but displaced to the concluding sections of two-part finales, evidence of Dittersdorf's determination to preserve the model of the four-movement symphony with minuet regardless of the structure of Ovid's tales.

He has an ingenious solution for integrating the dances into the stories. Excepting the trio of *Les Paysans changés en grenouilles*, a tone-painting of peasants splashing in a pond, each movement sets out to express emotions, usually two contrasting emotions in the minuet and trio respectively (Table 1.2). The Brazen Age is exemplary: although the topic of the minuet, "despotism," is not obviously an emotion, Dittersdorf's music is mostly concerned to create an atmosphere of authoritarian aggression, and the trio plumbs its affective complement of sorrowfulness. In effect, they are "character pieces" in the sense that Reichardt understood the term (see pp. 4–5), and indeed the minuets in the *Metamorphoses* share not only the expressive basis of that tradition but also some of its subjects: C. P. E. Bach wrote a "L'Irresoluë" (cf. the minuets of *Actéon*, *Jason*, and *Hercule*), and Reichardt and others treated sorrow, joy, and contentment. The connection is ironic inasmuch as the same northern German circles that cultivated the character piece in the later eighteenth century resisted the inclusion of

Table 1.2 *Expressive subjects of the minuets in the* Metamorphoses *symphonies*

Les Quatre Ages du monde	
minuet	despotism of the Brazen Age
trio	sorrows of the victims of despotism
La Chute de Phaéton	
minuet	Phoebus' anger at himself for granting Phaethon's wish to drive the sun-chariot
trio	Phaethon's joy at the granting of his wish
Actéon changé en cerf	
minuet	Actaeon's indecision over whether or not to enter Diana's grotto
trio	beauty of Diana bathing, which "sends [Actaeon] into ecstasy"
Andromède sauvée par Persée	
minuet	collective joy over Andromeda's rescue
trio	Andromeda's gratitude to Perseus
Phinée avec ses amis changés en rochers	
minuet	Perseus' joy over winning the battle with Phineus
trio	(no trio)
Les Paysans changés en grenouilles	
minuet	Latona's lament for water and the peasants' rude denial
trio	the peasants splashing in a pond
Jason qui enlève la toison d'or	
minuet	Medea's conflicting feelings as she contemplates betraying her father
trio	Medea's "ideal . . . that in the future many gods of love will flutter about her on their wings"
Hercule changé en dieu	
minuet	Deianira's conflicting feelings as she contemplates Hercules' rumored infidelity
trio	continuation of same
Ajax et Ulisse qui se disputent les armes d'Achille	
minuet	Ulysses' victory
trio	Ajax's discontent

minuets in symphonies. As late as 1802 Koch defined the symphony as a three-movement genre despite making approving references to Haydn, who had not written a symphony without minuet since 1765.[45] The underlying objections were outlined in 1792 by the Berlin music critic Carl Spazier, who complained that minuets transgressed the familiar ideal of unity, understood in this case as the necessity for symphonies to express a single "Gemüthsverfassung" (frame of mind) or "Hauptempfindung" (principal affect). First movements and finales could contribute by using similar tempos and styles, and slow movements by providing contrast, but minuets are inappropriate, "weil sie, wenn sie glattweg in dieser Form gearbeitet sind, schlechterdings zur Unzeit an den *Tanzboden* und an den Misbrauch der Musik erinnern; und, sind sie karikaturirt – wie dies mit den Haydn'schen und Pleyelschen öfters der Fall ist – das *Lachen* erregen" (since they, when incorporated wholesale into this genre, unavoidably trigger untimely reminiscences of the dance floor and the misuse of music; and if they are caricatured, as is often the case in Haydn's and Pleyel's, they give rise to laughing).[46] Dittersdorf turns the argument on its head, taking advantage of the great stylistic transformations to which eighteenth-century composers subjected minuets to create, not "caricatures," but movements that fit into a unified narrative and meet the expressive demands of Spazier's aesthetic.

Making emotion the focus of the minuets also brings yet another kind of drama to the symphonies. A movement such as the Brazen Age may seem as inimical to plot development as a repeat sign in a hunting symphony: with a battle coming up in the Iron Age, surely this meditation on the nature and effects of violence is a needless digression. But the parallels in contemporary stage works are even more obvious than in the case of movements that mix action with reflection. Even as Gluck, Calzabigi, and other mid-century reformers introduced more dramatic action into *opera seria*, and as plot-driven *opera buffa* began to surpass the older genre in popularity, reflective arias and other moments of more or less static expression continued to play a crucial role in deepening characterizations and allowing singers and audience time to react to the events. Equally important, in the theoretical context within which the *Metamorphoses* were conceived expression was itself considered dramatic, even a form of action. As an exemplary tableau for both spoken and musical theater, Diderot proposes Clytemnestra's reaction to the threatened sacrifice of Iphigenia. The scene seems to lack the element of action (in addition to repose) that he requires of tableaux, but his description of the

---

[45] Koch, *Musikalisches Lexikon*, cols. 1385–88.
[46] Spazier, "Über Menuetten in Sinfonien," in *Studien für Tonkünstler und Musikfreunde*, ed. Reichardt and Friedrich Ludwig Aemilius Kunzen (Berlin, 1793), 91–92. See also Zaslaw, *Mozart's Symphonies*, 415–16.

relevant passage from Racine's *Iphigénie en Aulide* (1674) finds dynamic movement in the "variété des sentiments et d'images" (variety of feelings and images) through which a composer might portray "la plainte . . . la douleur . . . l'effroi . . . l'horreur . . . la fureur . . . " (the lament . . . the grief . . . the fear . . . the horror . . . the fury . . .) – in short, a dramatic progression of emotional states.[47] More striking yet is Noverre: "L'*action* en matière de Danse est l'Art de faire passer par l'expression vraie de nos mouvements, de nos gestes & de la physionomie, nos sentiments & nos passions dans l'âme des Spectateurs" (Where dancing is concerned, *action* is the art of conveying, by the true expression of our movements, of our gestures and of the physiognomy, our sentiments and passions into the soul of the spectators).[48] A *ballet d'action* can be dynamic even if it lacks an emotional plot such as Diderot invents for Clytemnestra: what matters is the communication of emotions, what passes between stage and house rather than what transpires on stage.

Seen in this light, Dittersdorf's adaptation of the minuet to expressive purposes seems particularly appropriate. Minuet–trio movements involve more repetition than any other contemporary instrumental form. Depending on whether or not the repeat signs are observed during the *da capo*, the first strain of the minuet will be heard three or four times, and if the opening measures are reprised during the second half of the form – as they are in most of Dittersdorf's movements – the number of hearings rises to six or eight. In several cases Dittersdorf also brings back part of the trio in a coda, so that its music recurs nearly as often. Such copious repetition might be thought to enact Noverre's "conveying . . . sentiments and passions into the soul of the spectators." The orchestra presents an emotional state to its listeners, repeats the presentation one or more times to reinforce comprehension, then repeats it again after contrasting music to encourage comparison and reflection. In some cases the feeling may seem to develop, like Clytemnestra's; an example is the intensification that occurs at the reprise in the second half of the minuet of the Brazen Age (Example 1.9b). In most of the minuets and trios, however, what changes is the relationship between the audience and the music. Each programmed rehearing spreads the affective meaning of the movement into further precincts of the listener's consciousness.

The minuet also allows Dittersdorf again to communicate with his audience by implying familiar physical motions, although he uses the minuet somewhat differently than other characteristic rhythms. One

---

[47] Diderot, *Entretiens sur le Fils naturel,* 157 (see also 93); *Selected Writings on Art and Literature,* 74.

[48] *Lettres sur la danse,* 262. Noverre's definition was reprinted in Charles Compan, *Dictionnaire de danse* (Paris, 1787), s.v. "Action."

reason the minuet found its way into so many thousands of later eighteenth-century instrumental works was presumably that its choreography was so flexible. Two dancers trace "Z" patterns from opposite ends of the floor, passing one another in the middle; how many patterns they complete and how long each one takes is up to them, and neither the beginning nor end of the performance need be synchronized with the strains of the accompanying music.[49] Composers could thus write phrases and sections of any length without fear of contradicting an actual or – as in symphonies – imagined choreography. They exercised a similar freedom of style: as in any comparable collection of eighteenth-century symphonies, minuets in the *Metamorphoses* range from the military (*Quatre Ages, Phinée*) to the pastoral (*Actéon*, trio), from the tragic (*Quatre Ages*, trio) to the comic (*Phaéton* and *Jason*, trios), from the high and noble (*Phaéton, Ajax et Ulisse*) to the low and base (*Les Paysans*, trio). Each one leads listeners through what amounts to a different walk. Unlike the gavotte, the minuet has no springing or hopping steps but rather two unadorned *pas marchés* preceded by two *demi-coupés* in which the dancer bends the knee and rises while stepping forward.[50] The choreography emphasizes grace, but in the absence of actual dancers Dittersdorf and other composers could suggest all sorts of variations. The minuet of the Brazen Age marches along in big, bold strides that reproduce the hemiola of the dance, in which each group of steps consumes six beats with an accent on the first and third (as indicated in Example 1.9a). The trio, by contrast, creeps along on soft feet and does not imply any hemiola, emphasizing instead each smaller, shorter step of the 3/4 measure. Just as the Golden- and Silver-Age nobility had their signature walk, so now do despots and their victims.

But what different walks they are. The despots retain some trappings of nobility in the militarism of their dotted rhythms, but otherwise Dittersdorf denies his listeners the idealized self-representations of the preceding movements: the Brazen Age exaggerates military steps into the movements of an unbridled aggression, replacing the poise so valued among eighteenth-century elites with a series of unmannered kicks and lunges, and the trio goes to the opposite extreme, all but tiptoeing in its quiet lament. Neither motion can have felt as comfortable as the confident marching of the Golden or Silver Ages, which has implications not only for Ovid's narrative but also for the strategy of *Les Quatre Ages* as a whole. The people who move to the strains of the Brazen Age have begun to obey the impulses of feeling rather than the dictates of a rational

---

[49] Wendy Hilton, *Dance of Court and Theater: The French Noble Style 1690–1725* (Princeton: Princeton Book Publishers, 1981), 291–94.

[50] Ibid., 191.

society – violence is causing both physical and social bodies to run out of control. The degradation of a social ideal has begun.

Iron: symphonies and history

de duro est ultima ferro.
protinus inrupit venae peioris in aevum
omne nefas: fugere pudor verumque fidesque;

– Hard Steel succeeded then:
And stubborn as the Mettal [sic], were the Men.
Truth, Modesty, and Shame, the World forsook:
Fraud, Avarice, and Force, their places took.

(*Metamorphoses* 1: lines 127–29)

To convey the full horror of the Iron Age, Ovid inverts motifs from the Golden. Humans discover the mineral gold, but this leads to greed and deception; they learn to travel, but this causes border disputes. Worst of all, they destroy their natural relationships with one another through murder and war: hosts kill their guests, wives their husbands, sons their fathers. Such is the moral chaos that "virgo caede madentis / ultima cae-lestum terras Astraea reliquit" (Justice, here opprest, to Heav'n returns; 1: lines 149–50).

Dittersdorf responds with an inversion no less radical (Example 1.10a). Identified in his pamphlet as a battle (11), the finale, marked Presto, begins with unison strings descending by half-step from tonic to dominant and accelerating from whole notes all the way to sixteenths, a propulsive but ominous opening in that the falling chromaticism is reminiscent of lamenting music and used elsewhere by Dittersdorf to suggest poison spreading through the body of Hercules (in the finale of *Hercule*). Next comes a brash fanfare in the trumpets (m. 9), a call to arms that unleashes an unprecedented juggernaut of orchestral energy (m. 13). The next seventy-seven measures contain neither rests, nor any cadences that feel remotely like stopping places, nor, most surprising, any periodicity or distinct melodic profiles. Each successive passage is based on one- or two-measure constellations of melodic and rhythmic motives repeated across an ever-widening spectrum of tonalities. First, after a brief crescendo to *fortissimo* (mm. 13–26), syncopations in the vi-olins and arpeggios in the bass underpin motion from the tonic through the dominant to V/V (mm. 27–38). Second, the basses switch to a slic-ing scale motive and, still accompanied by syncopations, lead down by thirds from the dominant G to A minor then back through the domi-nant to E minor, the mediant (mm. 39–50). Third, the syncopations are replaced by interlocking fanfare rhythms in the lower strings and slash-ing sword strokes in the first violins, which stage their own inversion of the bizarre opening: with the violins fixed on the pitches G and B♭, the rest of the orchestra rises on a chromatically ascending bass from the tonic to the subdominant (Example 1.10b gives the first six mm.). And fourth, after a return through the tonic to a dominant pedal, arpeggios of the dominant and the tonic minor bring the section to a close.

The appended, entirely different Allegretto in the tonic major will be discussed in due course. What precedes it abandons altogether the "style d'aujourd'hui" that Dittersdorf claimed to be preserving by writing symphonies with minuets. The Presto lacks everything one associates with later eighteenth-century instrumental forms: recognizable musical

Example 1.10a   Dittersdorf, The Iron Age (*Les Quatre Ages du monde*, iv), mm. 1–41

(*cont.*)

Example 1.10a (*cont.*)

ideas, articulated phrases, large-scale repetitions, closure, tonal goals arranged into a familiar pattern. Equally unusual is the temporality. Where the first three movements all have repetitions of one kind or another, here time seems to pass linearly, as if Dittersdorf had finally come around to a "realistic" conception of drama. Enhancing the effect, while the other movements make clear distinctions between one musical event and the next, the Presto runs everything together in an unbroken torrent

Example 1.10b   Dittersdorf, The Iron Age, mm. 59–64

of rhythmic continuity. Changes in texture mark a few moments but are too rare to suggest the attacks, counterattacks, and other elements of a battle: this is music of pure forward motion. Most astonishing of all, the six *Metamorphoses* symphonies played at Dittersdorf's first concert include four additional finales as well as yet another (fast) second movement of very similar structure (Table 1.3). Some of these incorporate more recognizable events than the Iron Age does: in *La Chute de Phaéton*, for instance, Phaethon's ride ends with a straightforward tone-painting of the thunderbolt that knocks him from the sun chariot (see Example 3.2, p. 139 below). Yet even with this dramatic anchor, what the movement mostly communicates is the idea of irreversible and ultimately catastrophic action. The audience's experience is like that of Phaethon himself, dragged through uncharted territory by horses run off their appointed path; so the listener, too, is spun through featureless musical paragraphs by an orchestra bent on ignoring the conventions established in previous movements.

Dittersdorf had predecessors in representing swift-moving violence, although, as in his idyllic movements, he transformed as much as perpetuated existing traditions. An important model was again Gluck, who repeats motivic and rhythmic patterns in much the same way in the storm overture to *Iphigénie en Tauride* and the "Dance of the Furies" at the

Example 1.10c   Dittersdorf, The Iron Age, mm. 92–113

end of *Don Juan*. The latter also prefigures Dittersdorf in its avoidance of repetition and suggestion of linearly unfolding events. Although Gluck reprises his opening measures four times, their unpredictability leads to more chaos than formal balance (Example 1.11). A simple, chord-outlining tremolo builds a four-measure phrase on tonic and dominant but stalls soon thereafter on three measures of oscillation between V/V and its upper neighbor, obscuring the harmonic direction as well as any periodicity that may have been established (mm. 7–9). Listeners are hard pressed to know where or for how long the tremolo will continue, an uncertainty Gluck capitalizes on in the reprises by expanding the original three measures of oscillation first to six and then to eight measures, and also by adding ornamentation, chordal harmonization, and abrupt changes in dynamics. Along with the *Schreckensfanfare* – diminished

Table 1.3 *Action movements*

Les Quatre Ages du monde	
iva	war in the Age of Iron
ivb	celebration of the victors, laments of the conquered
La Chute de Phaéton	
iva	Phaethon's fatal chariot ride
ivb	"voluptuous sensations ... after a big storm"
Actéon changé en cerf	
iv	Actaeon hunted by his own hounds
Andromède sauvée par Persée	
iva	Perseus' battle to save Andromeda from the sea monster
ivb	joy and gratitude over Andromeda's rescue
Phinée avec ses amis changés en rochers	
ii	battle between Perseus and Phineus
....	
iva	battle between Perseus and Phineus continued
ivb	Perseus' joy over defeating Phineus

seventh chords sounded at climactic moments, often as vii^7 over a tonic pedal – the continuously changing theme propels the dance along a one-way trajectory.

This was probably Gluck's most celebrated ballet number, enjoying a second life as part of the underworld scene in the French version of *Orfeo* (1774) and also inspiring a symphonic homage by Luigi Boccherini, a finale entitled "Chaconne qui represente L'enfer et qui a été faite à L'imitation de celle de Mr. Gluck dans le Festin de pierre" (Chaconne which represents hell and which was composed in imitation of that of Mr. Gluck in *Don Juan*). Boccherini takes over the theme of Gluck's

Example 1.11   Gluck, Dance of the Furies from *Don Juan*, mm. 1–11

Example 1.12   Boccherini, *La casa del diavolo*, iv, mm. 30–46

dance along with the dissonant outbursts, but his alterations sap considerable energy from the original materials and structure and, in so doing, point up the challenge of using music like Gluck's in symphonic contexts. To begin with, Boccherini regularizes the tremolo into four-measure phrases confirming the tonic D minor (Example 1.12; the use of the oboes to highlight the sequential resolutions to v and iv reinforces the periodicity):

mm.	30–33	34–37	38–41	42–45
harmony	i–V	i–vii/v	v–vii/iv	iv–V–i (–V/V)

He also incorporates contrasting, relatively calm episodes and a repeat sign into the form and, most importantly, reprises his opening measures unchanged near the end, where they are followed by some fifty-six additional measures of tonic confirmation. In Gluck, by contrast, the final transformation of the theme is followed by a brief whirlwind of descending scales and a quiet *tierce de Picardie* tonic that alternates with the minor subdominant, a less than conclusive cadence inasmuch as the tonic is not reiterated enough to balance the harmonic instability of the rest of the movement, and the modal mixture suggests that all is not yet resolved (much like Mozart's similarly mixed ending in the banquet scene of *Don Giovanni*). The length of Boccherini's concluding tonic peroration and its unambiguous close in D minor signal, so to speak, that his Furies are finished dancing, an adjustment that seems motivated by the medium. In performances of Gluck's *Don Juan*, the sight of the Furies overcoming the hero (the scenario also calls for an earthquake[51]) would have helped compensate for any lack of finality in the music,

---

[51] Facsimile in Gluck, *Sämtliche Werke* (Kassel: Bärenreiter, 1951–), II/1: xxvi.

but Boccherini has to achieve closure without the help of stage action – hence the symphony must close more emphatically than the ballet.

In the years before 1780, other characteristic works follow suit. The most common subject with violent or catastrophic overtones, the storm, nearly always occurs in finales, where a combination of agitated rhythms, dissonant harmonies, brilliant passagework and quickly-changing dynamics provides an impressive and virtuosic curtain call (see Appendix 3c, p. 300 below). But a storm finale also has to provide unambiguous closure, which Haydn along with Simoni dall Croubelis, Franz Xaver Richter, Filippo Ruge, and Johann Baptist Vanhal manage by using sonata or binary forms with repetition and substantial concluding passages in the tonic. They do not always achieve the intensity of Gluck or even Boccherini, notwithstanding some remarkable experiments such as Richter's use of polymeter.[52] Only Haydn generates comparable energy, mainly by playing off the tonal dynamic of a quite "regular" (especially for him) sonata form: he saves his most chaotic music for the development, where it can be coupled with the most radical harmonies, and coordinates the attack of the storm with the most dynamic part of both the exposition and the recapitulation, the transition.[53] Even where the "natural" trajectory of the form is not taken advantage of, however, the tonally closed sonata and binary structures achieve satisfactory finality, and the same is true for the storms by Ignaz Holzbauer and Carl Stamitz, the first a finale and the second the end to a two-movement sequence occupying the first half of his *Le Jour variable* (1772). Both have through-composed forms not unlike those of Dittersdorf's finales, but both also incorporate tonal return and thematic reprise; Stamitz's, at nearly 300 measures the longest of all symphonic storms before 1780, caps off a long series of undifferentiated and aperiodic textures with some seventy measures of tonic confirmation, including two massive I–IV–V/V–V–I cadences. Long and unsettled as it is, there is no question of the movement leaving any energy uncontained.

Dittersdorf shares his contemporaries' concerns about closure but adopts a different solution. Only one of his finales, that of *Actéon changé en cerf*, ends Gluck-like with an overly brief return to the tonic (its inconclusiveness emphasized, again, by a concluding alternation between major tonic and minor subdominant). Elsewhere he couples passages like the Presto of the Iron Age with separate, tonally stable sections: *Andromède sauvée par Persée* and *Phinée avec ses amis changés en rochers* conclude with minuets, *Les Quatre Ages* with an Allegretto in march style,

---

[52] Throughout Richter's "Confusione," the first and second violins are in 2/4 and the viola and bass in 3/4. Phrasing and harmony are synchronized, but the conflicting downbeats of the two meters create disruptive cross-accents.

[53] See Will, "Programmatic Symphonies of the Classical Period," 412–15.

and *La Chute de Phaéton*, after the hero's death, with a lyrical *Doucement*. Always slower and less agitated than what precedes them and, in the case of the minuets and march, set in self-contained binary forms, the appended sections relieve Dittersdorf from having to effect closure within battles or other catastrophic scenes. Subsequent years saw increasing use of the same solution; Anton Wranitzky's *Aphrodite*, Louis Massonneau's *La Tempête et le calme* (1794), and Beethoven's *Pastoral* all couple turbulent and structurally anomalous storms with celebratory or idyllic movements in sonata or rondo form.

The *Metamorphoses* symphonies differ from those later works in that they associate their concluding dances and marches with tragedy. According to Dittersdorf, the Allegretto that follows the battle in the Iron Age expresses "les exclamations des vainqueurs en triomphe . . . [et] la douleur des vaincus" (the cries of the victors in triumph . . . [and] the sorrow of the vanquished [11]). The victors get a march in C major whose bright orchestral colors and sprightly duple rhythms vaguely recall the music of the Golden Age (Example 1.10c). But that movement was noble rather than militaristic, and it had nothing like the passage after the double bar of the march, in which the vanquished lament their fate in a dolorous C minor underpinned by a chromatic descending bass line – the opening gesture of the battle now brought into its regular emotional context (mm. 100–11). The strife of the Iron Age has made a return to the Golden Age impossible, creating a new world in which one group's joy comes at the price of another's sorrow. Comparable shadows fall over the rest of the *Metamorphoses*, only two of which end happily, *Andromède sauvée par Persée* and *Jason qui enlève la toison d'or*. The remainder show party after party meeting with catastrophe, whether the degeneration of the human race, as here; the deaths of Phaethon, Actaeon, Hercules, and Orpheus; or the metamorphoses of Phineus (turned into a stone), Scylla (bird; see *Le Siège de Mégare*), Ajax (flower), Midas (ass), and the Lycian peasants (frogs). Dittersdorf does not rescue Ovid's characters through divine intervention, as so many contemporary playwrights and librettists did, but follows them through to their original grim fates. More like classical than neoclassical texts, his symphonies tell of hubris punished.

He seems to have recognized that audiences might be taken aback, and in two instances he and Hermes explain the calm conclusions of the finales not as episodes in the stories but as palliatives for agitated nerves: "Mais comme cette scène [Phaethon's disastrous ride] sans quelques adoucissements n'auroit laissé dans l'âme des auditeurs que des impressions tristes et révoltantes, il [the composer] la tempére par le *Doucement* qui peint les sensations voluptueuses que nous éprouvons quand après un grand orage le ciel commence à s'éclaircir" (But since without any sweetening this scene would leave only sad and disgusting impressions

Example 1.13 Dittersdorf, Perseus celebrates victory (*Phinée avec ses amis changés en rochers*, iv), mm. 227–34

in the souls of the listeners, he balances it with a *Doucement* that paints the voluptuous sensations we experience when the sky begins to clear after a big storm [15]).[54] Really, though, Dittersdorf does not spare his listeners' feelings even when he does add denouements. The march at the end of the Iron Age is strictly Old Testament, an affirmation of humanity's self-destructive tendencies rather than a promise of redemption, and even worse is the minuet celebrating Perseus' victory over Phineus at the end of *Phinée avec ses amis changés en rochers*. This symphony has two battle movements, both comparable to the Iron Age in their through-composed forms, wide-ranging harmony, and lack of periodicity or distinctive musical ideas. The enormous energy of their combined forward drive empties out into a disturbingly bellicose dance (Example 1.13): scored for a marching band of horns, trumpets, and bassoons, the theme is a fanfare and the form a minuet with even more repetitions of the opening measures than usual, so that nothing disturbs a prevailing atmosphere of military self-congratulation.[55] According to Dittersdorf, who refers in his pamphlet to the head of Medusa with which Perseus turns his enemies to stone, "La satisfaction qu'il a de cet effêt du bouclier surpasse toutes les bornes, et l'induit à se moquer des métamorphosés par une ironie basse et effrénée" (The satisfaction he takes in the effect of the shield surpasses all bounds, and

---

[54] Hermes gives a similar explanation of a "douce & gaie" Allegretto at the end of *Orphée et Euridice* (*Analyse*, 179).

[55] The form is ||: a :||: b a :|| b a a, followed by a coda in which the fanfares of mm. 1–2 and 5–6 are repeated for an additional six measures, accompanied by increasingly forceful tonic chords.

leads him to mock the transformed ones with vulgar and unbridled irony [30]). The inspiration is Ovid, who has Perseus not only refuse clemency to a pleading Phineus but also gloat over the thought that his statue will be viewed every day by his former fiancée Andromeda – now Perseus' wife (*Metamorphoses* 5: lines 210–29). In the symphony, this bit of mean-spiritedness produces a concluding passage that, again, does not mitigate the horror of the preceding violence so much as emphasize it, exaggerating the victory celebration to communicate Perseus' unseemly pride.

This victory minuet also writes the final chapter of a preponderantly tragic story about human nature. Dittersdorf chose one myth from each successive book of Ovid's poem for his symphonies, and to judge from his pamphlet and the musical sources he imagined that they would be performed in the same order except for *Phinée avec ses amis changés en rochers*, whose tale comes from book 5 but which he places after the symphony based on book 6, *Les Paysans changés en grenouilles*.[56] At the first of the Viennese concerts and any other performance of the first six works together, this would have meant ending with Perseus' pompous minuet, arguably a more effective conclusion than the quiet croaking of frogs that fills the final measures of *Les Paysans* (see Example 3.3) but also one that would have sent listeners away with the darkest aspects of Dittersdorf's Ovid foremost in their mind. *Les Paysans* and the work that would have preceded it in performance, *Andromède sauvée par Persée*, represent comparatively bright spots in his vision of Antiquity; the latter ends happily, and the former is fundamentally comic from its opening bourrée to its amphibious finale (a point missed in the contemporary outrage over Dittersdorf's representation of frogs; see pp. 140–41). *Phinée avec ses amis changés en rochers* returns to the gloomier atmosphere of the first three symphonies, in all of which an initial state of pastoral happiness – or, in *La Chute de Phaéton*, the majestic self-confidence of Phoebus – gives way to violence, destruction, and death. Most particularly, *Phinée* re-tells the story of *Les Quatre Ages du monde*. It, too, begins with a *gavotte en rondeau*, one whose refrain explicitly recalls the $\hat{3}$–$\hat{5}$–$\hat{1}$ beginning of the Golden Age (cf. Example 1.14 and Example 1.1). Returned to its usual bright tempo, the dance now evokes a moment of real human happiness, the wedding of Perseus to Andromeda, whom he has just rescued from the sea monster. Thereafter, the sense of timeless joy engendered by the dance and its circular form is abandoned for the two battle movements, separated by an aria-like Longuement in which an innocent bystander, a musician soon to be killed himself, laments the violence around him. And after the second battle comes the boastful

---

[56] Only two sources preserve all six symphonies (at D-Dl and H-Bn); both indicate the same ordering as Dittersdorf's explanatory pamphlet.

Example 1.14   Dittersdorf, The Wedding of Perseus and Andromeda
(*Phinée avec ses amis changés en rochers*, i), mm. 1–8

minuet. This is the Four Ages of the World all over again, only worse: instead of the whole human race falling from an imaginary state of innocence, a sympathetic protagonist degenerates from heroic rescuer and happy bridegroom to arrogant, spiteful victor.[57]

Dittersdorf seems intent on drawing a moral lesson from this transformation and from the stories of Phaethon, Actaeon, and the Four Ages as well. If there is a moral to Ovid's *Metamorphoses*, it is only that mortals are subject to the whims of the gods and best advised to stay out of their way, a not unfamiliar message in classical texts. Dittersdorf's perspective seems closer to that of the Abbé Banier, who criticized Ovid for his indifference to even the most blameless victims of the gods:

> Some Mythologists . . . pretend to prove . . . that the Poets intended to shew us the Providence of those very Gods, who watched over all the Actions of Mankind; but what sort of Providence! A restless, morose, and revengefull Providence . . . has not Ovid represented Diana revenging herself in the most cruel and barbarous manner imaginable, for the Indiscretion of a young Prince [Actaeon] who had accidentally seen her in the Bath?[58]

Dittersdorf's invention of Perseus' "vulgar and unbridled irony," his attention to the victims of the Brazen and Iron Ages, even his effort to ameliorate the terror of listeners at the end of *La Chute de Phaéton* – all this recognizes the cost of Ovid's catastrophes in a way that the poet himself does not. Battle, in particular, becomes something other than an excuse for descriptive virtuosity, in whose service Ovid's warriors suffer gruesomely detailed deaths.[59] Dittersdorf presents war as a cause of moral decay, an evil that turns heroes into braggarts and a harmonious human race into parties of victors and victims.

---

[57] On *Phinée*'s relationship to *Les Quatre Ages* as well as its function as a concert closer, see also Rice, "New Light on Dittersdorf's Ovid Symphonies," 470–71.

[58] *Ovid's Metamorphoses in Latin and English, Translated by the Most Eminent Hands*, 87.

[59] See David Hopkins, "Dryden and Ovid's 'Wit out of Season,' " in Charles Martindale, ed., *Ovid Renewed: Ovidian Influences on Literature and Art from the Middle Ages to the Twentieth Century* (Cambridge: Cambridge University Press, 1988), 167–79.

What would his audience have made of such a stern judgment, and in general of a tragic Ovid? The eighteenth century did not always rescue its heroes from death, and German literature, particularly, had witnessed the recent bleak endings of Lessing's *Emilia Galotti* (1772) as well as of Goethe's *Die Leiden des jungen Werthers* (1774) and other works of the *Sturm und Drang*. In their obsession with catastrophe the *Metamorphoses* may have as much to do with the latter tradition as do the minor-key symphonies by Haydn and others more typically associated with it (although written largely before the literary movement),[60] yet the courtly milieu of Dittersdorf's Antiquity is a far cry from the contemporary bourgeois settings of Goethe and Lessing, and the metamorphoses his characters experience have little in common with the interiorized crises of a Werther. They better resemble a transformation being wrought on the symphonies' real-life listeners. The *Metamorphoses* reached Vienna at the end of a lengthy peace in the Habsburg empire, which had fought no major conflicts since the Treaty of Hubertusburg ended the Seven Years War in 1763. It was an era conducive to the sorts of idyllic scenes depicted in the Golden Age and other opening movements in the symphonies – courtly dances, weddings, hunts, contemplation of richly decorated palaces (as in *La Chute de Phaéton*). Dittersdorf himself would have participated, having served the Prince-Bishop Schaffgotsch of Breslau since late 1769 and since 1773 as *Amtshauptmann*, general manager of part of the bishop's territory, a position that required the composer's ennoblement.[61] Small wonder that he conceived Ovid's idyllic scenes as courtly rather than rustic; the march was his step, and although a countrified pastoral language was as available to him as it was to Beethoven two decades later in the *Pastoral* Symphony, he self-consciously refers to his sole essay in that vein, a vigorous bourrée representing the peasants at work in *Les Paysans changés en grenouilles*, as being "dans le goût trivial des chansons de paysans" (in the trivial style of peasant songs [25]). Otherwise his paradises are aristocratic, closer to Marie Antoinette's Petit Trianon than to the unsullied and potentially dangerous Nature of Werther or of contemporary rustic poets such as Salomon Geßner.

By the mid-1780s, however, Arcadia was beginning to crumble. The War of the Bavarian Succession of 1778–79, largely the project of the soon-to-be sole regent Joseph, disturbed the fifteen-year peace and, although not a major conflict in military terms, caused serious disruption where the armies marched, camped, and demanded supplies.[62] One

---

[60] See Landon, *Haydn*, II: 266–84.
[61] Dittersdorf, *Lebensbeschreibung*, 183–92, 204–05.
[62] The account in Derek Beales, *Joseph II*, vol. I, *In the Shadow of Maria Theresa 1741–1780* (Cambridge: Cambridge University Press, 1987), 386–422, includes Joseph's own dispatches testifying to the destruction being wrought at the front.

such area was Breslau, whose unfortunate situation between the opposing forces led Schaffgotsch to disband his court and put Dittersdorf in the position of defending his jurisdiction from would-be Prussian conquerors – perhaps the most remarkable episode in a life filled with them.[63] With Joseph's assumption of sole rulership in 1780 came the famous series of abruptly imposed imperial reforms, which promised greater political freedom but whose unintended consequences soon led to retractions.[64] In 1784 the government began pursuing the Masons, and by 1786 "Josephism" was in full crisis; just two months before Dittersdorf's concerts, in March 1786, the emperor's refusal to halt the brutal public execution of Franz Zaglauer von Zahlheim severely damaged his standing as an enlightened ruler. Political pamphlets accused him of exercising his absolute power at the expense of his own judicial code (he had convinced Maria Theresa to abolish torture and restrict capital punishment in 1776[65]), and a literary "fantasy" by the Viennese writer Paul Weidmann, *Der Eroberer*, offered a thinly disguised allegory for Joseph's "degeneration" by telling of a king who, although raised in idyllic and politically enlightened surroundings, falls into irrational despotism because of his addiction to conquering and bloodshed.[66] The Viennese *Aufklärer* had their gloomiest predictions fulfilled in the following year, when Joseph's reputation among Europe's monarchs as a "habitual expansionist" helped maneuver him into an unnecessary and disastrous war with the Turks.[67]

Symphonies in which violence results in tragedy, and in the moral downfall of ideal heroes, would not necessarily have suggested political critique even in such a fraught context. Opposition would have been uncharacteristic of Dittersdorf, defender of the empire and admirer of Joseph, and the emperor himself could not have objected to the works' essentially Christian ethic, which he considered his reforms to uphold.

---

[63] Dittersdorf, *Lebensbeschreibung*, 214–19.

[64] A useful summary of the Austrian reforms is Ernst Wangermann, "Reform Catholicism and Political Radicalism in the Austrian Enlightenment," in Roy Porter and Mikulás Teich, eds., *The Enlightenment in National Context* (Cambridge: Cambridge University Press, 1981), 127–40. The effect of Joseph's reforms on the arts is discussed in Leslie Bodi, *Tauwetter in Wien: Zur Prosa der österreichischen Aufklärung 1781–1795* (Frankfurt am Main: S. Fischer, 1977), and Volkmar Braunbehrens, *Mozart in Vienna 1781–1791*, trans. Timothy Bell (New York: Grove Weidenfeld, 1986), esp. 215–55.

[65] Beales, *Joseph II*, I: 236–38.

[66] Bodi, *Tauwetter in Wien*, 280–96, 354–65; Eduard Beutner, "Aufklärung versus Absolutismus? Zur Strategie der Ambivalenz in der Herrschersatire der österreichischen Literatur des Josephinischen Jahrzehnts," in Gerhard Ammerer and Hanns Haas, eds., *Ambivalenzen der Aufklärung: Festschrift für Ernst Wangermann* (Vienna: Verlag für Geschichte und Politik; Munich: Oldenbourg, 1997), 241–52.

[67] Charles Ingrao, *The Habsburg Monarchy 1618–1815* (Cambridge: Cambridge University Press, 1994), 207.

What Dittersdorf does suggest is a lament, an elegy for a way of life that had begun to vanish, for him, during the struggle with the Prussians in Breslau. He began composing the *Metamorphoses* symphonies in the following year, by which time he seems to have doubted whether the legislated calm of the *ancien régime* would endure; that, in any event, is the implication of a series of works in which human aspirations and jealousies, played out through violence, repeatedly overpower idyllic repose. In one instance he even has the quintessential pastime of an aristocratic peace provide the means for its own destruction: having hunted his way cheerfully through the first movement of *Actéon changé en cerf*, the hero finds himself pursued by his own hounds in the finale. Perhaps fittingly, this is the only concluding action movement with no soothing denouement.

With the way of life went a sense of self whose disintegration is all the more vivid thanks to the many references to dance and ballet. Diderot's tableaux, writes Michael Fried, provided the writer with "an external, 'objective' equivalent for his own sense of himself as an integral yet continuously changing being."[68] The tableau-like movements of the *Metamorphoses* subscribe to a related psychology in the sense that their music changes from measure to measure but also, through formal clarity and repetition, produces a unified portrait. The "integral yet . . . changing being" also inheres in the physical movements implied by the music. The traditional French choreographies required the body to remain poised even while in motion; in the minuet, for instance, the body was held so that the head would trace an elegant wave through the air as the steps progressed.[69] Furthermore, dancers often walked symmetrical paths that ended, in relation to the other bodies in the pattern, back where they began. The opening movements of the *Metamorphoses* symphonies enshrine this delicate balance between movement and stasis – the finales destroy it. Their battles and hunts and other violent scenes plunge the self into a world of unending change that, once experienced, cannot be escaped, making the real "irony" of the victory minuet in *Phinée* its effort to restore a traditional sense of time and movement. It insists on its stately rhythms, repetitions, and closed form, but the exaggeration alone proves that it is too little, too late. After so much tragedy, so much exposure to a one-directional unfolding of events – two whole movements, in this case – the listener cannot hear this minuet as representing the easy mediation between motion and stillness exemplified by the Golden Age. Perseus' celebration enforces a sense of permanency from outside; the character's true inclinations are for action

---

[68] Fried, *Absorption and Theatricality*, 91.
[69] See the description in William Hogarth, *The Analysis of Beauty* (1753), 147; quoted in Foster, *Choreography and Narrative*, 24.

and change. Perseus belongs to history, as must, in the end, the auditor of the *Metamorphoses* symphonies.

Dittersdorf's Viennese audience and indeed all of European society would soon have intimate knowledge of history's irreversible changes, thanks not only to Joseph II's military adventures but even more to the French Revolution and, in the realm of art, to Romantic fascinations with psychological progress and transcendence. The *Metamorphoses* symphonies mark a dawning awareness of impending trouble and an intense nostalgia for past security. They do not represent the incursion of historical process as a good thing; on the contrary, they associate it with death and the degeneration of the human spirit, while linking scenes of happiness and moral rectitude with greater or lesser measures of an older, neoclassical "Stille." Dittersdorf's is the music of a real Golden Age coming to an end.

2

Preaching without words: Reform Catholicism versus divine mystery in Haydn's *Seven Last Words*

The Seven Last Words of our Savior on the Cross posed still greater challenges to contemporary listeners than had the *Metamorphoses* symphonies. Commissioned to write music for a Good Friday observance in Cádiz, Spain, Haydn produced seven slow movements based on the utterances or "words" of the crucified Christ. In the original service each movement followed a reading and explication of the associated text, with an *Introduzione*, also slow, at the beginning, and a Presto, a depiction of the earthquake triggered by Christ's death, at the end. In concert, as the work was soon heard in Vienna, Paris, Berlin, London, and elsewhere, it proposed that music could guide listeners through the narrative crux of Christianity with only minimal assistance from language.[1] It also stepped square into a debate over religion and religious music that was raging throughout Europe and particularly in Josephinian Austria, not the milieu for which Haydn's movements were originally intended but the one in which he, like Dittersdorf, lived and worked. Joseph extended his reforms of the empire to the church, putting special emphasis on preaching as a medium for conveying religious truth and recommending that homilies take a single lesson from the day's Gospel reading and explain it in such a way as both to engage the intellect and to touch the heart.[2] The advice was founded on the principles of classical rhetoric and quite similar to that given in contemporary manuals on

---

[1] By 1793 performances were also recorded in Bonn, Breslau, and the United States. On the commission and early performance history see Landon, *Haydn*, II: 616–18, 690; and Jonathan Drury, "Haydn's 'Seven Last Words': An Historical and Critical Study" (Ph.D. diss., University of Illinois, 1976), 27–28.

[2] See pp. 99–100 below. The standard account of the Austrian church reform is Eduard Winter, *Der Josefinismus: Die Geschichte des österreichischen Reformkatholizismus 1740–1848* (Berlin: Rütten & Loening, 1962); see also Jean Bérenger, "The Austrian Church," in William J. Callahan and David Higgs, eds., *Church and Society in Catholic Europe of the Eighteenth Century* (Cambridge: Cambridge University Press, 1979), 88–105; Ernst Wangermann, "Josephinismus und katholischer Glaube," in Elisabeth Kovács, ed., *Katholische Aufklärung und Josephinismus* (Munich: Oldenbourg, 1979), 332–41;

composition, which called for each section of a musical work to elaborate a main idea or *Hauptsatz* and with it an associated emotion.[3] In one respect *The Seven Last Words* and its closest relatives among characteristic pieces, mid-eighteenth-century pastoral symphonies, combine the two ideals. Through unusually concentrated motivic and harmonic development, they explore the musical and emotional potential of *Hauptsätze* that are themselves signs for the words of Christ or other Gospel texts, so that exemplary composition and exemplary sermon seem to become one.

In another respect, however, they run against the grain of Austria's "Reform Catholicism." The pastoral symphonies evoke the music of rural Christmas celebrations and a realm of popular piety, of pilgrimages and relics and rocking the baby Jesus in the crèche, that reformers condemned as superstitious. And *The Seven Last Words* appeared four years after Joseph II had limited the use of orchestras in church to Sundays and major feasts and withdrawn a major source of support for large ensembles by banning Catholic brotherhoods of the type that commissioned Haydn's work from Cádiz.[4] Undoubtedly one of the larger Viennese churches could still have mounted a performance, but the concert premiere, at a private event in the palace of Prince Auersperg, better suited the prevailing climate. Sacred instrumental music was simply at odds with Joseph's mission to produce a laity better educated in the faith, for which he believed the ideal sacred music to be congregational hymns in the vernacular. Rhetorical clarity notwithstanding, Haydn's movements cannot match the directness of the emperor's hymnbook, which favors blunt moral lessons in rhyming verse[5] – if anything the lack of text in *The Seven Last Words* and, as we shall see, aspects of its formal and harmonic structure enhance the mystery of the crucifixion even as rhetorical development clarifies its emotional meanings.

Pastoral symphonies and *The Seven Last Words* thus betray some ambivalence toward "enlightened" Christianity, acknowledging the desire for lucidity but also pointing both backward and forward to a faith

James Van Horn Melton, *Absolutism and the Eighteenth-Century Origins of Compulsory Schooling in Prussia and Austria* (Cambridge: Cambridge University Press, 1988), 200–30; and Frank A. J. Szabo, *Kaunitz and Enlightened Absolutism 1753–1780* (Cambridge: Cambridge University Press, 1994), 209–57.

[3] Bonds, *Wordless Rhetoric*, 90–102.

[4] Bruce C. MacIntyre, *The Viennese Concerted Mass of the Early Classic Period* (Ann Arbor: UMI Research Press, 1986), 14–17.

[5] The hymnbook is Johann Kohlbrenner, *Der heilige Gesang zum Gottesdienste in der römisch-katholischen Kirche* (1777; revised 1781 by Michael Haydn). A representative text reads: "Ergab ich mich dem Saufen? / Beherrschte mich der Frass? / Und hielt ich beim Verkaufen / Das festgesetzte Maass?" (quoted in Reinhard Pauly, "The Reforms of Church Music under Joseph II," *Musical Quarterly* 43 [1957]: 375).

based more in revelation and ritual than in reason. Haydn's work also sounds another note of anxiety amid the official optimism of Josephinian Austria, not so loudly as the *Metamorphoses* but with a special urgency given the subject matter. The Passion of all stories should end with hope for the future, and some eighteenth-century passion oratorios do, but the finale of *The Seven Last Words* is as violent as Dittersdorf's battles and equally lacking in reassuring denouement. Criticisms of this conclusion and efforts to rewrite it after 1790 illustrate how important affirmation becomes under a new aesthetic regime; while a textless portrayal of Christ may have appealed to a generation that placed increasing value on the indefinite, it had also to satisfy a growing demand for transcendence. The darkness of Haydn's original ending suggests, like the violence of Dittersdorf's Iron Age, an undercurrent of doubt regarding the inevitability of redemption.

Pastoral symphonies and the rhetoric of emotion

The second of the six symphonies published by Huberty as Johann Stamitz's Opus 4 begins with more energy than one might expect given its title, "Pastorale." A tremolo in the first violins accompanies descending scales in the lower strings and then a vigorous melody in the winds, all at a tempo of Presto: this is not the languid grotto of Dittersdorf's or Pichl's Diana (Example 2.1). On the contrary, Stamitz signifies the opposite of retirement and repose: the melody in the winds recalls several eighteenth-century Christmas carols, most notably the Bohemian song known later in German as "Kommet ihr Hirten" and in English as "Come All Ye Shepherds" or "Bells are Ringing in the Tower," whose defining trademark is the repeated descent through

Example 2.1   Stamitz, *Sinfonia pastorale*, i, mm. 1–15

Example 2.2 "Come All Ye Shepherds"

Kommet, das Hir-ten, ihr Män-ner und Frau'n   Chri-stus, der Herr, ist heu - te ge-bo-ren, den Gott zum Hei-land euch hat er-ko-ren. Fürchtet euch nicht!
kom-met, das lieb-li - che Kindlein zu schau'n.

scale degrees $\hat{3}$–$\hat{1}$–$\hat{2}$–$\hat{5}$ (Example 2.2).[6] Comprising pitches available on the natural horn, this pattern and its associations turn the beginning of the symphony into a dramatic "Wachet auf," a call to action by an implied shepherds' horn that announces the miracle of the Nativity.

Christmas music of central and southern Europe in the eighteenth century abounds in shepherds waking one another, journeying to the manger at Bethlehem, and soothing the infant Jesus with music, particularly among the vocal and instrumental works termed "pastorella" by Geoffrey Chew and others.[7] These share a common origin in popular, predominantly rural Nativity customs: some have texts in local dialect and call for hurdy-gurdies, bagpipes, or real wooden shepherds' horns, while others quote carols or evoke rural instruments through drone accompaniments, horn fanfares, and prominent use of winds. Most of the several dozen mid-century orchestral works entitled "pastorella," "pastorale," or "pastoritia" can be counted part of this tradition (see Appendix 2, pp. 294–98 below). All of them use or imply rustic instruments, and others quote familiar songs, including "Come All Ye Shepherds" (in symphonies by Pichl, Leopold Hofmann [Kimball D1], and Franz Xaver Pokorny [Angerer C18] as well as Stamitz) and perhaps the most popular melody in the pastorella repertory, the "Night-Watchman's Song" (in two works by Pokorny [Angerer D33, D58]). The shorter examples in particular, those with only two or three movements or sections, also give evidence of having been used in church: Michael Haydn's *Pastorello* bears the date 23 December 1766 and the inscription "Ein Heiligthum"; Joseph Friebert's *Symphonia pastoralis* includes a list of Christmas Eve performances in 1774–78; Haydn, Friebert, Christian Cannabich, Remigius Falb, and Greggor Rößler all

---

6   The similarity between Stamitz's melody and the Bohemian carol "Nesem vám noviny" is identified in Eugene K. Wolf, *The Symphonies of Johann Stamitz: A Study in the Formation of the Classic Style* (Utrecht and Antwerp: Bohn, Scheltema and Holkema, 1981), 303–04. Other pastoral carols featuring the $\hat{3}$–$\hat{1}$–$\hat{2}$–$\hat{5}$ pattern are found in Jan Němeček, *Zpěvy XVII. a XVIII. století* (Prague: Státní Nakladatelství, 1956), 132; and Karl M. Klier, *Schatz österreichischer Weihnachtslieder*, 5 vols. (Klosterneuburg: Augustinus-Druckerei, n.d.), I: 14, 37, and V: 23, 34.

7   Chew, "The Austrian Pastorella and the *stylus rusticanus*: Comic and Pastoral Elements in Austrian Music, 1750–1800," in David Wyn Jones, ed., *Music in Eighteenth-Century Austria* (Cambridge: Cambridge University Press, 1996), 133–93; Mark Germer, "The Austro-Bohemian Pastorella and Pastoral Mass to c1780" (Ph.D. diss., New York University, 1989).

score for organ; and Hofmann uses trombones, found in the theater and church but not typically in the concert room of this period.

These works reference rural customs from a distance, surviving primarily in the archives of courts, monasteries, or urban churches where the resources were available to perform them and where composers such as Stamitz, Cannabich, Michael Haydn, and Pokorny were employed.[8] When Stamitz and others produced four-movement pastoral symphonies, they took a further step away from popular sources and complicated the semantic associations of their pastoral references; while such examples may also have been used in sacred contexts (with minuets omitted if they were deemed too worldly for church[9]), thanks to their length, movement order, and scoring for a normal complement of winds and strings they could also have taken the usual place of symphonies at the beginnings and ends of secular concerts – as Stamitz's symphony must have done during a long career that saw it published in Paris, Amsterdam, and in London as late as c. 1790.[10] Listeners in the know may have continued to connect its Christmas carol with the shepherds of Bethlehem, but others will have attributed the call to the shepherds' horns found also in Arcadia. Pastoral offered a meeting ground for sacred and secular, a point to which we shall return.

All listeners would have heard Stamitz elaborate his melody so systematically that the definition of "Hauptsatz" in Sulzer's *Allgemeine Theorie* some two decades later might have used the first movement of the symphony as an illustration. "Ist in einem Tonstük eine Periode, welche den Ausdruk und das ganze Wesen der Melodie in sich begreift, und nicht nur gleich anfangs vorkömmt, sondern durch das ganze Tonstük oft, in verschiedenen Tönen, und mit verschiedenen Veränderungen, wiederholt wird" (A *Hauptsatz* is a period in a musical work that incorporates the expression and the whole essence of the melody. It appears not only at the beginning of a piece, but is repeated frequently, in different keys and with different variations).[11] Echoes of

---

[8] The same is true of instrumental pastorellas generally (Germer, "Austro-Bohemian Pastorella," 114). Instrumental pastoral music of the first half of the eighteenth century, including Nativity-related works, is discussed in Hermann Jung, *Die Pastorale: Studien zur Geschichte eines musikalischen Topos* (Bern: Francke, 1980), 144–95.

[9] Cf. Zaslaw, "Mozart, Haydn, and the *Sinfonia da chiesa*," 116.

[10] Wolf, *The Symphonies of Johann Stamitz*, 400.

[11] Sulzer, *Allgemeine Theorie*, II: 488, trans. Bonds, *Wordless Rhetoric*, 94–95. Johann Philipp Kirnberger and Johann Abraham Peter Schulz assisted Sulzer with (and in some cases authored or co-authored) the musical articles in the *Allgemeine Theorie*. The difficulty of distinguishing their work and the authority of Sulzer as editor have led me, like other recent authors, simply to credit all entries to Sulzer himself (see Baker and Christensen, *Aesthetics and the Art of Musical Composition*, 14; and Mark Evan Bonds, "The Symphony as Pindaric Ode," in Elaine Sisman, ed., *Haydn and His World* [Princeton: Princeton University Press, 1997], 150–51n.).

"Come All Ye Shepherds" linger into the period following the initial quotation, in a figure whose fall by third, leap up, and fall by a larger interval recall the trademark motive of the carol (i.e., $\hat{3}$–$\hat{1}$–$\hat{2}$–$\hat{5}$; cf. Example 2.1 and 2.3a, mm. 18 and 22). The strings then bring the original version back in a contrapuntal texture after a half-cadence on the dominant (Example 2.3a, mm. 31–34), as well as the modified version, with rhythm extended, at the pause in the dominant halfway through the movement (Example 2.3b). All versions return again in the second

Example 2.3a   Stamitz, *Sinfonia pastorale*, i, mm. 15–39

Example 2.3b   Stamitz, *Sinfonia pastorale*, i, mm. 62–66

half of the movement as Stamitz reprises his materials in reverse tonal order, beginning in the dominant and ending in the tonic.

Likening the *Hauptsatz* to the Gospel verse used as the basis for a sermon, Joseph Riepel suggested analogies for musical ideas not derived from the main theme: "Ein Prediger kann ja das Evangelium nicht immer wiederholen und vorlesen; sondern er muss es auslegen. Er macht eben Uebergänge oder transitiones &c. Er hat nebst dem Satz aufs allerwenigste noch einen Gegensatz" (A preacher cannot constantly repeat the Gospel and read it over and over; instead, he must interpret it. He in fact makes transitions, etc. In addition to the thesis, he has at the very least an antithesis).[12] The half-cadence early on in Stamitz's movement is an obvious example of "transition." Turns, a descending scale, and a fanfare rhythm in the horn neither develop the carol melody nor establish a new contrasting *Satz*; rather, they punctuate the first key area and open the second (Example 2.3a, mm. 23–26). Other passages expand on the pastoral character of the *Hauptsatz* without elaborating it directly, particularly the oboes' descent in thirds and sixths over a drone in the basses and horns (Example 2.3a, mm. 35–39; the full period lasts eight measures). As for an "antithesis," the best candidate is a striking transformation of the *Hauptsatz* midway through the second half of the movement. Although Stamitz's form is more like a binary than a sonata, with the second part repeating the first rather than dividing into a development and recapitulation, he does allow for a recapitulation-like moment by withholding the carol melody until just before the tonic return. There it is heard first in the relative minor, sounding like a ghost of its former self thanks both to the key and to the absence of the unison, high-register voices of the winds (Example 2.3c). When they enter immediately afterwards, they wrest the melody away from the strings and restore it to the tonic, like an orator showing that what

---

[12] Joseph Riepel, *Anfangsgründe zur musikalische Setzkunst* vol. II: *Grundregeln zur Tonordnung insgemein* (Frankfurt and Leipzig, 1755), 76; trans. Bonds, *Wordless Rhetoric*, 99.

Example 2.3c   Stamitz, *Sinfonia pastorale*, i, mm. 89–97

looks like a contradiction is actually a proof. The shadow is dispelled with a single stroke.

Returning to Riepel, one might ask how this apparent confutation and the other tonal and thematic developments of the *Hauptsatz* "interpret" its message of Christmas joy. It is tempting to connect them to a rudimentary plot: the shepherds awake, feel the excitement of the moment (Example 2.3a, mm. 15–22), fall into discussion (imitation, mm. 30–34), experience doubt (minor key, Example 2.3c, mm. 90–92), and return to certainty (major key, mm. 93–96). One might even pursue the story into the following movements: the Larghetto could be a lullaby, slow and calm and with a new elaboration of "Come All Ye Shepherds" that recalls the musical cradle-rocking found in many pastorellas (Example 2.4), while the minuet, trio, and finale all suggest celebratory dancing, the last transforming the carol yet again into a gigue (Example 2.5). In a pastoral context, a dance is as fitting a parallel as any for the "glorifying and praising God" that concludes the account of the Nativity in Luke (2:20). However, repetitions and reprises pose the same obstacles to a narrative reading that they did in the sonata-form movements of Dittersdorf's *Metamorphoses*, forcing Stamitz's shepherds to awake, fall into discussion, or rock the cradle several times in succession. It seems more likely that the movements' twists and turns serve to persuade or, as in rhetorical conceptions of music, to touch the heart. According to Sulzer, musical works "kommen alle darin überein ... dass der Hauptsatz mit diesen Zwischengedanken in verschiedenen Harmonien und Tonarten, und auch mit kleinen melodischen Veränderungen, die dem Hauptausdruck angemessen sind, so oft wiederholt wird, bis das Gemüth des Zuhörers hinlänglich von der Empfindung eingenommen ist" (all have this in

Example 2.4   Stamitz, *Sinfonia pastorale*, ii, mm. 65–71

Example 2.5   Stamitz, *Sinfonia pastorale*, iv, mm. 1–8

common . . . that the *Hauptsatz* and [its] interpolated ideas are repeated often enough, in different harmonies and keys, and with small melodic variations appropriate to the governing mood, for the spirit of the listener to be captivated by the emotion).[13] Stamitz "captivates" listeners with joy through an extended play on the functional implications of the main motive. The horn call or bell figure of $\hat{3}$–$\hat{1}$–$\hat{2}$–$\hat{5}$ resolves most naturally to scale degree $\hat{1}$ over the harmonies I–V–I, and in other Christmas carols as in "Come All Ye Shepherds" it tends to reinforce cadences. As Stamitz transforms the motive, creating the pattern $\hat{4}$–$\hat{2}$–$\hat{5}$–$\hat{5}$, the accompanying ii–V–I progression pushes strongly toward closure (Example 2.3a, mm. 18 and 22), and when this version returns at the final cadences of both halves of the form, the elongation of its final two pitches allows for still more decisive cadential motion, ii–I$_4^6$–V–I (Example 2.3b, mm. 62–66). Pastorellas since the early eighteenth century had combined evocative motives with drones to punctuate cadences and imbue them with a sense of quietude;[14] Stamitz's endings rely on drones as well as harmonic closure to deliver the *Hauptsatz* to a state of rest it has implied all along.

The remainder of the movement explores other, less peaceful nuances of joy. Just before the first entrance of the winds, the tremolo in the first violin shifts from the tonic to the fifth scale degree, injecting additional energy into what already sounds like an uncommonly lively drone (Example 2.1, mm. 9–13). The winds themselves sound assertive rather than restful, particularly the high unison horns, and they repeatedly renew the melodic impetus by following the bell motive with leaps back up to a higher octave. In the ensuing period, the eighth notes of the opening accelerate to sixteenths and the cadential reworking of the main motive alternates with an upward-shooting arpeggio that eventually sparks the half-cadence on the dominant (Example 2.3a, mm. 15–26). The imitations on the motive (mm. 31–34) hint at the sobriety of the *stile antico* and introduce the clearest reference yet to authentic, restful pastoral music, the lilting passage for oboes (mm. 35–38) – but eighth notes turn

---

[13] *Allgemeine Theorie* II: 488, trans. adapted from Bonds, *Wordless Rhetoric*, 95.
[14] Chew, "Haydn's Pastorellas: Genre, Dating, and Transmission in the Early Church Works," in Otto Biba and David Wyn Jones, eds., *Studies in Music History Presented to H. C. Robbins Landon on his Seventieth Birthday* (London: Thames and Hudson, 1996), 22–23.

Example 2.6a Gossec, "Pastorella" (Symphony in D [Saceanu 27], i), mm. 78–86

Example 2.6b Gossec, "Pastorella," mm. 1–7

to sixteenths again in the next section, sparking yet more fresh energy. In short, the whole movement oscillates between excitement and calm in a way best understood as a means of impressing an emotional state upon listeners, who confront joy alternately as full-throated excitement, quiet calm, or varying degrees in between. Transforming the *Hauptsatz* creates the musical diversity necessary to hold the attention while at the same time focusing the soul on a single governing *Empfindung*.

That a pastoral joy such as this could be both sacred and secular is evidenced not only by the probable performance of Stamitz's movement in both contexts but also by the music of some less kinetic examples. Gossec published a "Pastorella" (the first movement of the Symphony in D, Saceanu 27) that is in many respects a homage to Stamitz, whose symphony he may have heard during the Mannheim composer's visit to Paris in the 1750s; the French composer takes over the repeated eighth notes of the beginning, uses a *Hauptsatz* derived from elements of "Come All

Example 2.6c Gossec, "Pastorella," mm. 152–74

Ye Shepherds,"[15] and even copies Stamitz's confutation midway through the second half of the form, to the point of having the winds enter on the second beat when they reclaim the main theme, exactly as in the other work (cf. Example 2.6a and Example 2.3c). Yet the fact that Gossec has the tonic follow the dominant at this rhetorical high point, rather than the more distant relative minor of Stamitz's movement, is symptomatic of a generally less dramatic and energetic conception evident also in a slower tempo, Allegro rather than Presto; a slower harmonic rhythm in the *Hauptsatz*, one rather than two chords per measure; and a softer orchestral timbre, with flutes rather than oboes used throughout. The movement is also framed by passages whose restfulness Stamitz never matches. Gossec begins with a slow introduction in which the repeated

---

[15] $\hat{3}$–$\hat{1}$–$\hat{2}$–$\hat{5}$ becomes $\hat{1}$–$\hat{3}$–$\hat{2}$–$\hat{5}$, preceded by an additional $\hat{1}$–$\hat{5}$ and followed by $\hat{4}$–$\hat{2}$ (as in Example 2.6a). The similarity is noted by John A. Rice in *The Symphony 1720–1840*, vol. D-3 (New York: Garland, 1983), xvii–xviii.

eighth notes are scored so that the violins must cross back and forth between the G and D strings, producing a murmur reminiscent of the streams and brooks of musical idylls that accompanies a relaxed neighboring progression, I–IV–I, occupying four long measures of the slow tempo (Example 2.6b). The final cadence uses the same plagal motion to cap off an extraordinary coda in which the eighth-note pulse of the Allegro slows to half and whole notes and the first violins descend unhurriedly through two octaves over a chain of suspensions (Example 2.6c). A more explicit reference to ecclesiastical counterpoint than Stamitz ever attempts, the long descent also draws a veil over the movement's already restrained excitement.

Even more restful is the first movement of the pastoral symphony by Pichl, which begins with a luxuriant setting of "Come All Ye Shepherds" that has murmuring eighths in the second violins, pulsing quarter notes on a root-fifth drone in the lower strings, and a melody whose initial notes have been stretched out to fill entire measures (Example 2.7). A half-cadence tries to spark some action (mm. 8–14) but results only in a repetition of the opening measures made even more lush by the addition of the winds. Most significant about this work is that it was composed contemporaneously with Pichl's neoclassical works and entitled, in one source (D-Rtt), not only *Pastorella* but also *Polymnia*, Muse of religious poetry. Hence the idyllic texture seems calculated to evoke as much the neoclassical paradises of Gluck and Dittersdorf as any Nativity scene, and with them the stillness of Winckelmann's ancient Greece. Composed in the wake of Winckelmann's first publications, the opening and closing of Gossec's movement and the equally peaceful second movements of several other pastoral symphonies, notably Pokorny's, may have triggered related associations, the result of which would have been an ever greater entanglement of sacred and secular meanings. "Stille" itself had religious overtones inasmuch as God, Christ, and (in some minds) the believer could display the same self-possession and calm that Winckelmann attributed to the denizens of Antiquity.[16] When Archbishop Colloredo of Salzburg, a dedicated proponent of church reform, oversaw the removal of side altars, statues, and other objects from his churches, his purpose was to promote more concentrated learning and reflection; he says that "alles, was die Stille der Seele stören, die Gedanken zerstreuen und die hochachtungsvolle Aufmerksamkeit auf göttliche Wahrheiten schwächen kann, soviel wie möglich entfernt werde" (everything that can disturb the stillness of the soul, scatter the thoughts, and weaken the respectful attentiveness to divine truths is so far as possible removed).[17] For similar reasons, he

---

[16] Nisbet, ed., *German Aesthetic and Literary Criticism*, 5; see p. 39 above.
[17] Pastoral letter of 29 June 1782, quoted in Günther Heinz, "Veränderungen in der

Example 2.7   Pichl, *Sinfonia pastorella*, i, mm. 1–14

preferred contemplative to narrative subjects in religious painting. Not quite so austere as his churches, which in any event lay some years in the future, the more relaxed of the pastoral symphonies likewise reduce the stimuli to the heart. Static harmonies and unchanging rhythms invite the listener to notice the simplest lines and progressions, the falling chord tones of "Come All Ye Shepherds" or the neighboring motion of tonic and subdominant, and in so doing provide both object and accompaniment for reflection. Meanwhile the *Empfindung*, the quietude of a pastoral idyll, can be both religious and profane, so that a Muse can sing Christmas carols – as the double title of Pichl's symphony implies – without fear of contradiction.

In the decades following Stamitz's, Gossec's, and Pichl's examples, composers of pastoral symphonies continued to develop both carols and other appropriate topics, most importantly the triadic fanfares imitating the call of the shepherds' horn or *tuba pastoritia*. The tradition reaches its apogee in the first movement of a symphony by Rosetti, which combines horn calls and a melodic fragment suggestive of the "Night-Watchman's Song" in a rhetorical display of remarkable complexity (cf. Examples 2.8 and 2.9).[18] Rosetti plays the two topics one off the other and at one point superimposes them; he also complicates matters by pitching his horns in two different keys (which allows the calls to be played in both tonic and dominant) and by having the

religiösen Malerei des 18. Jahrhunderts mit besonderer Berücksichtigung Österreichs," in Kovács, ed., *Katholische Aufklärung und Josephinismus*, 364–65.

[18] Rosetti's movement and further examples from Pichl's *Pastorella* and Haydn's *Le Matin* are discussed in Will, "Programmatic Symphonies of the Classical Period," 193–229.

Example 2.8 Rosetti, *Sinfonia pastoralis*, i, mm. 1–26

"Night-Watchman"-like exordium slip downward to the flatted sixth (one step beyond the song; see Example 2.8, m. 4).[19] This tonal swerve is recapitulated and resolved to the tonic late in the movement, adding

19 Additional eighteenth-century versions of the tune are given in Geoffrey Chew, "The Night-Watchman's Song Quoted by Haydn and its Implications," *Haydn-Studien* 3 (1973–74), 109–10.

Example 2.9   "Night-Watchman's Song," from Pokorny, *Pastorella* (Angerer D33)

a second developmental thread to the already elaborate interchange between horn calls in the tonic and dominant. The movement suggests a sermon in which the foundational Gospel verse is repeated while the preacher also demonstrates how the text can be applied in different situations, combined with a second text, or rescued from misinterpretation. In a court or aristocratic church, where the urge toward reform was strongest, such a sophisticated development of popular sources may have served not only to communicate emotional meanings but also to defend the sources themselves, for one of the principal objections to popular religious practice was that it did not encourage sufficient reflection: if altars to favorite saints filled churches with too many distractions, as Colloredo complained, then pilgrimages, cradle-rocking, and similar devotions required too much action, ritual movement taking precedence over contemplation and objects over principles. Action trumped reflection in many pastorellas as well, which enlivened the Christmas story with humor, local color, and vivid characters, and their survival into the later eighteenth century was possible only because reformers did not entirely succeed in suppressing popular impulses. The related tradition of pastoral symphonies may have been further protected by their emphasis on elaboration over narrative; in the hands of Stamitz or Rosetti, the music of carols or the *tuba pastoritia* proves worthy of extended and serious contemplation.

On the other hand, given the dependence of orchestral pastorals on upper-class patronage it comes as no surprise that they largely disappear, at least from Habsburg lands, at the peak of the reform movement in the 1780s. Pastoral movements that may have been intended for church survive in Italy as late as 1791, and in the early nineteenth century Franz Anton Schubert produced eleven one-movement *Pastorales* for the Catholic court at Dresden, including four "della Notte Santa di Natale." Otherwise the fanfares, drones, and other signatures of the earlier works pass into symphonies with elaborate programs such as Knecht's *Portrait musical de la nature* or Beethoven's *Pastoral* Symphony, or into works neither labeled nor exclusively concerned with pastoral: Haydn's later symphonies, for instance, continue to elaborate rustic dances, as in the finales of Nos. 82 and 104, and the call of the *tuba pastoritia*, in the slow movement of No. 93. Composers did not stop discoursing on pastoral topics, but the impetus for the rhetorically conceived pastoral symphony had passed.

The "Seven Last Words" and the enlightened Christ

Just as the reforming zeal reached its apex, however, the brotherhood in Cádiz inspired Haydn to a new and far more ambitious effort at rhetorical development in a sacred instrumental work than was ever attempted in a pastoral symphony. The circumstances were propitious inasmuch as the Good Friday devotion for which he was commissioned to write music, known as the *Tres horas* (Three Hours), was not among those that the enlightened church targeted for suppression. Instituted by Jesuits in Peru following the 1687 earthquake at Lima, it became widely known through an explanatory pamphlet authored by its creators and received the official sanction of Pope Pius VI in 1789.[20] Reformers could hardly complain. Organized around the seven utterances that Gospel concordances attribute to the crucified Christ, the service could not be accused of over-emphasizing a peripheral saint or relic, and the Jesuit tradition of enacting sacred narratives had also given way, in this instance, to the encouragement of contemplation. During the hours from noon to three from which the devotion takes its name, readings of each word are followed by sermons and choruses, and while the choral texts printed in the pamphlet mention a few events – the darkening of the sky during the crucifixion, for instance – mostly they expound the underlying themes of suffering, forgiveness, and redemption. The passion story becomes an excuse for the reflection that reformers held so dear.

In Spain at least one composer before Haydn was contracted to write instrumental movements for the service, presumably to take the place of the usual choruses.[21] When Haydn agreed to provide music for the same purpose, he undoubtedly assumed it would appeal to more than just his patrons in Cádiz, for not only were the *Tres horas* celebrated elsewhere in Catholic Europe, but their core texts formed an important link to Protestantism. Lutheran preachers such as Johann Jacob Rambach, a follower of Philipp Jakob Spener, founder of Pietism, published meditations on the Seven Words,[22] and in 1750 the Berlin poet Karl Wilhelm Ramler incorporated the Words into his oratorio *Der Tod Jesu*, which became widely known in German-speaking Europe through the 1755 setting by Carl Heinrich Graun: Vienna alone heard this work in 1784, 1785,

---

[20] The pamphlet is Alonso Messia Bedoya, *Devocion á las tres horas de la agonia de Christo*, published throughout the eighteenth and nineteenth centuries in Spanish, Italian, German, and English. For a concise history see Magda Marx-Weber, " 'Musiche per le tre ore di agonia de N.S.G.C.': Eine italienische Karfreitagsandacht im späten 18. und frühen 19. Jahrhundert," *Die Musikforschung* 33 (1980): 137–39.

[21] Robert Stevenson, "Haydn's Iberian World Connections," *Inter-American Music Review* 4/2 (1982): 10.

[22] Rambach, *Betrachtungen über die sieben letzten Worte des gecreuzigten Jesu* (Halle, 1726).

and 1787.[23] As in the Catholic devotion and the published meditations, Ramler does not dramatize the passion so much as reflect on it, replacing the evangelist and cast of characters familiar from J. S. Bach's passions with an unnamed witness, soloists, and chorus of believers who comment on the unfolding events. Even Christ does not speak directly, but is instead quoted by the witness as he describes the scenes before him.[24] With such a precedent, it is not surprising that Haydn's similarly contemplative *Seven Last Words* was soon performed in Protestant Berlin, and that an affinity between the two works was recognized by the Passau cathedral composer Joseph Friebert when he added vocal parts to Haydn's work in 1792. His text uses several lines from Ramler that were preserved when Haydn and Baron van Swieten revised the arrangement in 1796,[25] and they also strengthened the connection to *Der Tod Jesu* by replacing Friebert's text for the earthquake movement with part of the oratorio's concluding chorus.[26]

Friebert must have sensed that Haydn's movements, like those of the pastoral symphonies, offer a relatively clear musical analogy for the enlightened sermon. By 1787 the precepts of traditional rhetoric had become Austrian state policy on preaching, with Joseph II warning priests to teach the Gospel lessons without "doppelsinnige Ausdrücke oder ungeziemende Anspielungen ... undienliche Nebendinge ... überflüssige und oft schädliche Einwürfe und Kontroversen" (ambiguous expressions or improper insinuations ... pointless side issues ... unnecessary and often harmful objections and controversies), and to ensure that "Die Predigten nicht nur zur Aufklärung des Verstandes, sondern, und zwar vorzüglich, zur Pflanzung und Wirkung der Tugenden und zur Besserung des Herzens einrichten" (Sermons work not only toward the enlightenment of the intellect, but also, and indeed primarily, toward the cultivation and effectiveness of the virtues and the improvement of the heart).[27] A state-sponsored journal emerged, the *Wöchentliche Wahrheiten für und über die Prediger in Wien*, to inspire a clergy used to

---

[23] Andreas Holschneider, "C. Ph. E. Bachs Kantate *Auferstehung und Himmelfahrt Jesu* und Mozarts Aufführung des Jahres 1788," *Mozart-Jahrbuch* (1968–70): 277.

[24] *Der Tod Jesu* belongs to a tradition of "lyric" libretti typical for mid-eighteenth-century Protestant Germany (Howard E. Smither, *A History of the Oratorio*, vol. III, *The Oratorio in the Classical Era* [Chapel Hill: University of North Carolina Press, 1987], 361–69).

[25] Lines 256–61 of *Der Tod Jesu* are used, with some alteration, as the text for mm. 13–40 of "In manus tuas, Domine, commendo spiritum meum" (Adolf Sandberger, "Zur Entstehungsgeschichte von Haydns 'Sieben Worten des Erlösers am Kreuze,'" in *Ausgewählte Aufsätze zur Musikgeschichte*, 2 vols. [Munich: Drei Masken, 1921–24], I: 278).

[26] *Haydn: Werke* XXVIII/2: vii; on the genesis of the vocal version see also Dénes Bartha, "A 'Sieben Worte' változatainak keletkezése az Esterházy-gyüjtemény kéziratainak tükrében," *Zenetudományi tanulmányok* 8 (1960): 107–86.

[27] Decree of 4 February 1783, quoted in Winter, *Der Josefinismus*, 127.

Example 2.10   Haydn, *The Seven Last Words*

	Introduzione *Maestoso ed Adagio*	Dm	c
Sonata I	Pater, dimitte illis, quia nesciunt, quid faciunt *Largo*	B♭	3/4
Sonata II	Hodie mecum eris in Paradiso *Grave e Cantabile*	Cm	¢
Sonata III	Mulier, ecce filius tuus *Grave*	E	¢
Sonata IV	Deus meus, Deus meus, utquid dereliquisti me? *Largo*	Fm	3/4
Sonata V	Sitio *Adagio*	A	¢
Sonata VI	Consummatum est *Lento*	Gm	¢
Sonata VII	In manus tuas, Domine, commendo spiritum meum *Largo*	E♭	3/4
	Il Terremoto *Presto e con tutta la forza*	Cm	3/4

delivering its homilies, if at all, not during mass but before or after or at some other time altogether.[28] Haydn, of course, was not subject to such edicts, but his approach to the Words reflects a similar concern for clarity and expression. Each of his seven "Sonatas," the movements devoted to the Words themselves (Example 2.10), begins with a theme that "sets" the associated text to an appropriate melody, as if it were to be sung: in "Consummatum est" (It is finished), for instance, not only the rhythm and accentuation of the phrase but also its meaning are quite clearly captured by a unison cadence in the *alla breve* of the church style (Example 2.11a). At Haydn's request, the earliest editions of the orchestral parts and of his arrangements for string quartet and keyboard printed the words under the appropriate themes, so that performers, at least, were aware of the connection between verbal and musical utterance.[29] What the music gains is not simply a semantic connotation

---

[28] Bernhard M. Hoppe, *Predigtkritik im Josephinismus: Die "Wöchentlichen Wahrheiten für und über die Prediger in Wien" (1782-1784)* (St. Ottilien: EOS Verlag, 1989).

[29] Letter to Artaria, 14 February 1787 (Haydn, *Briefe*, 158).

Example 2.11a   Haydn, *The Seven Last Words*, "Consummatum est,"
mm. 1–31

(cont.)

but a specific implied text, a musical equivalent for the Gospel verses that were to form the *Hauptsätze* of sermons.

Haydn also develops his themes without introducing what might be considered, in musical terms, "pointless side issues." Following the three-measure exordium of "Consummatum est," a transformed version of the cadential motto leads into imitations decorated by a countersubject in eighth notes and eventually settling on a dominant half-cadence (Example 2.11a, mm. 4–13). There follows an abrupt shift to the relative major, a homophonic texture, and a lyrical and rhythmically variegated melody (mm. 14–21), yet the *Hauptsatz* lurks in the bass and becomes the principal voice again when the harmony wanders from the relative major into its parallel minor and beyond (mm. 22–28). When major is regained at the end of the exposition, the tune returns again (Example 2.11b), and in partnership with the comparatively active closing theme (i.e., mm. 38–39) it forms the basis for the densely

Example 2.11a (*cont.*)

Example 2.11b Haydn, *The Seven Last Words*, "Consummatum est,"
mm. 36–41

contrapuntal development section. None of the other Sonatas concentrates quite so intently on a single idea, but they all show signs of an essentially rhetorical conception.[30] The two additional movements

---

[30] Thematic and rhythmic elaborations in all the Sonatas are analyzed in Theodor Göllner, *"Die Sieben Worte am Kreuz" bei Schütz und Haydn* (Munich: Bayrische Akademie der Wissenschaften, 1986), 38–59. Different in developmental technique but no less rhetorically effective is Haydn's earlier symphonic treatment of two themes with sacred overtones, as shown in Marianne Danckwardt, "Zu zwei Haydnschen Sinfoniesätzen mit liturgischer Melodien (Sinfonien Nr. 30, 1. Satz und Nr. 26, 2. Satz)," in Norbert Dubowy and Sören Meyer-Eller, eds., *Festschrift Rudolf Bockholdt zum 60. Geburtstag* (Pfaffenhofen: Ludwig, 1990), 193–99.

Example 2.11c   Haydn, *The Seven Last Words*, "Consummatum est,"
mm. 95–99

in minor ("Hodie mecum eris in Paradiso" and "Deus meus, utquid
dereliquisti me?") likewise proceed from dominant half-cadences directly into transformed, relative-major versions of their opening themes;
the major-key "Mulier, ecce filius tuus" divides its opening measures
into two halves that return separately at several points; "Pater dimitte
illis" and "In manus tuas, Domine" use distinctive rhythmic figures to
connect passages throughout both movements.[31]

For the earliest reviewer of *The Seven Last Words*, the composer
and critic Johann Friedrich Christmann, Haydn succeeded not only in
achieving clarity but also in affecting the heart by unveiling the inner life of his protagonist: "Wenn der Hr. Verf[asser] unmittelbar aus
der Seele des sterbenden Mittlers herausgeschrieben hätte: so würde
er kaum im Stand gewesen sein, die Empfindungen desselben wahrer
und feierlicher darzustellen" (If the Herr Composer had written directly
from the soul of the dying Savior, he would hardly have been in a position to represent His emotions with more truth and solemnity).[32] The
feelings of Christ took on special significance in a theological context
where his moral teachings and devotion to helping others were valued
as much if not more than his performance of miracles or his miraculous
existence as both man and God.[33] Many eighteenth-century vocal texts
portray him as a distinctly human figure subject to the same emotional

---

[31] "Pater dimitte illis" is discussed in Peter Ackermann, "Struktur, Ausdruck, Programm:
Gedanken zu Joseph Haydns Instrumentalmusik über *Die Sieben letzten Worte unseres
Erlösers am Kreuze*," in Anke Bingmann, Klaus Hortschansky, and Winfried Kirsch, eds.,
Studien zur Instrumentalmusik: Lothar Hoffmann-Erbrecht zum 60. Geburtstag (Tutzing:
Schneider, 1988), 253–60.

[32] *Musikalische Realzeitung* "Probeblatt" (5 March 1788): 1. For Christmann's authorship of
this review (signed "Zx") see Hans Schneider, *Der Musikverleger Heinrich Philipp Boßler
1744–1812* (Tutzing: Schneider, 1985), 159.

[33] Karl Barth, *Protestant Theology in the Nineteenth Century: Its Background & History*, trans.
Brian Cozens and John Bowden (London: SCM Press, 1972), 100–13.

vicissitudes as his mortal companions, particularly the cantata and oratorio libretti influenced by Pietism[34] but also Metastasio's *La passione del Gesù Cristo*, which received numerous settings in Italy and Catholic Germany in the eighteenth and early nineteenth centuries.[35] Taken to the extreme, as in Ramler's *Tod Jesu*, the human Christ becomes a sentimental hero worthy of Richardson or Rousseau. As he is crucified, "Er leidet es mit Geduld, bleibt heiter" (He suffers it with patience, remains cheerful), and shortly thereafter he utters the first of the Seven Words, "Father, forgive them, for they know not what they do." But soon, "fällt der aufgehaltne Schmerz / des Helden Seele wütend an: Sein Herz / hebt die gespannte Brust. In jeder Ader wühlet / ein Dolch ... Er fühlet des Todes siebenfache Gräuel" (the suppressed pain strikes the soul of the hero with fury: his heart pounds in his tortured breast. In every vein twists a dagger ... He feels the sevenfold horrors of death).[36] This provokes the fourth and most despairing Word, "My God, why have you forsaken me?" Throughout the oratorio he journeys not only to Calvary but also through the chambers of the human soul.

Haydn effects a Ramleresque mood swing at the shift from minor to relative major in "Consummatum est" (Example 2.11a, mm. 13–14); indeed, so radical is it that his reviewer thought he had gone too far. Taking aim at the rhythmically active closing theme, itself a variation on the initial major-key music (cf. Example 2.11b, mm. 38–39 and Example 2.11a, mm. 18–21), Christmann writes: "Nur dünkt Rec[ensent] die in den sechs letzten Takten ... enthaltene Figur, die wir in der Musik den *Schwärmer* zu nennen pflegen, und deren man in unsern Opernarien schon so sehr gewohnt ist, für den Schluß dieser Sonate nicht passend, und für die Würde der Sache selbst nicht edel genug zu sein" (It seems to the reviewer only that the figure contained in the last six measures, which we customarily call the *enthusiast* in music, and which one is already so used to in our opera arias, is not appropriate for the end of this sonata, and not noble enough for the dignity of the topic itself).[37] Visitors to Vienna's churches in the 1770s and 80s frequently complained about the use of operatic styles and performers,[38] and while one might question

---

[34] Ingeborg König, *Studien zum Libretto des "Tod Jesu" von Karl Wilhelm Ramler und Karl Heinrich Graun* (Munich: Katzbichler, 1972), esp. 56–67; Klaus Langrock, *Die Sieben Worte Jesu am Kreuz: Ein Beitrag zur Geschichte der Passionskomposition* (Essen: Blaue Eule, 1987), 44–46.

[35] *New Grove* XII: 217–18 lists nine settings between 1730 and 1811. The text as well as the 1749 setting by Jommelli are treated in Smither, *The Oratorio in the Classical Era*, 54–58, 114–37.

[36] Quoted from Carl Heinrich Graun, *Der Tod Jesu*, ed. Howard Serwer (Madison: A-R Editions, 1975).

[37] *Musikalische Realzeitung* "Probeblatt" (5 March 1788): 2.

[38] Heartz, *Haydn, Mozart, and the Viennese School*, 15–23.

whether this particular motive, played Lento, really triggers the associations Christmann thinks it does, there can be no doubt that the music in major not only brightens the emotional atmosphere but also departs from the explicitly ecclesiastical style of the preceding. What he missed, or perhaps could not discuss in a review that devotes only a paragraph to each movement, is that a dialectic between "sacred" counterpoint and "secular" accompanied melody, and by implication between opposing emotional states, governs the whole of "Consummatum est." Given the example of Ramler's Christ, who weeps during much of his ordeal, it is not difficult to hear a tear starting in the exposed entry for flute and violin in Haydn's fourth measure: shed for a life lost or for companions left behind, the teardrop or some related frame of mind is carried into all registers and instruments by the ensuing imitative entries. By contrast, the music in major suggests memories from a happy life, or, perhaps, as the cadential half notes remain in the bass, premonitions of the divine reunion that will follow death. The two sides of the emotional coin then interact throughout the rest of movement: the exposition lapses once more into minor before regaining the major, and the development returns to imitation, setting Christmann's "enthusiast" as a countersubject to the *Hauptsatz*. Not unlike Ramler, Haydn portrays a Christ torn between suffering and happiness, darkness and light, earth and heaven, the confusion seeming all the more intense given that feelings of the earthly here-and-now are expressed by a religious *stile antico*, and thoughts of a heavenly future by worldly lyricism.

Opposing moods run through two other Sonatas as well. "Hodie mecum eris in Paradiso" (Today you will be with me in paradise) parallels "Consummatum est," with a minor-key *Hauptsatz* (Example 2.12a) giving way, after a half cadence, to an emotionally transformed version of the same theme in the relative major (Example 2.12b). Appoggiaturas, throbbing chords, and a pattern of upward leaps falling downwards link the opening measures to the suffering of Christ and of the crucified thief to whom he makes his promise. The passage in major, by contrast, stretches the *Hauptsatz* into a long, lyrical line that exorcises the dispirited strong–weak phrase endings of the original version (mm. 2, 4, 6, 8) as well as its concluding harmonic minor scale (m. 7). Accompanied by the familiar middle-texture murmuring of the musical idyll and reinforced, in the recapitulation, by the woodwinds and horns, these measures are quite explicitly, as Christmann says, "Aussichten für die Zukunft" (visions of the future), depictions of paradise.[39] "Sitio" (I thirst) inspires roughly the opposite psychological progression. It begins with an unexpectedly restful and quiet cadence; in the melody falling over the pizzicato accompaniment one can perhaps hear water

---

[39] *Musikalische Realzeitung* "Probeblatt" (5 March 1788): 1.

Example 2.12a   Haydn, *The Seven Last Words*, "Hodie," mm. 1–8

Example 2.12b   Haydn, *The Seven Last Words*, "Hodie," mm. 21–36

Example 2.13a   Haydn, *The Seven Last Words*, "Sitio," mm. 2–6

Example 2.13b   Haydn, *The Seven Last Words*, "Sitio," mm. 18–25

dropping onto an "arid" texture, but even so the governing sense of calm seems at odds with the only reference to physical suffering in all the Words, as if Christ were seeing the solution to his pain rather than the pain itself (Example 2.13a). The continuation corrects his vision as the orchestra, following the usual half cadence, launches into the parallel minor of the dominant (Example 2.13b). The falling melody becomes a sigh figure outlining dissonant and chromatic harmonies, the quiet pizzicati turn to *fortissimo* repeated eighths bearing both strokes and a *staccato* marking, and the basses undergird the whole with a strident figure emphasizing the leading tone and flatted sixth. Alternations between one music and the other fill the remainder of the movement, leaving a further impression of a spirit divided between suffering and relief, present and future.

The Christ of the remaining Sonatas does not experience such polarized feelings. Although Haydn elaborates his *Hauptsätze* no less thoroughly, he aims less to transform the associated emotions than to vary or intensify them – explore their "modifications," in eighteenth-century terminology. The best comparison is the remaining minor-key example, "Deus meus, Deus meus, utquid dereliquisti me?" (My God, my God, why have you forsaken me?). For nearly twenty measures it follows

107

Example 2.14a Haydn, *The Seven Last Words*, "Deus meus,"
mm. 1–32

Example 2.14b Haydn, *The Seven Last Words*, "Deus meus,"
mm. 119–27

the same trajectory as its counterparts: theme in the tonic, half-cadence on the dominant, same theme in the relative major (Example 2.14a, mm. 1–18). It also perpetuates the contour, the upward-moving sequence of a two-measure motto, the short phrases with strong–weak endings, and the concluding scalar descent of the opening theme of "Hodie" (cf. Example 2.12a). But this text allows no thoughts of paradise; the only Word given by the New Testament both in Aramaic and in translation (Matt. 27: 46; Mark 15: 34), it has a special status reflected by its position at the center of the Seven Words. It is the nadir of Christ's emotional journey, the point in *Der Tod Jesu* where a dagger twists in his every vein, and in Bach's *St. Matthew Passion* where his "halo" of accompanying strings temporarily deserts him.[40] Accordingly, Haydn counters the brightness of the relative major in the second group with the uncertainty of a search for resolution. Passages of imitation based on the end of the *Hauptsatz* lead successively to a first inversion tonic on a weak second beat (Example 2.14a, mm. 18–26), to a deceptive cadence (m. 32), and to a root-position tonic reached at different times by independent contrapuntal voices (m. 49). At two points, the imitations begin with disorientingly flattened pitches that themselves deny the promise of a pre-cadential chord (e.g., Example 2.14a, m. 27), and only near the end of the exposition does a rhythmically strong root-position cadence finally occur. In the recapitulation, matters grow worse. Imitation begins right away with the first, minor-key version of the theme, and major is never heard at all; alone of the minor-key movements, "Deus meus" does not conclude in the parallel major. And after all the avoided resolutions from the exposition are repeated, the final cadence also turns deceptive, triggering off a last passage of imitation that simply peters out after only two entrances – it requires a fresh start in the first violins to achieve closure (Example 2.14b). Christ continues to experience emotional development even when not racked by conflict, discovering, in this case, something like the agony of displacement: seeing no home on earth or in heaven, he wanders in search of an elusive reassurance.

In the preface to the vocal arrangement of *The Seven Last Words*, published in 1801, Haydn recalled, "Die Aufgabe, sieben Adagio's . . . aufeinander folgen zu lassen, ohne den Zuhörer zu ermüden, war keine von den leichtesten" (The task of having seven Adagios follow one after the other without wearying the listeners was hardly among the easiest).[41] Aware that the orchestral version had its critics – a year later, Hans Georg Nägeli would say it was "ein verunglückter Versuch" (an unfortunate mistake)[42] – he argued that it could only be judged

---

[40] Langrock, *Die Sieben Worte Jesu am Kreuz*, 40.   [41] Haydn, *Briefe*, 359.
[42] *AmZ* 5 (29 December 1802): col. 234.

in light of the intended performance during the *Tres horas*, which he described in some detail. Certainly to have heard each Sonata after a sermon on its text would have eased comprehension and broken the potential monotony of successive slow movements. Haydn's earlier publication of the instrumental versions, however, ensured that there would be concert performances where the responsibility for teaching and engaging listeners would fall on the music alone. Insofar as it proved up to the task, as Christmann believed it was, the clarity of the rhetoric was largely responsible. The few specific passages discussed by the reviewer include some of the most striking elaborations of *Hauptsätze*, among them the depiction of paradise in "Hodie" and the first imitative passage of "Deus meus" (Example 2.14a, mm. 18–24). "Wie natürlich und gefühlvoll der Ausdruk einer steigenden Sehnsucht nach Trost und Stärkung!" (How natural and full of feeling the expression of a growing longing for comfort and strength!), he writes of the latter, a comment that can only have been triggered by the melody's dissolution into multiple voices and inability to reach tonal closure.[43] Like the ideal sermons described in the *Wöchentliche Wahrheiten für und über die Prediger*, Haydn's Sonatas seek to elucidate Gospel texts through rational discussion, or as close an approximation as instrumental music can manage. Viewing each of Christ's words from a variety of perspectives, they argue the emotional significance of successive moments in the crucifixion. The Passion comes alive through the human feelings of its hero, the favorite topic of enlightened theology and the most obvious channel to the hearts of Haydn's listeners.

Wordless music, unfathomable harmony, and the divine

What critics objected to in *The Seven Last Words* was summed up in Breitkopf und Härtel's 1801 advertisement for the vocal arrangement: "auch wenn diese Instrumentalsätze noch so vollendet ausgeführt – mit andern Worten: wenn sie das wären, was sie waren, würden sie doch nimmermehr (wie keine Instrumentalmusik) die eigentlichen Worte des Erlösers, ohne Kommentar jedem verständlich, geben können" (Even if these instrumental movements were perfectly executed – in other words, if they were what they were – they would never be able to make the actual words of the savior understandable to everyone without commentary; no instrumental music could).[44] Already in 1787, a correspondent to Cramer's *Magazin der Musik* had declared, "Ich will nicht untersuchen, ob einem einzigen Zuhörer beym fünften Adagio das Wort: Sitio, (mich dürstet) einfallen kann und wird" (I do not

---

[43] *Musikalische Realzeitung* "Probeblatt" (5 March 1788): 2.
[44] *AmZ Intelligenz-Blatt* 12 (July 1801): col. 45.

wish to investigate whether in the fifth Adagio the word Sitio can or will occur to a single listener).[45] The comment misconstrues Haydn's purpose, which was not to conjure words out of thin air but to interpret texts that were printed in the music and known to listeners from other sacred works, published sermons, and the *Tres horas* devotion itself. Still, it is undeniable that even so lucid an instrumental work as *The Seven Last Words* cannot "speak" with the directness of a vocal Passion, and there are consequences for its theology as well as for comprehensibility. To begin with, despite the secure links between music, Word, and affect in the opening measures of each Sonata, the image of a human Christ experiencing worldly feelings is constantly threatened by intimations of divinity. Emanating from instruments rather than a human throat and bypassing language to communicate emotion directly, Christ's "voice" appears bodiless, unencumbered by either the physical or the intellectual limits of human communication. At the same time it seems to possess the power of God's voice in the book of Genesis, where things happen simply because they are commanded: Christ promises, "Today you will be with me in paradise," and paradise appears, presided over by an unearthly presence that makes itself known through violins and cellos in octaves (Example 2.12b).[46] The tangible sufferer of Ramler's *Tod Jesu* is forever dissolving into the ether of pure sound.

Haydn also endows nearly every Sonata with events that exceed the rhetorical goal of expressing human feelings, as for instance near the end of "Consummatum est." The development section ends by repeating, over a dominant pedal, the contrapuntal beginning of the movement up to and including the half-cadence (i.e., mm. 5–13) – at once retransition and recapitulation, this prepares a reprise of the second group, now in the tonic major. All continues as before until what was, in the exposition, a quiet statement of the *Hauptsatz* just before the closing theme (cf. Example 2.11b and c), at which point the orchestra bursts out with a new harmonized version in repeated eighths and sixteenths marked with strokes (mm. 97–98). The interjection sounds the note of triumph detected in the statement "It is finished" by Ramler, the Pietist commentator Rambach, and the Jesuit authors of the *Tres horas* service; if the sacrifice of Christ achieves the salvation of humanity, as Christianity believes, then his acceptance of death amounts to a declaration of

---

[45] *Magazin der Musik* 2 (1786): 1385. A similar concern was expressed about the same movement in the *Erlangische gelehrte Anmerkungen* (22 April 1788), quoted in Morrow, *German Music Criticism*, 130–31.

[46] In the seventeenth and early eighteenth centuries, the simplicity and effectiveness of God's commands in Genesis were held up as an alternative to overly artful sermons (Urs Herzog, *Geistliche Wohlredenheit: Die katholische Barockpredigt* [Munich: Beck, 1991], 191–94).

Example 2.15a   Haydn, *The Seven Last Words*, "Mulier," mm. 3–8

Example 2.15b   Haydn, *The Seven Last Words*, "Mulier," mm. 92–99

victory. But the passage suggests more than simply triumph or closure (Example 2.11c). It sounds quite exaggerated in a movement that otherwise alternates between sorrow and contentment, especially since it erupts at a point of rest, where a quiet finish is clearly imminent. That it disappears so quickly – the closing theme returns, *piano*, after only two measures – adds to its uncanniness; it passes like a flash, as if Christ has not merely sensed his impending victory over death but seen it, envisioned the miracle of the resurrection. Equally striking is a *fortissimo* midway through the recapitulation of "Mulier, ecce filius tuus" (Mother, behold your son), a movement otherwise marked by quiet lyricism. A reference to the anointing of the Beloved Disciple as guardian of Mary, the Word becomes a limpid four-measure melody with a continuation that relaxes toward the subdominant (Example 2.15a). The second key area develops the falling third in similarly calm surroundings and ends with a leisurely, twice-repeated cadence (mm. 36–40, 49–52), followed by the only slightly disruptive element in the whole exposition, an augmented sixth that oscillates with the dominant and hints at the minor in the last measures of the exposition (mm. 53–58). Precisely that chord, or more exactly its bass C♮, leads the recapitulation from a quiet pause on the relative minor into a wholly uncharacteristic explosion on the flatted sixth and its dominant, effected, as in "Consummatum est," by strings hammering away at repeated notes marked with strokes (Example 2.15b). Order returns only with the augmented sixth and following resolution to the dominant. In this case an emotional or visual referent such as the resurrection does not readily spring to mind, and the same can be said for the less forceful but equally surprising tonal detours in the very first Sonata, "Pater, dimitte illis, quia nesciunt, quid faciunt" (Father, forgive them, for they know not what they do). At what promises to be the cadence of the exposition in the dominant F major, the harmony drops to F minor and from there to D♭ major; there follows a full cadence and caesura, so that the exposition seems to end in the key of the flatted third (Example 2.16). Haydn rewrites the passage in the recapitulation so as to move again to D♭, this time from the tonic minor (mm. 81–87), and the key sounds all the more significant given its equally surprising entrance midway through the preceding *Introduzione* (m. 25). But its expressive purpose is unclear: what thought leads Christ to such remote regions, and what feeling for his mother, in "Mulier," provokes him to cry out with such intensity?

It helps to keep in mind that the human Christ and reasoned exegeses of enlightened theology were always contested, and that the Catholic hierarchy in Vienna, particularly, fought a running battle against the arrogation of its authority by the state and the effort to rationalize belief. Cardinal Migazzi supported the modest reforms initiated by Maria Theresa, mother and predecessor of Joseph II, but resisted the son's much more radical program with a series of memoranda that target reformers for ignoring the revelatory dimensions of faith. He argues that moral principles are revealed in the Gospels and need no imprimatur from modern philosophy, as Joseph assumed, and he also demands the dismissal of a theology professor who had discussed baptism and communion without recognizing them as sacraments.[47] He states his position best in a letter on education: "nach der damahligen Methode zu katechisieren . . . ist zu besorgen, daß Kinder sonst nichts für wahr annehmen, als was sie selbst einsehen und begreifen; wobey das katholische Glaubenssystem leiden könnte, welches Wahrheiten enthält,

---

[47] Cölestin Wolfsgruber, *Christoph Anton Kardinal Migazzi, Fürsterzbischof von Wien* (Saulgau: Hermann Ritz, 1890), 504–23.

Example 2.16   Haydn, *The Seven Last Words*, "Pater, dimitte illis," mm. 32–40

die über unsere geschwächte Vernunft erhaben sind" (It is a matter of concern ... regarding the current method of catechizing that children will not take anything for true except that which they themselves observe and understand, thanks to which the Catholic belief system, which contains truths that are elevated beyond our weakened reason, could suffer).[48] He had little luck turning back Joseph's edicts, but religious practice remained to a large extent in his corner, acknowledging the enigmas of Christianity in many ways. As we have seen, popular traditions expressed a faith in the miraculous so strong as to blur the line between religion and magic, and further up the social scale, even the seemingly "human" and "realistic" Seven Words could take on an otherworldly aura. The *Tres horas* in Cádiz took place in a church whose walls, windows, and columns were covered with black cloth, creating a "heilige[n] Dunkel" (religious gloom), as Haydn called it, that represented the miraculous darkness which fell during the crucifixion and would have heightened the impression that the wordless music emanating from the orchestra communicated "truths elevated beyond our weakened reason." Other performances of sacred music strove for a

---

[48] Letter of 9 December 1789, quoted in ibid., 522–23.

similar effect; in Milan and Kassel, Pergolesi's *Stabat Mater* was played with the orchestra hidden behind a curtain so that its accompaniment emerged, as if from nowhere, to support the visible singers,[49] and in Vienna as well as Salzburg, Kremsmünster, and elsewhere, oratorios were performed during Holy Week before a model of Christ's sepulchre, a reminder of his miraculous sacrifice and resurrection.[50]

Like the darkness of the Cádiz church, the unexpected outbursts and tonal surprises of *The Seven Last Words* would have strengthened a sense of mystery already raised by the absence of text and also by the general portent of orchestral music as it was understood in the eighteenth century. An oft-cited passage from Sulzer's *Allgemeine Theorie* includes a list of qualities that make symphonies "zu dem Ausdruk des Großen, des Feyerlichen und Erhabenen vorzüglich geschikt" (most excellently suited to the expression of the grand, the festive, and the sublime); among them are "anscheinende Unordnung in der Melodie und Harmonie, stark marquirte Rhythmen von verschiedener Art, kräftige Bassmelodien und Unisoni, concertirende Mittelstimmen, freye Nachahmungen … plötzliche Uebergänge und Ausschweifungen von einem Ton zum anderen, die desto stärker frappiren, je schwächer oft die Verbindung ist, [und] starke Schattirungen des Forte und Piano" (apparent disorder in the melody and harmony, strongly marked rhythms of different types, robust bass melodies and unison passages, concerting middle voices, free imitations of a theme … sudden modulations and digressions from one key to another that are all the more striking the more distant their relation, [and] strong gradations of loud and soft).[51] The description applies to symphony first movements, but its elements can all be found in the Sonatas of *The Seven Last Words*: powerfully emphasized rhythms, unisons, textures in which all the voices are active, free counterpoint, distant tonal relations, stark dynamic contrasts. They, too, would have been suggestive of the grand and sublime, which is significant in that the exalted genres or realms to which those terms referred had sacred implications; Sulzer's point of comparison is the odes celebrating athletic victories by the Greek poet Pindar, but the

---

[49] *Musikalische Realzeitung* (10 December 1788): col. 190.

[50] Smither, *The Oratorio in the Classical Era*, 341–44.

[51] Sulzer, *Allgemeine Theorie*, IV: 478–79; trans. adapted from Baker and Christensen, *Aesthetics and the Art of Musical Composition*, 106. "Symphonies" in several senses of the term (see above, p. 1) were associated with the sublime throughout much of the eighteenth and early nineteenth centuries. See Nicolas Henri Waldvogel, "The Eighteenth-Century Esthetics of the Sublime and the Valuation of the Symphony" (Ph.D. diss., Yale University, 1992); Elaine R. Sisman, *Mozart: The "Jupiter" Symphony No. 41 in C major, K. 551*, Cambridge Music Handbook (Cambridge: Cambridge University Press, 1993), 13–20; and Bonds, "The Symphony as Pindaric Ode," 131–53.

paradigms of sublimity in German literature were the religious odes and epic, *Der Messias*, of Friedrich Gottlieb Klopstock, and the most frequently cited examples in music were the oratorios of Handel.[52] An orchestral movement with complex textures and sometimes startling turns of events would by its very nature have evoked the immeasurable power and space associated with a religious sublime (see also below, pp. 177–81).

More specifically, a connection between unexpected harmonies and divine realms is suggested by several well-known sacred works from the second half of the eighteenth century. In Graun's *Tod Jesu*, a reference to hell at the end of the first chorus provokes a startling chromatic interruption of the final cadence,[53] and similar moments occur in C. P. E. Bach's *Die Auferstehung und Himmelfahrt Jesu*, set to another Ramler text and performed in Vienna in 1788 with Mozart directing.[54] The best examples, however, are in the dialogue between the "Chor der Engel" and "Chor der Völker" in the central section of C. P. E. Bach's motet *Heilig*. Each time one chorus pauses, the other continues with a remote chord reached by half-step ascent in the bass: C♯ major gives way to D major, D major to B in first inversion, F♯ to G, G to F minor in first inversion (the most unsettling move), and finally B to C. Further emphasizing the distance between the two groups, the people's music is diatonic and marked *forte* or *fortissimo* while the angels are chromatic and predominantly *piano*. Reichardt was reminded of the motions between root-position sonorities in Palestrina, an association Richard Kramer rightly terms anachronistic, but Reichardt's notion that such progressions suggest unheard transitional harmonies not only helps clarify the harmonic puzzle (as Kramer points out) but also attributes a sublime vastness to the spaces between the juxtaposed sonorities: "Die übergegangenen Zwischenaccorde, die wir immer so geflissentlich hören lassen, und als nothwendige kleine Brücken ... von einem Arme des Stroms zum andern so sorgfältig hinpflanzen, die geben hier jedem Schritte eine Riesengrösse, und lassen die Seele nur dunkel den Weg ahnden, den die Harmonie genommen" (The omitted transitional harmonies, which we ever so diligently supply and painstakingly plant out ... as indispensable little bridges from one branch of the stream to the other – these [ellipses] lend an enormity to each step and allow the mind only

---

[52] On the oratorio see Waldvogel, "The Eighteenth-Century Esthetics of the Sublime," 77–78; and Bonds, "The Symphony as Pindaric Ode," 139.

[53] "Sein Odem ist schwach," mm. 47–54; the harmony moves from the dominant of C minor directly to a dominant seventh on E, then down through a circle of fifths back to the tonic C.

[54] On the Vienna performance see Holschneider, "C. Ph. E. Bachs Kantate *Auferstehung und Himmelfahrt Jesu*," 264–76.

dimly to surmise the path that the harmony has taken).[55] To the rational harmonist, gaps in the tonal logic reveal the equally incomprehensible gulf between angels and people, heaven and earth.

In addition to the flat-side ventures discussed above, *The Seven Last Words* incorporates juxtapositions comparable to those in *Heilig* although based on third rather than half-step relations: at the juncture between first and second groups in the exposition, the minor key movements all drop by third from the home dominant to the relative major, and in "Mulier" and "Sitio" a comparable step from V/vi to the tonic links development and recapitulation. Some instances suggest obvious referents. In "Hodie mecum eris in Paradiso," the leap from V to III works on the same principle as Bach's moves by half-step, shifting the tonal landscape to match the scene change from earth to heaven. Similarly, on either side of the fractures in "Sitio" and "Consummatum est" are passages expressing starkly opposed moods, whose unmediated juxtaposition emphasizes the breadth of Christ's own emotional experience.

Yet tonal and dynamic surprises alike may be better heard to express a larger theological point. For Ramler, the story of the crucifixion became problematic when he felt obligated to write, "Ach seht! er sinckt, belastet mit den Missethaten von einer ganzen Welt" (Ah, look, he sinks, weighed down by the sins of an entire world). The divine Christ who takes responsibility for the sins of the world conflicted with his vision of a human teacher, and in a letter to Johann Wilhelm Ludwig Gleim he expressed his preference for words omitting the reference to sin: "Ach seht! er sinckt, der Held! – Sein Hertz in Arbeit" (Ah look! he sinks, the hero! His heart in stress).[56] The choral texts used in the *Tres horas*, by contrast, begin to meditate on sin already after the first Word, "Father, forgive them, for they know not what they do," to which the chorus responds, "Di mille colpe reo / Lo so, Signore, io sono / Non merito perdono . . . Lascia, Signor se puoi / Lascia di perdonar" (Guilty of a thousand sins, I know, Father, that I am not worthy of being pardoned . . . Father, if you are able, let me be pardoned). They go on to promise, after the fourth Word, no longer to sin, and to declare, after the sixth, that sinners are unworthy of God's kingdom.[57] Rambach's commentary on the Seven Words likewise dwells on sin and forgiveness, and indeed the themes are so central to the Passion that it is remarkable Ramler would even have tried to avoid them. In the end, as he admitted to Gleim, to mention

---

[55] *Musikalisches Kunstmagazin* 2 (1791): 55; trans. and discussed in Kramer, "The New Modulation of the 1770s: C. P. E. Bach in Theory, Criticism, and Practice," *Journal of the American Musicological Society* 38 (1985): 568–69.

[56] Letter of 27 October 1754, quoted in König, *Studien zum Libretto des "Tod Jesu,"* 59.

[57] Marx-Weber, "Musiche per le tre ore di agonia de N.S.G.C.," 139–41.

sin was obligatory, "weil ich sehe wie wichtig sie den meisten Lesern dünckt" (because I see how important it appears to most readers). He had come face to face with what Karl Barth considered one of the chief obstacles to enlightened "rationalizing" of Christianity, the enduring belief that Christ saved humanity through his death.[58]

The Seven Last Words would have invoked redemption simply by virtue of its subject matter, but one piece of evidence connects this central mystery of the crucifixion specifically to the harmonic digressions and tutti outbursts. When Friebert added vocal texts to the Sonatas, he aligned most such passages with references to sin and especially to redemption, an aspect of his arrangement that survived Haydn's revisions. In the first Sonata, for instance, the entire text ruminates on sin but Friebert saves redemption for the slide into F minor and D♭ at the end of the exposition (Example 2.16): "Das Blut des Lamms schreit nicht um Rach'; es tilgt die Sünden" (the blood of the Lamb does not cry for revenge; it redeems sin). These lines are not repeated in the recapitulation, leaving the peculiar mediant end of the exposition as a focal point of mystery. In "Mulier" Friebert devotes the exposition to the sufferings of Mary but in the development begins to describe her as the "Zuflucht aller Sünder" (refuge for all sinners), an image that blossoms into a plea for intercession at the departure to the flatted sixth in the recapitulation (Example 2.15b): "Wenn wir mit dem Tode ringen und aus dem beklemmten Herzen unsre Seufzer zu dir dringen, laß uns, Mutter, da nicht unterliegen" (When we struggle with death and urge upon you sighs from our oppressed hearts, Mother, let us not succumb). Although followed by a return to familiar territory in the music, in this case the departure transforms the text, which thereafter prays repeatedly for intercession as if the opening of remote regions had reminded the chorus that death could mean grace. Friebert's words for "Sitio" pair the image of mercy with another swerve to the flatted sixth in the recapitulation, complete with the by-now familiar repeated notes and *fortissimo* dynamic (see mm. 101–06), while those for "Consummatum est" turn its gestures toward minor and the flatted sixth into an exhortation to repentance (Example 2.11a, mm. 22–31): "Weh euch Bösen, weh euch Blinden, weh euch allen, die ihr Sünden immer häuft auf Sünden! Menschen, denket nach! Werdet ihr Erbarmung finden wenn er kommt in seiner Herrlichkeit und Macht?" (Woe to the wicked, woe to the blind, woe to all who pile sin upon sin. People, think! Will you receive mercy when he comes in his magnificence and power?) The last sentence is set to the final appearance of the *Hauptsatz*, the *tutti* reiteration that leads to such a memorable outburst in the recapitulation (Example 2.11c). In the vocal arrangement, Haydn

---

[58] Barth, *Protestant Theology*, 132–34.

adjusts the dynamics so as to render this reference to resurrection as a triumphant *fortissimo* in the exposition as well.

The mysteries of *The Seven Last Words* do not create such ambiguity as to overwhelm rhetorical clarity; with *Der Tod Jesu* in the background and Haydn's elaboration of emotionally loaded *Hauptsätze* in the work itself, there was ample justification for Christmann to write as if the Sonatas expressed Christ's feelings, in all their particulars. Their sublime overtones, however, do show the paradox of a religious culture at once explanatory and revelatory, humanly expressive and divinely mysterious: in effect, *The Seven Last Words* captures both the reforming spirit of Joseph II and the resistance of Cardinal Migazzi. Its fate after Joseph's death in 1790 illustrates the decline of reform and a contemporaneous transformation in musical aesthetics. The Catholic church retrenched just as the *Frühromantiker* began to celebrate the arts, especially music, for opening the transcendent spaces dubbed "das Unendliche" (the infinite) by Friedrich Schlegel and others. As we saw in the Introduction (see pp. 15–17), they continued to hear emotions in music as well, but there is a marked distinction in emphasis between a critic like Christmann, who lauds the transparency of Haydn's expression, and Wackenroder, who writes that music "wohl überhaupt um so mächtiger auf uns wirkt, und alle Kräfte unsers Wesens um so allgemeiner in Aufruhr setzt, je dunkler und geheimnißvoller ihre Sprache ist" (generally affects us more powerfully, and throws all the forces of our being more generally into uproar, the darker and more secretive its language is).[59] Significantly, he and many of his contemporaries became enamored of Catholicism, not because it had been reformed – their native Protestantism had undergone a far longer and more thorough rationalization – but because it still emphasized ritual and spectacle over textual exegesis. The mysteries of a revealed faith were what art was to express, and Wackenroder devotes many of his comments to sacred music as well as to the religious paintings of Michaelangelo and Raphael.

Friebert's reading of *The Seven Last Words* takes a step in this direction, attributing emotions to the Sonatas but finding redemption in them as well, the miracle that Christmann never once mentioned. The Prussian dilettante Baron Otto von Kospoth went a good deal further in creating the most singular document in the reception history of *The Seven Last Words*, the *Composizioni sopra Il Pater noster consistenti in sette sonate caratteristiche con un' introduzione* (1794). For what context he designed this work, if any, is unknown, but he emulated Haydn closely, dividing the "Our Father" into nine sentences that serve as titles for an *Introduzione*, seven slow "Sonatas," and an Allegro spirituoso that, like Haydn's earthquake, follows the last Sonata without break

---

[59] Wackenroder, *Werke und Briefe*, I: 134.

Example 2.17   Kospoth, *Composizioni sopra Il Pater noster*

	Introduzione *Grave* Pater noster, qui es in coelis	F	c
Sonata I	Sanctificetur nomen tuum *Largo*	F	3/4
Sonata II	Adveniat regnum tuum *Andante sostenuto maestoso*	A	c
Sonata III	Fiat voluntas *Largo*	Gm	3/4
Sonata IV	Panem nostrum da nobis hodie *Adagio*	Eb	¢
Sonata V	Et remitte nobis debita nostra sicut *Adagio molto*	C	c
Sonata VI	Et ne nos inducas *Largo molto lento*	G	6/8
Sonata VII	Sed libera nos a malo *Largo con espressione*	Dm	3/4
	Quia tuum est regnum et potentia et gloria in saecula saeculorum. Amen *Allegro spirituoso*	D	c

(Example 2.17). He means the movements to be understood as meditations on the prayer, and by choosing what was probably an even more familiar text than the Seven Words and giving it in Latin, he aimed to appeal to the whole of Christian Europe. Despite resemblances that extend even to similar themes, however, the two works weight expression and transcendence far differently. Kospoth does not "set" his texts as Haydn does, perhaps because they do not obviously emanate from a protagonist; although spoken by Christ in the Gospels, the words are intended for the "we" of communal prayer. But whatever the reason, absent the direct connection between words and theme the movements stand at a further remove from language than Haydn's, and the handling of form widens the gap. While Kospoth develops some of his musical ideas and even uses one of them in two separate movements, his elaborations are never so concentrated as Haydn's, and indeed he frequently abandons his *Hauptsätze* altogether. "Sanctificetur nomen tuum" (Hallowed be your name) begins much like "Hodie" or "Deus meus," with a brief first group ending on a half-cadence and followed by music of a radically

120

different character; the strong–weak ending of the first phrase even recalls the rhythmic structure of the first themes of the Haydn movements (Example 2.18a). Much as in "Hodie," furthermore, the music
after the half-cadence consists of the sustained chords, murmuring
arpeggios, and lyrical melody of a classic musical idyll. The difference
is that Kospoth does not derive the new melody from the opening measures, or develop it; the exposition continues with several additional
ideas. Paradise is not the logical outcome of a promise, as in Haydn, but
a sudden and mystifying apparition.

The effect is compounded later. Kospoth colors the dominant at the
end of his development section with eye-opening strokes of C♯ minor
and A minor, reached by a common-tone move from C to A♭/G♯ that
warns of surprises ahead (Example 2.18b, mm. 63–66). And indeed, the

Example 2.18a   Kospoth, *Il Pater noster*, "Sanctificetur nomen tuum,"
mm. 1–20

first group lapses into minor, setting up a return to major like that at the parallel point in "Hodie," only it is not the original second group that returns (mm. 82–89). Sustained chords, arpeggios, and lyrical mood remain, but the melody is new, shorter than before, and played by the winds rather than the strings. What is more, the recapitulation goes on to introduce a second previously unheard idyllic passage and to return to similar textures at the final cadence, which the exposition had not. Where Haydn's recapitulation drives the point home, fulfilling the promise of paradise in the tonic major, Kospoth's travels further and further into the unknown. Sparked by sublimely irrational harmony, his movement ends in a world unimagined by the exposition.

The remaining Sonatas of *Il Pater noster* follow a similar trajectory: exposition, tonally wide-ranging development, recapitulation with one or more new ideas, most often long-breathed melodies for the winds enfolded by lush, idyllic accompaniments. Sometimes paradise arrives with even less preparation than in "Sanctificetur nomen tuum"; in "Fiat voluntas" (Your will be done), there is no recapitulation of any

Example 2.18b   Kospoth, *Il Pater noster*, "Sanctificetur nomen tuum," mm. 61–89

(*cont.*)

Example 2.18b (*cont.*)

exposition material but only a new theme that transforms minor to major and instantiates the final word of the text: "on earth as it is in heaven." An even grander apotheosis accompanies the last two lines, "Sed libera nos a malo, quia tuum est regnum et potentia et gloria in saecula saeculorum" (Deliver us from evil, for yours is the kingdom, the power and the glory for ever and ever), set in two sections that accomplish a dual shift from minor to major and slow to fast: the D minor Largo unfolds only through a highly chromatic development section, upon which the D major Allegro follows as a recapitulation substitute (Example 2.19). Solidly diatonic, it carries listeners into a heaven both

Example 2.19 Kospoth, *Il Pater noster*, "Quia tuum est regnum," mm. 1–10

triumphant and graceful, where vigorous march rhythms alternate with further idyllic melodies and a quiet, plagal cadence reminiscent of Gossec's *Pastorella*. Intimated so many times, paradise is ultimately achieved in an "Our Father" that is less a plea for intercession than a journey to salvation.

The contrast with *The Seven Last Words*, particularly its ending, could not be more stark. Haydn's concluding Sonata, "In manus tuas, Domine, commendo spiritum meum" (Into your hands, Lord, I commend my spirit), has a richly scored and balanced eight-measure *Hauptsatz* as well as a calm "farewell" horn call to invoke a spirit confident of its imminent ascension (mm. 1–12). On the other hand, lengthy passages for the first violins alone, broken up by rests as in settings of the last chorus of the *Tres horas*,[60] offer the less reassuring spectacle of Christ gasping his final breaths (mm. 29–36, 81–88). After the final horn call, moreover, restfulness and self-possession give way to the earthquake, perhaps the most terrifying musical cataclysm between Gluck's Dance of the Furies and the storm in Beethoven's *Pastoral* Symphony. Trumpets and timpani enter for the first time in the entire work, adding a blustery edge to the sound and wrenching the key from E♭ down into C minor. The opening measures are rent by diminished seventh chords, angry trill and scale figures, and rhythmic uncertainties caused by missing downbeats and hemiolas; the apparent second group, articulated by a thematic fragment that begins to suggest four-measure periodicity, is rudely broken off by a unison trill (Example 2.20a, m. 53). Disruption then mounts, with hemiolas twice implying a two-measure hypermeter (mm. 57–58 and 60–61) but running aground on missing downbeats (mm. 59 and 62), leaving the orchestra simply to reiterate the tonic and dominant scale degrees (mm. 65–69). Eventually the opening measures and even the second group theme are reprised in the tonic, suggesting a binary or sonata form, but again the surface action prevents any sense of resolution (Example 2.20b). The violins break off in their highest register on a subdominant (m. 108), then plunge to a Neapolitan chord whose Phrygian second, present in the main theme since the beginning, now remains to the bitter end (the opening measures are quoted in mm. 115–18). The concluding unisons barely effect closure, even at triple-*forte*; like Gluck's Furies, the earthquake generates more energy than its final cadence can contain.

Heard after this, the end of *Il Pater noster* sounds like a reproach, a rejection of darkness that is not entirely explained by the difference in subject matter. In and of itself the "Our Father" does not suggest the foretastes of paradise that Kospoth reads into every line, or the triumphant affirmation of his finale. Conversely, Haydn's story need not finish with

---

[60] Marx-Weber, "Musiche per le tre ore di agonia de N.S.G.C.," 146.

Example 2.20a Haydn, *The Seven Last Words*, "Il Terremoto," mm. 50–70

such gloom and violence. He might have ended with the meditation on the seventh Word, as the *Tres horas* devotion does, or with the expressions of sorrow and repentance found in many Passion libretti. Ramler even adds a declaration of victory, "Weinet nicht! Es hat überwunden der Löwe vom Stamm Juda!" (Weep not! The lion from the tribe of Judah has overcome!), which leads Graun to interrupt his otherwise somber concluding lament with a series of brisk and cheerful bass solos. Friebert tried to inject a similar note of hope into *The Seven Last Words* themselves, interpolating eight measures of *a cappella* singing just before the final cadence of the earthquake (i.e., after m. 114), on the text, "Ach lass uns beym Auferstehn als Erbe im Himmel eingehn" (Oh let us enter heaven as the heritage of the resurrection).[61] But Haydn did not preserve this startling innovation, and although he adopted Ramler's final chorus as

[61] Bartha, "A 'Sieben Worte,'" 152.

Example 2.20b   Haydn, *The Seven Last Words*, "Il Terremoto,"
mm. 102–23

a text for the movement, he cut it off after only nine lines, before the reference to the lion's victory. As in the instrumental version, the lingering image is of the destruction wrought by Christ's death rather than the salvation it promises.

Kospoth and Friebert were not the last to wish the ending were different. The *Musikalisches Taschenbuch*, a short-lived periodical (1803–05) distinguished by its precocious adoption of Romanticism, rejected Haydn's earthquake as inconsistent with the new aesthetic: "ich [kann] mich nicht genug wundern, wie der Componist, der durch die angehängte Darstellung des Erdbebens die Realität dem Idealen entgegensetzen sollte, von seiner Höhe in eine so gemeine, widrige, und die heilige Wirkung des Ganzen vernichtende Natürlichkeit gefallen ist" (I find it surprising that the composer, who undertook to counter the ideal with reality through the attached representation of the earthquake, fell from his heights to a naturalness that is so common, contrary, and destructive of the holy effect of the whole).[62] One might have expected the earthquake to suggest different connotations. It does, after all, represent a divine intervention in human affairs, and Haydn's curt and chaotic setting has as much right to be called sublime as the storm in the *Pastoral* Symphony, which another Romantically inclined critic would soon hear as expressing the voice of God (see p. 179 below). But the earthquake is "natural," "realistic," like the birds and other earthly phenomena that critics would attack in Haydn's *Creation* and *Seasons* (see pp. 143–46 below). The paradox is only partly explained by the music's physical tangibility, so striking after the ethereal farewell of the preceding Sonata; nevertheless, Beethoven's storm is no less material. What matters is that the *Pastoral* Symphony has another movement, a shepherds' hymn that would presumably have lifted the *Taschenbuch*'s critic back into the realm of "the ideal," a catchword (like "the infinite," to which the journal refers with equal frequency) for a transcendence that does not admit the darker side of the supernatural – or, if it does, requires that it be dispelled. Wackenroder may have celebrated the dark mysteries of musical language, but symphonies and sacred music inspired him to envision King David and "ein munteres Chor von Jünglingen und Mädchen [die] auf einer heitern Wiese tanzen" (a merry chorus of youths and maidens who dance on a cheerful meadow), images of nobility and light.[63] The earthquake invokes powers that threaten humanity rather than save or elevate it: crush the soul rather than free it from the body. Christ, redemption, and transcendence are all swallowed up by a blackness as profound as that of the church in which *The Seven Last Words* was originally performed.

---

[62] *Musikalisches Taschenbuch* (1805): 61–62.
[63] Wackenroder, *Werke und Briefe*, I: 133.

Despite enormous differences in subject matter, musical structure, and means of representation, Haydn's orchestral Passion thus has at least one thing in common with Dittersdorf's symphonic Ovid. Both are products of an age that believed in the perfectibility of humankind, and more specifically of a society whose leader tried to legislate this central ideal of the Enlightenment into practice, in no small part by turning his church into a house of moral instruction. Yet both works leave some question as to whether the emperor's hopes are realistic, and they use similar means to do so: fast, violent finales that depart to a greater or lesser extent from the conventions of form, phrase, and rhythm observed in the preceding movements. Haydn's is the more complex work in that it engages critically with religious practice all along: Christ speaks, teaches, and feels, as he is supposed to do in the enlightened church, but he also has visions, makes promises about the hereafter, and loses his humanity in the ambiguities of wordless sound. Yet the result is not dissimilar, as the unknowables that Christ acknowledges, like the violence of Ovid's characters, eventually turn against the listeners. At the end of *The Seven Last Words*, the sublimity glimpsed so many times bursts out to disavow the possibility of reform.

3

The boundaries of the art: characteristic music in contemporary criticism and aesthetics

The subtitle of Beethoven's *Pastoral* Symphony, "More the expression of emotions than painting," reveals two curious facts about characteristic music.[1] Long before the nineteenth century put the *Pastoral* on stage or discovered extra birds in its second movement (see p. 18 above), attaching texts to instrumental works raised expectations that physical objects or events would be represented, whatever the stated subject. Beethoven was not alone in trying to challenge the assumption; Hermes, too, begins his *Analyse* of Dittersdorf's *Metamorphoses* by declaring that they are not "imitations de la nature" but "le résultat de ce que le compositeur a senti chaque fois lorsque frappé de la lecture d'un poème d'Ovide, il a versé sur le papier le feu dont il se trouvoit enflammé" (the result of that which the composer felt each time that he, struck by the reading of a poem of Ovid, set onto paper the fire in which he found himself enflamed).[2] The music is said to embody passion, feeling, creative rapture, anything but physical nature, for that – and here is the second fact – would invite criticism. Adherents to the doctrine of mimesis in the eighteenth century felt that "tone-painting" literally transgressed the boundaries of music, appropriating practices more properly left to the other arts. The Romantics objected to its apparent materialism, the "reality" of Haydn's earthquake that so disturbed the *Musikalisches Taschenbuch* as it contemplated the otherwise "ideal" *Seven Last Words* (see p. 127 above). Without some preemptive defense, characteristic works were doomed, associated by default with violations of taste.

And yet composers continued to write them, and to meet a surprisingly favorable reception in light of the apparent obstacles – why? For

---

[1] The phrase is found on the title page of the first violin part used at the symphony's premiere (Gustav Nottebohm, *Zweite Beethoveniana* [Leipzig: C. F. Peters, 1887], 378) and on the verso of the title page of Breitkopf und Härtel's first edition of 1809 (*Ludwig van Beethoven: Thematisches Verzeichnis von Gustav Nottebohm nebst der Bibliotheca Beethoveniana von Emerich Kastner, ergänzt von Theodor Frimmel* [Wiesbaden: Sändig, 1969], 62).

[2] Hermes, *Analyse*, 168.

one, although the rejection of tone-painting was sincere, it was colored by issues of morality and nationality that turned a debate on musical representation into a forum on the social function and political identity of art. The consequences affected vocal even more than instrumental music, and the discourse surrounding various operas and oratorios, most notably Haydn's *Creation* and *Seasons*, became so heated that tone-painting acquired an even more dubious reputation than either a mimetic or a Romantic viewpoint really warranted. Beethoven's caution, and that of Hermes, stems partly from this exaggeration of the dangers of material representation, which opened composers who "painted" to accusations not simply of poor taste but of moral decrepitude and worse. In addition, while tone-painting was assumed to be fundamentally different both from expression and from evocations of the ideal, critics addressing actual examples found it difficult to maintain the distinctions; as we have seen in the preceding chapters, emotive outpourings can come in the form of dances, and natural phenomena with overtones of repose or agitation. Characteristic works benefited from a paradox not unrelated to the status of music as semantically both definite and indefinite; seemingly so independent, their physical and emotional attributes collapse into one another once they are considered closely.

Tone-painting versus expression

With the adoption of mimesis as the basis for musical aesthetics in the early eighteenth century, tone-painting and expression were set up as separate categories of imitation.[3] To express meant to imitate emotions, conceived of as the discrete, tangible states of mind called "characters" in the keyboard pieces of Reichardt and others; to paint meant to copy the sounds or motions of storms, running water, wind, birds, and battles, or simply to suggest motion per se, especially ascent, descent, swiftness, and slowness. Expression ranked higher from the beginning, declared the proper goal of music in the foundational texts on art as mimesis by Jean-Baptiste DuBos and Charles Batteux.[4] This left tone-painting open to criticism, and indeed by the middle of the century writers were

---

[3] On mimesis in eighteenth-century musical aesthetics see Hosler, *Changing Aesthetic Views of Instrumental Music*, 31–141; James Anderson Winn, *Unsuspected Eloquence: A History of the Relations between Poetry and Music* (New Haven: Yale University Press, 1981), 194–286; Neubauer, *The Emancipation of Music from Language*, 60–75; and Lippman, *A History of Western Musical Aesthetics*, 59–136.

[4] DuBos, *Réflexions critiques sur la poësie, la peinture et la musique* (Paris, 1719); Batteux, *Les Beaux-arts réduits à un même principe* (Paris, 1746); the relevant passages from both are trans. in Peter le Huray and James Day, eds., *Music and Aesthetics in the Eighteenth and Early-Nineteenth Centuries* (Cambridge: Cambridge University Press, 1981), 21–22, 50–53.

already going out of their way to emphasize its inferiority. When Charles Avison, for instance, arrives at the section "On Musical Expression, So Far As it Relates to the Composer" in his *Essay on Musical Expression* (1752), he begins by telling composers not what they should *do* to achieve expression but rather what they should *not* do – namely, conjure up thunder, laughter, birdsong, and other subjects assumed to be pictorial. Lest anyone mistake his meaning, he adduces a series of cautionary examples from Handel's oratorios and only then goes on to discuss the representation of emotion.[5] So critical is the problem that it is worth displacing what appears to be the main subject of both chapter and book.

English and German writers propound related views throughout the rest of the century, but with variations that both broaden the implications of tone-painting and confuse its definition. Nowhere is this more evident than in Sulzer's *Allgemeine Theorie*, one of two texts that were frequently cited as being so authoritative on the subject as to render further discussion superfluous (the other, by Johann Jakob Engel, is discussed below).[6] The entries on "Ausdruk in der Musik," "Mahlerey (Musik)" and "Gemähld (Musik)" (Expression in Music, Painting [Music], Picture [Music]) intensify earlier critiques such as Avison's or that of Christian Gottfried Krause, whose description of expression as "der wahre und höchste Zweck der Musik" (the true and highest goal of music) hints that tone-painting, which merely "ergötzet ... den Zuhörer" (charms the listener), has an air of falsehood or superficiality.[7] Sulzer says outright, "Mahlereyen sind dem wahren Geist der Musik entgegen, die nicht Begriffe von leblosen Dingen geben, sondern Empfindungen des Gemüths ausdrüken soll" (painting violates the true spirit of music, which ought to express the sentiments of feeling, not convey ideas of inanimate objects),[8] and he inaugurates a pair of derogatory terms for

---

[5] Avison, *An Essay on Musical Expression*, 2nd edn. (London, 1753), 56–106. On similar criticisms of Handel in Germany see Schmenner, *Die Pastorale*, 45–46.

[6] Sulzer and Engel are referred to in numerous reviews as well as in Johann Nikolaus Forkel, *Allgemeine Geschichte der Musik*, 2 vols. (Leipzig, 1788 and 1801), I: 56, and in didactic works such as Daniel Gottlob Türk, *Von den wichtigsten Pflichten eines Organisten* (Halle, 1787), 23, and Ernst Wilhelm Wolf, *Musikalischer Unterricht für Liebhaber und diejenigen, Welche die Musik treiben und lehren wollen*, 2 vols. (Dresden, 1788), I: 73. The dissemination of their views was encouraged by an annotated reprinting of Engel's pamphlet and of two of the three relevant articles by Sulzer ("Mahlerey" and "Gemähld") in the *Magazin der Musik* 1 (1783): 1139–83.

[7] Krause, *Von der musikalischen Poesie* (Berlin, 1752), 53, quoted in Adolf Sandberger, "'Mehr Ausdruck der Empfindung als Malerei,'" in *Ausgewählte Aufsätze zur Musikgeschichte*, II: 208.

[8] Sulzer, *Allgemeine Theorie*, II: 357; trans. Baker and Christensen, *Aesthetics and the Art of Musical Composition*, 90. Further references in the text (the second page number indicates the translation, if necessary).

the practice that would become favorites of future critics: "Kindereyen" (childish tricks [III: 357]), and "kindische Künsteleyen" (childish artificialities [II: 357]). His condemnation seems especially strong given that his "true spirit of music," the expression of emotions, is promoted elsewhere in the *Allgemeine Theorie* as the means by which art will not only entertain but also, by triggering emotional responses in its audience, strengthen and shape the moral sense. Criticized as old-fashioned even in Sulzer's own day, this notion of art as moral lesson retained some currency in the second half of the eighteenth century thanks in no small part to the success of the *Allgemeine Theorie*, and the consequence for tone-painting was to saddle it with failings beyond the merely aesthetic.[9] A representation that did not speak to the soul did nothing to better the listener, and, worse, it might have the opposite effect if it crowded out opportunities for expression.

The moral turn of Sulzer's thinking reverberates in later years, when, as we shall see, seemingly innocuous references to animals or natural phenomena are taken to threaten the very status of music as a fine art. But he also qualifies his position in ways that would prove equally important. Blanket condemnations notwithstanding, his real concern is with the abuse of tone-painting in vocal music, especially in arias, which – ideally, in his view – should represent the dominant emotion of the character on stage. Objective images too often disrupt psychological coherence; when a joyful character mentions a storm by way of remembering past tribulations, for instance, musical allusions to thunder or lightning exaggerate the metaphor and obscure the reigning affect (III: 357).[10] Avison voiced caution on the same point, and after Sulzer it became a critical cliché to fault storms or birdcalls for distracting the attention from a governing mood.[11] Sulzer goes still further and recognizes that musical figures he defines as expressive can be similarly abused; if the same joyful character says "do not weep" instead of "be joyful," musical figures associated with weeping will cause no less distortion than a thunderclap (I: 274). The overriding

---

[9] Sulzer's most prominent critics were Karl Philipp Moritz and Goethe (Dahlhaus, *The Idea of Absolute Music*, 5; Nicholas Boyle, *Goethe: The Poet and the Age*, vol. I, *The Poetry of Desire* [Oxford: Oxford University Press, 1992], 128). See also Robert E. Norton, *The Beautiful Soul: Aesthetic Morality in the Eighteenth Century* (Ithaca: Cornell University Press, 1995); Hosler, *Changing Aesthetic Views of Instrumental Music*, 145–52; and Ruiter, *Der Charakterbegriff*, 64–66. Among writers on music, Koch is particularly indebted to Sulzer's moralism, e.g., in the *Versuch einer Anleitung zur Composition*, 3 vols. (Leipzig, 1782–93), II: 16.

[10] Similar complaints are found already in DuBos (Le Huray and Day, *Music and Aesthetics*, 21), and are reinterpreted from a formalist perspective by Winn, who argues that tone-painting detracts not from expression but from structural coherence (*Unsuspected Eloquence*, 217–24).

[11] Avison, *Essay on Musical Expression*, 68–69.

purpose of his articles turns out to be not the prohibition of tone-painting so much as the education of composers in how to read texts.

Illustrating that "expressive" and "pictorial" representations can transgress the same rule of unity also suggests that the two categories overlap, a possibility made more evident by the examples themselves. A storm symbolic of remembered troubles has built-in expressive connotations, whether or not they are appropriate in a context of joy, and, conversely, weeping in eighteenth-century music nearly always involves the imitation of sorrowful sounds such as sobbing or sighing, or of physical motions such as the falling of tears or the marching of mourners (see pp. 216–17 below). To judge from a further passage, even the distinction between natural event and human activity, storm and crying, does not always suffice to separate tone-painting from expression. "Es geht... an, Mahlereyen aus der leblosen Natur in Musik zu bringen: nicht nur solche, die in der Natur selbst sich dem Gehör einprägen, wie der Donner oder der Sturm, sondern auch die, welche das Gemüthe durch bestimmte Empfindungen rühren, wie die Lieblichkeit einer stillen ländlichen Scene" (It is appropriate to incorporate paintings of inanimate nature in music, not just those that in nature impress the ear, like thunder or a storm, but also those that move the soul with specific feelings, like the tenderness of a quiet countryside scene [III: 357, my trans.]). No less part of the natural world than the storm, the rural scene nevertheless provides moral stimulus where the other does not, a difference that does not obviously follow from the musical conventions associated with the two subjects; the shepherds' horns, birdcalls, and bubbling brooks of eighteenth-century pastoral music seem as "objective" as a flash of lightning or rainy downpour. Here as elsewhere Sulzer argues for the importance of words, "die uns das Gemählde, dessen Würkung wir durch das Gehör empfinden, zugleich der Einbildungskraft vorstellt" (by which the painting whose effect is sensed by the ear also presents itself to our imagination [III: 357, 90]),[12] another point with broader resonance inasmuch as the fate of characteristic works depended greatly on whether their texts were accepted as constitutive of the work. Where they were, a written declaration that a pictorial passage also communicated "tenderness" would tend to be taken as evidence that it did, as seems to have happened in the case of Sulzer's rural scene. But another text might equally well present a storm as expressive of agitation or fear, as storms often were in contemporary dramatic music, so that image and feeling would again unite. The difficulty of keeping them apart is implicitly recognized by Sulzer and would be used by

---

[12] See also Hosler, *Changing Aesthetic Views of Instrumental Music*, 159–64.

composers and critics to defend tone-paintings against his accusation of moral emptiness.

In his essay *Über die musikalische Malerei*, the only text on the issue of representation to rival the influence of the *Allgemeine Theorie*, Johann Jakob Engel concurs with Sulzer that music should touch the heart, and that expression is therefore the highest form of mimesis. He also portrays references to inappropriate images in vocal music as a particularly egregious offense and concludes, Avison-like, with a list of cautionary examples. But the grounds for his viewpoint are practical rather than moral, which prevents him from rejecting tone-painting out of hand and from taking Sulzer's sanctimonious tone. Like the Englishman James Harris, Engel argues that music can better represent emotions than objects because, whereas all of the former possess musically imitable sounds and motions, only some of the latter do.[13] This is in large part because music and feeling are both perpetually in flux, an analogy drawn also by Carl Friedrich Junker and Johann Nikolaus Forkel and a testament to the growing influence in Germany of Lord Kames and other English writers, who saw the emotions as mutable and fluid rather than as "characters" experienced one at a time.[14] The inner life is therefore a more fitting match for the rhythmic variability of music than physical objects or movements, and its imitation allows the medium to meet a different but no less potent standard than moral education: "man soll mit jeder Kunst dasjenige am liebsten ausführen wollen, was man damit am besten, am vollkommensten ausführen kann" (one should prefer to execute with every art whatever it allows one to execute best – most perfectly).[15] The reference point is the *Laokoon: oder über die Grenzen der Malerei und Poesie* (1766) of Lessing, which held that artists should devote their energies to the form of representation most appropriate to their genre – painters should describe, and epic poets narrate. Engel's extension of the criterion to music was welcomed by critics who hoped it would encourage young composers to consider "das Gebiet und die Grenzen ihrer Kunst" (the province and boundaries of their art),[16] and who may have seen *Über die musikalische Malerei* as a substitute for the

---

[13] Engel, *Über die musikalische Malerei* (Berlin, 1780), repr. *J. J. Engel's Schriften*, vol. IV (Berlin, 1802), 307–08. Cf. Harris, *Three Treatises Concerning Art* (London, 1744), in Lippman, *Historical Reader*, I: 181–83.

[14] Engel, *Schriften*, 312–18. On Engel's contemporaries see Hosler, *Changing Aesthetic Views of Instrumental Music*, 172–73 and 178–80; the important texts are Forkel, *Allgemeine Geschichte*; and Junker, *Tonkunst* (Bern, 1777), and *Betrachtungen über Mahlerey, Ton- und Bildhauerkunst* (Basel, 1778).

[15] Engel, *Schriften*, 320; trans. Wye Jamison Allanbrook in Leo Treitler, gen. ed., *Source Readings in Music History*, rev. edn. (New York: Norton, 1998), 959. Further references in the text (the second page number indicates the translation).

[16] Spazier, "Über das Oratorium Hiob," *Studien für Tonkünstler und Musikfreunde*, 42.

never-completed second and third parts of *Laokoon*, which were to have treated music.[17]

Yet no matter how powerful his reasons for thinking that music should express, Engel recognizes the uses of tone-painting and acknowledges what Sulzer only implied, that subjective and objective representation cannot always be distinguished. In his view, the emotions differ in how they relate to the things that trigger them. Some, like fear, invert the shape and magnitude of their source: "Die Größe, die Stärke, die im Object wahrgenommen wird, ist gegen das Subject gerichtet: je größer, je stärker also jenes, desto nichtiger, desto schwächer dieses" (The greatness and strength that are perceived in the object are directed against the subject. The grander and stronger the one, the baser and weaker is the other [333, 963]). Such "heterogeneous" passions must be represented without reference to their stimulus, or else contradictions will arise; to portray the crash and bluster of a thunderstorm would be to ignore the frightened whimpering of the people cowering before it. "Homogeneous" emotions, by contrast, put mind and body in sympathy with that which they see, as in the case of admiration: "Das betrachtende Subject nimmt so viel, wie möglich, die Natur und Beschaffenheit des betrachteten Objects an: die Stimme wird voll, die Brust erweitert sich . . . wenn man große Gegenstände denkt. Denkt man erhabene, so richtet man das Haupt empor, erhebt Stimme und Hände" (The contemplating subject assumes as much as possible the nature and quality of the contemplated object. When one thinks on great objects . . . the voice becomes full, and the breast expands. People who are thinking exalted thoughts raise their heads and lift their voices and hands [332–33, 962–63]). Now the cause of the reaction may be imitated without fear of distortion, a point Engel illustrates with an example from an oratorio on a Metastasio text, *Sant'Elena al Calvario*, by Johann Adolf Hasse (1746; revised 1772). At the entrance of Draciliano, Prefect of Judea, Hasse "malt die Ankunft der großen Heerführer durch einen prächtigen marschmäßigen Satz, der zu der freudig erhabenen Empfindung, welche durch's Ganze der Arie herrschen soll, gar nicht übel zu passen scheint" (paints the arrival of the great commanders-in-chief with a magnificent phrase in march style, which seems remarkably well suited to the joyously exalted feeling that should dominate the whole of the aria [339, 964]; see Example 3.1a). In fact, as Engel surely knew, Hasse's swinging *alla breve* theme not only "depicts" the character's physical entrance but also "expresses" his dignified excitement at the prospect looking out from Calvary when the march is taken up in the vocal part – but this is acceptable if the emotions

---

[17] Lessing, *Laocoön: An Essay on the Limits of Painting and Poetry*, trans. Edward Allen McCormick (Indianapolis: Bobbs Merrill, 1962), xxv.

Example 3.1a   Hasse, *Sant'Elena al Calvario*, "Del Calvario già sorger le cime," mm. 1–6

Example 3.1b   Hasse, "Del Calvario già sorger le cime," mm. 27–32

associated with exalted or sublime sights are taken to be "homogeneous" (Example 3.1b).[18] Hence where action and feeling coincide, so, too, do the seemingly so polarized categories of representation, allowing Engel to make the remarkable statement that "painting is expression" (334, 963). Moreover, and significantly, the congruence between external and internal in Hasse's Draciliano permits Engel to justify a tone-painting by one of the most prestigious composers in Europe and specifically in Germany. His is the first of many critical interventions to give as much weight to the hierarchies of contemporary taste as to the demands of aesthetic doctrine.

As commentators approached characteristic works in the 1780s and 1790s, they had to consider the categories of musical representation laid out by Sulzer and Engel and also a further issue, comprehensibility, which provoked an important if less heated discussion of its own. Regarding instrumental music in general, most German writers felt that it could best communicate definite meanings when it abided by the principle of affective unity that underlay the character piece for keyboard.

---

[18] The entire text reads: "Del Calvario già sorger le cime / Veggo altere di tempio sublime, / E i gran Duci del Rè delle sfere / Pellegrini la tomba adorar!" (Already from Calvary I see the proud spires of the lofty temple rising, and the grand Dukes of the King of the heavens coming as pilgrims to worship at the tomb!), trans. *Source Readings*, 964n.

As Engel wrote: "Eine Symphonie, eine Sonate ... sobald es mehr als bloss ein angenehmes Geräusch, ein liebliches Geschwirre von Tönen seyn soll – muss die Ausführung Einer Leidenschaft, die aber freilich in mannichfaltigen Empfindungen ausbeugt ... enthalten" (If a symphony or sonata ... is intended to be more than just an agreeable noise, a pleasing buzz of tones – it must contain the realization of a single passion, although certainly that realization can take the form of a variety of feelings [323–24, 960]).[19] The dangers of representing too many and, especially, overly diverse emotions were considerable, potentially as great as painting inappropriate objects inasmuch as both Engel and Reichardt heard exaggerated affective changes in instrumental movements as suggestive of madness: "die wilden Phantasieen eines Fieberkranken" (the wild fantasies of a person delirious with fever [322, 960]) is what Engel imagined he would hear if an accompanied recitative or melodrama were performed without its text, and he attributes a similar effect to a familiar kind of characteristic work, the opera overture that summarizes several personalities or actions of the following drama.[20] Needless to say, depicting an insane mind could do no more for the moral education than creating pictures bereft of feeling, and although their reactions are not recorded one suspects that the more ambitious characteristic symphonies of the day, the *Metamorphoses* or *Télémaques* with their numerous characters and panoply of sentiments, would have caused Engel, Reichardt, and Sulzer all to recoil. More to their taste would have been Dittersdorf's *Il combattimento delle passioni umane*, in which the composer not only sets out to depict emotional allegories such as *Il Malinconico* but also avoids, to a large extent, the stylistic heterogeneity of Italian comic opera that was the basis of contemporary instrumental discourse and a source of discontent for many German writers in addition to Engel and Reichardt (see p. 4 above).

But characteristic music raised a further question, which was whether written words could be considered integral to instrumental works and therefore in a position to influence their meaning, like the text that changed Sulzer's rural scene from a painting to an expression of tenderness. Reichardt assumed that listeners would read the titles or, in one case, the sonnet of Petrarch printed at the top of his character pieces and interpret the associated music accordingly.[21] Not surprisingly, most other composers and enthusiasts of characteristic music took the same

---

[19] Sulzer and Junker expressed similar views (Hosler, *Changing Aesthetic Views of Instrumental Music*, 162, 175).

[20] Reichardt compares character pieces that try to express several contrasting emotions to the monologue of the mad Ophelia in *Hamlet* (*Musikalisches Kunstmagazin* 2 [1791]: 39).

[21] *Musikalisches Kunstmagazin* 1 (1782): 24–33, 64–68. Ruiter quotes earlier statements in favor of titles by Krause and Friedrich Wilhelm Marpurg (*Der Charakterbegriff*, 48–49).

view, in the absence of which works like the *Metamorphoses* could hardly achieve the desired effect. As we have already seen, however, critics of *The Seven Last Words* wondered whether the music could suggest "thirst" to a listener not already aware of the subject, a question that can only be asked if the text is considered separable from the music, as an appendage with no role in the act of reception (see pp. 110–11 above).[22] Heinrich Christoph Koch makes just this assumption and thereby dismisses all characteristic music as unable to speak to the heart or the intellect,[23] and others suggest that only those subjects should be represented that can be recognized without text, such as battles or hunts.[24] Although it figures only occasionally in discussions of specific characteristic pieces, the idea that they ought to be able to communicate without words undoubtedly colored many unrecorded reactions, and it prefigures the frequent nineteenth- and twentieth-century criticism of program symphonies and symphonic poems that their subjects cannot be divined without verbal aid.

It is not surprising, then, that Hermes like Reichardt is quite explicit about the importance of text in understanding Dittersdorf's *Metamorphoses*, urging listeners to read not only his own interpretive descriptions of the movements but also the original stories in Ovid. They can then approach the symphonies in a frame of mind where events like the death of Phaethon, struck from Apollo's chariot by Jupiter's thunderbolt, will be unmistakable: "ce qui met le comble à l'horreur de l'ensemble, c'est l'éclair ... Je n'ai garde d'expliquer comment cela se fait; il me suffit de prévenir que c'est l'ouvrage d'un clin-d'œil, & que sur cent auditeurs vous n'en trouverez pas un seul peut-être, qui se soit douté de l'instrument d'où sort la foudre, & qui ne s'effraye & ne pousse des hauts cris au moment que le feu tombe" (what forms the peak of horror in the scene is the lightning ... I am wary of explaining how it is done; it is sufficient for me to warn that it is the work of an instant, and that in a hundred listeners you will find perhaps not one who has suspected from which instrument the thunderbolt appears, and who is not frightened

---

[22] A similar query surfaces in a review of a characteristic sonata by E. W. Wolf in the *Allgemeine Verzeichniß neuer Bücher* (1779): 599, quoted in Morrow, *German Music Criticism*, 130.

[23] Koch, *Versuch*, II: 41. In the *Musikalisches Lexikon*, s.v. "Simphonies à programmes," col. 1385, Koch is less dismissive but still wonders whether "historische Gegenstände" (historical events) can be communicated in music "ohne Beyhülfe der Dichtkunst" (without the assistance of poetry), which assumes, again, that characterizing texts have no role in reception.

[24] *AmZ* 2 (1800): cols. 749–50; see also Schulin, *Musikalische Schlachtengemälde*, 232. A similar debate took place over the propriety of using programs to clarify the action of ballets (Brown, *Gluck and the French Theatre in Vienna*, 290–92; Foster, *Choreography and Narrative*, 115–16).

Example 3.2   Dittersdorf, thunderbolt (*La Chute de Phaéton*, iv, mm. 89–91)

and does not cry out at the moment the fire strikes).[25] His confidence in the clarity of the passage is not unjustified; Dittersdorf sets the thunderbolt as two sweeping *tirades* for violins alone, separated by grand pauses from some ninety measures of rhythmic confusion depicting Phaethon's chaotic ride, and, on the other side, from a descrescendo and descent representing his fall to earth (Example 3.2). The meaning can hardly be missed. But most interesting is Hermes' claim for the psychological impact of a moment that is, in and of itself, as paradigmatic an example of tone-painting as occurs anywhere in eighteenth-century music. Sensitive to the criticism it might provoke, Hermes endows it with the moral efficacy that Sulzer demanded by proposing a realism so exact as to provoke an emotional response even though the representation remains strictly objective.

Neither Sulzer nor Engel is likely to have agreed – the latter might have argued that a "heterogeneous" emotion like fear required music that precisely did *not* resemble its source. But the rationale for the thunderbolt is only one of several employed by Hermes that betrays their influence. He emphasizes Dittersdorf's own predilection for setting the most psychologically rich scenes from Ovid, from the spectacles of social contentment or disarray discussed in Chapter 1 above to monologues and dialogues such as take place between the confident Phaethon and a fearful Apollo before the tragic ride.[26] Hermes rightly asserts that such movements are both compatible with an aesthetic of expression and semantically lucid – provided, as always, one accepts the descriptive aid of the texts. More subtle and ambitious is his remark, quoted at the beginning of this chapter, that construes Dittersdorf's music as a reflection of the creative ardor brought on by reading Ovid. Used also by Reichardt to describe his own composition of character pieces,[27] the image of the artist working in the throes of inspiration not only connects the work to additional emotions – in this case, those of the composers themselves – but also invokes a mythology of genius with roots in the early eighteenth century, when Alexander Pope as well as Johann Mattheson and other music theorists portrayed artistic brilliance as flowering from the

---

[25] Hermes, *Analyse*, 171.
[26] Dittersdorf's dialogue movements are discussed in Will, "When God Met the Sinner," 186–91.
[27] *Musikalisches Kunstmagazin* 1 (1782): 64.

Example 3.3   Dittersdorf, frogs (*Les Paysans changés en grenouilles,* iv, mm. 215–18)

immersion in emotional states.[28] Anticipating Romantic enthusiasts of Haydn and Beethoven, Hermes appeals to the growing authority of a transcendent musical gift to sanction any representational practice.

The effect of the *Analyse* on the reception of the *Metamorphoses* is difficult to judge since they were never formally reviewed. They do seem to have provoked an incident, however, that clarifies why Hermes and defenders of other works would mount such elaborate justifications. In the 1789 volume of his *Musikalischer Almanach*, Forkel reported news of a concert at which Dittersdorf had imitated frogs, a reference, presumably, to the finale of *Les Paysans changés en grenouilles*. Like most of the more literal representations in the *Metamorphoses*, the passage itself seems as intent on conjuring a mood as on imitating a sight or sound; against the sustained murmuring chords of an outdoor idyll, alternating horns suggest the voices of the frogs without any undue effort at naturalism (Example 3.3). Nevertheless, Forkel's reaction summons the language and substance of Sulzer's most categorical rejections: "Auch glauben wir, daß ein Mann, der fähig ist, eine so äußerst abgeschmackte, und für die Kunst erniedrigende Kinderey öffentlich zu begehen, gar nicht im Stande ist, in irgend einem Werke der Kunst würdigen Ausdruck zu erreichen" (We also believe that a man capable of publicly committing such childishness, utterly tasteless and degrading to the art, is not in the position to achieve worthy expression in any work of art whatsoever). He also embroiders his judgment with an anecdote about two farmers who, having paid hard-earned money to hear Dittersdorf play, stalk out in disgust when they realize they are hearing "weiter nichts als ein Froschgeschrey; so was hören wir zu Hause alle Tage!" (nothing

[28] Winn, *Unsuspected Eloquence*, 197–98.

140

more than the croaking of frogs; we hear that every day at home!).[29] So self-evident are the shortcomings of tone-painting, apparently, that they are recognized even by untutored peasants, whose homespun wisdom is echoed by later tales blaming the pictorial organ improvisations of Georg Joseph Vogler for bad harvests and soured milk.[30] As if moral and practical limitations were not enough, tone-painting now transgresses the natural order and, equally problematic for those trying to promote favorite works, becomes a butt for jokes. A defense can scarcely be mounted if its object is not taken seriously.

The 1788 review of *The Seven Last Words* by Johann Friedrich Christmann has little difficulty showing how Haydn upholds the superiority of expression, assuming, again, that the music is understood in terms of its texts (see p. 103 above); the movements concentrate almost exclusively on the feelings of a single experiencing subject, and the exception, the earthquake that later upset the *Taschenbuch*, is simply finessed: "Zwar schauerlich schön" (Horribly beautiful indeed) is all Christmann says.[31] More difficult was the task of justifying Vogler, whose tours around Europe improvising battles, pastoral idylls, the heroic death of the Duke of Brunswick, the meanings of Rubens' *Last Judgment*, and several other subjects provoked more controversy than any effort at musical representation before Haydn's oratorios.[32] Not surprisingly, the prosecution was led by Forkel, who published a series of derisive reports from around Europe in the same volume of his *Almanach* that contained the attack on Dittersdorf.[33] His correspondents employ still stronger terms than the editor or Sulzer, not only calling the performances "Kindereyen," "kindisches Klimpern" (childish tinkling), and "Schwärmerey" (effusion), but also referring to Vogler himself as a "Charlatan." The moral shadow over tone-painting extends to touch its creator, as it would, later, the composers of battle pieces,[34] and his implied fraud or fakery is made all the worse by the fact that, as an organist, he must give his concerts in church, where "Würde, Ernst und

[29] Forkel, *Musikalischer Almanach* 4 (1789): 129.

[30] *Musikalische Korrespondenz der teutschen Filharmonischen Gesellschaft* 38 (21 September 1791): col. 304; *AmZ* 17 (1815): col. 524.

[31] *Musikalische Realzeitung* "Probeblatt" (5 March 1788): 2. Composers of characteristic pieces could also be criticized for expressing a stated emotion poorly (Morrow, *German Music Criticism*, 130).

[32] On Vogler's tours see Floyd K. Grave and Margaret G. Grave, *In Praise of Harmony: The Teachings of Abbé Georg Joseph Vogler* (Lincoln: University of Nebraska Press, 1987), 227–37.

[33] *Musikalischer Almanach* 4 (1789): 133–44. Vogler seems to have taken revenge with his *Verbesserung der Forkel'schen Veränderungen über das englische Volkslied God Save the King* (Frankfurt am Main, 1793).

[34] Schulin, *Musikalische Schlachtengemälde*, 238–39.

Feyerlichkeit" (dignity, seriousness, and solemnity) should reign.[35] An admirer of Vogler's who nevertheless had his own doubts about the organ concerts was moved to redeem at least the composer's personal reputation by arguing that the double pressure of his musical and religious duties (Vogler was also a priest) had led him down unfortunate artistic paths.[36] Improbably, the debate on musical representation has become a battle over moral integrity.

That Vogler should have incited such passion is all the more ironic given that his writings on music offer one of the few eighteenth- and early nineteenth-century conceptions of musical meaning to go beyond the moral and aesthetic terms set by Sulzer and Engel. Although his *Betrachtungen der Mannheimer Tonschule* require that music stimulate the emotions, he argues that visual representations work equally as well as emotional: "das Herz . . . wird von lebhafter Vorstellung entweder eines malerischen Bildes oder einer gut getroffenen Leidenschaft gerührt" (the heart . . . is moved by the lively presentation of either a pictorial likeness or a well-rendered passion).[37] He even ranks pictures over feelings in a remarkable passage that goes on to obliterate the boundary between mind and soul by lifting both into transcendence:

Wenn der Ausdruk der Leidenschaften auch stark ist: so nehmen wir Antheil an der Freude oder dem Leide des Schauspielers; ist aber das Gemählde richtig, werden die Bilder mit Tönen lebhaft geschildert: so sind wir nicht mehr unser. Die Gewalt der Harmonie erhebt uns in die Sphäre, wir hören die Engel singen – wir singen mit – . . . es war nur eine Täuschung, eine hinreissende Täuschung, die uns die Kräften des Verstandes benahm, blos um mit dem fühlbaren Herzen, fühlbar zu denken, statt denken, zu fühlen.

If the expression of passions is powerful, we take part in the joy or the sorrow of the actor. But if the painting is correct, if the images are clearly depicted with tones, we lose ourselves. The power of the harmony lifts us into the heavens, we hear the angels sing – we sing along . . . it was only an illusion, a captivating illusion that robbed us of the powers of intellect, in order to think sensitively with our sensitive hearts; instead of thinking, to feel.[38]

Hermes speaks in passing of the power of "illusion" to impress auditors of the *Metamorphoses*, but he seems to have thought the idea too much at odds with contemporary opinion to pursue.[39] Vogler proceeds undeterred into new territory, preceding Wackenroder by some twenty years

---

[35] *Musikalischer Almanach* 4 (1789): 138.

[36] *Musikalische Realzeitung* (3 September 1788): cols. 76–78.

[37] *Betrachtungen der Mannheimer Tonschule*, 3 vols. (Mannheim, 1778–81), II: 243. In the *Deutsche Encyclopädie* (Frankfurt am Main, 1778), s.v. "Ausdruck," Vogler includes a list of tone-paintings such as rain, thunder, and the sea (Grave, *In Praise of Harmony*, 296n.).

[38] *Betrachtungen*, I: 293–94.   [39] Hermes, *Analyse*, 169.

in hearing music as a window on divine vistas and proposing that, once elevated beyond the mundane, meaning crosses freely between the pictorial and the emotional as well as the definite and the indefinite. Listening is a matter no longer of being instructed but of being transformed, swept up by an enthusiasm not unlike that experienced by the inspired genius – whose presence, of course, would have been especially strong at a program of improvisations. For the few who were to follow Vogler, among them Christmann, Daniel Schubart, and the composer Justin Heinrich Knecht, both his works and the project of characteristic music generally appeared in a positive light; the two critics authored the only unqualified praise of his concerts, and Knecht wrote both organ pieces and symphonies on some of the same subjects.[40] But they were a minority. Anecdotes condemning Vogler's performances continued to appear as late as 1815,[41] suggesting that his ultimate legacy was to cement the dubious status of tone-painting as well as its association with characteristic music. The two assumptions carry on unchallenged into the nineteenth century.

Imitation and the ineffable

Within the first few years of the century, in fact, sentiment against tone-painting rose to new heights thanks to the provocation of Haydn's *Creation* (1798) and *Seasons* (1801). The seriousness of the subject matter of the two oratorios, especially the first, and the popularity and prestige of their composer seem to have made their imitations of animals and natural phenomena a particular affront to critical orthodoxy, one that attracted not only the usual complaints about childishness but also, from one particularly outraged writer, an accusation that "thirty or forty years" of "music's enlightenment" had been negated.[42] The works also brought to the surface a long-running political undercurrent in German critical discourse. Engel's chief example of the misuse of tone-painting had been another aria from Hasse's *Sant'Elena al Calvario*, one in which the heroine, while expressing her joy at seeing Calvary, refers passingly to the sea ("mar") she has crossed to reach it. Hasse responds with a long, waving melisma, which not only privileges an image at the expense of an affect but also does so, according to Engel, in the service of

---

[40] Christmann's and Schubart's remarks appear in the *Musikalische Korrespondenz* (13 October 1790): cols. 118–20, and (20 October 1790): cols. 122–23. Knecht's works include *Die durch ein Donnerwetter unterbrochne Hirtenwonne* (1794) for organ as well as the symphonies listed in Appendix 1, of which *Le Portrait musical de la nature* (1785) is dedicated to Vogler.

[41] See n. 30, p. 141 above.

[42] *Zeitung für die elegante Welt* (22 December 1801); trans. Landon, *Haydn*, IV: 601.

displaying the singer's virtuosity.[43] Many of the specific tone-paintings with which German critics took issue were faulted for the same reason, which had a political subtext inasmuch as melismatic word decoration, and coloratura generally, were associated overwhelmingly with Italian singers and vocal practice. Some of the most vociferous criticism came from England and from Italy itself,[44] but "der Italiänische Singsang", as Engel called it, provoked a distinctly chauvinist response from those concerned with the establishment of a German national opera.[45] Most eloquent was the composer Joseph Martin Kraus, who, in an essay of 1777, savages the recently premiered German-language *Alceste* of Anton Schweitzer for its "Italian liberties," among them a setting of the word "Strahlen" (sun-rays) to a long stretch of illustrative coloratura.[46] He compares Schweitzer unfavorably with the "Germans" Gluck and Grétry, whose reformed operas or, in Grétry's case, vocally unadorned *opéras comiques* avoid the pitfalls of the Italian manner, and he laments that Germany, by failing to recognize native talent, forces its greatest composers to write for the French and leaves its own stage vulnerable to Italianization.[47]

As late as 1798 Dittersdorf perpetuated this connection between word-painting and Italy with a folksy anecdote reminiscent of the one with which he had himself been criticized in Forkel's *Almanach*; as a singer in Venice improvises a lengthy cadenza on the words "Un fulmine improvviso" (sudden flash of lightning), a gondolier leaps up from the audience to challenge his taste, confirming the wisdom of untutored instinct and leading Dittersdorf, by his own account at least, to guard more vigilantly against similar errors of taste.[48] The reception of Haydn's oratorios gave birth to a new and more problematic national affiliation.

[43] Engel, *Schriften*, 335–36; see Hasse, *Sant'Elena al Calvario*, in Joyce L. Johnson and Howard E. Smither, eds., *The Italian Oratorio 1650–1800*, vol. XXVIII (New York: Garland, 1987), fol. 11r.

[44] E.g., in Francesco Algarotti, *Saggio sopra l'opera in musica* (Livorno, 1755) and subsequent Italian texts excerpted in Enrico Fubini, *Music and Culture in Eighteenth-Century Europe: A Source Book*, ed. Bonnie Blackburn (Chicago: University of Chicago Press, 1994), 231–69.

[45] See Friedrich Wilhelm Marpurg, *Der critische Musikus an der Spree* 1 (4 March 1749): 1–8; Heinrich Wilhelm von Gerstenberg, "Schlechte Einrichtung des Italienischen Singgedichts. Warum ahmen Deutsche sie nach?", *Briefe über Merkwürdigkeiten der Litteratur* 1 (1766): 116–36; and Christoph Martin Wieland, "Versuch über das Deutsche Singspiel und einige dahin einschlagende Gegenstände," *Der Teutsche Merkur* (1775), repr. *Sämmtliche Werke*, vol. XXVI (Leipzig, 1796), 229–342.

[46] *Etwas von und über Musik fürs Jahr 1777* (Frankfurt am Main, 1778), 64, 68; for Kraus's authorship of this anonymous pamphlet see the reprint, ed. Friedrich W. Riedel (Munich: Katzbichler, 1977), i. The offending melisma is in Schweitzer, *Alceste*, ed. Thomas Bauman, *German Opera 1770–1800*, vol. III (New York: Garland, 1986), 106–07.

[47] *Etwas von und über Musik*, 81–83. [48] *AmZ* 1 (1798): cols. 202–03.

In a correspondence that was supposed to remain private, the composer wrote that the imitation of frogs in *The Seasons* "ist nicht aus meiner feder geflossen; es wurde mir aufgedrungen diesen französischen Quark niederzuschreiben" (did not come from my pen; I was forced to write down this French trash) – the perpetrator having been the author of the text, Baron van Swieten.[49] Haydn's own intention does not seem to have been unfriendly. He had recently received a valuable medal from a group of French musicians and considered visiting Paris,[50] and his biographer Georg August Griesinger reports that "French trash" referred to a specific frog-painting passage from a French opera – one by Grétry, ironically enough, the same composer whom Kraus had celebrated as a "German" genius.[51] Blaming librettists for tone-painting was also a time-honored strategy that had already been directed at Metastasio as well as the authors of Handel's oratorios.[52] Still, Haydn's comment had unintended consequences when it was leaked to the critic A. G. Spazier and quoted in an 1801 review of *The Seasons*,[53] infuriating the composer and van Swieten and linking tone-painting to a country that posed far more tangible political dangers to German-speaking Europe than Italy and its singers ever had. Despite the Treaty of Lunéville of early 1801, Napoleon's imperial ambitions remained a source of concern throughout Europe, and a reputation for being "French" can only have stacked the odds further against a sympathetic reception of tone-painting.[54]

Nor did Haydn's imitations of nature enjoy one, even among those favorably disposed to the oratorios such as Carl Friedrich Zelter, who could write only, "obgleich er selber sichs nie unterziehn würde quakende Frösche, zirpende Grillen, Wachtelschlag und dergl[eichen] durch musikalische Mittel zu idealisieren; so ist doch dieser Umstand in Haydns Jahreszeiten keinesweges als anstössig zu erweisen, und kann nur ... komischen Gemüthern komisch erscheinen, für welche

---

[49] The remark is found on a corrected proof sent by Haydn to the arranger of the piano-vocal score of the *Seasons* on 11 December 1801 (*Briefe*, 389). See also Georg Feder, "Haydns Korrekturen zum Klavierauszug der 'Jahreszeiten,'" in Thomas Kohlhase and Volker Scherliess, eds., *Festschrift Georg von Dadelsen zum 60. Geburtstag* (Neuhausen-Stuttgart: Hännsler, 1978), 104, 107–08.

[50] Landon, *Haydn*, V: 67–74, 80; Otto Biba, ed., *"Eben komme ich von Haydn ...": Georg August Griesingers Korrespondenz mit Joseph Haydns Verleger Breitkopf & Härtel 1799–1819* (Zurich: Atlantis, 1987), 91, 97.

[51] Griesinger, *Biographische Notizen*, 72.

[52] "Etwas über die Oper *Olimpiade*" (unsigned), *Studien für Tonkünstler und Musikfreunde*, 10; James Beattie, *Essay on Poetry and Music as They Affect the Mind* (London, 1776), in Lippman, *Historical Reader*, I: 222.

[53] *Zeitung für die elegante Welt* (31 December 1801); see Landon, *Haydn*, V: 89, 187.

[54] Efforts by German critics to define both tone-painting and characteristic music as "foreign" are further discussed in Schmenner, *Die Pastorale*, 46–50.

dann auch diese komische Tendenz sogleich verschwinden würde, wenn man ihnen die Worte wegnehmen und die Musik allein fortschreiten lassen wollte" (and though he personally would never stoop to idealize croaking frogs, chirping crickets, the quail's call, etc., by musical means, this circumstance in Haydn's *Seasons* is by no means proved to be repellent. It can only appear ... comical to a person of a comical disposition, for whom this comical tendency would at once disappear if one took away the words and let the music continue by itself).[55] Trying to put the best face on the matter, he manages both to condescend to Haydn and to expose his real desire that the animals be extirpated, which would be the net effect of removing their verbal identifiers. On the other hand, that he tempers his criticism at all suggests that something is working to protect the oratorios despite what now seem like virtually insurmountable obstacles – and indeed it is: as will be true of Beethoven's *Pastoral*, the *Creation* and *Seasons* benefit from the greatly enhanced authority granted to genius around the turn of the century. Where Hermes pictured Dittersdorf in the flames of inspiration as a way of emphasizing the emotional origins of his music, Zelter takes Haydn's brilliance as proof that his decisions are simply not to be questioned: "Der Recens[ent] bekennt sich als so überzeugt, wie es jemand seyn kann, dass dieses schöne Werk ... nur allein als ein Werk des Genie's und keiner spekulativen Intention zu beurtheilen sey" (The reviewer is as persuaded as anyone can be that this beautiful work [*The Seasons*] ... can only be judged as a product of genius and not speculatively).[56] Running parallel to the assertion, made most eloquently in Goethe's essays on Shakespeare,[57] that great writers and painters were not bound by "rules" of taste, this faith in compositional instinct sways even some of Haydn's harsher critics, who distinguish their low opinion of the oratorios from their respect for his other music or blame the tone-paintings on van Swieten.[58] Challenging Haydn directly would have undermined a hierarchy that ranked him as the greatest composer in Germany (however construed) and indeed all of Europe, and thereby the standard against which musical aesthetics itself had to be measured.

Zelter goes to particularly great lengths to develop criteria that can recognize both oratorios as "products of genius" even in their

---

[55] *AmZ* 6 (1804): col. 526; trans. Landon, *Haydn*, V: 193. Zelter reviewed both *The Seasons* (*AmZ* 6 [1804]: cols. 513–29) and *The Creation* (*AmZ* 4 [1802]: cols. 385–96) and wrote separately on the "Chaos" introduction to the latter work (*AmZ* 3 [1801]: cols. 289–96).

[56] *AmZ* 6 (1804): col. 526; trans. Landon, *Haydn*, V: 193.

[57] Goethe, *Zum Shakespeares-Tag* (1771), *Shakespeare und keine Ende* (1815–16).

[58] E.g., in *AmZ* 3 (1801): col. 409, or *Zeitung für die elegante Welt* (22 December 1801) (Landon, *Haydn*, IV: 591, 601).

most imitative moments. The ambivalence of the above-quoted passage notwithstanding, he finds ways of defending, for instance, the bird-calls in "Auf starkem Fittiche schwinget sich"/"On mighty pens up-lifted soars" (in *The Creation*), which contribute to the expression of "Reinheit und Unschuld" (purity and innocence), or moments in the spring and hunting episodes of *The Seasons* that he says are not superficial but "serious."[59] Both arguments accept the old demands that music be expressive and morally instructive (Zelter even calls the grape harvest in *The Seasons* "eine wahre moralische Bachanalie" [a true moral bacchanal]),[60] and they had seen use in earlier justifications of the *Metamorphoses* and *The Seven Last Words*. More novel is the suggestion that material representations communicate the kind of fleeting, indeterminate meaning the early Romantics associated with music and especially with instrumental music. Zelter begins his review of *The Creation* by praising the developmental textures of Haydn's symphonies and quartets, which offer the intellectual challenges heard in instrumental music by Adam Smith and others (see pp. 14–15) and also conjure an image of limitlessness: "Dieses Spiel der leichten Fantasie ... giebt dem kleinsten Fluge des Genius eine Keckheit und Dreistigkeit, die von allen Seiten abwärts geht und das Feld ästhetischer Kunst bis in's Unendliche erweitert" (This play of easy imagination ... lends to the smallest aspect of a genius a boldness and confidence which spread over all its parts and enlarges into the infinite the field of aesthetic art).[61] In the instrumental works the favorite realm of the Romantics is reached by a customary path, the suggestive but semantically unfixed elaboration of musical ideas without words. The oratorios, Zelter argues, are to be understood in the same spirit, in part because they have so few conventionally expressive scenes, especially *The Creation* in which no human characters enter until near the end.[62] The descriptions of divine invention that take their place, or, in *The Seasons*, of such activities as hunting and harvesting, are grist for the imagination rather than the heart, and the same holds true for even the most definite pictures of natural phenomena and creatures. They allow for a wide range of interpretation; the potential associations of the "Winter" prelude to *The Seasons* include the sight of falling snow, the sound of howling wind, the fear of winter's dangers, and the comfort of a safe fireside.[63] More importantly, all such images lose substance when translated from language into the indefinite and ephemeral medium of sound: "Die ganze Intention also ist sinnlich, soll sinnlich wirken und dem Sinne verschwinden, wie sie ihm

---

[59] *AmZ* 4 (1802): col. 394, *AmZ* 6 (1804): cols. 520, 524.
[60] *AmZ* 6 (1804): col. 525.   [61] *AmZ* 4 (1802): col. 387; Landon, *Haydn*, IV: 593.
[62] *AmZ* 3 (1801): col. 294.   [63] *AmZ* 6 (1804): cols. 518–19.

erscheint; sie ist ein höheres Spiel für das Gehör, das sich zugleich mit einem Schattenspiel und mit einem Feuerwerke vergleichen lässt" (The whole intention [of *The Seasons*] is therefore sensuous, is supposed to act sensuously and to disappear from the senses even as it appeared; it is a higher play for the ear and may be compared to a shadow-play and to fireworks).[64] The eighteenth-century metaphor of music as firework (see p. 15) is joined by a comparison to shadow-play that Zelter uses to emphasize the intangibility of both oratorios: Haydn, the analogy suggests, represents not animals or storms but only their silhouettes, leaving listeners to fill in the details. If more determinate in meaning than untexted instrumental music, tone-paintings nevertheless require an exercise of the imagination that may well lead toward the infinite.

Reminiscent of Vogler's claim that musical pictures elevate the beholder to a plane on which thought and emotion unite, Zelter's justification is more modern in that it rejects the necessity of feeling altogether; what he sees in *The Creation* and *The Seasons* is a genius taking bold steps toward abandoning the aesthetic of expression. Unlike Vogler, he also admits that music can be semantically ambiguous even where its meaning appears most highly determined, a nod toward Romantic and idealist thinking that produces perhaps the most honest description of tone-painting to be found anywhere in the eighteenth or early nineteenth centuries. Haydn's most notorious imitations, the series of animal sounds and movements as well as weather phenomena that occur in the accompanied recitatives of the oratorios, tumble out so rapidly and bear so little actual resemblance to the things they represent that the result is less like a parade than a mosaic, a colorful but indistinct survey of natural wonders. The lightning stroke in Dittersdorf's *Phaéton* is similar, so fleeting and musically generic that its concrete referent disappears as quickly as the scale itself, leaving only a general impression of climax, turning point, pause for emphasis (Example 3.2, p. 139 above). Especially in characteristic works, where the connection between sound and text is already loose, the effect of representation is always more like scene- than word-painting; the music opens expansive vistas, the details of which blur into broadly meaningful textures, rhythms, or forms. Zelter is the rare writer to recognize the difficulty of maintaining precise image–music relationships in a representational medium that lacks substance and changes constantly over time.

Yet in his own words he personally would never stoop to imitating animals, suggesting that he did not convince even himself of the entire legitimacy of tone-painting; if silhouettes were better than pictures, they were still too material for an art that challenged the mind

---

[64] Ibid., cols. 515–16; Landon, *Haydn*, V: 189; in *AmZ* 4 (1802): col. 389, *The Creation* is said to be like "ein höheres Schattenspiel."

to comprehend the infinite. Nor did many subsequent reviewers of characteristic pieces see birdcalls or storms as alluding to vast fields of Romantically indeterminate meaning. On the contrary, the earthquake of *The Seven Last Words* reminded the Romantic listener all too vividly of the "external, sensuous world" from which E. T. A. Hoffmann segregated music in his review of Beethoven's Fifth Symphony, which itself cites the *Metamorphoses* and battle symphonies as examples of what not to do, much as eighteenth-century texts listed inappropriate word-paintings (see p. 17 above). What the furor over Haydn's oratorios produced was mainly a newly dismissive attitude, according to which Hoffmann and others exchange the moral and aesthetic outrage of earlier criticism for the humor of the anecdotes about farmers and gondoliers: in the pages of the *Allgemeine musikalische Zeitung*, now the most influential German periodical on music, "lächerlich" (laughable) replaces "kindisch" as the favorite epithet, and a typical review suggests "caricatured" as a more accurate title than "characteristic" for a battle sonata by Jan Ladislav Dussek.[65] From the lofty perspective of infinity, efforts at material representation seem so trivial as to be unworthy of serious criticism.

But as in the eighteenth century, what appear to be inviolate principles of taste do not produce the uniformity of opinion one might expect. For one thing, even in the *AmZ* Romanticism does not supplant the aesthetic of expression so much as coexist with it during the first decade of the nineteenth century, so that works may be praised or decried on the basis of quite different criteria. A keyboard sonata by Vanhal celebrating the Treaty of Lunéville, as well as a battle piece for keyboard trio by Daniel Steibelt, are rebuked for being incomprehensible without the aid of their texts, testifying to the continuing validity of the notion that music should refer to definite, perceivable subjects.[66] Equally viable is the ideal of expressivity; in the same year that Dussek's battle piece was deemed laughable, his *Elégie harmonique sur la mort de S. A. R. le Prince Louis Ferdinand de Prusse* was lauded for depicting the composer's feelings about the prince's death in battle rather than the event itself.[67] More Romantically-inclined critics could also find reason to approve of representation even where the subject was relatively concrete. Just two years after dismissing the *Metamorphoses*, Hoffmann wrote in favor of the overture to Méhul's *Chasse du jeune Henri* although its galloping rhythms and *sonneries* are as "realistic" as anything in Dittersdorf; nevertheless, by his lights they suggest the Romantic vastness of the woods rather than any too detailed plot, essentially the

---

[65] *AmZ* 10 (1807): col. 224. For representative uses of the terms "lächerlich" or "Lächerlichkeit," see also the reviews cited in n. 68 below.
[66] *AmZ* 3 (1801): col. 564; *AmZ* 6 (1803): col. 178.   [67] *AmZ* 9 (1807): col. 744.

same argument that had been made about a hunting piece by C. L. Ruppe a few years earlier.[68] In a familiar critical about-face, the particulars of the given work overwhelm the generalities of the governing aesthetic.

Beethoven had the multiple perspectives of contemporary criticism very much in mind as he worked on the *Pastoral* Symphony, which would provide the next focus for debate. His sketches record two attempts to formulate the sentiment that would eventually wind up in his subtitle, "Auch ohne Beschreibungen wird man das ganze welches mehr Empfindung als Tongemählde erkennen" (Even without descriptions one will recognize the whole, which [is] more emotion than tone-painting), and "Pastoral Sinfonie Worin keine Malerej sondern die Empfindungen ausgedrückt sind" (Pastoral Symphony, in which [there is] no painting but rather the emotions are expressed).[69] The appeal in both cases is to an older, mimetic conception of meaning, whose principles are apparent in the reference not only to emotion but also to semantic clarity, said to be so marked that explanatory texts, to which writers like Koch objected, are unnecessary. Dealing with a beloved subject and a well-known set of musical topics, Beethoven had reason to trust in the lucidity of his work, and at one point he toys with the idea of withholding characterizations altogether: "Man überläßt es dem Zuhörer sich selbst die Situationen auszufinden" (one leaves it to the listener to discover the situations for himself).[70] But this comment suggests his awareness of newer currents of thinking as well, of the value placed by writers like Wackenroder or Hoffmann on the imaginative challenges of instrumental music. Allowing an audience to interpret the symphony on their own ensures a multiplicity of meanings being read into even the most familiar of subject references, bringing the music closer to Zelter's ambiguous shadow-play and freeing it from the requirement of moral or communicative efficacy. Similarly cognizant of the powers of imagination is the second half of Beethoven's eventual title, *Erinnerung an das Landleben* (Memory of Country Life), which phrase is also drafted in

---

[68] *AmZ* 14 (1812): col. 743; *AmZ* 11 (1808): cols. 95–96.

[69] The first remark appears on a leaf formerly in the *Pastoral* Symphony sketchbook and now in the sketch miscellany Landsberg 10, p. 77 (*Ein Skizzenbuch zur Pastoralsymphonie*, I: 17); the second is in Grasnick 3, fol. 16v (*Ein Skizzenbuch zur Chorfantasie op. 80 und zu anderen Werken*, ed. Dagmar Weise [Bonn: Beethovenhaus, 1957], 92). The comments written in the sketches to the *Pastoral* are also discussed in Jones, *Beethoven: "Pastoral" Symphony*, 33–34 (with somewhat different translations). Beethoven may have been especially sensitive on the issue of tone-painting inasmuch as he had been, according to Ferdinand Ries, among the critics of Haydn's oratorios (Ferdinand Ries and Franz Gerhard Wegeler, *Biographische Notizen über Ludwig van Beethoven* [Coblenz: K. Bädeker, 1838], 77–78).

[70] *Pastoral* Symphony sketchbook, fol. 2r (*Ein Skizzenbuch zur Pastoralsinfonie*, II: 5 and the first facsimile page).

the sketches.[71] Displaced to the mind, the pastoral setting becomes as much internal as external, a place that each listener pictures according to his or her own experience as well as Beethoven's musical depiction. In a sense the words capture the whole duality of characteristic music, where the tangibility of a stated subject is balanced by the polysemy of a medium with so few words; not only are the texts brief in the *Pastoral*, but what they refer to exists only in the imaginary space of memory, whose representation of past places and events is itself always variable and imperfect.

Fittingly enough, Beethoven's largely sympathetic reviewers proceed from alternately "expressive" and "Romantic" viewpoints, liking the symphony but for different reasons. In the *AmZ*, Michael Gotthard Fischer adopts an essentially eighteenth-century attitude that is reflected in his opening gloss on Beethoven's subtitle: "Allerdings sind wir jetzt so ziemlich damit im Reinen, dass die Darstellung äusserer Gegenstände durch die Musik höchst geschmacklos . . . sey. Allein dieser Ausspruch passt gar nicht auf vorliegendes Werk, welches nicht eine Darstellung *räumlicher* Gegenstände des Landes, sondern vielmehr eine Darstellung der Empfindungen ist, welche wir bey dem Anblick ländlicher Gegenstände haben" (Certainly we are now tolerably in agreement that the representation of external objects in music is the utmost in tastelessness. Yet this pronouncement absolutely does not apply to the present work, which is not a representation of *physical* objects of the countryside, but rather a representation of the emotions that we have on contemplating rural objects).[72] Significant is not only the predictable assertion that the symphony expresses feelings but also the use of the first-person plural, which implies a community united both in aesthetic principle and in its understanding of the pastoral: this is no silhouette to be filled in by the individual listener, but a mirror of universally experienced reactions to the outdoors. A similar ethos reigns throughout the review, which goes so far as to claim that the music itself represents a society coming to consensus: when the lilting thirds of the first few measures of the second movement return at the end of its exposition (cf. mm. 1–4 and 50–54), Fischer imagines an "unvermuthete[s] Zusammentreffen unserer Freunde" (unexpected meeting of our friends), who relate "ihre verschiedenen Schicksale, die das

---

[71] Ibid.

[72] *AmZ* 12 (1810): col. 242; italics original. Further column references in the text. On Fischer's authorship of this review, which has also been attributed to Hoffmann, Amadeus Wendt, and Friedrich Rochlitz, see Hans von Müller and Friedrich Schnapp, eds., *E. T. A. Hoffmanns Briefwechsel*, 3 vols. (Munich: Winkler, 1967–69), I: 292n., and Peter Schnaus, *E. T. A. Hoffmann als Beethoven-Rezensent der Allgemeinen musikalischen Zeitung* (Munich and Salzburg: Katzbichler, 1977), 21n.

allgemeine Interesse und das Band der Freundschaft vereinigt" (their diverse destinies, united by general interest and the bonds of friendship [246]). The *Pastoral* promotes as well as reflects mutual feeling. By the same token, when Fischer arrives at the birdcalls at the end of the movement he stigmatizes potential critics by putting them into the singular, declaring that "die Stimmen der Nachtigall, der Wachtel und des Kukkucks... von Niemand getadelt werden *wird*,... weil die Stelle... von Niemand getadelt werden *kann*" (the voices of the nightingale, the quail and the cuckoo... *will* be made fun of by no one... because the passage *can* be made fun of by no one [248]). Rather than justify an obvious instance of tone-painting – by arguing, say, that the birds carry emotional overtones – he simply excommunicates discordant voices from the harmonious collective formed by Beethoven's music.

He works harder to legitimate the other obvious pictorialism in the symphony, the storm, elevating his community to Vogler's higher plane where the physical and the emotional blur. The change comes suddenly, after the material effects of the movement have been catalogued with surprising candor: "das ununterbrochene, den heulenden Sturm ausdrückende Schreyen der Hoboen, Hörner, Fagotte und Trompeten; die anstrebenden Sechzehntheilfiguren in den Bässen, welche das Rollen des Donners nachahmen; die häufigen Dissonanzen, vorzüglich der verminderte Septimenaccord mit seinen Verwechselungen – ein getreues Bild der Gefühle des Grausens und Entsetzens – alles erfüllt mit grossen und erhabenen Empfindungen" (the uninterrupted shrieking of the oboes, horns, bassoons and trumpets, expressing the howling storm; the struggling sixteenth-note figures in the basses, which imitate the roll of thunder; the frequent dissonances, especially the diminished seventh and its inversions – a true picture of the feelings of horror and dread – all filled with great and sublime emotions [250–51]). The sentiments remain generic, available to every listener, but they are magnified by the imagery of the description and by its syntax, whose accumulation of parallel clauses and then of fragments separated by dashes would have been recognized as belonging to a "sublime" style of descriptive prose.[73] So graphically detailed at the beginning of the sentence, Beethoven's "pictures" are swept by grammar into a realm where the mind no longer distinguishes spectacle from response.

Equally enthusiastic, the review by Friedrich Mosengeil published in the same year in the *Zeitung für die elegante Welt* nevertheless reads the *Pastoral* very differently, right from its opening not with a statement about the music's expressivity but rather with an evocation of the

---

[73] See Waldvogel, "The Eighteenth-Century Esthetics of the Sublime," 97–105, 160–66; Sisman, *Mozart: The "Jupiter" Symphony*, 15–16; and below, p. 198.

artist: "Von seiner Phantasie in die lieblichen Auen einer arkadischen Hirtenwelt getragen, begeistert von ihren unschuldsvollen Genüssen, ruft er seine himmlische Muse, die Harmonie, zu sich hernieder, und gibt sich ihren süßen Tönen hin" (Drawn by his fantasy into the lovely pastures of an arcadian shepherd's world, spellbound by its innocent delights, he calls down to him his heavenly muse, harmony, and abandons himself to her sweet tones).[74] The experience of nature is understood as something personal, not communal, and the symphony as a kind of autobiography: in the second movement, "Der Dichter ruht am Bache" (The poet rests by the brook), alone, and, in the scherzo, "Wir sehen den Dichter sich erheben . . . um nun fröhlich zu seyn mit den Fröhlichen und gleich kommt ein lustiger Schwarm von Landleuten heran, die ihm alles bieten, was er wünscht" (We see the poet now arouse himself in order to be glad with those who are glad, and immediately a happy swarm of country folk comes and offers him everything that he wishes [1050–51]). People other than Beethoven figure in the story only as servants, like the *Landleute*, or as beneficiaries of his unique vision, like the listener who grows "mit ihm heimisch in diesen reizenden Thälern" (at home with him in these charming valleys [1050]). The contrast to Fischer's social interpretation becomes particularly evident in the description of the storm, although Mosengeil proceeds with the same grand imagery and dash-laden grammar and even outdoes the *AmZ* reviewer in sublimity by hearing the voice of God in Beethoven's thunder, the significance of which will be discussed in the next chapter. More striking in the present context, however, is what follows his reference to divine intervention: "Doch nicht bloß da, wo der Stral seiner Wetterwolke erglüht, und ihr Donner die Berge beben macht, – auch da ist Gottes Finger, wo der Geist eines begünstigten Sterblichen, sich seiner göttlichen Herkunft bewußt, mitten in den wilden Strömen mächtiger Töne fest und lenkend steht, und all diese vielfachen Laute, welche, wenn sie regellos durcheinander fließen, das Ohr zerreißen und das Gefühl empören, melodisch zügelt und vereinigt" (But not just there, where the lightning of his thundercloud burns, and its thunder makes the mountains shake – God's finger is also there, where the spirit of a blessed mortal, aware of his divine origins, stands firm and ruling amidst the wild currents of powerful tones, and melodically tames and unites all of these various sounds, which if they flowed about unruled would rend the ear and outrage the feelings [1052]). The genius is now the Creator, or at least the controller of creation, a role in which critics had also cast Haydn but with caveats about his seeming tendency to create so many mundane things. Mosengeil's picture of an all-powerful Beethoven relegates both material and

---

[74] *Zeitung für die elegante Welt* (5 July 1810): col. 1049. Further column references in the text.

emotional representation to purely subsidiary status; lightning, thunder, and wind are important only as symbols of the vast natural forces over which the composer has dominion, and feelings are the property of a listener whose ears must be protected by superior force. "In diesem Gewitter des *Shakespears* der musikalischen Welt" (In this storm by the *Shakespeare* of the musical world [1052]), the presence of the artist is so strong that a single superhuman "character" replaces the "characters" of the symphony's texts – human, emotional, scenic – as the subject of the music. Other meanings pale beside the projection of what Körner called the "ordering power" of the creative mind (see p. 5 above).

Between them Mosengeil and Fischer demonstrate, again, how flexible aesthetic criteria could be when applied to concrete examples. The more pictorial aspects of the *Pastoral* Symphony ought to have offended "expressive" and "Romantic" sensibilities alike, at least as much as the similar passages in Haydn's oratorios did, but instead the semantic imprecision of characteristic music and the consequent freedom of interpretation result in whole-hearted endorsements. If further evidence were needed, this sanctioning of even the most material of Beethoven's representations would answer the question posed at the beginning of this chapter, as to why composers continued to imitate "physical" sounds and motions given the likelihood of criticism; in fact, from Sulzer onwards it was clear that "painting" could be defended on the grounds that it communicated more than mere objective meanings – that it expressed or triggered emotions or, later, revealed the hand of the creator. Even Vogler had his defenders, and less controversial figures were as likely to be commended as condemned.

But the reception of the *Pastoral* does more than sum up a tradition of critical maneuvers; it also shows an opposition taking shape that will soon overshadow the traditional pairings of object and emotion or real and ideal. Critics before Mosengeil who heard individual agents in music tended to be inspired by the subject matter, as we have seen with Christmann's response to *The Seven Last Words*, and to assume that the experience of the protagonist was in some sense universal, especially with regard to emotion. The listener is invited to identify with Christ or with Phaethon, whose sorrows and joys are extreme but not unrelated to those of the rest of humanity; feeling is "social" in the same way that Fischer imagined the *Empfindungen* of the *Pastoral* to be, even when only a single character is on stage. Mosengeil, by contrast, not only finds a hero where none is explicitly indicated but also, like Hoffmann, raises his feelings and abilities to a level no ordinary mortal can hope to attain. In addition, even if the listener can follow the composer into the infinity opened up by the music, the journey will be as personal as that of the composer himself; no two people will find the same meanings in a limitless expanse. Radical individualism replaces shared experience as the basis for both representation and comprehension, with results that echo through many characteristic symphonies of the post-Revolutionary period. The *Pastoral* could be annexed by both viewpoints and thus enjoy universal admiration, but in other works the relationship between individual and collective ideologies would prove more difficult. The moral and political meanings of musical representation become increasingly fraught in a culture that wants to idealize both the solitary genius, the Beethoven or the Napoleon, and more elusive constructs such as the harmonious pastoral collective or the nation united in war.

4

Paradise regained: time, morality, and humanity in Beethoven's *Pastoral* Symphony

Three decades after the premiere of Dittersdorf's *Metamorphoses*, another audience gathered in Vienna to hear Beethoven's now-legendary academy of 22 December 1808. As in 1786, the program began with an orchestral representation of paradise, the first movement of the *Pastoral* Symphony.[1] The setting was contemporary, a place that real people might visit rather than a distant Golden Age: this, in any event, is the implication of the movement title, "Erwachen heiterer Empfindungen bei der Ankunft auf dem Lande" (Awakening of happy feelings on the arrival in the countryside), which echoes references in Beethoven's letters to escaping the city for rural retreats.[2] Yet there is no mistaking the effort to conjure a world protected from violence, degradation, human foible – a desire to transport listeners into a haven of calm, in the tradition not only of *Les Quatre Ages du monde* but also of other works both pastoral and, as we shall see in Chapter 5, military. In retrospect, after the second half of the concert had opened with Beethoven's Fifth Symphony, the initial repose in the countryside must have seemed all the more idyllic.

The *Pastoral* goes on to follow an equally familiar trajectory among characteristic symphonies, a passage from calm to turmoil and back, or from calm to turmoil to celebration. As we saw, Dittersdorf's *Metamorphoses* never quite complete this journey, but military and other

---

[1] The concert program is reprinted in the *AmZ* 11 (1809), cols. 267–68; see also Jones, *Beethoven: "Pastoral Symphony,"* 1–3.

[2] Excerpted in ibid., 19–20, and contextualized within contemporary discourses on nature as therapeutic retreat in Schmenner, *Die Pastorale*, 192–95. Related is Wieland's description of the rural Schloß Warthausen, where he and Knecht (see p. 175 below) escaped the pressures of urban Biberach (quoted in Hermann Jung, "Zwischen *Malerey* und *Ausdruck der Empfindung*: Zu den historischen und ästhetischen Voraussetzungen von Justin Heinrich Knechts *Le Portrait musical de la Nature* [1785]," in Annegrit Laubenthal, ed., *Studien zur Musikgeschichte: Eine Festschrift für Ludwig Finscher* [Kassel: Bärenreiter, 1995], 420–21).

politically related works always do, and the same is true of such pastoral antecedents of Beethoven's work as *Le Portrait musical de la nature* (1785), by Justin Heinrich Knecht, and *Aphrodite* (1792), by Anton Wranitzky. Beethoven accepts the convention but intensifies it in ways that give the end of the *Pastoral* a quality distinct from that of other characteristic works. The difference lies partly in scale, not of length so much as stylistic and emotional range; the *Pastoral* contains the most "rustic" music outside eighteenth-century pastorellas, but also moments of exaltation fit for an oratorio; an extraordinarily placid brook, but also vigorous dancing; an uplifting hymn of thanks, but also a storm so disruptive as to recall not other storm music so much as battles. The contrast between calm and turmoil is also magnified by a more self-conscious manipulation of symphony norms than can be found in any comparable work. Dittersdorf, the Wranitzkys, and others retain elements of the contemporary three- and four-movement symphony, but Beethoven writes four movements so typical of the genre that Tovey could speak of "normal" forms (see p. 19), thanks to which the "abnormal" exception, the storm whose violence and grandeur the critics Fischer and Mosengeil already found so sublime, stands out all the more from its surroundings. In effect, the *Pastoral* sits halfway between a symphony with independent and formally closed movements, and a characteristic symphony of the type representing series of scenes or emotions, where the penchant is for continuity and formal freedom in moments of action. The transition between paradise and trouble becomes a passage not simply from one musical style to another but between genres.

Stylistic breadth and mixed generic identity highlight questions about time, morals, and human agency in the idyllic world of the *Pastoral*. Notwithstanding the many juxtapositions of slow- and swift-moving music in other characteristic symphonies, even other pastoral symphonies, no work so vividly dramatizes the shifts and thereby the implied problem: what happens to a pastoral retreat when it is gripped by unfolding events? The *Metamorphoses* offered one, pessimistic answer; Beethoven's finale proposes another, matching the sublimity of the storm with a religious tone suggestive of a community inspired by terror to redeem itself. Most singular of all is the nature of the people involved. In an age that tended to glorify proactive heroism, whether its ideal was individual or communal action, the *Pastoral* Symphony celebrated a comparatively passive, reactive mode of being. The inhabitants of Beethoven's countryside do face a crisis, but they survive thanks not to their own deeds but to the apparent intervention of a higher power. The beginning of the 1808 academy freed listeners not merely from urban surroundings but from a heroic imperative that would be powerfully articulated in the concert's second half.

An unsettling storm

Just how far the *Pastoral* upped the ante on musical storms can be seen by setting it beside a work Beethoven and some of his listeners may well have heard, Anton Wranitzky's *Aphrodite*. Wranitzky was a member – and, from 1797, Kapellmeister – of the musical establishment of Beethoven's future patron Prince Lobkowitz, and he composed *Aphrodite* for Lobkowitz's wedding in 1792, the year of Beethoven's arrival in Vienna.[3] The structure and dramatic context of its storm anticipate those of the *Pastoral* in several respects. A brief section falling into no conventional form and ending on the dominant, the storm is sandwiched between an idyllic binary form for the winds and horns, "Das ruhige, sanfte Meer" (the peaceful, gentle sea), and an equally idyllic ternary form, the emergence of Aphrodite and "Entzüken der Seegötter" (enchantment of the sea-gods; see Example 4.1). Together with a concluding sonata form (expressing further enchantment), the episodes make up a single continuous movement not unlike the run-on complex at the end of the *Pastoral*, with – again as in the later work – the idyllic movements in major and the storm in the parallel minor. Yet Wranitzky's storm projects nothing like the same violence, notwithstanding some powerful C minor tuttis undergirded by flying sixteenths and a triple eighth-note anacrusis that propels the music forward (Example 4.2, mm. 55–58). The motion remains predictable, contained within an almost invariable two- or four-measure periodicity that goes along with a clear succession of key areas: tonic, relative major, submediant, and dominant. Representative are the opening measures, whose *Figaro*-like trills creeping up a chromatic scale create palpable nervous tension, but whose repetition after the initial orchestral outburst puts a considerable restraint on the excitement (mm. 40–48/49–54). Like Boccherini's adaptation of Gluck's "Dance of the Furies" (see pp. 72–74 above) the music has the topics to evoke a "brausende Gährung" (raging storm) but not the irregularity to render it frightening.

Beethoven's storm also begins with a repetition, and of an eight-measure passage at that (extended to ten on the second hearing), but in this case the harmony begins on a mysterious submediant and climbs steadily toward the tonic (mm. 3–20). The bass continues to rise through the ensuing tutti, screwing the tension up further, and the orchestral attacks resemble less the directed tonic and dominant alternations of Wranitzky than the chaotic onrush of one of Dittersdorf's battles. Not without reason does Roland Schmenner argue that the movement

---

[3] Eva Hennigová-Dubová, *The Symphony 1720–1840*, vol. B-12 (New York: Garland, 1984), xxxiv.

Example 4.1   Anton Wranitzky, *Aphrodite*, first movement

(all sections are continuous)

tempo:	*Adagio*	*Allegro con fuoco*	*Poco adagio*	*Allegro*
form:	binary		ternary	sonata
program:	calm seas	storm	celebration of Aphrodite's appearance	continuing celebration
measure:	1	40	134	170
key:	C major	C minor	C major	C major

Example 4.2   Anton Wranitzky, storm (*Aphrodite*, i), mm. 40–58

(*cont.*)

Example 4.2 (*cont.*)

seeks to "simulate" rather than imitate a storm;[4] particularly since their descending arpeggios are not integrated into a coherent melody as in Wranitzky, the initial tuttis of the *Pastoral* seem instead to assault listeners with the sheer force of orchestral sound – these are thunderclaps as cannon fire (see pp. 196–97 below). Nor is a pattern of keys or repetitions established that would allow for events in the following music to be predicted in advance.[5] A network of relationships does connect the three *fortissimos* that serve as the main points of articulation (mm. 21–40, 78–94, and 106–18): the first and third begin with the same massive chords underscored by rumbling, superimposed quadruplet and quintuplet sixteenths (compare mm. 21–32 with 106–10, and see Example 4.3a); the first and second conclude with the same unison arpeggio figure in the strings (mm. 35–40 and 89–94, Example 4.3b); and the second and third incorporate another, tremolo arpeggio figure (mm. 78–88 and 119–29, Example 4.3c). The passages preceding the *fortissimos* also share similarities, the first two emphasizing the same suspenseful staccato motive (mm. 3–18 and 56–77; Example 4.3d), and the third referring back to a preliminary, subverted crescendo that preceded the second *fortissimo* (mm. 51–55 and 103–06).[6] None of these connections, however, brings the stability of a recapitulation or reprise, chiefly because none coincides with any kind of tonal return. Far from establishing a series of keys, after departing the F minor tonic the harmony modulates continuously until reaching the dominant plateau on which the storm ends (mm. 136–53).

Rendering the storm still more unsettling is the ambiguous status of its structure, which has neither the independence of a movement nor the dependence of a slow introduction (Tovey's analogy[7]) or of a passage like Wranitzky's storm, which most nearly resembles a sonata-form

---

[4] Schmenner, *Die Pastorale*, 70.

[5] Inattention to the storm's structure throughout much of its twentieth-century reception history may have contributed to critics' unwillingness to recognize its unconventionality (see pp. 19–20 above); Tovey, for example, analyzes the first three movements of the *Pastoral* in considerable detail but passes over the storm with only a few remarks on its tone-paintings (*Essays in Musical Analysis*, I: 46–55). In-depth discussions of its structure have appeared more recently in Jones, *Beethoven: "Pastoral Symphony,"* 73–76; Schmenner, *Die Pastorale*, 58–62; Rudolf Bockholdt, *Beethoven: VI. Symphonie F-dur op. 68 Pastorale*, Meisterwerke der Musik 23 (Munich: Fink, 1981), 50–58; and Carl Schachter, "The Triad as Place and Action," *Music Theory Spectrum* 17 (1995): 158–69.

[6] In both mm. 51–55 and mm. 103–06, the melodic gestures accent the second beat, the harmonic rhythm begins at one change per measure and then doubles at the peak of the crescendo, the harmonies shift from diminished to dominant sevenths through half-step descents in the bass, and the basses mark the chord changes with isolated punctuations.

[7] Tovey, *Essays*, I: 45, and *Musical Articles from the Encyclopaedia Britannica*, 168.

Example 4.3a–e   Beethoven, *Pastoral* Symphony, storm motives

exposition separated from the rest of its form. Clearly the storm of the *Pastoral* cannot stand on its own. It needs the surrounding movements both to make sense of its opening D♭, which follows directly on the last dominant of the scherzo, and to resolve its own concluding dominant, which leads, through V/V, straight into the finale (mm. 154–55). To extract and perform the movement separately, as one could the scherzo and finale with only minor adjustments, would be impossible. Yet in other respects it asserts a surprising degree of independence. The link to the scherzo notwithstanding, the tonal structure is distinct from that of the preceding movement. By the time the storm breaks in, the scherzo has cadenced so emphatically (mm. 255–57) that the deceptive D♭ seems to prevent only the scherzo's final dominant seventh from resolving: the overall tonal process of the movement sounds already finished. A few measures later, furthermore, the storm returns to a tonic chord in the same register and scoring as the dominant left hanging at the end of the scherzo (cf. the scherzo, m. 264, and storm, m. 21). This arrival concludes the last unfinished business of the scherzo, and all of the subsequent music is heard in relation to the storm's own, F minor tonic.[8]

The storm cannot separate itself so decisively from the finale, for only that movement's return to F major can resolve the passage's final dominant. Nevertheless, its concluding measures still achieve some independence from what follows by implying resolutions other than tonal ones. The lengthy diminuendo and *pianissimo* at the end suggest dramatic closure: as the final *fortissimo* (mm. 106–11) fades through pulsating *sforzati* (mm. 112–18) and diminishing tremolo figures (mm. 119–35), the storm seems to subside, and by the point at which only faint rumblings in the double basses remain (mm. 144–53), it seems to have dissipated entirely. As an episode in the program, in other words, it seems to end *before* the finale begins, an impression heightened by motivic and harmonic events. During the concluding *pianissimo,* the orchestra transforms a series of motives in such a way as to lend them a calmness or stability contrasting sharply with the agitation of their earlier appearances. Over a stable dominant harmony, the violins repeat an upward-leaping arpeggio (Example 4.3e; cf. m. 140) heard earlier in the context of modulations (e.g., mm. 33–34 and 51–55); the basses, similarly, reduce the low-register rumblings (Example 4.3a; cf. mm. 130–53) from the first *fortissimo* and elsewhere to a simple tremolo. Most radically of all, the oboes turn the staccato motive from the first two *fortissimos* into a song-like legato (Example 4.3d; cf. mm. 146–53).[9]

Meanwhile the harmony settles on a dominant that itself functions unexpectedly like a resolution. After the initial outburst on F minor, the music proceeds to the dominant through tonicizations of both the subdominant and the dominant (Example 4.4a), and much of the remaining tonal business consists of unsuccessful attempts to repeat this motion.[10] In the two crescendos preceding the second *fortissimo*

---

[8] Schachter calls m. 21 "the true tonal beginning" of the storm ("The Triad as Place and Action," 159, and see also m. 21 in his Examples 9a and 9b). By concluding whatever remains of the scherzo's tonality, the F minor chord in m. 21 also distinguishes the storm from another passage to which it has been compared, the transition between the scherzo and the finale in Beethoven's Fifth Symphony (Bernstein, *The Unanswered Question*, 186). The transition essentially prolongs the final dominant of the preceding scherzo until the finale arrives. Because the storm resolves the corresponding dominant, its own concluding dominant is heard not as a prolongation of the scherzo's final chord but as the dominant of the new, F minor tonic.

[9] Grove (*Beethoven and His Nine Symphonies*, 219), was apparently the first of numerous commentators to note the derivation of mm. 146–53 from Example 4.3d.

[10] Cf. Schachter, who characterizes the bulk of the storm as an "extended dominant prolongation" because of its repeated returns to dominant-related chords, including V/V (m. 78) and vii^7/i (mm. 95–103) as well as major and minor chords on the dominant itself (mm. 35, 39, 55; "The Triad as Place and Action," 161–65).

Example 4.4a–d   Beethoven, *Pastoral* Symphony, approaches to V

vii/iv iv vii/v V	°7 V/iv iv V/V v V⁴₂ v	°7 V/iv iv V/V v	°7 V/iv iv V/V v V
(a) mm. 21-35	(b) mm. 50-55 (c) mm. 55-80		(d) mm. 106-36

(Example 4.4b and 4.4c), and again during the final *fortissimo* and following diminuendo (Example 4.4d), applied dominants lead first to the subdominant and then almost to the dominant, only to have the penultimate V/V give way each time to a minor V chord.[11] The deferrals become progressively more frustrating: in the second instance (Example 4.4c), a prolongation of V/V beyond what the harmonic rhythm predicts (mm. 72–79) serves to heighten expectations of the dominant just before they are again thwarted;[12] and on the last time around (Example 4.4d) an accompanying diminuendo signals the end of the storm and presumably of its harmonic process as well – but V/V again moves to C minor (m. 124) and must be re-established before it can at last give way to the dominant (m. 136). This long-sought arrival brings with it a sense of stability and finality that, like the *pianissimo* dynamic and the transformed motives, suggests that the storm achieves some resolution in its own concluding measures, independently of the finale. Only a cadence to the tonic would provide full closure, but the passage ends definitively enough that whether it is dependent or independent remains a confusingly open question.

Form, genre, and time

To say that the *Pastoral* mixes "characteristic" and "symphonic" practices simplifies somewhat. Unusual movement forms and run-on connections

---

[11] The progressions in Examples 4.4b–d also share a series of preliminary steps; in all three cases, an initial C in the bass drops by tritone to F#, which in turn drops by half-step to the F that serves as the bass of V/iv. This highly characteristic motion – which, as Schachter notes, the violins forecast in their C–Gb–F motive at the very beginning (mm. 5–6; "The Triad as Place and Action," 165–68) – provides a further link between the three passages. Schachter reads the progressions in my Examples 4.4c and 4.4d as leading toward G and F, respectively (his Example 9, mm. 55–78 and 106–11); I hear them rather in the context of an overall effort to regain the dominant first reached in m. 35.

[12] In mm. 72–77, each stage of the progression (V/iv–iv–V/V) occupies two measures, leading one to expect the dominant at m. 78. Instead, V/V is tied over into the *fortissimo* (m. 78) and its resolution to the minor V (m. 79) overshadowed by the rising bass motion to V/VI (mm. 78–81). See Bockholdt, *VI. Symphonie*, 55; and Schachter, "The Triad as Place and Action," 165.

between passages in different tempo, although often found in character-istic music, are nevertheless also encountered in the larger repertories of dramatic music. Frequently the situations involve storms: there are well-known examples in Gluck's *Iphigénie en Tauride* (1779), Mozart's *Idomeneo* (1781), Haydn's *The Seasons*, and Beethoven's own ballet *Prometheus* (1800–01).[13] The composer may well have had this last work in mind while composing the *Pastoral* inasmuch as its storm sequence looks like a draft for the symphony's concluding movements: the beginning of the storm breaks off the final cadence of the ballet's overture, the end leads through a dominant directly into the first dance, and the form lacks a conventional key structure and pattern of repetition.[14] Furthermore, run-on connections between movements, and movements consisting of sections in different tempo ("compound" movements), are not uncom-mon in instrumental music generally in the later eighteenth and early nineteenth centuries;[15] a dozen of Haydn's later string quartets and piano trios, along with ten of Beethoven's pre-*Pastoral* piano sonatas and string quartets, contain examples.[16] They are found in symphonies as well, for the most part before 1780 but also, of course, in Beethoven's Fifth, where the link between scherzo and finale provides a vital tran-sition between the unstated but readily apparent moods of anxiety and affirmation.[17]

[13] In *Iphigénie en Tauride*, see the overture; in *Idomeneo*, the Act 1 chorus "Pietà! Numi, pietà!"; and in *The Seasons*, the chorus No. 17, "Ach, das Ungewitter naht!" Run-ons also connect storms and similar scenes in Cherubini's operas, which enjoyed great popularity in Vienna at the beginning of the nineteenth century and whose influence on Beethoven's middle-period music has been well documented (for a summary see Broyles, *Beethoven*, 119–26). See especially Act 2, Scene 6 of *Eliza* (1794) and the conclu-sion of *Lodoïska* (1791), the second of which has not a storm but an instrumental battle movement that leads directly into a multisectioned ensemble finale.

[14] Maynard Solomon calls the *Prometheus* storm a "first sketch" for that of the *Pastoral* (*Beethoven*, 2nd rev. edn. [New York: Schirmer, 1998], 247). Two motivic ideas from the earlier movement reappear in the *Pastoral*, descending tremolo arpeggios in the strings (cf. mm. 28–46 with Examples 4.3b–c) and a sixteenth-note "lightning" arpeggio (cf. mm. 18–20 with Example 4.3e; see also Bockholdt, *VI. Symphonie*, 53).

[15] "Run-on" and "compound" are used in the sense defined by Webster in *Haydn's "Farewell" Symphony*, 186–87.

[16] Webster lists the Haydn works in *Haydn's "Farewell" Symphony*, 188, 192. The Beethoven examples include the sonatas Opp. 13 (first movement), 27/1 and 2, 31/2 (first move-ment), 53, 57, and 81a, and the quartets Opp. 18/2 (second movement), 18/6 (fourth movement), 53/1 and 3, 74, and 95.

[17] Similar movements had all but ceased to appear in Haydn's and also in Mozart's symphonies after 1780. Of the ten Haydn examples, only Symphony No. 79 in F (c. 1782) dates from after 1780 (Webster, *Haydn's "Farewell" Symphony*, 191–94). Of the works that Zaslaw includes in *Mozart's Symphonies*, run-ons occur only be-fore 1780 and then primarily in three-movement works whose structures are based on the Italian opera sinfonia: K. 74 in G (probably 1770), K. 126 + 161/63 = 141a in

Characteristic symphonies remain an apposite point of comparison for the *Pastoral* because they use run-ons and unconventional forms for the most closely analogous purpose, conveying a subject without the assistance of singing or staging. Equally important, they highlight Beethoven's determination to employ such devices within a strongly symphonic framework and thereby to endow them with special significance. Composers who set out to represent a series of scenes tended to alter or abandon not only the movement forms most typically found in contemporary symphonies but also established norms regarding the number, tempo, and order of movements (Tables 4.1 and 4.2).[18] Examples range from Dittersdorf's *Metamorphoses*, where re-ordered fast and slow movements and compound finales fit into recognizable four-movement frameworks, to the pastoral works of Anton Wranitzky and Knecht, which exhibit only the faintest outlines of any familiar movement pattern. Still other composers recapitulate music from one movement of a work in the course of another, a practice with only rare precedent outside the characteristic tradition.[19] Beethoven, by contrast, does not re-order movements, replace single-tempo with compound movements, bring back movements that have already concluded, or

---

D (1772–74; = overture to *Il sogno di Scipione* plus new finale), K. 181/162b in D (1773), K. 184/166a in E♭ (1773), K. 208 + 102 = 213c in C (1775–76; = overture and No. 1 from *Il Rè pastore* plus new finale), and K. 318 in G (1779). The only examples not directly related to opera sinfonias are K. 213a in D (1775; = movements from the serenade K. 204), and the possibly authentic K. 95 in D (date unknown).

[18] The tables omit those works whose unusual structures may be said to have resulted from special circumstances, such as Haydn's *Seven Last Words*. On the equally unusual movement plans of battle symphonies see Example 5.1, p. 192 below. It is worth emphasizing that Beethoven and his audiences may have known many of the works in Tables 4.1 and 4.2. Those by Dittersdorf, Massonneau, Knecht, and Paul Wranitzky circulated widely; Wranitzky was as well known in Vienna as his brother Anton; and the *Metamorphoses* retained enough of a reputation to be mentioned in E. T. A. Hoffmann's 1810 review of Beethoven's Fifth Symphony (see p. 17 above). Circumstantial evidence also connects Beethoven with Knecht's *Portrait*, which Heinrich Philipp Boßler published in the same year that he issued Beethoven's piano sonatas WoO 47, 1785, and which both he and Traeg listed alongside music by Beethoven in their catalogues (Heinz-Werner Höhnen, *The Symphony 1720–1840*, vol. C-12 [New York: Garland, 1984]: xviii). This may help to explain why the *Pastoral*'s earliest reviewers never felt obliged to justify the storm or the run-ons. They do not even characterize them as unconventional, perhaps because they had already encountered similar passages in other characteristic works (reviews and reports through 1830 are reprinted in Stefan Kunze, ed., *Ludwig van Beethoven: Die Werke im Spiegel seiner Zeit. Gesammelte Konzertberichte und Rezensionen bis 1830* [Laaber: Laaber-Verlag, 1987], 115–29).

[19] I know of only two symphonic examples where there is no characterizing text, Beethoven's Fifth and Haydn's No. 46 in B (1772). Characteristic symphonies with similar recapitulations include Boccherini's *La casa del diavolo*, Brunetti's *Il maniatico*, Knecht's *Portrait*, Kraus's *Symphonie funèbre*, Paul Wranitzky's *Grande Sinfonie caractéristique*, Leopold Kozeluch's *L'Irrésolu*, and Romberg's *Trauer-Symphonie*.

Table 4.1 *Run-on and compound structures*

Composer	Symphony	No. of mvts.	Run-on mvts.	Compound movements
Beecke, Ignaz von	*Sinfonia di caccia* (ca. 1786)	4	ii–iii	i: ABA'; fast exposition and recapitulation frame slow middle section
	Pastorale sinfonie (1787)	3	i–iii	i: ABA': slow sections frame fast sonata form
Beethoven, Ludwig van	*Pastoral Symphony* (1808)	5	iii–v	
Brunetti, Gaetano	*Il maniatico* (1780)	4	i–ii	iv: ABA'; fast exposition and coda frame slow middle section
Dittersdorf, Carl Ditters von	*Les Quatre Âges du monde* (prob. 1781)	4		iv: free-form fast section followed by binary-form march
	La Chute de Phaéton (prob. 1781)	4		iv: fast followed by slow section; both free forms
	Andromède sauvée par Persée (prob. 1781)	4		iv: free-form fast section followed by minuet–trio
	Phinée avec ses amis changés en rochers (prob. 1781)	4	i–ii	iv: free-form fast section followed by minuet (without trio)

(cont.)

Table 4.1 (*cont.*)

Composer	Symphony	No. of mvts.	Run-on mvts.	Compound movements
Dittersdorf	*Les Paysans changés en grenouilles* (prob. 1781–82)	4	ii–iii	iv: prelude-fugue-prelude-coda, all continuous
Haydn, Joseph	*Le Matin* (1761)	4		ii: Adagio sections surround Andante for concertante violin/cello
	Le Midi (1761)	4		ii: recitative followed by double concerto mvt. for concertante violin/cello
	Symphony No. 45, "Farewell" (1772)	5	iv–v	
Knecht, Justin Heinrich	*Le Portrait musical de la nature* (1785)	3	ii–iii	i: sonata form interrupted by two binary-form dances ii: see Example 4.6 iii: slow theme and variations with a fast, binary-form chorale inserted within Variation 1
Kozeluch, Leopold	*L'Irrésolu* (1780–90?)	4		i: fast sonata form followed by recitative iv: march- and dancelike sections interspersed with recitative and concluded by recit. from mvt. 1
Marsh, John	*La Chasse* (1790)	3	i–iii	

Massonneau, Louis	La Tempête et le calme (1794)	3	i–ii	
Pichl, Václav	Diana (1765–70)	3		i: long slow section (not an introduction) followed by fast sonata form
Romberg, Bernhard	Trauer-Symphonie (1810)	2		i: long slow section (not an introduction) followed by fast sonata form ii: 5 run-on sections, slow–fast–fast–slow–slow
Stamitz, Carl	Le Jour variable (1772)	4	i–ii, iii–iv	
Wranitzky, Anton	Aphrodite (1792)	3		i: see Example 4.1 ii: slow sonata form followed by two dances iii: quasi-binary slow section followed by fast sonata form
Wranitzky, Paul	Grande Sinfonie caractéristique (1797)	4		i: sonata form with binary-form marches inserted into exposition and development iii: two binary-form marches followed by free-form battle iv: slow binary form followed by fast sonata form

Table 4.2 *Unusual movement orders*

Composer	Symphony	Movements					
		i	ii	iii	iv	v	vi
Beethoven, Ludwig van	*Pastoral* Symphony (1808)	F	S	Sch –	F –	F	
Brunetti, Gaetano	*Il maniatico* (1780)	int–S –	F	F	F–S–F		F
Dittersdorf, Carl	*Les Quatre Ages du monde* (prob. 1781)	S	F	M	F–S		
Ditters von	*Andromède sauvée par Persée* (prob. 1781)	S	F	S	F–M		
	Phinée avec ses amis changés en rochers (prob. 1781)	S –	F	S	F–M		
Haydn, Joseph	"Farewell" Symphony (1772)	F	S	M	F –	S	
	Il distratto (no later than 1774)	int–F	S	M	F	S	F
Knecht, Justin Heinrich	*Le Portrait musical de la nature* (1785)	F–S–F–S–F	S–F–S –	S–F–S			
Romberg, Bernhard	*Trauer-Symphonie* (1810)	S–F	S–F–S–S	S –	F		
Stamitz, Carl	*Le Jour variable* (1772)	S –	F	S –	F		
Wranitzky, Anton	*Aphrodite* (1792)	S–F–S–F	S–F	S–F			
	Symphony in D (1796)	F	S	M	S	F	
Wranitzky, Paul	*Grande Sinfonie caractéristique* (1797)	F	S	Marches–Battle	S–F	F	

int = slow introduction; F = fast; S = slow; M = minuet–trio; Sch = scherzo. Multiple letters for a single movement indicate a compound structure; dashes indicate run-on movements or sections.

eliminate any of the standard movement types of the four-part model – on the contrary, he remains within conventional practice except at the juncture between the scherzo and the finale. Of his predecessors, only Dittersdorf and Haydn had attempted anything similar, the former in *Actéon* and *La Chute de Phaéton* and the latter in *Le Matin* (1761), *Le Midi* (1761), and the *Farewell* Symphony (1772). In all five works run-ons, extra movements, compound movements and the like occur only in one place within otherwise unexceptional (at least as regards the order and number of movements) symphonies.[20] Yet they are the exceptions: as a rule, narrative or semi-narrative programs like Beethoven's led his contemporaries much further afield from symphonic forms.

As has been argued about other recently discussed examples of generic mixture,[21] the purpose of situating "characteristic" elements within a "symphonic" context is most likely to convey meaning. If tone-paintings and musical topics serve to represent the storm, the brookside idyll, and the other scenes described in the program of the *Pastoral*, its deployment of multiple formal conventions suggests something the movement titles do not describe, the relationship *between* the scenes and, in particular, their unfolding in time. The symphony effectively falls into two halves, a "symphonic" one consisting of the first and second movements, in which run-ons and related devices play no role, and a "characteristic" one consisting of the scherzo, storm, and finale. Time seems to run differently in each half. The run-ons between the scherzo, storm, and finale link the country dance, the storm, and the thanksgiving after the storm into a single unbroken narrative. Beethoven reinforces their connectedness by calling the finale "Frohe, dankbare Gefühle nach dem Sturm" (Glad, thankful feelings after the storm), which ensures that the storm and finale will be understood as successive scenes. In the first two movements, by contrast, neither the music nor the text indicates whether the scenes they represent happen in succession, with a pause in between, or at different times altogether. As independent, tonally closed movements, surrounded by silence, they could just as well stand for widely separated moments as consecutive ones. Nor do their titles settle the question. "Awakening of happy feelings on the arrival in the countryside" does suggest a beginning; whatever else happens in the

---

[20] The Haydn works exemplify his general tendency in characteristic works to use unconventional structures sparingly (Will, "Programmatic Symphonies of the Classical Period," 404–20). On the movement order of the "Farewell" see Webster, *Haydn's "Farewell" Symphony*, esp. 13–16.

[21] Jeffrey Kallberg, *Chopin at the Boundaries: Sex, History, and Musical Genre* (Cambridge, MA: Harvard University Press, 1996), 3–29 (a revised version of "The Rhetoric of Genre: Chopin's Nocturne in G Minor," *19th-Century Music* 11 [1988]: 238–61); James A. Hepokoski, "Genre and Content in Mid-century Verdi: 'Addio, del passato' (*La traviata*, Act III)," *Cambridge Opera Journal* 1 (1989): 249–76.

countryside, it must presumably follow the arrival there. But how long after, and in what order? The titles of the second movement, "Szene am Bach" (Scene by the brook), and of the following scherzo, "Lustiges Zusammensein der Landleute" (Cheerful gathering of country folk), do not specify when they take place in relationship either to the first movement or to one another. The second half of the title of the symphony, *Memory of country life*, creates perhaps the most ambiguity (see pp. 150–51 above). If the program is being constructed out of past events, then the progression from first to second movement, or from second movement to concluding sequence, could as well represent the artist drifting from memory to memory as a series of contiguous events.

As the discrete, disconnected scenes of the symphony's first half give way to the dramatic continuity of the second, the rate at which time passes seems also to change. Numerous commentators have noted that the first two movements unfold deliberately rather than driving toward their conclusions in the manner of so many other products of Beethoven's middle period.[22] The first movement lingers over its opening theme, reiterating both the theme and its constituent motives many times before finally moving to the transition (mm. 1–53); the second movement likewise repeats the expansive principal ideas of both its first and second groups before going on (mm. 1–6/7–12, and 33–40/41–48). Harmonies change slowly: most strikingly, the first movement begins with three measures of drone on the tonic, continues with four more after a brief pause on the dominant (mm. 5–8), then expands the drone to epic proportions both in the repetition of the main theme (mm. 29–42) and in the long blocks of B♭, D, G, and E chords in the development (mm. 151–220). And in neither movement does Beethoven establish the kind of powerful tonic–dominant polarity that propels others of his contemporary instrumental works seemingly headlong toward their final cadences. Instead, he moderates the dominant's drive for resolution through frequent use of the subdominant, even at normally tense moments such as the approach to the recapitulation in the first movement (mm. 275–78).

The following two movements could hardly differ more. The storm races through the most adventurous harmonic progressions and sharp dynamic contrasts in the entire symphony in a far shorter time than is taken up by either of the first two movements: it has only 155 measures in 4/4 time, marked Allegro, as opposed to the first movement's 512

---

[22] Bockholdt, *VI. Symphonie*, 13–41; Jones, *Beethoven: "Pastoral Symphony,"* 54–67; Wolfram Steinbeck, "6. Symphonie F-Dur Pastorale op. 68," in Albrecht Riethmüller, Carl Dahlhaus, and Alexander L. Ringer, eds., *Beethoven: Interpretationen seiner Werke*, 2 vols. (Laaber: Laaber-Verlag), I: 506–09; Philip Gossett, "Beethoven's Sixth Symphony: Sketches for the First Movement," *Journal of the American Musicological Society* 27 (1974): 253; Broyles, *Beethoven*, 198–204; Burnham, *Beethoven Hero*, 153–54.

(with repeat, 650) measures in 2/4 time, marked Allegro ma non troppo, or the second movement's 139 long measures in 12/8 time, marked Andante molto mosso. And the scherzo already anticipates the storm's frantic pace, in part through its own deviations from formal convention. Its first section begins like a rounded binary form (see Example 4.5): although the first, sixteen-measure unit cadences on the submediant major rather than V or I, the passage is repeated and, after a brief excursion to the dominant (a'), the opening measures return and lead to a cadential theme in the tonic (a").[23] Where one expects a repeat of the second half of this binary form, however, it instead proceeds directly into the trio (c d c'); the trio then also behaves like a rounded binary until the end of *its* second half, where, once again, the expected repeat is forsworn in favor of a new section (e e' e"). Evidently a second trio, and in duple rather than triple meter, this new section ends on the dominant without tonal closure. All three sections are then played again, after which a compressed version of the first leads to a final tonic cadence.

Commentators have tended to downplay the idiosyncrasy of this structure, much as they have that of the storm.[24] Admittedly, the *da capo* of the trios along with the scherzo recalls Beethoven's characteristic twist on A B A dance movements, in which he repeats both the main movement and the trio to create a five-part form, A B A B A'.[25] Nevertheless, the repetitions in the *Pastoral* result in the unprecedented order of A B C A B C A', and, more importantly, the parts of the movement lack the independence typical of contemporary dances: the first section runs into the second with no double bar and virtually no pause; the first two sections end too abruptly, without the tonal closure that a

---

[23] There is ample precedent for Beethoven's writing out the repeat rather than using a sign, for instance in the scherzos of Symphonies Nos. 3 and 7, and in both the scherzos and trios of Symphonies Nos. 4 and 5.

[24] See, however, Alain Frogley, "Beethoven's Struggle for Simplicity in the Sketches for the Third Movement of the Pastoral Symphony," *Beethoven Forum* 4 (1995): 99–134, which not only emphasizes the differences between the movement's formal design and those found in Beethoven's earlier scherzos, but also shows that the scherzo–two trio structure is present throughout the sketches for the movement. Tovey called the movement "a very typical Beethoven scherzo," locating the beginning of the trio at m. 91 and offering no explanation of how the 2/4 section fit into the form (*Essays*, I: 45 and 52–54; cf. Frogley, 106n.).

[25] In the symphonies whose scherzos follow this pattern – Nos. 4, 7, and possibly 5 – Beethoven also shortens the final repetition of the main movement as he does in the *Pastoral* Symphony. On No. 5 see Sieghard Brandenburg, "Once Again: On the Question of the Repeat of the Scherzo and Trio in Beethoven's Fifth Symphony," in *Beethoven Essays: Studies in Honor of Elliot Forbes*, ed. Lewis Lockwood and Phyllis Benjamin (Cambridge, MA: Harvard University Press, 1984), 146–98; and Clive Brown, *A New Appraisal of the Sources of Beethoven's Fifth Symphony* (Wiesbaden: Breitkopf und Härtel, 1996), 59–67.

Example 4.5 Beethoven, *Pastoral* Symphony, scherzo

meter:	3/4			3/4			2/4			3/4		
section:	A (Scherzo)			B (Trio 1)			C (Trio 2)			A' (Coda)		
phrase:	a	a'	a''	c	d	c'	e	e'	e''	a	a'	a''
mm:	1–16 / 17–32	33–52	53–86	87–106 / 107–22	123–32	133–64	165–72 / 173–80	181–88	189–204	205–21	222–34	235–64
harmony:	I–VI♯ / VI♯–V	I	I	I	V	I	I	V	V	I–V	I	I

(repeat signs ‖: … :‖ enclose the score)

Example 4.6 Knecht, *Le Portrait musical de la nature*

movement:	i	ii				iii
tempo:	*Allegretto*	*Tempo medemo*	*Allegro*	*Tempo medemo*		*Andantino*
program:	idyll	storm approaches	storm	storm recedes	idyll restored →	hymn: nature praises heaven
measure:	1	321	411	637	687	723
key:	G major	G major	D major		G major	G major

repetition of their second halves would provide; and the third section makes no pretense at closure at all but simply leads directly back into the scherzo. Each section comes in too soon, it seems, creating a sense of haste that is heightened by an acceleration to Presto in the movement's final measures (mm. 235–64). The storm continues in the same vein, and only in the finale does the symphony seem to slow again, beginning with a three-fold repetition of the opening theme and proceeding with similar deliberation throughout. Its unhurriedness signals, as much as the movement's major harmonies and repeated pastoral horn calls, a restoration of the world of the first two movements.

Time undergoes similar transformations in Knecht's *Portrait musical de la nature*, long recognized as an important predecessor of the *Pastoral* and with a program that even more closely approximates Beethoven's than does that of Wranitzky's *Aphrodite*.[26] Like the *Pastoral*, the *Portrait* falls clearly into two halves (Example 4.6). First comes a long sonata-form movement representing a natural paradise, into which Knecht interpolates two binary forms that introduce, respectively, a piping shepherd and a singing shepherdess. Then follows a series of continuous sections and movements depicting the approach, arrival, and departure of a storm as well as a concluding "hymn" of thanksgiving. The two halves contrast less sharply with one another than Beethoven's, for Knecht, rather than opposing the "characteristic" to the "symphonic," instead uses run-ons and unconventional movement forms throughout. As in the *Pastoral*, though, the first half represents a single scene in a single independent movement, while the second links several scenes into a continuous progression, and Knecht's music also creates the sensation of a broad acceleration and deceleration. The first movement advances slowly through the successive sections of its sonata form, and the interpolations delay things still more by slowing the tempo from an already moderate Allegretto to Andante and Un poco adagio. The ensuing storm unfolds much more quickly, while the hymn, like Beethoven's finale, restores something resembling the pace of the first movement.[27]

While neither Knecht's nor Beethoven's characterizing texts mention time, the way in which it seems to pass more quickly or slowly, continuously or discontinuously, contributes as much to their representations of pastoral as the references to shepherds' horns, storms, and feelings of happiness or gratefulness do. Mikhail Bakhtin writes of "the special relationship that time has to space in the idyll: an organic fastening-down,

---

[26] The similarity between Knecht's and Beethoven's works was noted by François-Joseph Fétis, "Deux symphonies pastorales," *Revue et gazette musicale de Paris* (28 October 1866): 337–38, and has since been mentioned in numerous commentaries on the *Pastoral*.

[27] Claus Bockmaier analyzes Knecht's storm movement in *Entfesselte Natur in der Musik des achtzehnten Jahrhunderts* (Tutzing: Schneider, 1992), 267–91. On the background of the *Portrait* see also Jung, "Zwischen *Malerey* und *Ausdruck der Empfindung*."

a grafting of life and its events to a place . . . where the fathers and grand-fathers lived and where one's children and their children will live."[28] Living perpetually with no change in circumstances, the characters of an idyll do not experience time in the normal, linear sense: "This unity of place in the life of generations weakens and renders less distinct all the temporal boundaries between individual lives and between various phases of one and the same life."[29] If time enters the idyll at all, it does so only in the form of such renewable cycles as are represented by the generations of the family, the seasons, or the hours of the day. Too much linear time forces the landscape and its inhabitants to change, at which point the idyll ceases to function as a retreat from the outside world. Both the *Pastoral* and the *Portrait* have moments in which time seems to pass, not just slowly, but in this cyclic fashion. The finales provide the most obvious examples; Beethoven writes a rondo and Knecht a theme and variations, forms that return repeatedly to their starting points and thus suggest only temporary or gradual change. Even the sonata forms of the opening movements seem cyclic, however, inasmuch as both frequently repeat their themes and motives and also recapitulate their expositions with relatively few alterations.

But the two symphonies also suggest quickly-moving and linear time: the two storms and Beethoven's scherzo seem literally to rush by, and the second half of each work depicts a one-directional, non-cyclical series of scenes. In this respect they recall contemporary literature that likewise juxtaposes the "timelessness" of the idyll with the "historicity" of the real world, and that itself reflects a new awareness of history linked to a perceived acceleration in the passage of time in the wake of the French Revolution.[30] Goethe's *Hermann und Dorothea* (1797) and Wordsworth's "Michael" (1800) provide two particularly good examples.[31] In the first, history, in the guise of war refugees, fan-tastically accelerates the heretofore idyllic pace of Hermann's life with

---

[28] Mikhail Bakhtin, "Forms of Time and Chronotope in the Novel," trans. by Michael Holquist and Caryl Emerson in *The Dialogic Imagination: Four Essays*, ed. Holquist (Austin: University of Texas Press, 1981), 225.

[29] Ibid.

[30] The new temporal consciousness is discussed in Schmenner, *Die Pastorale*, 97–102, and Reinhold Brinkmann, "In the Time of the *Eroica*," in Scott Burnham and Michael P. Steinberg, eds., *Beethoven and His World* (Princeton: Princeton University Press, 2000), 8–10. Temporal juxtapositions were also the result of the growing later eighteenth-century interest in "realistic" idylls, populated not by mythical shepherds but by real human characters who involved themselves in historical events. On the origins and effects of pastoral realism see Renate Böschenstein, *Idylle* (Stuttgart: Metzler, 1968), 68–78; and Renato Poggioli, *The Oaten Flute: Essays on Pastoral Poetry and the Pastoral Ideal* (Cambridge, MA: Harvard University Press, 1975), 31–34.

[31] Bakhtin offers an equally relevant but less well-known example, the 1811 story "Unverhofftes Wiedersehen" (Unhoped-for Reunion) by Johann Peter Hebel ("Forms of Time and Chronotope in the Novel," 228n.). A woman loses her fiancé to a mining

his parents; having fallen in love with a refugee, he must marry her on the very same day or lose her forever. And while the betrothal restores a measure of equilibrium, Dorothea's arrival will permanently change the relationships within Hermann's family. In "Michael," the shock of real time comes when the fortunes of a city-dwelling nephew collapse and Michael, a farmer living in pastoral reclusion, is held liable. Events again speed out of control; having decided to make good the debt by sending his own son to work in the city, Michael becomes obsessed with haste: "let us send him forth / Tomorrow, or the next day, or tonight: / – If he could go, the Boy should go tonight."[32] But haste shatters the cycle of generations on the farm, for the son falls prey to urban vice and flees overseas rather than return home to face his parents.

The *Pastoral* and the *Portrait* tell comparatively abstract stories; even if one hears them as portraying an individual in nature – perhaps Beethoven, as in Mosengeil's review (see pp. 152–54 above) – the protagonist still experiences a relatively generic set of events: idyll, dance, storm, thanksgiving. What the symphonies lack in narrative specificity, however, they more than make up for in temporal immediacy. Prose and poetry can describe time quickening or slowing down and can also, to some extent, use language and formal proportions to emphasize mimetically a temporal shift. But they cannot match music's capacity to control the perception of time, which proves to be, here as elsewhere in characteristic symphonies, a critical means of representation. Abstraction notwithstanding, the *Pastoral* and the *Portrait* may well have provided the period's most vivid accounts of the uneasy relationship between idyllic and historical time.

An idyll redeemed

Beethoven's mixture of formal conventions in the *Pastoral* may also have influenced the semantic connotations of the storm. Because the first, second, and final movements of the work are so manifestly "symphonic," at least as regards tempo, form, and movement order, and because the scherzo departs only partially from symphonic practice, they contextualize the storm as a startling generic deviation. They suggest a parallel between its programmatic meaning and its formal function – as the storm disrupts the idyll, so the music representing it disrupts the genre – that in turn imbues the scene with considerable force. In the world of

---

accident but remains unalterably in love until, fifty years later, she gets the chance to bid a proper farewell when the fiancé's perfectly preserved body is exhumed from an icy cavern. Hebel explicitly contrasts the timelessness of her love with the real time of history by using a litany of world events to describe her years of waiting.

[32] William Wordsworth, *Lyrical Ballads*, ed. Michael Mason (London and New York: Longman, 1992), 351, lines 286–88.

the *Pastoral*, it would appear, the stability of the idyll depends on the observance of symphonic convention, as witnessed in varying degrees by the movements other than the storm. Accordingly, the storm's break with convention seems not merely to disturb the idyll but to challenge the very premises on which it rests.[33]

It will be remembered that Fischer described the movement as being "erfüllt mit grossen und erhabenen Empfindungen" (filled with great and sublime feeling; see p. 152 above). Beyond the critic's own desire to lift the movement onto an exalted plane, there is much about the storm itself that could have moved him to such a statement. Its brevity is a quality thought crucial to successful evocations of the sublime in the eighteenth and early nineteenth centuries,[34] and its harmonic language and overall dramatic structure could hardly correspond more closely to the following description from an 1805 essay by Christian Friedrich Michaelis:

Der Componist bedient sich auch des *Wunderbaren* zum erhabenen Ausdruck. Dies entspringt aus dem Ungewohnten, Befremdenden, mächtig Ueberraschenden, oder Frappanten in der harmonischen und rhythmischen Fortschreitung. Wenn nämlich der herrschende Ton plötzlich eine unvermuthete Wendung nimmt, ein Akkord sich ganz anders auflöset, als nach der Regel sich erwarten ließ, oder wenn die gehoffte Beruhigung nicht eintritt, sondern von manchen stürmischen Bewegungen noch aufgehalten wird, so entsteht Verwunderung und Staunen, eine Stimmung, die den Geist tief bewegt, und erhabene Ideen in ihm weckt oder unterhält.

The composer also expresses sublimity through the use of the *marvelous*. This is achieved by the use of unconventional, surprising, powerfully startling, or striking harmonic or rhythmic progressions. If, for instance, the established tonality suddenly veers in an unexpected direction, if a chord is resolved quite differently than the rules would lead one to expect, or if the longed-for calm is delayed by a series of stormy passages, then astonishment and awe result and in this mood the spirit is profoundly moved and sublime ideas are stimulated or sustained.[35]

---

[33] Hepokoski argues that in Verdi, "structural conventions stand for the artificial, operatic world in which the characters move and act," and departures from convention signal a challenge to, or abandonment of, "the axioms underpinning that world" ("Genre and Content in Mid-century Verdi," 256).

[34] Sisman, *Mozart: The "Jupiter" Symphony*, 13–18.

[35] Michaelis, "Einige Bemerkungen über das Erhabene der Musik," *Berlinische Musikalische Zeitung* 1 (1805), 180; trans. adapted from Le Huray and Day, *Music and Aesthetics*, 289. Michaelis's essay concludes by discussing the symphonies of Haydn, Mozart, and Beethoven, and the symphony in general was connected with the sublime by numerous writers (see p. 115 above, n. 51). The comments of Michaelis and others are discussed in Sisman, *Mozart: The "Jupiter" Symphony*, 13–20, 74–76; Dahlhaus, "E. T. A. Hoffmanns Beethoven-Kritik und die Ästhetik des Erhabenen," *Archiv für Musikwissenschaft* 38 (1981): 80–92; and Schwartz, "Periodicity and Passion in the First Movement of Haydn's 'Farewell' Symphony," 319–31.

Most important in the present context, the storm would also have invoked the sublime by virtue of its departure from the conventions governing the rest of the symphony. Eighteenth- and early nineteenth-century writers regularly associate sublimity with phenomena external to an established frame of reference. Michaelis writes, "Die erhabenen Töne, Figuren und Akkorde sind ihr [der Imagination] angemessen; sie muß sich anstrengen und *ungewöhnlich erweitern*, um sie festzuhalten, zusammenzufassen und wieder zurückzurufen" (Sublime notes, figuration and harmonies stimulate the imagination, which must exert itself and expand *beyond its normal bounds* to grasp, integrate, and recall them).[36] Speaking of all the arts, Sulzer says similarly, "Es scheinet, daß man in den Werken des Geschmaks überhaupt dasjenige Erhaben nenne, was in seiner Art weit größer und stärker ist, *als wir es erwartet hätten*" (It appears that in works of taste, the term sublime is generally applied to whatever in its way is much greater and more powerful *than might have been expected*).[37] In the context of the *Pastoral*, Beethoven's storm has not only an unexpected form but also unprecedentedly irregular rhythms and phrases as well as previously unheard or rarely heard harmonies: the preceding movements entirely avoid diminished seventh chords and even, to a remarkable extent, minor tonalities, both very prominent in the storm. It also has a fuller scoring than the rest of the symphony; piccolo, trombones, and timpani enter for the first time during the storm, so that its *fortissimos* are literally "much greater and more powerful" than any heard before.[38]

Mosengeil went a step beyond Fischer and associated the storm with the sublime event of a theophany – "Groß und wunderbar ist der Herr der Natur!" (Great and wondrous is the Lord of Nature!), he cries during his description of the passage, as if its music spoke with the voice of God.[39] The interpretation is neither as extravagant as it might seem nor rooted entirely in his own efforts to cast Beethoven as a divine creator, for the connection between storms and God has deep roots in Western culture. He appears in or as a storm in both the Old and the New Testaments: Moses, for instance, receives the Ten Commandments in a cloud that

---

[36] Michaelis, "Einige Bemerkungen," 180, trans. Le Huray and Day, *Music and Aesthetics*, 290. Italics mine.

[37] Sulzer, *Allgemeine Theorie*, II: 97, trans. Le Huray and Day, *Music and Aesthetics*, 138. Italics mine.

[38] On the symphony's orchestration and distribution of diminished and minor harmonies, see Bockholdt, *VI. Symphonie*, 50–52; and Jones, *Beethoven: "Pastoral Symphony,"* 49, 52–53, and 73. Emphasizing the sublime quality of "suddenness" in the storm (64–67), and what he calls its "complete repeal of the compositional principles valid in the unfolding of the symphony thus far" (226), Schmenner reads the storm as an "apotheosis of violence" whose reference points include, ultimately, the violence of the French Revolution (*Die Pastorale*, 211–27).

[39] *Zeitung für die elegante Welt* 10 (1810): 1052.

thunders and flashes with lighting and fire, and in Revelation, John the Divine describes thunder and lightning as emanating from God's throne.[40] Numerous eighteenth-century writers used similar imagery specifically in pastoral contexts, most famously Friedrich Gottlieb Klopstock in his ode "Das Landleben" (Country Life, 1759), later revised as "Die Frühlingsfeier" (Celebration of Spring, 1771). After celebrating God as the creator of nature, Klopstock then calls on his pastoral characters to recognize him in a storm, using a "sublime" tone that he was in large part responsible for establishing in German letters:

> Seht ihr den neuen Zeugen des Nahen, den fliegenden Strahl?
> Höret ihr hoch in der Wolke den Donner des Herrn?
> Er ruft: Jehova! Jehova!
> Und der geschmetterte Wald dampft! (93–96)

(Do you see the sign of His approach, the fleeting lightning? Do you hear high in the clouds the thunder of the Lord? He calls: Jehovah! Jehovah! And the shattered woods smoke!)[41]

Klopstock's ode gained particular fame via Goethe's reference to it in *Die Leiden des jungen Werthers*; having themselves watched a thunderstorm cross an idyllic landscape, Werther and Lotte think spontaneously of "Die Frühlingsfeier."[42] And readers would have encountered the same topos in Christoph Christian Sturm's oft-reprinted and translated *Betrachtungen über die Werke Gottes im Reiche der Natur* (*Reflections on the Works of God in the Realm of Nature*, 1772), a series of short meditations, one for each day of the year, in which Sturm reads every aspect of nature as a sign for God or his beneficence. Storms are mentioned frequently, and God himself invariably either appears in or controls them.[43]

According to the *Betrachtungen*, storms provide the means for God not only to water the earth and rid the air of vapors but also to

---

[40] Deuteronomy 5: 22, Exodus 19 and 20, Revelation 4: 5. See also Psalm 18 and John 12: 28–29, in both of which God speaks through thunder.

[41] Klopstock, *Ausgewählte Werke*, ed. Karl August Schleiden (Munich: Carl Hanser, 1962), 92.

[42] See Werther's letter of 16 June 1771.

[43] See esp. Sturm's discussions of summer thunderstorms in the entries for 26 June, 8 July, 11 July, and 19 August. While Sturm's book is unquestionably relevant to the reception of the *Pastoral*, it would appear that Beethoven himself encountered it only after completing the symphony; his personal copy, which survives with passages marked in his hand, is of an 1811 Reuttlingen edition (see Eveline Bartlitz, ed., *Die Beethoven-Sammlung in der Musikabteilung der Deutschen Staatsbibliothek* [Berlin: Deutsche Staatsbibliothek, 1970], 208–09). Schindler possessed Beethoven's copy after the composer's death and wrote repeatedly of the composer's fondness for Sturm (*Biographie von Ludwig van Beethoven*, esp. 151–52).

frighten sinners, a frequently encountered theme within the complex of associations between God and storms. In *The Seasons* (1748), for instance, James Thomson says in connection with a destructive summer thunderstorm, "Guilt hears appalled, with deeply troubled thought," the implication of which is that the sinner recognizes God's wrath in the storm.[44] In *The Seasons*, whose text van Swieten based on Thomson, the storm provokes the closely related idea that the morally righteous will be shielded from its destructive power; following the storm, the chorus calls its survivors to a repose they have earned through their "reines Herz, gesunde[n] Leib und Tagesarbeit" (pure heart, healthy body, and day's work; from "Die düstren Wolken trennen sich"). And in Jérôme-Joseph de Momigny's "Picturesque and Poetic Analysis" of the first movement of Haydn's Symphony No. 103, the peasants whom he imagines populating the movement interpret the drumroll in the slow introduction as God's thunder, which prompts them to pray for redemption. The danger seemingly past, they tease one another in the main movement for having been scared, but return to prayer after the drumroll recurs in the recapitulation. Having learned their lesson at last, they cease in the concluding measures to torment one another and instead celebrate together the end of the storm.[45]

Events in the finale support the idea that the storm in the *Pastoral* might carry similar connotations. Mosengeil, the same critic who read the storm as a theophany, heard in the following movement "eine Freude, die sich von der in den drei ersten Sätzen empfundenen, durch die beigemischten Gefühle des religiösen Dankes unterscheidet" (a joy which is distinguished from that felt in the first three movements by added sentiments of religious thanksgiving).[46] He seems to have sensed a quality of the movement that was not made explicit in its published text. In his sketches for the finale, Beethoven made the note "Ausdrucks des Danks O Herr wir danken dir" (Expression of thanks, O Lord, we thank you),[47] and in both the autograph score and the parts used at the first performance, he titled the movement "Hirtengesang. Wohlthätige mit Danck an die Gottheit verbundene Gefühle nach dem Sturm" (Shepherds' hymn. Grateful feelings combined with thanks to

[44] Thomson, *The Seasons*, "Summer," line 1169; quoted from J. Logie Robertson, ed., *The Complete Poetical Works of James Thomson* (London: Oxford University Press, 1908), 95.
[45] Momigny, *Cours complet d'harmonie et de composition*, II: 600–06; trans. in Bent, ed., *Music Analysis in the Nineteenth Century*, II: 137–40.
[46] *Zeitung für die elegante Welt* (5 July 1810): col. 1053. A. B. Marx wrote of the movement: "Natur und Menschen bringen dem Herrn, der im Wetter segnend vorüberzog, das Opfer ihres Danks" (Nature and men offer their thanks to the Lord, who passed over with blessings in the storm; *Ludwig van Beethoven: Leben und Schaffen*, 2 vols. [Berlin: Otto Janke, 1859], II: 109).
[47] Landsberg 10, p. 164 (*Ein Skizzenbuch zur Pastoralsymphonie*, I: 17).

God after the storm).[48] Sometime during preparations for the first edition of 1809, this title was replaced by the shorter and grammatically simpler "Shepherds' hymn. Glad, thankful feelings after the storm," but the original version and the comment in the sketches show clearly that Beethoven himself attributed sacred meaning to the finale.[49]

Two aspects of the movement's music have religious connotations. First, Beethoven in certain respects treats the principal theme as if it were a church hymn: it always occurs twice or three times in succession, as if accommodating a series of verses, and it appears in a striking passage toward the end of the movement in a scoring that recalls the texture of a chorale (mm. 237–44).[50] Second, arpeggiated horn calls like those that open the movement and form the basis for the principal theme have a long lineage in religious pastoral music, not only in the eighteenth-century Christmas pieces discussed in Chapter 2, but also in examples such as "Der muntre Hirt" from Haydn's *Seasons* (cf. mm. 5–8 with mm. 21–25 in Example 2.8), where the context is not Christmas but a more general celebration of God in nature.[51] Beginning a sequence of summer scenes that will lead eventually to the storm, Haydn's shepherd goes out with his flock to greet the sunrise.[52]

Beethoven's shepherds likewise greet the return of the sun, or at least of calm, after a passage of darkness as profound as night itself. Moreover, if one accepts that both the storm and the finale have sacred overtones, then the latter's horn calls can be heard to initiate the last episode in a

---

[48] Nottebohm, *Zweite Beethoveniana*, 378; Hans Schmidt, "Die Beethovenhandschriften des Beethovenhauses in Bonn," *Beethoven-Jahrbuch* 7 (1969/70): 238.

[49] The shorter title is entered as a correction to the original in the 1808 printer's exemplar for the work; Sieghard Brandenburg, "Die Stichvorlage zur Erstausgabe von Beethovens Pastoralsymphonie op. 68: eine neuaufgefundene Primärquelle," in Ernst Herttrich and Hans Schneider, eds., *Festschrift Rudolf Elvers zum 60. Geburtstag* (Tutzing: Schneider, 1985), 57. Grove translates "Hirtengesang" as "shepherds' hymn," which better reflects Beethoven's original conception of the movement than the now-standard "shepherd's song" (*Beethoven and His Nine Symphonies*, 220).

[50] Cf. Kirby, "Beethoven's Pastoral Symphony as a *Sinfonia caracteristica*," 617–19; and Owen Jander, "The Prophetic Conversation in Beethoven's 'Scene by the Brook,'" *Musical Quarterly* 77 (1993): 549–50. Jones discusses mm. 237–44 in connection with the "O Herr wir danken dir" comment from Beethoven's sketches (*Beethoven: "Pastoral Symphony*," 38–39).

[51] Alexander Hyatt-King claimed that Beethoven's theme "is obviously taken from [a Swiss herding tune known as] the Rigi Ranz" ("Mountains, Music, and Musicians," *Musical Quarterly* 31 [1945]: 403). Jones, however, is surely correct in saying that "given the wide distribution of such themes and the propensity of art music to invent themes in this mode when appropriate . . . it is likely that the resemblance is generic rather than particular" (*Beethoven: "Pastoral Symphony*," 77).

[52] Jones also notes the similarities between this passage and the opening of the *Pastoral* finale, as well as the importance of pastoral in church music of this period generally (*Beethoven: "Pastoral Symphony*," 12–16).

narrative not unlike that which Momigny invented for the first movement of Haydn's Symphony No. 103. The *Pastoral*'s first two movements suggest a beautiful and emotionally untroubled countryside; the music or the associated images may inspire religious thoughts inasmuch as writers like Klopstock and Sturm saw God everywhere in nature, but they do not make them explicit. The scherzo then populates the countryside with decidedly profane inhabitants, *Landleute* so frantic about their reveling that they cannot even finish one dance properly before beginning another. The storm, like the drumroll in Momigny's story, reminds them of the wrath of God and frightens them into prayer – or, put more positively, it reveals the sublime magnitude of God, after which the horn signals call the *Landleute* to prayer.

Knecht's *Portrait* also ends with a hymn, and the work as a whole enacts a similar scenario: a storm dramatizes the power of God over life and/or landscape, after which he receives thanks both for creating life and landscape and for withholding more severe destruction. The differences between Knecht's and Beethoven's plots, however, throw a further revealing light on the *Pastoral*. Rudolf Bockholdt points out that the *Portrait*, according to its program at least, tells a story more abstract than human. The only characters are the shepherd and shepherdess of the first movement, who disappear thereafter, leaving only a personified "Nature" to sing the hymn of thanks: "La Nature transportée de la joie éleve sa voix vers le ciel et rend au createur les plus vives grâces par des chants doux et agréables" (Transported by joy, Nature raises her voice to heaven and gives the Creator the most lively thanks through sweet and pleasant songs).[53] In Beethoven's story (and in Momigny's), by contrast, the characters remain through the end, and it is they, not an anthropomorphized landscape, who give thanks. Furthermore, owing to a simple but important difference between Beethoven's and Knecht's symphonies, the former's storm seems to effect a more profound transformation than the latter's. Following the storm in the *Portrait*, Knecht recapitulates part of his idyllic first movement, suggesting that everything has reverted to the way it was before the storm (Example 4.6, m. 687). After the storm in the *Pastoral*, by contrast, Beethoven restores the mood, the topics, and the unhurried pace of the first two movements, but he does not literally repeat any of their music. Knecht's storm seems

---

[53] Bockholdt, *VI. Symphonie*, 66–69. He also contrasts Knecht's use of "Nature" in his program to Beethoven's "Land" ("Landleben," "Landleute"). The latter term suggests a countryside separate from another sphere of human life, the city; as Bockholdt points out, Fischer heard the beginning of Beethoven's first movement as a journey "von der Stadt nach dem Lande" (from the city to the country; *AmZ* 12 [1810]: col. 243). Knecht's "nature," by contrast, populated only by the conventional shepherd and shepherdess, suggests the traditional pastoral retreat, cut off from the world of man altogether. See also n. 2 above.

to pass through, leaving no permanent mark, but Beethoven's ensures that nothing will ever be as it was before.

The religiosity of the two finales takes on a different meaning as a result. Knecht's sounds like an independent idea, a reaction that takes hold after God has restored the idyll to its original state. Beethoven's sounds like a new element in the idyll itself. It is as if his pastoral inhabitants have realized that their existence depends on God's grace, and have thus tried to achieve something like the harmony between Momigny's peasants at the end of his story, or the "pure hearts" of Haydn's and van Swieten's peasants in the *Seasons*. To ward off further storms, and to regain and preserve their pastoral innocence, they transform their natural paradise into a moral one.

The humanity of the "Pastoral" Symphony

This reading of the *Pastoral*, as a progression from idyll through destruction to moral redemption, triggers some unexpected associations. First, it recalls the familiar narrative of humankind's fall and return to grace, which is to say: rather than end with the pessimism of Dittersdorf's *Quatre Ages*, or simply continue the Christianized celebration of nature found in Haydn's *Creation*, the *Pastoral* seems to finish the story, to guide its pastoral innocents through the Fall to a new paradise rather than leave them bereft or, as in *The Creation*, content in Eden. This is "Ausdruck der Empfindung" in Sulzer's sense, where the emotional experience leads to edification and redemption (see pp. 132–34 above). And the journey through tribulation to paradise suggests a second, equally familiar narrative as well: the story of a hero's triumph over adversity, a paradigmatic representation of which has traditionally been found in the *Eroica* and other instrumental works that Beethoven composed in the years surrounding the *Pastoral*. This second association poses problems, however, for in fact no one has ever heard the *Pastoral* as heroic, and for good reason. Those elements of Beethoven's middle-period style that its first, second, and final movements abjure are precisely those that typify the heroic style: most importantly, dynamic tonal motion and the emphasis on driving toward long-term goals. The comparatively static and nonteleological music of the *Pastoral*, combined with a program worded in such a way as never to introduce an individual protagonist, have caused great difficulty for commentators who would read the symphony as portraying the kind of active hero attributed to the *Eroica* Symphony and related works. Even Mosengeil, who transformed Beethoven from countryside observer into heroic artist, could not sustain his interpretation to the end of the piece; after the composer wins his vividly described battle with the forces of nature and music (see pp. 153–54 above), he disappears. Not he, but only "die wackeren Hirten" (worthy shepherds) celebrate the return of pastoral calm. Taming the storm evidently reveals Beethoven to be the semi-divine protector of the idyll, a role he cannot fill without relinquishing his residency there.[54]

It is not that the *Pastoral* lacks heroic dimensions altogether. As Schmenner notes, Goethe and others thought neoclassicizing pastoral landscapes, especially those of Claude Lorrain, to be expressive of a generalized sense of striving and achievement associated with Antiquity. To the extent that the symphony brought up related visions of the past, it, too, may have reminded some listeners of ancient social or artistic ideals which they felt the modern world should struggle to attain.[55] Still, the *Pastoral* suggests no specific heroic narrative, no protagonist with whom one might identify and thereby experience the self-affirming journey through trials to triumph discussed in the Introduction (see p. 22 above). The symphony presents only collections of characters, peasants and shepherds – or, if in fact God enters the story through the storm, a subject whose actions one can hardly take part in vicariously. And even if one identifies with an imaginary "Beethoven-in-nature," this character still does not undergo the trials of, say, the protagonist of the *Eroica*. The scherzo and storm certainly threaten the idyll and, by extension, whoever is thought to inhabit it, and they do so with music that has all the tonal dynamism, affective intensity, and forward propulsion of the heroic style itself. Nevertheless, this music occupies but a small proportion of the work compared to the corresponding music in the first movement of the *Eroica*, where the "hero's tribulations" fill all but the very last measures of a gigantic sonata form. The storm also sounds so different from the rest of the symphony, so much like an intrusion from another genre, that it gives the impression of posing a purely external obstacle; it would be difficult to conceive of the storm as the sort of spiritual crisis that, along with worldly challenges, heroes typically have to overcome. By heroic standards, consequently, the *Pastoral* sounds unrealistic and even slightly impersonal. It devotes so little time to crisis, and the crisis it does present belongs so clearly to the natural rather than the emotional world, that it never suggests the specifically psychological drama, so often heard in heroic-style works, that has led commentators to attribute a uniquely "human element" to Beethoven's music.[56]

---

[54] *Zeitung für die elegante Welt* (5 July 1810): cols. 1052–53.

[55] Schmenner, *Die Pastorale*, 256–59.

[56] The term "human element" (das Menschliche) comes from a 1922 essay on Beethoven by Ferruccio Busoni, cited and discussed in Hans Heinrich Eggebrecht, *Zur Geschichte der Beethoven-Rezeption: Beethoven 1970* (Mainz: Akademie der Wissenschaften und der Literatur, 1972), 8–9; and in Burnham, *Beethoven Hero*, xiii. Over the course of their studies, Eggebrecht and Burnham discuss numerous additional manifestations of the belief that Beethoven's music is uniquely human.

For modernist critics such as Tovey (see pp. 19–20 above), this seeming distance between the *Pastoral* and human experience was probably as powerful a motivation for proving the work's "normality" as were its tone-paintings or association with program music; emphasizing the self-sufficiency and coherence of its forms, or the complexity of its motivic development, imbued the *Pastoral* with qualities that were by Tovey's day inextricably associated with works like the *Eroica* and the Fifth Symphonies.[57] At the same time, by pronouncing the irrelevance of Beethoven's pastoral subject matter, they freed listeners to associate the music with subjects different from and – potentially at least – more psychologically dramatic than the experience of nature. Other twentieth-century interpreters, also sensing a lack of human drama in the piece, have chosen to amplify rather than to compensate for it. The famous *Pastoral* Symphony episode in Disney's *Fantasia* (1940), for instance, bears a striking similarity to early nineteenth-century readings in that, during the storm, Jove appears in a cloud and hurls down thunderbolts. The entire sequence, however, takes place in an explicitly unrealistic Arcadia populated by centaurs rather than people, and even the storm ends with an image of Jove retiring contentedly, as if it had all been merely an amusing diversion. And in André Gide's *La Symphonie pastorale* (1918), Beethoven's music is likewise taken to represent a world of pure fantasy, albeit now a dangerous one. A well-intentioned but naive clergyman uses the *Pastoral*, along with carefully selected passages from the Bible, to inculcate a young blind woman with an idealized view of human relations. Again the symphony takes on religious connotations, this time prelapsarian, in that it is taken to depict "non point le monde tel qu'il était, mais bien tel qu'il aurait pu être, qu'il pourrait être sans le mal et sans le péché" (not the world as it was, but as it could have been, as it could be without evil and without sin).[58] This perfect world leads to tragedy, however, when the young woman's sight is restored by an operation. She cannot accept the gulf between reality and her *Pastoral*-inspired imaginings and shortly thereafter commits suicide.

To dismiss these readings as misreadings would ignore the very different and complex motivations behind them, but the *Pastoral's* failure to tell a heroic story need not be taken to mean that it tells no human story at all. Like the pastoral writings of Klopstock or Goethe, it dramatizes fundamentally human concerns about morality and about the effect of time's passage on the paradises, real or imagined, that

---

[57] Burnham argues that many of the most influential nineteenth- and twentieth-century criteria for interpreting and evaluating instrumental music had their origins in analyses by A. B. Marx, Schenker, and other theorists of Beethoven's Fifth Symphony and other heroic-style works (*Beethoven Hero*, 66–111).

[58] André Gide, *La Symphonie pastorale*, ed. Claude Martin (Paris: Lettres modernes, 1970), 46.

people value. To recognize that the symphony addresses such concerns serves to illuminate the work, but also – perhaps more importantly – it urges us to reconsider the very notion of the "human element" in Beethoven's music. Not all humans are heroes, and the *Pastoral* Symphony reminds us that Beethoven, too, told more than just heroic stories. His vision extends beyond individual to collective experience, and beyond active undertakings such as are suggested by the *Eroica* (or imputed to the *Pastoral* by readers from Mosengeil to the modernists) to the comparatively passive acceptance of events both earthly and divine. Humanity cannot be circumscribed by a single metaphor.

5

Making memories: symphonies of war, death, and celebration

The *Eroica* Symphony has a subtitle at once similar to the *Pastoral*'s "memory of country life" and more immediate in its connotations: *composta per festiggiare il souvenire di un grand Uomo* (composed to celebrate the memory of a great man). More often than country life, great men were memorialized throughout the French Revolution and Napoleonic Wars in funerals, festivals, concerts, theater presentations, and art exhibits, which remembered their deeds and deaths and a great deal else besides, most notably the battles fought and the treaties signed by Europe's warring parties.[1] Such occasions inspired works in all media, some seeking to reenact events and others aspiring to be, in Schiller's words, "Nicht unwert des erhabenen Moments / Der Zeit, in dem wir strebend uns bewegen" (not unworthy of the sublime moment in time in which we act and strive):[2] a symphony like the *Eroica*, originally to have been entitled "Bonaparte," or a historical play like Schiller's *Wallenstein* idealized the age and its actors while paintings or stagings of battles set down its history.[3] Instrumental music pursued both aims, assuming

---

[1] On memorial concerts see the sources cited below concerning individual events. Among numerous studies of related memorial occasions, most useful have been Conrad L. Donakowski, *A Muse for the Masses: Ritual and Music in an Age of Democratic Revolution 1770–1870* (Chicago: University of Chicago Press, 1972), 33–53; Mona Ozouf, *Festivals and the French Revolution*, trans. Alan Sheridan (Cambridge, MA: Harvard University Press, 1988); Jean-Louis Jam, "Marie-Joseph Chénier and François-Joseph Gossec: Two Artists in the Service of Revolutionary Propaganda," in Malcolm Boyd, ed., *Music and the French Revolution* (Cambridge: Cambridge University Press, 1992), 221–35; Gillian Russell, *The Theatres of War: Performance, Politics, and Society, 1793–1815* (Oxford: Clarendon Press, 1995); Christopher Clark, "The Wars of Liberation in Prussian Memory: Reflections on the Memorialization of War in Early Nineteenth-Century Germany," *Journal of Modern History* 68 (1996): 550–76; and Christopher Prendergast, *Napoleon and History Painting: Antoine-Jean Gros's "La Bataille d'Eylau"* (Oxford: Clarendon Press, 1997).

[2] Schiller, "Prolog" to *Wallenstein* (1799), lines 55–56; quoted from *Sämtliche Werke*, IV, ed. Jochen Golz (Berlin: Aufbau, 1984), 8.

[3] Beethoven's intention of entitling the *Eroica* "Bonaparte," his subsequent change of heart, and the symphony's relationship to Napoleon generally are extensively

roles previously reserved for opera and sacred vocal music as it marked battlefield victories and the deaths of rulers, or spoke to a culture of war in "military" symphonies. What Beethoven's subtitle reiterated was the common goal of such works to put people and events into the past and thereby to shape understanding: as the political and social transformations after 1789 passed into memory, there to help interpret them was the discriminating hand of artistic representation.

Orchestral works remember both the specific and the ideal and also both the individual and the communal, categories that frequently but not always align with the first pair. The *Eroica*, at least in its first movement, and some other symphonies on political topics project single protagonists onto a plane of myth, transforming earthly biographies into the narratives of overcoming and self-fulfillment whose representation in the *Eroica* has been so often discussed. Less familiar are the collective effort and emotion apotheosized by musical reenactments of battles, funerals, or victory celebrations, which belonged to a populist strain of wartime rhetoric that emphasized less the achievements of military or political leaders than those of regular soldiers, or citizens in the newly-minted "imagined communities" of the nations.[4] Such works helped construct the shared memories on which communal identities depend,[5] showing a united populace – or at least, a society of concert-goers who believed in the existence of such a thing – what it had accomplished. To the modern listener they also demonstrate intimate links between memory, public performance, and movement. Much like Dittersdof in the *Metamorphoses*, composers gave expression to political subjects chiefly by implying physical actions, the marching of soldiers or the dancing and singing of victors. As Paul Connerton has written of social memories in general, such "bodily practices ... contain a measure of insurance against the process of cumulative questioning entailed in all discursive practices ... Every group ... will entrust to bodily automatisms the values and categories which they are most anxious to conserve."[6] So amorphous a community as the early nineteenth-century "nation" lacked the names, titles, and private possessions that stood for the past

discussed in Geck and Schleuning, *"Geschrieben auf Bonaparte,"* 15–189; Carl Dahlhaus, *Beethoven: Approaches to his Music*, trans. Mary Whittall (Oxford: Clarendon Press, 1991), 19–30; Solomon, *Beethoven*, 173–85; and Sipe, *Beethoven: "Eroica Symphony,"* 30–53.

[4] The term is from Benedict Anderson's classic study, *Imagined Communities: Reflections on the Origin and Spread of Nationalism*, 2nd rev. edn. (London: Verso, 1991).

[5] John R. Gillis, "Memory and Identity: The History of a Relationship," in Gillis, ed., *Commemorations: The Politics of National Identity* (Princeton: Princeton University Press, 1994), 3–4.

[6] Paul Connerton, *How Societies Remember* (Cambridge: Cambridge University Press, 1989), 102.

in aristocratic families,[7] to say nothing of written histories; memories had instead to be enacted publicly and on the body. To represent people marching or dancing was to show a society perpetuating its self-image through the remembered physical synchrony of its members.

Symphonies on politically related subjects repay consideration of their somatic memory-making, for it influences not only the most material and communal examples but the whole repertory: even the *Eroica*, which begins with such exemplary heroic individualism, ends with its own tribute to the governing rhythm of eighteenth- and early nineteenth-century social celebration, the contradance. Heroes and societies do not so much oppose one another as engage in dialogue, sometimes in one and the same work. Symphonies carried on the debate of a political culture itself divided over who and how many should be remembered.

The war of soldiers

Instrumental music's most direct response to current events, its answer to the paintings and dramas and odes that told of recent military victories, was the battle piece. Composers had depicted battles since the Renaissance, but the later eighteenth century brought the remarkable success of Franz Kotzwara's *Battle of Prague* (pub. c. 1785–88), which spread across Europe and the United States in multiple editions and undoubtedly helped inspire the more than 150 similar compositions produced after 1789.[8] About half of these advertise themselves as representations of specific engagements – Trafalgar, Austerlitz, Waterloo – while the rest are simply called "battle" even where they are known to have been written with particular events in mind: the orchestral *La Bataille* (1789) of Franz Christoph Neubauer was conceived as a depiction of the Austrian victory at Martinesti but publicized as such only in some sources.[9] With hundreds of engagements laying claim to the public imagination, composers and publishers undoubtedly hoped to broaden the appeal of their works by making them appropriate to multiple occasions, and similar considerations probably account for the relatively small number of orchestral battles, some sixteen of which only seven were published (see Appendix 3e, pp. 301–02 below); the

---

[7] Maurice Halbwachs, *On Collective Memory*, trans. and ed. by Lewis A. Coser (Chicago: University of Chicago Press, 1992), 123–28.

[8] The best account of this tradition is Schulin, *Musikalische Schlachtengemälde*. RISM A/I lists forty-one editions of Kotzwara's work.

[9] Ernst Ludwig Gerber, *Historisch-biographisches Lexikon der Tonkünstler*, 2 vols. (Leipzig, 1790–92), II: col. 20, reports that Neubauer intended to commemorate Martinesti, which agrees with the descriptions accompanying a set of manuscript orchestral parts (now lost) as well as the published arrangement for keyboard. The two orchestral editions, however, are entitled only *La Bataille* (see Appendix 1, p. 274 below).

expense of printing orchestral parts and even the effort of composing for large ensemble would have been difficult to justify when a
piece could so quickly become outdated. Yet none of this detracts from
the immediacy of the genre; however titled, battle pieces were meant
to remember recent history and were performed, at least in the case
of the symphonies, at concerts commemorating specific engagements.
Anchoring them further in current affairs, the performances sometimes
raised money for those most affected by the fighting, the wounded and
widowed.[10]

Given this context, it is surprising at first to find that battle pieces
give so little weight to historical accuracy. To be sure, keyboard or
chamber works sometimes include detailed narratives of the fighting and even, in one case, a map, but Karin Schulin shows that the
relationship between actual events and musical representation rarely
amounts to more than the use of appropriate marches and songs to identify the combatants.[11] Otherwise composers boil down even the most
complicated engagements to three or four stages found already in the
Battle of Prague: marches and other preparations, fighting, laments for
the dead and wounded, and celebration (Example 5.1). Orchestral battles
are especially prone to simplification as their stories had to be followed
primarily by ear. Even if aided by printed or declaimed programs, concert audiences unlike the performers of battles for keyboard or chamber
ensemble did not have the luxury of referring to a score marked up
with explanations, the consequence of which is that composers rely
heavily on conventionalized and easily understood scenes. They in
turn produce some impossibly straightforward narratives. The battle of
Leipzig was fought on several fronts over two days by Austrian, French,
Prussian, Saxon, and Russian troops among others, but for his com-
memorative *Schlacht-Symphonie* Reichardt wrote simply a march, a sup-
plicatory chorale, a one-movement battle, a thanksgiving chorale, and
another march (Example 5.1a). All the confusion is contained by an arch
form even more symmetrical than the movement layout would suggest: the battle movement divides into an exposition and recapitulation,
between which lies, as a sort of keystone of the keystone, a brief passage in minor expressing the sorrows of the wounded. The line of the
architecture smoothes out even the hardest bump in the story.

---

[10] Examples include the 1813 premieres of *Wellington's Victory*, as reported in the *Wiener
allgemeine musikalische Zeitung* 1 (1813), repr. in Kunze, *Ludwig van Beethoven: Die Werke
im Spiegel seiner Zeit*, 269; and of Peter von Winter's *Schlacht-Sinfonie*, *AmZ* 16 (1814):
cols. 74–76. A "militair[ische] Symphonie" of Friedrich Witt, probably the *Sinfonie turque*
listed in Appendix 1, was performed at a benefit for volunteers in Frankfurt (*AmZ* 17
[1815]: col. 437).

[11] Schulin, *Musikalische Schlachtengemälde*, 176–79. The work with map is *The Battle of Belle
Alliance* by Johnson (first name unknown), facsimile in ibid., 362.

Example 5.1 Battle symphonies

a. Reichardt, *Schlacht Symphonie* (1814)	**March**	**Chorale** • Jesus, meine Zuversicht	**Battle**	**Chorale** • Nun danket alle Gott	**March**

b. Beethoven, *Wellingtons Sieg*, Op. 91 (1813)	**Marches** • "Rule Britannia" • "Marlborough" (each preceded by drum & trumpet signals)	**Battle** • trumpet signals • *Allegro* (4/4) • *Meno allegro* (3/8) • *Sturmmarsch* (¢) • *Presto* (¢) • "Marlborough" reprise (*Andante*)	**Victory/Song** • Intrada • *Allegro con brio* (march-like) • "God Save the King" (*Andante grazioso*) • Tempo I • "God Save the King" (*Tempo di minuetto moderato*) • Fugato (based on "God Save the King")

c. Neubauer, *La Bataille* (1789)	**Preliminaries** • Le Matin • Allarme au camp • Harangue aux Guerriers	**March**	**Battle**	**March** • Retour a la camp	**Victory** • Celebration de la victoire

Reichardt and his contemporaries could simplify so drastically because musical unlike pictorial or dramatic memorials sought to embody more than to recount the events on the field. Even their marches go beyond identifying armies or suggesting maneuvers, although those functions are important in a work like Reichardt's or like Beethoven's *Wellington's Victory*, with its English and French marches at the beginning and "Sturmmarsch" (double-time attack) midway through (Example 5.1b). Yet equally important is the invocation of a military and social ideal of synchronized motion. Marching and other forms of rhythmic drill had been the foundation of military discipline since their introduction in the 1590s, the means by which soldiers of diverse origins learned to coordinate their efforts and to develop *esprit de corps*.[12] Those tasks became more urgent as the ranks of post-revolutionary armies swelled with draftees and volunteers,[13] and it was according to routines that broke each action down into a series of movements, performed to a beat, that the inexperienced learned how to walk, run, fire muskets, and handle pikes together. An American military manual of the period (based on British practice) goes so far as to explain how to make a metronome from a musket ball and a piece of string, to ensure that each exercise is done in the correct tempo.[14] Marches in battle symphonies call up the spectacle or, for those who had experienced it, the feeling of bodies "keeping together in time" (McNeill), of soldiers subordinating their personal interests to the functioning of the whole. Looking ahead for a moment to the scenes of celebration with which the works end, we shall see that their dances and songs evoke similar associations from contexts beyond the army. When François Devienne quotes "Ça ira" and "La Carmagnole" at the end of his *Bataille de Gemmapp* (c. 1794), these most popular of the French revolutionary tunes recall the communal performances around Liberty Trees and elsewhere that helped forge the new political communities of the republic.[15] Likewise the chorales in Reichardt's *Schlacht-Symphonie*, or "God Save the King" in *Wellington's Victory* and the *Grande Bataille* (1810) of Ferdinand Hauff, or the patriotic strophes in Peter von Winter's *Schlacht-Sinfonie* (1813; performed by an actual chorus, in this case) – all refer to performances on the French model conducted elsewhere in Europe at concerts and

---

[12] William H. McNeill, *Keeping Together in Time: Dance and Drill in Human History* (Cambridge, MA: Harvard University Press, 1995), 3–11.

[13] Ibid., 136.

[14] Edward Gillespy, *The Military Instructor, or, New System of European Exercise and Drill as Now Practised by the British Army According to General Dundas* (Boston, 1809), 9.

[15] Ozouf, *Festivals and the French Revolution*, 172; McNeill, *Keeping Together in Time*, 59–60; Jean Mongrédien, *French Music from the Enlightenment to Romanticism, 1789–1830*, trans. Sylvain Frémaux (Portland: Amadeus, 1996), 39–45.

Example 5.2a   Beethoven, *Wellington's Victory*, mm. 74–77

* = French Cannon
Ü = English Cannon

other public occasions.[16] The song in the battle symphony complements the image of armies marching with the equally physical spectacle of a society breathing and enunciating in unison.

Representations of fighting appeal similarly to the physical, in the first instance by undermining the rhythmic unity of marches and songs. In *Wellington's Victory*, the battle begins with superimposed triplets and sixteenth notes and with unsettling syncopations on the second beat of each measure (Example 5.2a). As time goes on, the cannons and muskets enter at increasingly unpredictable intervals, and even the strongest bastion of stability, the repeated two-measure unit, breaks down sporadically

---

[16] On the German states see Hanslick, *Geschichte des Concertwesens in Wien*, I: 170–84; and the *AmZ* 16 (1814): cols. 329–30, 356, 695; 17 (1815): cols. 437, 487–90, 507; and 18 (1816): col. 422. On London see Russell, *The Theatres of War*, 65–66; and Landon, *Haydn*, III: 259–61.

Example 5.2b   Beethoven, *Wellington's Victory*, mm. 162–77

into one-measure fragments (e.g., mm. 86–89). With the metric certainty of the preceding marches vanishes also their regular proportions and shape: "Marlborough," the march used by Beethoven to identify the French army, comprises two statements of an eight-measure theme separated by a four-measure interlude, with the theme itself divided into four-measure phrases and two-measure groups all based on the same melodic motive and ending on tonic chords. Not every march is so perfectly predictable, but none departs very far from the orderliness of four- and eight-measure phrases, tonic and dominant harmonies, statements balanced by counterstatements – all of which then collapses in battle. Rent by competing note values and metric emphases, the two-measure

195

units of Beethoven's battle have little in common with the half-phrases of "Marlborough," and they also build no larger shape but simply follow one after the next in a sequence with no obvious beginning or end. The bass line pulls steadily downward but does not arrive at its destination in the way that a march arrives at the end of a phrase; the ear may remember a C minor stage toward the beginning of the sequence as adumbrating the eventual pause there (mm. 82–85), but with the passage beginning in B major and referring to numerous additional keys along the way, there is little way of knowing in advance where it will end.[17] Adding to the confusion, the entire descent is traversed without caesura or articulation, the very antithesis of a song or march in which regular pauses mark off sections or allow for breathing.

The sheer loudness of the movement, marked *fortissimo* throughout and broken only occasionally by reductions in texture, extends its physicality into another dimension. All symphonic battles are comparably raucous, a result not only of dynamics but also of scoring. Even where they do not call for two orchestras, as in the pre-revolutionary works by Johann Friedrich Klöffler and Georg Druschetzky, composers consistently require oversized ensembles: Devienne uses trombones and piccolo, familiar in sacred and dramatic music by 1794 but not in symphonies; Beethoven scores for six trumpets (two offstage), trombones, and two complete wind bands; and everyone uses percussion, sometimes in great quantities as in *Wellington's Victory* where the score calls for a "Turkish" battery of bass drum, triangle, and cymbals along with side drums, ratchets (for musket fire), and two more bass drums specified as "die größten Gattungen ... welche man gewöhnlich in den Theatern braucht, um einen Donnerschlag zu bewirken" (the largest variety ... which are generally used in theaters to produce a thunderclap).[18] The rest of the orchestra, the instructions continue, "muß natürlicherweise verhältnißmäßig so stark als möglich besetzt werden; je größer der Saal, desto stärker die Besetzung" (must naturally comprise as many members as possible; the bigger the room, the larger the ensemble): *Wellington's Victory* was premiered by an orchestra of over 100 players; Winter's *Schlacht-Sinfonie,* by a combined orchestra and chorus numbering 300.[19] Volume tried to approximate what was commonly understood to be the overwhelming noise of battle, especially the roar of artillery, and consequently to produce the related physiological

---

[17] Albrecht Riethmüller likens the "unpredictable, unstable, widely modulating harmonic unfolding" of Beethoven's battle to a fantasy ("*Wellingtons Sieg* op. 91," in Riethmüller et al., eds., *Beethoven: Interpretationen seiner Werke*, II: 41).

[18] From the foreword to the first edition, repr. in *Beethoven: Werke* (Munich: Henle, 1961–), II/1: 124.

[19] Kunze, *Ludwig van Beethoven*, 268; *AmZ* 16 (1814): col. 75.

effects. Goethe attributed the experience of "cannon fever" entirely to aural stimuli:

It seemed as though I were in a very hot place, and thoroughly permeated by that same heat, so that I felt completely at one with the element in which I found myself. My eyes lost nothing of their strength or clarity of vision, yet it was as though the world had a certain reddish brown tone, which made my own condition, as well as the objects around me, still more ominous ... [I]t is still remarkable how whatever causes such terrible anxiety is conveyed to us solely through our sense of hearing; for it is the thunder of the cannon, and the howling, whistling and blasting of cannon balls through the air that is actually the cause of these sensations.[20]

A half-century earlier Edmund Burke used cannon fire as an example of "excessive loudness [which] alone is sufficient to overpower the soul, to suspend its action, and to fill it with terror": he would have diagnosed Goethe's fever as a result of confronting the sublime.[21] With symphonies in general already connected with sublimity, high-volume battle symphonies would have had little trouble evoking similar associations, and indeed even the second movement of Haydn's *Military Symphony*, not a battle but a march with brief interludes suggesting violence, inspired one writer to describe "the hellish roar of war increas[ing] to a climax of horrid sublimity!"[22] Another pointed specifically to the "discordant, grating, and offensive" sound of the cymbals, whose ear-splitting crash and saturation of pitch space might be thought of as a synecdoche for the registral, timbral, and dynamic power of the battle orchestra as a whole.[23]

Sublimity looms out of rhythm as well, both within the measure and beyond. To the tremolo, rapid scales, syncopations, and polyrhythms with which all musical battles obscure beat and meter are added larger-scale uncertainties caused by irregular groupings or unpredictable sequences of events. In the second section of Beethoven's battle (Meno

---

[20] Goethe, *Campaign in France 1792*, trans. Thomas P. Saine, in Saine and Jeffrey L. Sammons, eds., *Goethe's Collected Works*, vol. V (New York: Suhrkamp, 1987), 651–52. Portions of this passage as well as Burke's response to the sounds of war (see next note) are discussed in Thomas Röder, "Beethovens Sieg über die Schlachtenmusik: Opus 91 und die Tradition der Battaglia," in Helga Lühning and Sieghard Brandenburg, eds., *Beethoven zwischen Revolution und Restauration* (Bonn: Beethoven-Haus, 1989), 241–42.

[21] Edmund Burke, *A Philosophical Enquiry into the Origin of our Ideas of the Sublime and Beautiful* (London, 1757), ed. James Boulton (London: Routledge and Kegan Paul, 1958), 82.

[22] *Morning Chronicle* 7 April 1794; quoted in Landon, *Haydn*, III: 247.

[23] *Morning Chronicle* 5 May 1794; quoted in Landon, *Haydn*, III: 250–51 (see also p. 233 below). On this and the preceding quotation see also A. Peter Brown, "The Sublime, The Beautiful, and the Ornamental: English Aesthetic Currents and Haydn's London Symphonies," in Biba and Jones, eds., *Studies in Music History Presented to H. C. Robbins Landon*, 55.

allegro), the strings take up triple-meter galloping figures while trumpets on each side sound cavalry signals, the French in C (the key of "Marlborough") and the English in E♭ (the key of their march, "Rule Britannia"). They meet in a collision whose rhythm is not particularly unsettling, in and of itself – the trumpets trade signals first at four-, then at one-, then again at four-measure intervals – but whose seeming regularity is fractured by the repeated juxtaposition of the two tonalities without transition (Example 5.2b, p. 195). "The words burst forth without connectives, pour out, as it were, and the speaker himself cannot keep up with them. 'Shield on shield' – says Xenophon – 'they were pushing, fighting, killing, dying.' "[24] In the famous treatise on sublimity ascribed to Longinus, the author is describing the figure of asyndeton, which has parallels in similarly unprepared leaps between harmonic centers in many battle symphonies. To burden such passages with the niceties of modulation would hinder what Longinus calls the "impression of actuality" generated by images piling one upon the next with no evident logic. The regularity of rhythm in *Wellington's Victory* paradoxically enhances the effect, setting boundaries within which the lurches between tonalities seem all the more shocking.

Unpredictability typifies the order of events on the largest scale as well, whether the battle falls into several sections, like Beethoven's, or remains in a single tempo and meter throughout. In the first instance listeners have little chance of knowing what will happen next. Both *Wellington's Victory* and Pierre Jean de Volder's *La Bataille d'Jena* (1806) have cavalry charges, exchanges of cannon fire, and quick-time marches, but the two composers order and treat the components differently: Beethoven puts the cavalry (Meno allegro) before the march (*Sturmmarsch*) where Volder does the reverse, and Beethoven sets each action in a single section while Volder subdivides them into episodes in different tempos and meters. Single-tempo battles are not much more consistent despite a common indebtedness to sonata and binary forms. All three of Druschetzky's have discernible expositions, developments, and recapitulations, but the musical ideas are heard in a new order in the recapitulation and typically interrupted by new passages, including, in one case (the *Pataglia* Powley C13), an electrifying asyndetic plunge to the flatted sixth. In addition, the parts of the form are no better articulated than the measure groupings at the beginning of *Wellington's Victory*. There is no caesura in any of the movements, which roll on like the run-on sentences with which Horace sought to capture the sublimity of Pindar, or Sulzer the continuity of the "symphony style," or Fischer and Mosengeil the exalted

---

[24] *On the Sublime*, ascribed to Longinus, trans. by G. M. A. Grube as *On Great Writing* (Indianapolis: Bobbs-Merrill, 1957), 31.

chaos of the *Pastoral* Symphony storm.[25] Other sonata-based movements demarcate their sections more traditionally, notably Winter's
and Reichardt's, but different elements serve to thwart expectation:
Winter's clearly prepared recapitulation, for instance, begins in E
rather than the tonic C and thereafter introduces a previously unheard march to signal the final push against Napoleon at Leipzig.
The hallmark of battle music remains disorder in the large as in the
small.

The relationship between music and audience does not go unaffected.
If marches and songs invite participation – listeners might imagine
themselves marching or, as surely happened at some performances,
actually sing along with "God Save the King" and other familiar
melodies – battle music seeks to "overpower the soul" by means of
volume and irregularity. As Burke wrote:

when at any time I have waited very earnestly for some sound, that returned
at intervals, (as the successive firing of cannon) though I fully expected the
return of the sound, when it came, it always made me start a little; the ear-drum
suffered a convulsion, and the whole body consented with it. The tension of the
part thus increasing at every blow, by the united forces of the stroke itself, the
expectation, and the surprise, it is worked up to such a pitch as to be capable of
the sublime; it is brought just to the verge of pain.[26]

Any of the irregular movements of battle music, large or small, might
be thought to administer the half-unexpected impulses Burke describes,
and to the discomfort they produce must be added a sense of isolation
that comes with the demise of rhythmic synchrony: no longer an implied
member of a community, the listener becomes individually vulnerable
to the uncertainties of warfare. Visual aspects of the performance would
have reinforced the message, as listeners watched an orchestra initially
bound by uniformity (eighteenth-century observers regularly compared
well-disciplined orchestras to armies[27]) break down into constituent sections or even, in the percussion and the winds, into individual players.
Arms, fingers, and diaphragms all moving at different times, the musicians themselves enacted the confusion of soldiers on the field.

The spectacle of an orchestra "at war" would have enhanced one last
physical quality of musical battles, their embodiment of extreme effort.
The greatest military theorist of the era, Carl von Clausewitz, considered
physical exertion to be constitutive of the "climate of war," emphasizing

---

[25] See p. 152 above as well as Waldvogel, "The Eighteenth-Century Esthetics of the
Sublime," 160–66.

[26] Burke, *Enquiry*, 140.

[27] John Spitzer, "Metaphors of the Orchestra – The Orchestra as a Metaphor," *Musical
Quarterly* 80 (1996): 242–45.

that a victorious commander must persevere against the exhaustion of soldiers expending their energy against climate and terrain as well as the enemy.[28] He ranks danger, uncertainty, and chance as equally important, but where they have parallels in musical volume and disorder, exertion finds its correlate in technique. Performers of orchestral battles have to negotiate difficult passages at high speed and to play loudly for extended periods, often in extreme registers. Wind players have to sustain long tones, and, perhaps most symbolic, violinists and violists nearly always have to execute tremolo, the very picture of incessant muscular contraction and extension. Such an orchestra's *fortissimos* signify the noise of war but also the ensemble's own sweat, the triumph of will over matter that it, like an army, must achieve in order to "win" the "engagement." In the roaring of violence is heard also the pounding of hearts, the gasping of lungs, the straining of bodies under duress.

The war of heroes

Missing from most battle symphonies are the effects of violence. "Suddenly someone you know is wounded, then a shell falls among the staff. You notice that some of the officers act a little oddly; you yourself are not as steady and collected as you were: even the bravest can become slightly distracted . . . For a final shock, the sight of men being killed and mutilated moves our pounding hearts to awe and pity."[29] *Wellington's Victory* represents confusion but never the distraction that Clausewitz describes; however sublimely disordered, the fighting is uninterrupted and decisive and leaves no time for pity. Battle symphonies before 1800 often had lamentation movements, but by 1813 those had disappeared along with everything else that might impede the rush to victory. Even the earlier works, moreover, put sorrow into separate movements and rarely allowed it a role in the fighting itself. The combatants and the listeners who were invited to identify with them fought unencumbered by sadness, confusion, or fear.

When emotional nuance was introduced it complicated both the plots and the social meanings of the battle piece. The best example is Neubauer's *Bataille* for the Austrian victory over the Turks at Martinesti, signs of whose unusual aspirations appear already in the first movement, a relaxed pastoral entitled "Le Matin" (see Example 5.1c for an overview). While it has parallels elsewhere, in the sunrises beginning Volder's work and most particularly in the pastoral Andantes beginning

---

[28] Carl von Clausewitz, *On War* (1832), trans. and ed. Michael Howard and Peter Paret (Princeton: Princeton University Press, 1976), 115–16.
[29] Ibid., 113.

Example 5.3   Neubauer, *La Bataille*, "Le Matin," mm. 36–45

all three of Druschetzky's, the dawn before battle here expands into a regular Golden Age: in the rhythm of a slow minuet, a reference borne out by eight-measure phrasing and a rounded binary form typical of dance, a profusion of idyllic signatures conjures a beautiful retreat (Example 5.3 shows the reprise; elsewhere there are woodwinds in thirds, drones [mm. 21–24], middle-register murmuring [mm. 56–60], and even an apparent bird call in the flute [mm. 30–33]). The difference from beginning with a march, as so many battle pieces do, could not be more stark; the violence, when it comes, seems to disrupt not only the coordinated movements of the army but also a prelapsarian state of innocence, so that the real-life taking up of arms becomes an action of mythic significance, a descent from paradise into the Iron Age. The following movement has similar connotations. The Austrian army at Martinesti was led by General Coburg, celebrated as a hero in several tributes including a dance by Mozart (see p. 230 below). Neubauer gives him a "Harangue aux guerriers" for solo bassoon, not his most effective movement in its mixture of heroic dotted rhythms and triadic figures with offbeat pizzicati reminiscent of a serenade, but one that provides a grand protagonist to match the mythic locale. Recent history begins to sound like epic.

After a series of marches, the battle plays out the elevated tone of the opening movements in a dialectic between action and hesitation. The movement is in an adapted sonata form (exposition, marches, and

Example 5.4a   Neubauer, *La Bataille*, mm. 1–9

combined development/recapitulation), and it begins with the usual vigor: to the strains of tremolo, flying scales, brass fanfares, and a continuous roar in the bass drum and timpani,[30] two paragraphs crescendo from *piano* to *forte* without pause or caesura but for the return to *piano* following the crest of the first crescendo (Example 5.4a). Anticipation builds as the harmony turns toward the dominant, at which point the harmonic rhythm doubles to two changes per measure and the basses, having thus far played only chord roots, begin moving in

---

[30] According to Gerber, at the premiere Neubauer himself "soll dabei die Pauken auf eine noch nie gehörte originelle Art selbst schlagen" (is supposed [to have] played the timpani in an original manner, never heard before); *Historisch-biographisches Lexikon* II: col. 20.

counterpoint with the first violins (Example 5.4b). A climax seems imminent, but nothing from the more standard run of battle pieces could predict that the outer voices, after hovering between the dominant and its dominant for three measures, would introduce the parallel minor of the dominant, the C♮ in the upper line representing the first altered pitch in the movement other than the leading tone to the dominant (m. 35). Nor is there much precedent for the previously headlong forward motion giving way to an exchange between the violins and basses, who attack every other downbeat, and the winds and percussion, who answer on the second beats. With the inner strings adding an

Example 5.4b   Neubauer, *La Bataille*, mm. 31–57

(*cont.*)

Example 5.4b (*cont.*)

accompaniment of tense syncopations, the episode sounds in certain respects like the beginning of the battle in *Wellington's Victory*, but the diminuendo across each two-measure segment lowers the tension, and once C♮ has fallen back to B and the harmony returned to V/V, the texture unravels further until only the woodwinds and strings are left dialoguing on plaintive half-steps (mm. 43–46). Cannons and hurrying bodies are replaced by the sound of voices, and boldness by a note of hesitation, the half-steps moving in such small increments as to suggest that each move must be tested before taken. They hold off a cadence as well. The upper line rises to F♮ but falls back again to A minor (mm. 46–49), and only after both C♮ and F♮ are regained over successive diminished seventh chords does the orchestra reach the dominant proper (mm. 51–55). An inverted arch has been inscribed, with its nadir the plaintive *piano* and its climax the climb back to *fortissimo*, which is made all the more powerful by the chain of diminished sevenths (vii/E, vii/A) and by the transformation of the keening half-steps into a motive whose five eighth notes lunge forward across the bar lines into the second beats (mm. 51–54). Neubauer's soldiers are cautious and brave by turn, not only here but in the following measures where the *fortissimo* breaks down again on A minor and opens the way for a second dialogue in half-steps followed by a second triumphant return to action.

The shifts in emotional register continue throughout the movement and intensify the action, making each successive *fortissimo* seem all the more hurried and confused and recalling in certain respects the way in which battles unfold in epic or historical drama. Minor keys, diminished sevenths, motion by half-step, and emphasis on the "vocal" woodwinds figure in most musical laments of this period, evoking the feelings of those in mourning or, in military contexts, the sufferings of the wounded. Neubauer probably wants to trigger both associations, to suggest how the cries of the fallen awaken pity or fear in the survivors and, in turn, cause them to hesitate or reflect; his soldiers act like the characters in Homer and Shakespeare, whose battlefield deeds are always interspersed with reflections, farewells, and elegies, most of them followed by renewed calls to action. Heroes gain stature at such moments by showing the inner strength that enables them to persevere, and on a more general level the battle becomes more humanly comprehensible as it breaks down into individual dramas, sometimes, as in Shakespeare, involving more than just the noble protagonists. Given the precedent of Coburg's "Harangue," Neubauer's interludes might well suggest the Field Marshal absorbing his losses and pressing onward, overcoming inertia like one of Clausewitz's commanders. But it seems equally likely that one is getting a glimpse of his toiling fighters, whose suffering balances the mythic overtones of the opening movements: represented as destroying a Golden Age, the battle cannot proceed without its ill effects on everyone being noted.

Exploring the darker aspects of violence has a further consequence best seen when *La Bataille* is compared with its most closely related contemporary, the *Grande Sinfonie caractéristique pour la paix avec la République françoise* (1797) of Paul Wranitzky (see frontispiece). This is not a battle piece per se but a history of events leading up to the Treaty of Campo Formio, signed by Napoleon and Emperor Franz of Austria in October 1797 (Example 5.5). It was a difficult occasion for a Viennese composer to celebrate given that Austria had lost several engagements to the French and, by the terms of the treaty, conceded long-held territories in Italy

205

Example 5.5   Paul Wranitzky, *Grande Sinfonie caractéristique pour la paix avec la République françoise*

No. I: The Revolution. English March. March of the Austrians and Prussians.

Andante maestoso (Cm) – Allegro molto (Cm)
Slow introduction – Sonata form with marches
interpolated

No. II: The destiny and death of Louis XVI. Funeral march.

Adagio affettuoso (E♭-Cm-E♭)
Ternary form with funeral march as middle section

No. III: English March. March of the Allies. Confusion of a battle.

Tempo di Marcia movible (C) – Allegro (C)
Two binary-form marches followed by battle

No. IV: Peace negotiations. Cries of joy for the restoration of peace.

Andante grazioso (G) – Allegro vivace (C)
Slow introduction – Sonata form

and west of the Rhine.[31] Wranitzky not surprisingly exercised considerable poetic license, treating each of his chosen subjects from a distinctly Habsburgian perspective. The otherwise stormy first movement, representing the Revolution, is interrupted by Austrian and Prussian marches, a presumed reference to their 1792 invasion of France (during which Goethe experienced his cannon fever) that does not, however, recognize the catastrophic defeat of that campaign. Similarly in the finale, the celebration of peace, further reference to the Austrian march tends to forget that the imperial army had given little reason to rejoice. The "Tumulte d'une bataille" omits all mention of the enemy, quoting only Austrian, Prussian, and English marches before plunging into action, and the slow movement mourns Louis XVI, uncle by marriage to Emperor Franz, with a heroic funeral march embedded within an apotheosizing Adagio affettuoso. This was history as the Habsburgs might have liked to remember it, a fantasy of royal martyrdom and military redemption.

The resulting work may seem the very opposite of Neubauer's, an attempt to whitewash defeat where the other cast shadows over victory, but in fact they have much in common. Wranitzky also conjures an

---

[31] A concise account of the Austrian conflict with Napoleon is Ingrao, *The Habsburg Monarchy*, 220–42; on Campo Formio see 226–28.

idyll with a substantial slow introduction in siciliano rhythm preceding the finale: the paradise of neoclassicism returns, this time elevating the "Négociations de paix" to the status of myth. The slow movement exalts an individual hero, more effectively than Neubauer's "Harangue" in that there is no dissonance between the musical topics and the intended mixture of tragedy and nostalgia. Most obviously, Wranitzky probes the emotional complexities of violence, particularly in his "Revolution" where an adapted sonata form traces affective arches similar to Neubauer's but in the opposite direction. After a foreboding slow introduction, the first group and transition represent action at its most tortured, the antithesis of the brilliant scales and arpeggios with which Neubauer begins. The governing tonality is C minor and the texture polyphony, sometimes imitative but more often free, with independent ideas superimposed: both possibilities are instanced in the first few measures, whose competing figures in the bass and treble vividly evoke antagonists struggling for dominance (Example 5.6a). The brighter aspects of militarism shine forth only later, in homophonic march tunes heard first in the relative major and then, in an unusual twist toward the end of the exposition, in the parallel major (Example 5.6b). To call these passages contrasting would be an understatement, particularly in the second case where, apart from the premature introduction of the tonic parallel (there follows a transition to the dominant and a repeat sign, so that the entire succession is heard twice), the march is scored for *Harmonie* alone and contained in its own binary form. Yet Wranitzky fits it into his musical plot no less securely than Neubauer does his sorrowful interludes; the march melody falls from $\hat{6}$ to the leading tone, recalling the equivalent and ubiquitous descents that, along with the rhythmic figure of an eighth followed by two sixteenths, integrate the motivic web of the surrounding minor-key music (e.g., Example 5.6a, mm. 22–23). The composer probably planned all along to transform revolutionary confusion into military order, an appropriate nod to Habsburg sensibilities. On the other hand, while he does not emphasize Europe's failure to quell the Revolution, he does let all the marches disappear back into gloom, even the C major march which does not return in the recapitulation where its tonality would more easily fit. Like Neubauer but with poles reversed, he completes a journey from one emotional plane to the other and back.

Alternating moods lend both symphonies an epic quality that in turn affects their attitudes toward individual and communal endeavor. It is not simply that both composers devote movements to leaders as well as to soldiers and to the celebrants depicted in their happy contradance finales. They also represent themselves. The *Grande Sinfonie caractéristique* so obviously revises history that it cannot help calling attention to its creator, the presence behind the music who shapes its

207

Example 5.6a   Paul Wranitzky, The Revolution (*Grande Sinfonie caractéristique*, i), mm. 18–29

singular version of events. Idyllic scenes and mood swings point in the same direction by lending reality a specifically artistic grandeur. It is significant that Neubauer and Wranitzky also observe more conventions of the contemporary symphony than do most writers of battle pieces, using full-blown sonata forms and, in Wranitzky's case as in that of Dittersdorf's *Metamorphoses*, fitting the program to four more or less typical movement types. Emotional variety is the natural result, both

Example 5.6b   Paul Wranitzky, English March (*Grande Sinfonie caractéristique*, i), mm. 136–43

between movements and within the battles, where the changes in character are no more than what would be expected in a symphony fast movement – but the critical point is that similar changes do not occur in other battle pieces, which pause neither for classicizing utopias, nor for operatic inner struggles, nor for symphonic conventions. No more "truthful" than Wranitzky's or Neubauer's works, they nevertheless put less emphasis on their own interpretive role, submerging the creative persona in the rush toward victory and celebration. By contrast, *La Bataille* and the *Grande Sinfonie caractéristique* suggest the hand of the commemorator with each additional topic they introduce, the individual who is not a combatant but rather a bard who glorifies current events by mixing battlefield and paradise, death and immortality. Alongside the battlefield hero there begins to emerge a parallel figure in the arena of representation.

Something similar happens in the first movement of Beethoven's *Eroica* Symphony, but on such an expanded scale as to require some introduction. The movement bears a kinship to the works discussed thus far in that it has always been heard as suggestive of conflict, and, in the nineteenth century, specifically as a battle.[32] There was ample justification even at a time when only Beethoven's closest associates knew of the connection with Napoleon; with war a constant threat, reference to heroism and to a "great man" would have promised a representation of military deeds, and the music in many ways obliges, staging some of the most viscerally engaging moments of violence to be found anywhere. A short list would include the *tutti* outburst following the second horn's premature entry before the recapitulation, the equally stunning outbursts at the beginning of the coda, and the numerous passages rent by syncopations, especially the famous cataclysm in the middle of the development section. Here again are Burke's cannon shots, increasingly anticipated as they accumulate but still unexpected, cause for the hearing to convulse. With the events also driven forward by the energy

---

[32] For surveys of the *Eroica* reception see Geck and Schleuning, *"Geschrieben auf Bonaparte,"* 193–392; Sipe, *Beethoven: "Eroica Symphony,"* 54–75; and Burnham, *Beethoven Hero*, 3–28.

of Beethoven's heroic style, small wonder that an 1811 commentator heard "das Gemälde einer Schlacht . . . das muthige Gegeneinanderrennen, das wilde Toben, das unermüdliche Dreinschlagen und verworrne Wüthen" (the picture of a battle . . . the courageous assaults, the wild rage, the unremitting attacks and confused anger).[33]

On the other hand, as Thomas Sipe suggests, Beethoven's titles equally well suggest a portrayal of character, an alternative that is reflected musically, above all, in the intensive elaboration of the principal theme.[34] Among battle movements only Wranitzky's "Revolution" attempts anything similar, but without identifying its recurring motives with an individual protagonist. Elsewhere the tendency is to enhance confusion precisely by not integrating successive passages, as in *Wellington's Victory* where none of the battle music has distinctive enough themes even to allow for systematic development. The *Eroica* more closely resembles *The Seven Last Words*; if Christ, whose utterances begin as fully formed melodies that are thereafter varied, does not therefore make the celebrated journey toward wholeness that Beethoven's *grand Uomo* does, his identity coheres in a similar way. Thematic resemblances give the impression that every twist and turn in the implied plot, every emotional vicissitude, affects a single body.

Peculiar to the *grand Uomo* is the sheer number of ups and downs he experiences – active *fortissimos* alternate with lyrical *pianos* every thirty to forty measures in a movement as long as all of *Wellington's Victory* – as well as the affective distance he traverses, from the most dynamic action toward a repose that far outdoes the mere hesitation of Neubauer's soldiers. When the mysterious C♯ ascends to D in the opening measures, a subtle change from repeated notes to slurred figures in the second violins adds a familiar pastoral topic, the middle-register murmuring of Gluck's "Che puro ciel," to other signs of suspended action such as the smoothing out of the first-violin syncopations into long tones and the leisurely progress of both violins and cellos toward closure on the tonic (mm. 9–14). In the following restatement of the theme, the use of solo woodwinds and horn prolongs an idyllic atmosphere for a few measures before it is swept up in the ensuing drive to *fortissimo* (mm. 15–22). Each subsequent return to *piano* brings back the solo woodwinds or horn in combination with murmuring accompaniments (as in mm. 45–54) or with a threat of pastoral lassitude that reaches its apex in the pulsing chords following the powerful cadence midway through

---

[33] *Haude- und Spenerschen Zeitung* (1811), quoted in Geck and Schleuning, *"Geschrieben auf Bonaparte,"* 226; trans. Sipe, *Beethoven: "Eroica Symphony,"* 78.
[34] Sipe, *Beethoven: "Eroica Symphony,"* 83–95. Numerous interpreters of the *Eroica* first movement have equated the development of its theme with that of the protagonist (see Burnham, *Beethoven Hero,* 7–9; and Dahlhaus, *Beethoven,* 136–38).

the second group (m. 83 in the exposition, m. 486 in the recapitulation). After the directedness of a unison scale descending to the tonic (mm. 81–82), it is all the more surprising to hear only a succession of woodwind entrances on the tonic triad, a *Klangfarbenmelodie* whose melodic motion over four measures amounts to no more than a literal descent from $\hat{3}$ to $\hat{2}$ (mm. 83–86). The answering strings develop more energy, pushing up as high as $\hat{6}$, yet their descent to the tonic is not the rush to closure of before but a dying away, an expansion of the $\hat{3}$–$\hat{2}$ sigh with which the antecedent ended (mm. 87–91). Motion has given way to a sensuousness that wafts out of the woodwinds, out of the pulsing rhythms and the *messe di voce* spanning each phrase, and out of the passing chromaticisms, reminiscent of Mozart's *amoroso* moods in the similarly clarinet-heavy "Porgi amor" and elsewhere. The *grand Uomo* would appear to have strayed into one of those erotic idylls where the heroes of epic are forever losing their way, the palace of Armida or the island of Calypso. When the woodwinds continue inaction takes hold even more firmly via a threatened tonicization of Db, one of numerous references throughout the movement to the C♯ that first disturbed the course of the main theme (m. 94). This particular instance creates an impasse, an empty downbeat from which the music must reconstitute itself like the Turkish march in the Ninth Symphony: the basses fall to C and the woodwinds to the dominant F, over which the strings inch slowly upwards from a dissonant ninth chord (itself forecasting the similar regrouping that takes place after the breakdown in the development section [cf. mm. 99 and 280]). Soon enough the heroic journey has resumed (m. 109), prepared by the typically Beethovenian devices of an insistent dominant pedal, a crescendo, and a twofold acceleration from quarter to eighth notes and from two- to one-measure groups (mm. 102–08). But the detour has gone much farther afield than Neubauer or Wranitzky ever risk. In this movement especially, the pace can only slow so far before one begins to suspect that the protagonist has forgotten his goal: witness the recurring interpretation of the horn entry at the recapitulation as a "wake-up call" following a relaxation of tension that decrescendos to the point of inaudibility.[35] Silence is death, if not of the body then of the ideal that animates it, and the empty downbeat to which the pulsing woodwinds lead represents the brink of oblivion.

---

[35] Burnham, *Beethoven Hero*, 13–18. A. B. Marx heard "im Angesicht blutiger Entscheidung ... nachdenkliche Vorstellung" (reflective imaginings ... in the face of bloody resolution) in mm. 83ff. (*Ludwig van Beethoven*, I: 261; trans. Scott Burnham in Marx, *Musical Form in the Age of Beethoven: Selected Writings on Theory and Method* [Cambridge: Cambridge University Press, 1997], 162); for related interpretations see Sipe, *Beethoven: "Eroica Symphony,"* 100–01.

Another digressive idyll awaits at the beginning of the recapitulation, less dangerous but striking in that it involves the only substantial rewriting of exposition material (mm. 398–423). So forcefully asserted just a few measures before, the tonic disappears again after the disruptive C♯, which falls to C in preparation for a new statement of the theme in F major, in the horn. Yet another statement follows, in D♭, this time with virtually no transition to prepare it and with the solo in the flute. Both keys can be related to events elsewhere – especially, of course, D♭ – but the impression is once again that the tonal forces driving the form have been temporarily suspended. Rosen writes aptly of an "illusionistic color" and "exoticism" that result also from the quiet dynamics and solo scoring, both of which put the music at a further remove from its surroundings.[36] If paradise is elsewhere sensual, here it is ethereal, unreal, like a vision.

When at last the main theme reaches its final form in the coda – eight measures long, in the tonic, undisturbed by C♯s – it also internalizes, so to speak, the pastoral associations that have threatened to run the movement aground. Its triadic outline could in fact serve equally well as a military fanfare or a pastoral horn call, a point that is now made clear by orchestration. The horn plays the first iteration, grounding its earlier, "fictive" rendition in the "reality" of the tonic and also, through its dialogue with the second horn and first oboe, prefiguring the back-and-forth calling of shepherds at the beginning of the *Pastoral* Symphony finale (mm. 631–38). The second violins return to middle-register murmuring, against which the sixteenth-note figures in the firsts, so intense when they powered the development-section fugato (mm. 236–43) and other forward-striving passages (mm. 65–72 in the exposition or 186–219 in the development), become suddenly light, dance-like, the accompaniment to a polonaise. As the violins take up the theme, the clarinet and cello assume the role of the second violins and the horns that of the echo, while the texture acquires drones for a total effect quite similar to, again, the *Pastoral* Symphony finale (mm. 639–46; cf. mm. 17–24 of the *Pastoral* Symphony finale). Only with the third hearing does the scoring migrate toward the military, dropping the middle-register accompaniment in favor of trumpet and timpani flourishes as well as eighth-note syncopations reminiscent of earlier conflicts (mm. 647–54), and in the end the theme develops into a full-blown trumpet fanfare with a continuation that ventures away from the tonic only to return in greater triumph (mm. 655–73). Yet no longer does its heroism strive to overcome the lure of idyllic repose; the one topic grows seamlessly out of the other, portraying a character who is an amalgamation of both. The foil to the heroic identity

---

[36] Rosen, *Sonata Forms*, rev. edn., 293.

has become its foundation, the conscience on which its endeavors build.

Reconciling the *grand Uomo* with his pastoral inclinations enhances his mythic stature to the point of divinity. His exceptional grandeur is already ensured by the range of his emotions, which also extend to sorrow; not without its own pastoral overtones, including woodwind solos and an implied 6/4 meter with siciliano-like dotted rhythms, the theme first heard in E minor in the development section also recalls Neubauer's laments in its *pathétique* accents and descending chromatic counter-melody (mm. 284–91). Its recapitulation is the first business of the coda, as if a recognition of loss were necessary to clear the way for apotheosis (mm. 581–94). The added element of the pastoral brings a mythical setting kept separate by Neubauer and Wranitzky right into the action, transforming the hero and with him the meanings of idyllic stillness. If at first pastoral topics stand for distraction, for sensual or illusory retreats from duty, by the end they have become a landscape that inspires, like the Swiss mountains whose embedded history of freedom and justice motivate Schiller's Wilhelm Tell to his struggle against tyranny. False idylls give way to a genuine one, an exchange that even more strongly recalls another Schiller play, *Die Jungfrau von Orleans* (1801), in which Joan of Arc overcomes the main obstacle to her destiny, her love for an enemy leader, by remembering her life as a shepherdess, the idyllic circumstances in which she received her divine summons to military heroism. One thought replaces the other in a soliloquy (Act 4, Scene 1) in which, according to the stage directions, "weiche, schmelzende Töne" (soft, melting tones) in flutes and oboes strengthen the scene's pastoral associations, the familar woodwinds who also in the *Eroica* suggest first an erotic and later a heroic paradise. One of the earliest and most interesting reviewers of the *Eroica*, Heinrich Hermann, even heard traces of Joan of Arc's religious fervor in the coda of Beethoven's first movement, describing an "allmählig sich vorbereitende und heranschwellende Füllung mit dem blossen Thema, bis zum gewaltigen himmlischen Zusammenklang im höhern Chor – alles dies, in einer ganz neuen Art von Kirchenstyl ausgeführt" (gradual enrichment of the simple theme, which is prepared and built up to a powerful heavenly harmony in the higher instruments – all this executed in a wholly new manner of the church style).[37] Religious associations were always latent in pastoral music, and the strophic, hymnlike treatment of the main theme is yet another prefiguring of the *Pastoral* Symphony finale (see p. 182). The *grand Uomo* may not earn the sainthood of Joan of Arc, but to some ears his triumph must have sounded like a redemption.

---

[37] Ernst Woldemar (Heinrich Hermann), *Morgenblatt für die gebildeten Stände* 1 (9 July 1807), quoted in Geck and Schleuning, *"Geschrieben auf Bonaparte,"* 234.

Hermann also heard transcendence in Beethoven's many abrupt changes of topic. Where some of the composer's contemporaries objected to "das Zusammenstellen der heterogensten Dinge, wenn z.B. eine Pastorale im größten Stile durchgeführt würde, durch eine Menge Risse in den Bässen, durch drei Hörner u.a.d." (the combination of the most heterogeneous elements, as for instance when a pastoral in the largest style is ripped up by the basses, by three horns, etc.),[38] Hermann detected the *Humor* of Jean Paul, the "romantic comic" that results when the contrasts between juxtaposed subject matters, characters, or plot elements are so great as to evoke the infinite. His example is the dizzying fall from dissonant syncopations at the climax of the development section, which he terms a "herbes Leiden" (bitter suffering), to the "sanften Moll" (soft minor) of the subsequent theme, "wodurch wir uns in der Folge beynahe in eine Shakespear'sche Zauberwelt hingerückt fühlten!" (through which we feel called forth in the following passage into an almost Shakespearean world of magic!).[39] He develops the analogy no further and ultimately wonders whether music has the "System und Besonnenheit" (system and self-possession) to counter the disintegrating tendencies of *Humor*, but had he had E. T. A. Hoffmann's confidence in Beethoven's *Besonnenheit* he might have found a complement for his idea that the coda has a religious dimension.[40] Jean Paul's humorist has a divine ability to comprehend totalities: "[humor] recognizes no individual foolishness, no fools, but only folly and a mad world." Pitting "the small ... against the infinite world" or the comic against the tragic demonstrates mastery of the entire human condition and in turn "scorn for the world," an "annihilating" contempt not for humanity but for the "finitude" in which it is caught up, for reality itself.[41] The *Eroica* protagonist might be thought to evidence a similar disregard for earthly concerns in his leaps from action to inaction, militarism to sensuousness, heroism to pastoral. Long before the coda, he reaches a plane, unimagined by the less ambitious battle symphonies, where the extremes of human existence are traversed in an instant.

For Hermann as for Jean Paul, though, *Humor* was a property of artists rather than their creations, and it is the figure of Beethoven, as humorist, that most distinguishes the *Eroica* within the field of politically associated

---

[38] *Der Freimüthige oder Berlinische Zeitung für gebildete unbefangene Leser* 3 (26 April 1805), quoted in Geck and Schleuning, "*Geschrieben auf Bonaparte*," 230; trans. Weiss and Taruskin, *Music in the Western World*, 329.

[39] Geck and Schleuning, "*Geschrieben auf Bonaparte*," 233–34; trans. Sipe, *Beethoven: "Eroica Symphony*," 58.

[40] Hoffmann, review of Beethoven's Fifth Symphony, *AmZ* 12 (1810): cols. 633–34; see the discussion in Schnaus, *E. T. A. Hoffmann als Beethoven-Rezensent*, 80–83.

[41] *Jean Paul Richter's School for Aesthetics*, 88, 92–93.

symphonies. "We have defined the objective principle as a desired infinity; this I cannot conceive and posit *outside* myself . . . Consequently I place myself in the breach."[42] *Humor* foregrounds the author, its seemingly arbitrary juxtaposition of opposites emphasizing the intervention of the creative will so that Jean Paul's humorists are not the characters of Swift, Shakespeare, or Sterne but the writers themselves – and also Haydn, who "destroys entire tonal sequences by introducing an extraneous key and storms alternately between pianissimo and fortissimo, presto and andante."[43] A humorist's persona may well hover over any musical work in the contrast-ridden style of the later eighteenth and early nineteenth centuries, not only Haydn's, which were often singled out for their Sterne-like wit,[44] but even Neubauer's or Wranitzky's battle movements, where laments and marches reveal the composer's selective memory. The *Eroica* differs, as always, in scale, its contrasts so radical that their creator immediately displaced the title character as the focus of reception; to use Burnham's felicitous terms, "Beethoven's Hero" became "Beethoven Hero" as early as Hermann's review, even if his task was not yet to save music but only to evoke infinity.[45] In another review of the same year the composer is even more obviously identified with his protagonist, becoming a military leader himself: "With the bold flight of the eagle he overcame everything put in the way of his swift march."[46] The effect of the traditional musical battle, with its paradoxically consistent sublimity, is quite different. Dahlhaus called *Wellington's Victory* "a parody of the heroic style," but really it is more like the reverse, an imitation that, rather than exaggerating the original for the purposes of comedy, leaves out the exaggerations that would generate *Humor*.[47] With them goes authorial presence, as indeed it must; in the celebration of communal effort, of an army or of the society that supports it, neither the individual hero nor the artist can intrude too far. The music must move with the steps of many, speak with a collective voice. Those symphonies that read current events as myth, above all the *Eroica*, are distinguished less by their "realism" (the communal ethos of battle pieces was no less constructed) or even by their representation of discrete heroes than by their assertion of the artist's political role. The most individualizing aspect of the *Eroica* is its arrogation of a poet's authority to interpret history.

---

[42] Ibid., 94.   [43] Ibid., 93.

[44] See Mark Evan Bonds, "Haydn, Laurence Sterne, and the Origins of Musical Irony," *Journal of the American Musicological Society* 44 (1991), esp. 63–64 and 79–87.

[45] Burnham, *Beethoven Hero*, xvi; see also his discussion of the diegetic quality of the first movement coda and of the heroic style generally, 23–24, 142–44.

[46] *Les Tablettes de Polymnie* (1811), quoted in Geck and Schleuning, *"Geschrieben auf Bonaparte,"* 198.

[47] Dahlhaus, *Beethoven*, 17.

Death

If the regular run of battle pieces ignored death in favor of action and celebration, it was the genre that was responsible and not the political culture at large. Some of the era's most spectacular public ceremonies honored the deceased, from the Revolutionary burials of Mirabeau and Voltaire to the 1806 funeral of Admiral Lord Nelson.[48] There were concerts to match, perhaps most impressively a program given on the second anniversary of the death of Queen Louise of Prussia, which included not only Mozart's *Requiem* but also a memorial cantata by Friedrich Heinrich Himmel and a full-length *Trauer-Symphonie* by Bernhard Romberg.[49] Instrumental works simply tended to deal with mourning separately from fighting, whether in symphonies like Romberg's that paid tribute to royalty (Appendix 3h) or in the funeral marches that followed on the success of Gossec's Revolutionary *Marche lugubre* (1790). It should be remembered that even the most optimistic battle symphonies implicitly honored the fallen when they reenacted their deeds at concerts benefiting the wounded or widowed. The sacrifices of wartime remained a unifying image even when they were not directly represented.

Perhaps unexpectedly, mourning music returns us from the individualistic tendencies of the more mythologizing battle symphonies to a relatively communal ethos, for obsequies recognized social identities, symbolized in this case not by the joint effort of military endeavor but by the shared experience of grief. Their centerpiece was the procession, as at Nelson's funeral where a long train of sailors, officers, religious officials and political leaders accompanied the coffin on its way from the Admiralty to St. Paul's, watched by thousands of spectators. For Joseph II the path led from the Hofburg to St. Stephen's, and in his city less elaborate parades led humbler souls to their graves so often that the practice was satirized in J. E. Mansfeld's *Bildergalerie katholischer Misbräuche* (1784–85).[50] Walking to the church was the principal way in which grief was extended, on state occasions, to those members of the public too low on the social scale to attend the culminating church service. Mourning music implied a similarly broad participation by adopting the funeral march as its most frequently used and semantically charged topic, even

---

[48] According to Ozouf, "it was in the funeral festivals that the most determined expressionism of the Revolutionary festival was to survive"; *Festivals and the French Revolution*, 81. On Nelson's funeral see Russell, *The Theatres of War*, 80–87.

[49] *AmZ* 14 (1812): cols. 275–76. A list of (primarily vocal) mourning works from 1780 to 1801 is given in Friedrich W. Riedel, "Die Trauerkompositionen von Joseph Martin Kraus: Ihre geistes- und musikgeschichtliche Stellung," in Riedel, ed., *Joseph Martin Kraus in seiner Zeit* (Munich: Katzbichler, 1982): 156–61.

[50] See Landon, "Picture Essay: Aspects of Life in Austria in Mozart's Time," in *The Mozart Essays* (London: Thames and Hudson, 1995), plate 19.

though its objects of commemoration were nearly always individuals. References to actions or qualities of the deceased are not lacking, but they appear within the framework of a community's joining together in sorrow.

Mourners resemble soldiers in that they move together, but outside of marches meant for real or onstage processions their steps are usually complicated by additional gestures. This is especially true in symphonies, where march rhythms are nearly always developed and juxtaposed with other topics. Apart from the *Marcia funebre* of the *Eroica*, the most compelling example is the *Symphonie funèbre* (1792) of Joseph Martin Kraus, composed during the two weeks separating the death of Gustav III of Sweden on 29 March 1792 (he had been shot two weeks earlier) and his lying-in-state in Stockholm's Riddarholmskyrka, which began on 13 April with a ceremony at which the symphony was played.[51] Its four movements trace a choreography of grief that sets the march against several related or contrasting rhythms, beginning, in the very first measures, with long tones in the winds and syncopations in the strings (Example 5.7). The two topics each have their own connotations (exploited separately at the end of the symphony; see Example 5.9e), most obviously the winds who quite literally embody exhalation, a *suspiratio* emanating here not from a dying hero, as in the final Sonata of *The Seven Last Words* (see p. 124 above), but from the sighing onlookers. Comparable chords begin Romberg's symphony for Queen Louise as well as the *Mauerische Trauermusik* of Mozart.[52] Equally common in other funeral works are the accompanying syncopations, which betray the emotional turmoil rumbling under the controlled surface of the public ceremony. In the cantata prepared by Kraus for Gustav's funeral, held a month later on 14 May, similar figures first appear at the words "o grymma lagar" (oh grim laws), an outcry against the injustice of the assassination.[53] The offbeat accompaniment to the opening of Mozart's *Requiem* has a related effect, counterpointing the smooth choral proclamations of eternal peace with an anxious undercurrent. The association would appear to be visceral, its reference point the uneven pulse of a body beset by intense emotion, so that listeners already confronted by the physical actions of marching and breathing are also alerted to their own, fragile, life rhythms.

[51] Riedel, "Die Trauerkompositionen von Joseph Martin Kraus," 154; Bertil H. van Boer, Jr., *Dramatic Cohesion in the Music of Joseph Martin Kraus: From Sacred Music to Symphonic Form* (Lewiston, Lampeter, and Queenston: Edwin Mellen, 1989), 357–65.

[52] And the funereal overture to Gluck's *Alceste* (1767), as van Boer points out (*Dramatic Cohesion*, 375).

[53] In the duet No. 6, mm. 11ff; see the edn. by Jan Olof Rudén, *Monumenta Musica Svecicae* 9 (Stockholm: Riemers, 1979), which also includes the *Symphonie funèbre*. Text trans. in van Boer, *Dramatic Cohesion*, 435.

Example 5.7   Kraus, *Symphonie funèbre*, i, mm. 1–12

Kraus achieves an oppressive darkness in these measures, an equivalent to the purple and black cloths that draped Gustav's coffin and the
tables displaying his regalia in the Riddarholmskyrka.[54] Like Mozart in
both the *Requiem* and the *Mauerische Trauermusik*, he scores for only
the darkest woodwinds, bassoons and clarinets (Mozart uses basset
horns); the strings remain in their lowest register; and the brass are
muted, as are the timpani in the tradition of funeral drums. For some
measures it also appears that the weight of grief is holding the marchers
in place. Although each exhalation surges forth with an upward leap in
the basses, the music keeps returning to the muffled tap of the timpani
and to the tonic pedal, which persists through some four alternations.

---

[54] See the description quoted in ibid., 364–65.

Example 5.8   Kraus, *Symphonie funèbre*, iii (chorale)

Movement forward is implied only by the slowest and most incremental linear ascent, from $\hat{3}$ through an applied dominant of the subdominant to $\hat{4}$ (Example 5.7, mm. 4–8), which becomes dissonant over a following dominant and descends – at which point the harmonic rhythm doubles and the bass at last departs the tonic for the dominant (mm. 8–12). Yet it is typical of the symphony as a whole that the uppermost voice should now remain on $\hat{3}$ for four measures before falling to $\hat{2}$, where it remains, and that the concomitant half-cadence, although forward-looking to the extent that it requires resolution, is stretched out over eight additional measures that conclude with multiple reiterations of the dominant chord and a fermata. A rhyming pause occurs no less than four times in the finale, each time strengthening the impression that the mourners can barely keep walking. The sections of the form become like the initial woodwind chords, exhalations that follow one another with extreme deliberation and tail off repeatedly into silence.

Into this somber atmosphere Kraus injects a further contrast, the chorale "Lät oss thenna kropp begrafna" (Let us bury this body), which appears initially in the third movement in a four-part setting that may well have been sung (as it was at a later performance of 1797[55]) (Example 5.8). Again there are parallels in other mourning works, in the liturgical songs that brighten both the *Mauerische Trauermusik* and the first movement of the *Requiem*, and in the memories of happier times that leaven Kraus's and similar funeral cantatas, which include texts in the past tense relating exploits or celebrating character. The chorale offers consolation by suggesting Gustav's transcendence and, equally important, allowing listeners to rise above the breathing, pulsing, and halting that roil so much of the rest of the work. Its rhythms are uniform and its melodic line smooth and active; moreover, its key, A♭, as well as the cadence of the third phrase on the relative F minor serve to reinterpret elements of the preceding movements by bringing them into newly calm surroundings. A♭ is the secondary key of the first movement, a connection that is all the more noticeable given that the more usual choice would be the relative major E♭, and the pitch A♭ makes repeated appearances as the bass of pre-dominant chords, including a climactic

---

[55] *Monumenta Musica Svecicae* 9, xvn. Ibid., viii, identifies the chorale as No. 400 in the 1697 Swedish Lutheran chorale book.

German sixth heard just before the final cadence (m. 123; see also mm. 13, 17–19, 84, and 88–90). F minor is tonicized by the symphony's very first harmonic motion (Example 5.7, m. 8) and subsequently taken as the tonic of the second movement, shorter and swifter than the first but with the same syncopations, dissonances, and difficult pauses – and also the same emphasis on A♭, which serves as the headnote of the main theme and as the movement's highest pitch overall (mm. 1–2, 21–24, 33). Developing the two keys in the chorale integrates the work's tonal structure in a way that renders the confrontation between turmoil and tranquillity more direct. The new serenity of the third movement does not escape the earlier agitations but rather engages them, showing a different side of what seems to be a single experience of grief.

The finale is left to mediate the contrast. Much the longest and most complicated movement, it cannot in fact be understood except as the continuation of previous events, as becomes apparent when it begins not in the tonic C minor but in the subdominant F minor (Example 5.9a). With a five-note turn reminiscent of the first phrase of the chorale,[56] the violins plunge back into a mood close to that of the first two movements, replete with syncopations and, later (mm. 5–9), a venerable sign for lament, a descending chromatic bass line that here complements a Baroque ornateness in the melody. Thus far the darker side of grief prevails, its typically uneven motion enhanced by offbeat entrances in the violins and their eventual traversal of two-octave arpeggios and leaps. The same affect persists beyond the first of the movement's four half-cadences, into a second episode that abruptly reinterprets the dominant of F as the tonic of C minor, then descends through another chromatic bass line to its own dominant, G. The work could conceivably terminate its emotional journey at this point, continuing on in the tonic and consigning the brighter vision of the chorale to memory – but Kraus has a grander ambition: to lift listeners again toward transcendence before returning them to darkness, and at the same time to work out tonal issues that an overly quick return to C minor would abridge. Three episodes in as yet unheard major keys, E♭ and its dominant B♭, offer new consolations and topics. In the first, a solo horn soars over the strings and suggests for the first time an individual character, most likely Gustav himself, whose description in Kraus's cantata as both a warrior and "den mildaste bland alla / Som nånsin styrt ett söndrad land" (the kindest among all those who ever ruled our splintered land)[57] is an excellent match for the horn's mixture of heroic leaps and delicate appoggiaturas (Example 5.9b). Syncopations and still another chromatic descent in the

---

[56] Van Boer notes the similarity between the turn and the later fugue theme (see Example 5.9c) itself based on the opening phrase of the chorale (*Dramatic Cohesion*, 381).

[57] In the aria No. 5; trans. van Boer, *Dramatic Cohesion*, 434.

Example 5.9a   Kraus, *Symphonie funèbre*, iv, mm. 1–4

Example 5.9b   Kraus, *Symphonie funèbre*, iv, mm. 24–31 (horn solo)

Example 5.9c   Kraus, *Symphonie funèbre*, iv, mm. 50–52 (beginning of fugue)

bass lose their heaviness when heard in conjunction with the horn and with lightly pulsing arpeggiations in the violins, and a similar spirit animates the next two episodes, both of which return to the chorale tune. First it is played by woodwinds in the texture of a chorale prelude, its rhythm enlivened by flowing sixteenths in a solo cello that dispel both the uneven motion and the chromaticism of the sixteenths played by the violins at the beginning of the finale. Then comes a fugue, in which the strings at last remove their mutes and counterpoint the first phrase of the chorale with vigorous ascending scales (Example 5.9c). Syncopations become a source of upbeat propulsion in the subject itself, which in turn enjoys as predictable an exposition as could be wished despite its unusual five-beat length: after six successive entries on tonic

221

Example 5.9d   Kraus, *Symphonie funèbre*, iv, mm. 59–63 (return to A♭)

and dominant, the symphony now seems poised to end like an oratorio, sweeping Gustav and mourners alike into the familiar apotheosis of the learned style.

But by the time the fugue begins, many unanswered questions hang over its tonality in particular. The first two half-cadences of the finale were left unresolved, each succeeding episode taking the preceding dominant as a new minor-key tonic. The remaining two raised different problems, resolving normally but darkening the major-key episodes they concluded with shadows of the minor (as in Example 5.9b, mm. 30–31). In one sense the fugue seems all the more affirmative when it answers a sighing pause in the minor with lively counterpoint in the major, but one cannot forget those dominants left hanging, particularly given the importance of C and F minor elsewhere in the symphony. Nor does the newly achieved height of B♭ major feel entirely secure. It elevates the chorale tune into a loftier register than its original A♭ and culminates the finale's steady push up the circle of fifths, enhancing the effect of transcendence. But it also raises expectations of a balancing descent, the symphony having been altogether too well-integrated to end so far above where it began, and indeed it is not surprising when the first episode of the fugue turns downward toward A♭ in a modulation packed with allusions to previous events (Example 5.9d). A chain of dominants implies G minor, C minor, and F minor in quick succession, recalling the unresolved half-cadences of earlier and adumbrating, through the D♭s of the last step, the key of A♭ to come (mm. 58–59). Thereafter the dominant of G minor returns, followed by a deceptive move to E♭, the other key of the finale articulated here by the beginnings of an augmented fugue subject (mm. 60–61). At last A♭ sneaks in, announced only by the shift from D to D♭ in the bass but proving in retrospect to have been the goal, the home for two complete fugal entries on tonic and dominant and then a reprise of its first-movement

Example 5.9e   Kraus, *Symphonie funèbre*, iv, mm. 75–90 (return of
mvt. i)

role as a pre-dominant as it gives way to sequences that lead first to C
minor and then, through the familiar augmented sixth, to a dominant
pedal of the home tonic.

The final sound is of the mourners resuming their march, but
with differences reflecting the emotional distance they have trav-
eled (Example 5.9e). Exhalations and syncopations are now separated,
stretching the eleven measures of the original statement into sixteen
and also introducing, through new dynamics, what sounds like an effort to forestall the end: each of the first three wind entrances grows

louder, the second increasing all the way to *forte* as the harmony points one last time beyond the tonic toward the subdominant. Simply forcing the breath cannot dissipate the tonic pedal, however, and the resolution fades back to *piano* and the final cadence even further, to a nearly inaudible triple-*p*. Always difficult, the shared rhythm of the procession is finally unsustainable, even with a *tierce de Picardie* that harks back to the brighter moments of the chorale, horn solo, and fugue. Suggestive of the king's redemption and life after death, ultimately those passages provide cold comfort at best, and the abiding image is not of a transcendent Gustav but of mourners who end, their long journey toward calm and transcendence notwithstanding, freshly vulnerable to the uneven pulses of grief.

In ending with such faint hope the *Symphonie funèbre* is of a piece with its companion cantata. Again, no fugue awaits here to transform sorrow into celebration, only a prayer in chorale style begging protection from further catastrophes: "Men förtyng ej straffets hand, / Låt ej hämdens fasa stanna / Öfver ett olyckigt land" (But let not the hand of punishment, let not the horror of vengeance remain over an unhappy land). The shock of the assassination and its immediacy – Kraus knew Gustav well and attended the masked ball where he was shot[58] – was simply too great to allow for the more optimistic conclusions of many other funeral pieces. In his *Trauer-Symphonie* (1810) for Queen Louise of Prussia, by contrast, Romberg also returns to marching music toward the end, but unlike Kraus he appends a coda probably indebted to the C major interlude of Beethoven's *Marcia funebre*, with a solo oboe floating up the tonic triad and the texture filling first with the idyllic murmuring and later with the military fanfares both found also in Beethoven's movement (Example 5.10). The passage bears no separate characterization, but a "Prolog" to the symphony by C. A. Tiedge, which was read aloud, probably suggested images similar to those ending the same poet's *Die Wanderer*, a cantata performed on the same occasion.[59] Addressing the angels, the chorus demands: "Nennt Luisen / Beim Namen, der uns einst so süß, so festlich klang! / Umfeiert Sie in euern Paradiesen, / Und singet Ihr Triumph-Gesang!" (Call Luise by the name that once resounded so sweetly and nobly to us! Celebrate her in your paradises and sing her song of triumph!).[60] Romberg's oboe "names" the queen much as the horn did Gustav, but with the difference that she is thereafter enfolded by the transcendence of idyllic heroism. The mourners disappear.

Their presence to the last in Kraus marks an ideological difference as well as his personal involvement with the subject. Both Romberg's

---

[58] Ibid., 360–61.   [59] *AmZ* 14 (1812): col. 276.
[60] *C. A. Tiedge's Werke*, ed. A. G. Eberhard, vol. III (Halle, 1827), 117.

Example 5.10   Romberg, *Trauer-Symphonie*, mm. 218–23 (conclusion)

symphony and the second movement of Wranitzky's *Grande Sinfonie caractéristique*, his apotheosis of Louis XVI, are rather conventionally monarchic to the extent that they sound the grief of the community but keep the charismatic ruler to the fore; Wranitzky's funeral march for Louis, although deeply pathetic, is the central section of a ternary form whose outer parts are devoted to lyricism and nostalgia. Kraus shifts the balance so as to refer less to the top of the monument erected in the Riddarholmskyrka, where rested a bust of Gustav, than to the figure who sat weeping just below, Svea, the allegorical representative of the nation. Indeed, the feelings of those mourning the king so dominate both symphony and cantata[61] that they point forward to the burial monuments built by Antonio Canova in early nineteenth-century Italy, where large figures of the nation quite eclipse small reliefs of the deceased.[62] Not nationalist in the sense of emphasizing the "Swedishness" of Gustav or his subjects, Kraus's works nevertheless encourage listeners to construct a unity in grief, either by accepting a collective guilt as the cantata exhorts them to do, or by moving their bodies as one.

The apparent difficulty with which communal motion is sustained in the *Symphonie funèbre* is also the most important of several elements it shares with the *Marcia funebre* of the *Eroica*. Beethoven's movement also has its moment of apotheosis and a fugue, but the disintegration of its main theme in the final measures both intensifies Kraus's conclusion and clarifies its larger cultural meanings. In addition to breaks in continuity,

61 Van Boer contrasts the emotionalism of the cantata text with the "bombastic and allegorical" tone of the libretto by S. A. Averdonck on the death of Joseph II, set by Beethoven in 1790 (*Dramatic Cohesion*, 383–86).
62 David Irwin, "Sentiment and Antiquity: European Tombs 1750–1830," in Joachim Whaley, ed., *Mirrors of Mortality: Studies in the Social History of Death* (London: Europa, 1981), 139–41.

Example 5.11   Beethoven, *Eroica* Symphony, disintegration of funeral march (mvt. ii, mm. 238–47, compared to mm. 1–8)

the march theme is distorted at the end by variations in speed that make it appear as if all discipline has been lost (Example 5.11). It begins in the middle of a measure, seemingly late by a beat, and by its third step it breaks down as the E♭ of the melody enters unexpectedly in the bass and only afterwards, a further beat later, in the violin. Reduced to two lines and lacking the drum flourishes that earlier punctuated the rhythm, the texture seems no longer appropriate to a solemn tread and becomes even less so when the violins, already *sotto voce*, are directed to play still more quietly (m. 240). No longer do the feet fall to the ground, heavy and certain; each step has become hesitant, light, timid. This enables a compression of the original quarter–eighth rhythm of the E♭ and C into two eighths and, more striking, an acceleration of the march's three-measure melodic fall and rise, from G down to C and back up to A♭, into only three-and-a-half beats (mm. 240–42). Escaping the gravity of its midpoint half-cadence, the theme rather nervously reaches its high point more than a measure earlier than it ought. The ensuing descent is correspondingly reluctant, a measure longer than formerly so that the complete march occupies the same overall time that it did at the beginning of the movement, with horns, oboes, and finally the inner strings supplying the missing weight. At the very last, in the two-measure pendant to the cadence, the drum rhythm brings the march firmly back to earth, accompanied by a dramatic exhalation in the winds that recalls the final *forte* of the *Symphonie funèbre*. But the earlier loss of substance is equally evocative, suggesting an effort similar to that of Kraus's mourners to break free of grief – but now by absence rather than force. If only the corporeality of the march could be shaken, it seems, the mourners might be able to forget.

This moment is prepared throughout the second movement of the *Eroica*, which in a sense inverts the first by breaking down a theme heard fully formed at the beginning rather than building up to a complete statement at the end. The theme is an antecedent–consequent period with all the regularity of a military march, its two four-measure phrases shaped into similar melodic arches ($\hat{1}$–$\hat{5}$–$\hat{2}$, $\hat{2}$–$\hat{6}$–$\hat{1}$) and accompanied by parallel rhythmic patterns (emphasizing the measure, mm. 1–2 and 5–6, then the half measure, mm. 3 and 7, then the eighth, mm. 4 and 8). After the written-out repeat, what begins as an equally regular sequence gaps open to reveal an undercurrent of chaotic passion. The second iteration of the new descending motive does not end quietly on E♭, as one expects, but loudly on E♮ over the diminished seventh of F minor (m. 20), and after a pause a recitative-like outburst repeats the same chord on what ought to be the un-stressed final beat of a four-measure group. The B♭ in the first violin more properly belongs at the beginning of the next measure, where it would initiate a third stage in the sequence; instead the downbeat is empty, and the awaited A♭ and subdominant enter awkwardly after the rest (m. 21). References to other funeral music abound. Claude V. Palisca points out that the descending diminished fourth is found also in Gossec's *Marche lugubre*, and in fact Mozart, Kraus, and Romberg all use variations on the same figure, taking advantage of the double sigh of its two half-steps and of its possibility for use as $\hat{3}$–$\hat{2}$–$\hat{1}$–$\sharp\hat{7}$ in minor.[63] The motive is frequently coupled with pauses and heard in sequence, Gossec ascending in three stages to a diminished seventh outburst that has the same, if slower, short–long profile of Beethoven's recitative-like punctuation (Example 5.12, m. 31). Where Beethoven differs is in compromising well-established rhythmic certainties. The steps of Gossec's sequence are parallel in rhythm to one another and consistent in scoring with the entire march, throughout which the winds answer downbeats or whole measures played only by the percussion. Beethoven disrupts a reigning four-measure periodicity and introduces many more local discontinuities as well: the textural shift from connected lyricism to isolated attack, the sudden dynamic swell and equally sudden return to *piano*, the missing downbeat after the *forte*, the subsequent *sforzati* on competing eighth notes. Nor does the form ever entirely recover. The march theme returns, as in a rounded binary, but it echoes the breakdown on vii/iv both by resuming in F minor and by foundering, in its fourth measure, on another *forte* that emphasizes the first two eighths of the bar and leaves the subdominant hanging into empty space (m. 34). Its meter further obscured by syncopations, the ensuing cadence cannot balance the closure of the initial eight

---

[63] Palisca notes harmonic and rhythmic similarities between the passages as well ("French Revolutionary Models for Beethoven's *Eroica* Funeral March," in Anne Dhu Shapiro, ed., *Music and Context: Essays for John M. Ward* [Cambridge, MA: Harvard University Department of Music, 1985], 202–03).

Example 5.12   Gossec, *Marche lugubre*, mm. 25–33

measures, and it is not surprising that the repeat has a codetta tacked on, one that restores four-measure periodicity and admits syncopations only after the cadences, whose stability remains assured (mm. 56–68). It is equally unsurprising that after the C major interlude and the fugue, whose textural continuities work to dispel memories of rupture, the march stumbles again. Another syncopated diminished seventh breaks off the fugue and leads to the apparent beginnings of a statement in G minor (mm. 150–55), which, however, trails off to a high A♭ answered by a fanfare-laden *fortissimo*, a Burkean explosion recalling the violence that makes the funeral necessary (mm. 158–63). After this, and a reca-pitulation of the original binary form that ends with a second detour to A♭ (m. 209), the uneven steps of the final measures seem an inevitable consequence. Under pressure throughout, the controlled movement of dignified mourning at last succumbs to the ebb and flow of a too-powerful grief.

In the same moment, an image of decay reflects the subject of death back on the listeners. To some extent all pauses and unsettled motions in funeral music have this effect, including those in Kraus, in that they con-front the sad but animate body of the mourner with the possibility of its own distortion or demise. The *Marcia funebre* goes furthest, reducing the rhythms of mourning to fragments and revealing the commemorator to be as vulnerable as the one commemorated. It is not clear whose steps are compromised, whether Beethoven imagines the *grand Uomo* together with fellow warriors to be honoring his comrades, or the warriors themselves and their society to be mourning the *grand Uomo*.[64] Or perhaps the disruptions in the movement suggest again the hand of Jean Paul's humorist, memorializing his creation in his own eccentric way. But whatever persona one imagines, by the end it is face-to-face with its own ruin. The *Eroica* loses faith in its powers of myth-making and allows time to ravage a solidly built memorial, so that what seemed like a grim but noble procession, something out of David, ends up looking more like a decrepit cathedral in one of Caspar David Friedrich's gloomy canvases. Ruins were a potent sign for both personal and social decay in the eighteenth and early nineteenth centuries,[65] and as their spectre rises in the symphony, the immortality promised by burial sentiments falls. If at first the march stands for the endurance of memory, for the determination not to forget, by the end, steps forgotten, the mourner or mourners themselves approach oblivion, unconscious either of their dead or of their own existence. What in Kraus seems like a weight of grief halting a nation in its steps becomes in Beethoven the erosion of history. The second movement disintegrates an identity as completely as the first movement constructed one.

Celebration

Identities must be reconstituted by the end of politically inspired symphonies, for, whatever happens along the way, the era of war and revolution requires affirmation. Violence cannot leave the bitter aftertaste of an Iron Age, even if heroes or soldiers die; on the contrary, the sweet flavor of victory must be exaggerated, prolonged, so that even the most straightforward battle reenactments end not with the moment of triumph but with a march showing the winning army leaving the field, or, more commonly, with a full-scale finale representing the ensuing celebrations. The music redoubles its historical closure by collapsing function into subject matter, depicting events of which it is itself a part; to restore social harmony, as a march does after the confusion of a battle, or to depict rejoicing, is to put the threat of disruptive violence ever more firmly in the past.

---

[64] Sipe recounts the conclusions of earlier critics (*Beethoven: "Eroica Symphony,"* 59–63, 79–81, 104–05).

[65] See Laurence Goldstein, *Ruins and Empire: The Evolution of a Theme in Augustan and Romantic Literature* (Pittsburgh: University of Pittsburgh Press, 1977), esp. 1–10 and 232–40; and Stuart Semmel, "Reading the Tangible Past: British Tourism, Collecting, and Memory after Waterloo," *Representations* 29 (2000): 9–37.

Celebrations mine the populist vein of contemporary political rhetoric more obviously than any other kind of movement. Their governing topics are the patriotic song and the contradance, both of which invoked real-life public expressions of joy (see pp. 193–94 above). Communal singing punctuated victory festivals as well as concert and theater productions across the era, and when composers quoted the same tunes in symphonies, critics readily heard the implied voice of a populace: "eine[n] siegestrunkenen, ausgelassenen Volksjubel" (a boisterous, victory-drunk jubilation of the folk) was how one writer described the end of *Wellington's Victory*, where "God Save the King" is heard both in chorale style and in a fugato using the quick 3/8 meter of the popular "Deutsche" (Example 5.13).[66] If audiences sang along they would have identified themselves with this jubilant folk, and indeed they did so, in at least one instance, even where they could not literally participate: the patriotic choruses concluding Winter's *Schlacht-Sinfonie* were newly composed and performed by a choir on stage, but as they began, "Lautes Freudengeschrey erhob sich von allen Seiten des Saales, begleitete lange die feurige Musik . . . und verlohr sich erst, nachdem die Töne schon lange geschwiegen hatten" (A loud cry of joy arose from all sides of the hall and accompanied the fiery music for a long time . . . subsiding only after the tones had long since fallen silent).[67] Unable to sing, listeners nevertheless joined the rejoicing by roaring their approval.

The contradance, specifically the bright duple-meter variety associated with England, had always had less formal connotations than its principal counterpart in later eighteenth-century ballrooms, the minuet. It required regular changes of partner, so that participants mixed together, and it united, at least on occasion, dancers from different social classes.[68] During the 1780s and after, several examples intended for ballrooms (primarily Viennese) allowed attendees to remember military victories through dance, among them Mozart's "Sieg vom Helden Coburg," K. 587, which commemorates the same engagement as Neubauer's *Bataille*.[69] Meanwhile the sonata- or rondo-form finale based on contradance rhythms became the standard ending for orchestral battles, as well as for "military" and "Turkish" symphonies and for works such as Wranitzky's *Grande Sinfonie caractéristique* or Franz Anton Hoffmeister's *Festa della pace 1791*, the latter written to mark the cessation of hostilities between Austria and the Turks. Whether real or implied, the eight-measure patterns and what appear to have been the skipping

---

[66] *AmZ* 18 (1816): col. 248.   [67] *AmZ* 16 (1814): col. 76.

[68] Sarah Bennett Reichart, "The Influence of Eighteenth-Century Social Dance on the Viennese Classical Style" (Ph.D. diss., City University of New York, 1984), 226–35; see also Sipe, *Beethoven: "Eroica Symphony,"* 12.

[69] Schulin, *Musikalische Schlachtengemälde*, 130–32.

Example 5.13a   Beethoven, *Wellington's Victory*, mm. 425–30

Example 5.13b   Beethoven, *Wellington's Victory*, mm. 528–36 (fugato, at entrance of second voice)

or hopping steps of the "Englische"[70] became the choreography of joy for central Europe.

In music so strongly evocative of communal motion, the individual enters principally in the figure of the creator – the protagonists of the stories have been dealt with, if at all, in previous movements. The prominence of the artist depends, in turn, largely on the choice of song versus dance. Composers who use songs tend to absent themselves, exchanging the role of creator for that of arranger. They do not disappear entirely, of course, and at least one listener found the transformation of "God Save the King" into a "light-footed" fugato at the end of *Wellington's Victory* to be as good an example of *Humor* as anything else in Beethoven's music (and a tasteless one inasmuch as the "serious" tune is said to be "profaned" by Beethoven's treatment).[71] Yet there is no comparing that brief contrapuntal development to the comprehensive exhibit of variation technique in the last movement of the *Eroica*, which in turn is only the most self-conscious of many finales that subject contradance themes to highly sophisticated elaboration. Already Neubauer, for instance, integrates the concluding rondo movement of *La Bataille* by incorporating a rhythmic figure from the opening measures into each subsequent episode, turning what could be simply a string of dances into an elaboration of a *Hauptsatz* à la Haydn or

---

[70] Reichart, "Eighteenth-Century Social Dance," 235–38.
[71] Gottfried Weber, "Über Tonmalerei," *Cäcilia* 3 (1825), repr. Kunze, *Ludwig van Beethoven*, 287.

Example 5.14a Neubauer, victory celebration (*La Bataille*, finale), mm. 1–8

Example 5.14b Neubauer, victory celebration, mm. 53–77

Stamitz (Example 5.14a). The motivic connections help integrate both a quotation, of an Austro-Prussian march used also by Wranitzky (cf. Examples 5.14b, mm. 69–77, and 5.15a, mm. 67–75), and a swerve to the flatted mediant that is itself another sign of "artistry" inasmuch as it recalls the minor and flat-side laments of the battle movement (cf. Examples 5.14c and 5.4b). Likewise the finale of Wranitzky's *Grande Sinfonie caractéristique* harbors both references to the past – in this instance, the German march has appeared in both the first and the third

Example 5.14c   Neubauer, victory celebration, mm. 133–52

movements, the Revolution and the battle (see Example 5.5) – and motivic development (Example 5.15a). After emphasizing the high points
of the opening dance theme (mm. 55–56, 63–64), trumpet and drum fanfares absorb the directly following march quotation seamlessly into the
discourse (mm. 67–69). Later the brass and the rest of the orchestra trade
the fanfare rhythm back and forth in a closing theme that is lengthened
and intensified in the development section so as to suggest a memory of
battle (Example 5.15b). Even as it carries them into the thrill of a victory
dance, the movement asks its listeners to appreciate the composer's skill
in remembering what has gone before.

The same is true of the finale of Haydn's *Military* Symphony, so much
so that it raised an objection from the *Morning Chronicle*, the most assid-
uous and usually adulatory recorder of the composer's London visits.
Following the benefit concert of 2 May 1794, the newspaper criticized
the use of cymbals both in the last movement of the symphony and in the
"Finale" of the program (also by Haydn but unidentified), where their
military overtones and recollection of the symphony's second movement left too vivid an image of "the terror of ... thousands of men
meeting to murder each other."[72] If arguable, as will be seen, the critique testifies to the strength of the desire for affirmation and is worth
pondering for what it suggests not only about the *Military* Symphony
but about the contradance finale in Haydn's London symphonies generally. The continual references to his genius in the *Chronicle* and other
sources were undoubtedly due, as has been argued, to his ability to make
instrumental movements model rational discourse, *The Seven Last Words*
being a paradigmatic example.[73] At the same time, the topical content of
the new symphonies must have appealed to a country that found itself
increasingly embroiled in conflict. Allusions to war are not infrequent:

---

[72]   *Morning Chronicle* (5 May 1794), quoted in Landon, *Haydn*, III: 250–51.
[73]   See esp. David P. Schroeder, *Haydn and the Enlightenment: The Late Symphonies and
their Audience* (Oxford: Clarendon Press, 1990); and Leon Botstein, "The Demise of
Philosophical Listening: Haydn in the 19th Century," in Sisman, ed., *Haydn and His
World*, 255–85.

Example 5.15a   Paul Wranitzky, peace celebration (*Grande Sinfonie caractéristique*, iv), mm. 51–75

beyond the marches and cymbals in the *Military*, witness the fanfares that open No. 97 in C, the battle episodes in the slow movements of No. 103 in E♭ (mm. 109–34[74]) and (possibly) No. 94 in G (mm. 107–42),

---

[74] Noted by Ratner in *Classic Music*, 26.

Example 5.15b   Paul Wranitzky, peace celebration, mm. 235–47

and the march-like or Turkish passages in the finales of No. 95 in C minor (mm. 152–68), No. 99 in E♭ (mm. 68–103 and esp. its reprise, mm. 223–58), and No. 101 in D (mm. 138–88). Moreover, all the finales are based on contradances that Haydn varies and develops so as to allow, in many cases, for one or more triumphant arrivals of the main theme toward the end (e.g., in No. 101, mm. 261–80, No. 103, mm. 368–86, or No. 104 in D, mm. 309–34). Each symphony finishes by sweeping listeners into a communal dance that intensifies to a climax of joy, a rhetorical plan that cannot but have had political overtones given the circumstances of the original performances.

More than just cymbals may have prevented the *Morning Chronicle* from experiencing the finale of the *Military* Symphony similarly, for Haydn embeds several events that suggest a memory or even a continuation of violence, beginning with two surprises already within the rounded binary form that opens the movement. Its second half shifts abruptly to the relative minor, casting a shadow over the theme that lengthens as the answering statement continues in the parallel minor of the dominant (mm. 9–16). A few measures later, the upper and lower strings begin trading the theme in imitation, as if contending for dominance; they also descend a circle of fifths to the subdominant, from which the bass must climb back upward to the dominant (mm. 26–31). Both moments have echoes in the development and recapitulation. As Tovey noted, the former is unusually long and harmonically wide-ranging, coursing to the flat side as far as D♭ before heading back sharpwards through a mode shift to C♯ minor;[75] the jumping-off point is the familiar parallel minor of the dominant, preceded by a timpani roll startling enough to be sublime as well as witty, another hint of battlefield surprises (m. 122). More ominous is the brief interlude in C♯ minor, a duet in strict style reminiscent of the "Men in Armor" scene from Mozart's *Die Zauberflöte* (mm. 166–73). Through its relative major E, it provides a bridge back to the imitations between bass and treble and the original disruptive key, E minor, where the development climaxes on a descending contrapuntal sequence followed by a much-repeated but never concluded cadence in hammering eighth notes (mm. 182–202).

The cymbals and the rest of the Turkish battery do not enter until the second group of the recapitulation, which is prefaced by additional drama. As if to draw down the problematic E toward V, after returning to the tonic Haydn departs for E♭, where imitation on the dance theme ensues once again (mm. 235–50). He could fall to the dominant through an augmented sixth, but introduces instead a descent in thirds that takes the bass to B♮, not unlike the earlier drop to the subdominant (mm. 26–30) except that this time the following ascent leads scalewise all the way up through the dominant to the tonic (mm. 255–65). The deepest of all such bends in the movement (see also the closing theme, mm. 98–109), this fall away from the tonic and subsequent return prepare the kind of triumphant arrival more often reserved for a first theme, with the percussion recalling the battlefield once again and continuing to do so through the return of the main theme with which the movement does eventually end. The *Morning Chronicle* surely overreacted; the very turmoil that unsettles the celebration causes the Turkish instruments to sound as joyous as they do warlike, and their entry is like a victory all over again. There also are no further surprises, only previously heard music reinforcing the tonic, and certainly the many other composers who used percussion in their finales meant to add military glitter rather than to return to fighting. On the other hand, there is no denying a seriousness that to some extent distinguishes the *Military* Symphony finale from its counterparts among the other London symphonies, at once tempering and exalting its celebration; more obviously than Neubauer or Wranitzky, Haydn intervenes in the dance so as to recall its cause and broaden its emotional range, asserting his authority as commemorator to endow real-life events with the qualities of myth.

The artist is even more palpable in the last movement of the *Eroica*, thanks in no small part to the fermata that repeatedly brings the second half of the main theme to a halt, suspending the dancers comically in mid-step (first at m. 31). More serious is the systematic variation of the *basso del tema* and subsequently of the theme itself, including

[75] Tovey, *Essays*, I: 161.

two fugal episodes that put the dance in the unfamiliar context of a continuous texture enlivened by multiple voices in dialogue. The first (mm. 117–74) opens out into a pair of variations that come closest to invoking a real military past, one with marching band-like fifing in the flute (mm. 175–98) and the other with the minor key, dotted rhythms, and accented appoggiaturas of a Turkish march (mm. 211–56). The second fugato (mm. 277–348) leads to a passage without parallel in other celebratory finales, a Poco Andante in which the dance becomes a hymn. More than just another conversion of reality into myth, this passage and the coda that follows effect a transcendence that relies on the same mixture of topics as the first movement but seems to lift up a different body. Winds and strings suggest a sacred style with their initially hushed and homophonic texture (mm. 349–64), after which syncopations and the most plainly idyllic middle-register arpeggios in the entire symphony, played by the clarinet, turn the mood toward the pastoral (mm. 365–80). Idyll and hymn are then subsumed by a majestic statement led by the horn, an apotheosis that, by right of its basis in the dance theme, should sweep up the celebrants even as it recalls the hero's fulfillment in the first movement (mm. 381–96). Banishing the memory of the disintegrated funeral march, the drawn-out tutti confers an epic grandeur upon communal movement itself, allowing a society to achieve divinity alongside the protagonist and the artist both.

Songs in symphonies may have had a similar effect, as their corollary was not only the political singalong but also the congregational hymn, whose texture is imitated in all the orchestral battles written at the end of the wars: *Wellington's Victory* (see Example 5.13a), and the commemorations of Leipzig by Reichardt and Winter. Again, a community reaches the realm of the ideal, its synchronous action seemingly blessed with sacred associations. Missing, however, is an artistic or heroic agent to lead the transformation, for songs defined community in its broadest sense, as the people making up a nation. The most communally oriented political symphonies frequently drew an explicit connection to the nascent ideology of nationhood. Early on, during the Revolution, Othon Joseph Vandenbroek dedicated his *Prise de la Bastille* "à la nation," and Devienne made a similar statement by quoting the "Marseillaise" and other Revolutionary songs in his *Bataille de Gemmapp*. In central Europe it was at the end of the Napoleonic adventure, in the context of a pan-German nationalism originating from Prussia, that symphonies began to recognize nationhood and listeners to hear them in those terms; the chorus in Winter's *Schlacht-Sinfonie* sings of a "Vaterland" and "Volksverein" bounded by the Elbe, Rhine, and Danube rivers, and a witness to the premiere of *Wellington's Victory* saw the efforts of its performers, who had donated their services, as an example of "patriotischem Eifer und innigem Dankgefühl für den gesegneten Erfolg der allgemeinen Anstrengungen Deutschlands in dem gegenwärtigen Kriege" (patriotic pride and inner gratefulness for the blessed success of the general efforts of Germany in the present war).[76] Such an ensemble lifts itself to victory through no effort other than its own, bringing to mind the societies of gymnasts, or *Turnervereine*, founded in Prussia after the war. Veterans primarily of volunteer regiments, the *Turner* practiced physical routines based in military drill that remembered a conflict between common soldiers acting in unison rather than between heroic generals or emperors.[77] Likewise the performers of battle symphonies, and by implication their audiences, synchronized themselves musically to memorialize not any single person but a body politic.

On the other hand, the power of nationalist rhetoric in the early nineteenth century should not be overestimated, or allowed to obscure the competing claims of less broadly construed memories. "National" loyalty was unstable in a conflict of fluctuating alliances; despite its pan-Germanist cant, for instance, Winter's symphony was commissioned by and dedicated to King Maximilian Ludwig of Bavaria, who owed his kingship to Napoleon and joined the "German" coalition against him only when a French defeat appeared inevitable. A decade earlier, after the marriage of Maximilian's daughter to Napoleon's son, Vogler had celebrated quite a different national identity by adding a chorus to an existing work in C major and creating a *Bayrische nationale Sinfonie*, with a text reading "Ich bin ein Baier, ein Baier bin ich" (from a song also by Vogler).[78] In addition, works like Winter's as well as *Wellington's Victory* existed side by side with more traditional forms of tribute, *Te deums* or cantatas such as Beethoven's *Der glorreiche Augenblick* (1814), which mentions the "Volk" and its wartime travails but devotes far more energy to exalting Emperor Franz and the other monarchs gathered for the Congress of Vienna. The rulers did not object to giving their subjects credit, particularly not if it helped motivate them to further effort, but they and their artists expected that other forms of political expression would be pursued as well: Franz heard *Der glorreiche Augenblick* on the same program as *Wellington's Victory*, just as Maximilian did the heroic allegory *Timoteo*, also by Winter, alongside the *Schlacht-Sinfonie*.[79] Other than in Revolutionary France, it would have been inappropriate to

---

[76] *AmZ* 16 (1814): col. 70.

[77] Clark, "The Wars of Liberation in Prussian Memory," 559–76.

[78] Recent histories emphasize that political identity in the early nineteenth-century German states was inconsistent, and frequently more regional than national (David Blackbourn, *The Long Nineteenth Century: A History of Germany, 1780–1918* [Oxford: Oxford University Press, 1998], 88–90; Brendan Simms, *The Struggle for Mastery in Germany, 1779–1850* [New York: St. Martin's, 1998], 90–104).

[79] *AmZ* 16 (1814): cols. 74–75.

celebrate a general populace as the sole guarantor of victory, and indeed within a few years the *Turner*, whose leader Friedrich Ludwig Jahn was among the most strident of the pan-Germanists, would be suppressed for challenging the dynastic basis of power.

But however vulnerable the ideal of community, there is no doubt that songs, marches, and contradances in symphonies invoked it to varying degrees, as an alternative or a complement to the apotheosizing of military and political leadership. The patriotic culture of Napoleonic Europe had room for both, and so, too, did the musical horizons of composers such as Winter and Beethoven, who helped to articulate "popular" and "elite" sentiment alike. Such ecumenism would not long survive the wartime context. With music ever more firmly identified as a medium of expression at once personal and transcendental, it seemed increasingly unimaginable that the same composer could have written both *Wellington's Victory* and the *Eroica*, and criticism of the former work mounted quickly. When Gottfried Weber published the first extended attack in 1825 his concern was only partly the materiality that troubled so many earlier reviewers of characteristic works and other imitative music; to be sure, he says that cannon shots and musket fire comprise "die Trugkunststücke der scenischen Akustik" (the illusory tricks of acoustic scenery), simulations without any patina of artistic ennoblement, but what bothers him more is the combination of material representation and communal ethos in the *Sieges-Sinfonie*, from which he expects "Ein[en] Triumph, in Tönen idealisirt vom grossen Meister der Instrumental-Composition" (a triumph idealized in tones by the great master of instrumental composition) but gets instead the "Pöbelslustbarkeit" (mob festivity) of a fugato in dance rhythm. He longs for the exalted and individualized atmosphere of Beethoven's overture to *Egmont*: "der hohe Triumph seines Sterbens, vor dem jede Klage verstummt, und die hehre Glorie und Verklärung des ungebeugten Gefallenen – Welch ein Contrast von *solcher* Glorie zu dem belobten 'ausgelassenen Volksjubel'!" (the high triumph of his death, before which every lament falls silent, and the noble glory and transfiguration of the unbowed fallen one – what a contrast between *such* glory and the beloved "boisterous jubilation of the folk"!).[80] The quoted phrase comes from a review of 1816 (see p. 230 above) that found the happy crowd scene at the end of Beethoven's work a cause for admiration; during the intervening decade, it has become problematic for the composer to animate anyone other than the grand heroes in whose company he is himself thought to belong.

Related developments spell an end to the circumstances that fostered characteristic symphonies generally. As late as 1832 Louis Spohr

---

[80] Weber, "Über Tonmalerei," in Kunze, *Ludwig van Beethoven*, 286–88.

would call his fourth symphony, *Die Weihe der Töne*, a *Charakteristisches Tongemälde in Form einer Sinfonie*, an appropriate choice inasmuch as his four-movement scenario consists mainly of familiar situations and events: pastoral idyll with storm, cradle song with dance, battle with hymn of thanksgiving, funeral with chorale. Yet there is a dissonance between the music, also relatively traditional in its stylistic language and referential topics, and the poem by Carl Pfeiffer from which Spohr extracted his scenes and which he insisted be made available to listeners. It does include images of nature, battle, and death, but in a context where musical sounds are conceived as "schöne Träume / Aus dem unbekannten Vaterland" (beautiful dreams from the unknown homeland), signs for a noumenal space that gives birth to music and envelops the human subject in its progress through everyday life.[81] Spohr, by contrast, has music representing scenes from the real world, which are not without their transcendental dimensions – writing a symphony on the poem rather than a cantata, as Spohr originally planned, certainly helps mitigate semantic certainty – but nevertheless have too much solidity to fit Pfeiffer's ethereal soundscape.[82] More in tune with an intangible subject matter is Berlioz's *Symphonie fantastique* of two years earlier, which had already turned the symphony with text in a new direction. It, too, bears hallmarks of earlier traditions, including a dance, a pastoral scene, a march, and an infernal conclusion that may owe some conceptual debt to the underworld scenes of Berlioz's beloved Gluck. But the events all take place in the imagination of the drugged protagonist, whose privacy Berlioz insures with the bizarre orchestral atmospheres of the first and last movement openings. Unlike the murmuring idyllic textures found in so many characteristic symphonies, which help locate the action in the outdoors or on the plains of Antiquity, the luminous shimmering of Berlioz's woodwinds (in the first movement) and strings (in the finale) remove hero and listener into a world of dream.

Characteristic symphonies remain on earth, or, better, in the middleground between reality and the ineffable that was sketched in the Introduction and realized in musical and critical practice. If they seem most material when representing battle, imitating noise or the physical movements of fighters and a rejoicing populace, it should be remembered that the political communities celebrated by battle symphonies were as much products of the imagination as Beethoven's *grand Uomo*. Conversely, if the *Eroica* or *The Seven Last Words* most obviously portray idealized heroes, they ground them in actions and feelings tangible enough for commentators to speak of historical battlefields or of the

---

[81] See the complete poem in Joshua Berrett, ed., *The Symphony 1720–1840*, vol. C-9 (New York: Garland, 1980), 5–6.

[82] See the discussion in Ruiter, *Der Charakterbegriff*, 97–106.

human emotions of a divine Christ. Characteristic symphonies do not tend solely toward the infinite so valued by the early Romantics, but neither do they reflect only the military, or natural, or emotional realities contained in their subjects. Like individual and community, material and ideal coexist in a medium that refuses to grant priority to either of its constitutive parts, music or language.

Appendixes

Appendix 1 lists symphonies with characterizing texts c. 1750–1815; Appendix 2 gives additional symphonies and movements bearing only the title word pastoral, which, for reasons of space, are listed without instrumentation or incipits; and Appendix 3 categorizes symphonies by subject matter. Works by Beethoven, Joseph Haydn, and Wolfgang Amadeus Mozart are included only in Appendix 3 (for bibliographic information the reader is referred to the standard thematic catalogues and critical editions), as are a few examples with national or regional characterizations for only a single movement. While more works undoubtedly remain to be discovered, the Appendixes present the results of an extensive survey of library catalogues, lists of works and biographies for individual composers, and the publications and databases of the RISM project (A/I, A/II, B/II), as well as earlier studies by Frederick Niecks (*Programme Music*, 86–112), Otto Klauwell (*Geschichte der Programmusik*, 68–98), and F. E. Kirby ("The Germanic Symphony," 72–76).

Where possible, Appendixes 1 and 2 identify works according to the author and number from an available catalogue or index for the composer. In such cases the entries here are based on the published catalogues and include incipits and source information only where the catalogue is in need of substantial emendation (Pichl). Where sources have been discovered that were unknown to a published catalogue, they are noted in the comments and marked with an asterisk, and the entries also include all characterizing texts (as some catalogues do not), with significant variations between sources noted. Cited catalogues and indexes are listed on pp. 243–45 below. Incipits (in Appendix 1) are for first violin unless noted; dashes between movements or sections indicate that they are continuous. Manuscripts are located according to RISM library sigla, with shelf marks included where multiple sources reside in a single institution. All manuscripts are parts unless otherwise indicated. Numbers following prints refer to RISM A/I, which lists locations; where relevant, a RISM siglum in brackets acknowledges a particular print exemplar consulted for this book, e.g., [D-MÜu]. Cited sigla are listed on pp. 246–48 below. Modern editions are cited by place of publication, publisher, date, editor, and, if applicable, series (e.g., *Diletto musicale*).

CATALOGUES AND INDEXES

Altner, Vladimír. "František Xaver Dušek." In *The Symphony 1720–1840*, B-12.

Angerer, Hugo. "Franz Xaver Pokorny." In *The Symphony 1720–1840*, C-7.

"Joseph Touchemoulin." In *The Symphony 1720–1840*, C-7.

Bebbington, Warren A. "Johann Gottlieb Graun." In *The Symphony 1720–1840*, C-1.

Biondi, Michael. "Anton Zimmerman." In *The Symphony 1720–1840*, B-14.

Breitkopf, Johann Gottlob Immanuel. *The Breitkopf Thematic Catalogue: The Six Parts and Sixteen Supplements 1762–1787*, ed. Barry S. Brook. New York: Dover, 1966.

Brook, Barry S. "Othon-Joseph Vandenbroek." In *La Symphonie française dans la seconde moitié du XVIIIe siècle*, vol. II. Paris: L'Institut de musicologie de l'Université de Paris, 1962.

Brook, Barry S., gen. ed. *The Symphony 1720–1840*. 60 vols. plus *Reference Volume: Contents of the Set and Collected Thematic Indexes*. New York: Garland, 1979–86.

Brown, A. Peter. "Carlo d'Ordonez." In *The Symphony 1720–1840*, B-4.

Bryan, Paul. *Johann Wanhal, Viennese Symphonist: His Life and His Musical Environment*. Stuyvesant, NY: Pendragon, 1997.

Davis, Shelley G. "Johann Georg Lang." In *The Symphony 1720–1840*, C-1.

Downs, Annaliese. "The Symphonies of Friedrich Schwindl." Ph.D. diss., New York University, 1973.

Dunning, Albert. *Joseph Schmitt: Leben und Kompositionen des Eberbacher Zisterziensers und Amsterdamer Musikverlegers (1734–1791)*. Amsterdam: Heuwekemeyer, 1962.

Eisen, Cliff, ed. *Leopold Mozart: Sinfonien*. Denkmäler der Musik in Salzburg 4. Bad Reichenhall: Comes, 1990.

Fisher, Stephen C. "Friedrich Witt." In *The Symphony 1720–1840*, B-9.

Forsberg, Suzanne. "Joseph Camerloher and Placidus von Camerloher." In *The Symphony 1720–1840*, C-2.

Freeman, Robert N. "Johann Georg Zechner." In *The Symphony 1720–1840*, B-6.

Gérard, Yves. *Thematic, Bibliographical and Critical Catalogue of the Works of Luigi Boccherini*. London: Oxford University Press, 1969.

Gottron, A. and W. Senn. "Johann Zach, Kurmainzer Hofkapellmeister: Nachträge und Ergänzungen zum thematischen Verzeichnis seiner Kompositionen." *Mainzer Zeitschrift* 1 (1955): 81.

Der Göttweiger thematische Katalog von 1830. Ed. Friedrich W. Riedel. Munich: Katzbichler, 1979.

Götze, Ursula. "Johann Friedrich Klöffler, 1725–1790." Diss., University of Münster, 1965.

Grave, Margaret G. "Carl Ditters von Dittersdorf." In *The Symphony 1720–1840*, B-1.

Hatting, Carsten E., Niels Krabbe, and Nanna Schiøt. "Simoni dall Croubelis." In *The Symphony 1720–1840*, F-6.

Henderson, Donald G. "Peter von Winter." In *The Symphony 1720–1840*, C-11.

Hennigová-Dubová, Eva. "Antonín Vranický." In *The Symphony 1720–1840*, B-12.

Hickman, Roger. "Franz Anton Hoffmeister." In *The Symphony 1720–1840*, B-5.

Hill, Cecil. "Ferdinand Ries." In *The Symphony 1720–1840*, C-12.

Hill, George R. "Florian Leopold Gassmann." In *The Symphony 1720–1840*, B-10.

Höhnen, Heinz Werner. "Justin Heinrich Knecht." In *The Symphony 1720–1840*, C-13.

Jenkins, Newell. "Gaetano Brunetti." In *The Symphony 1720–1840*, A-5.

Kaiser, Friedrich Carl. "Carl Stamitz, 1745–1801: biographische Beiträge, das symphonische Werk, thematischer Katalog der Orchesterwerke." Diss., University of Marburg, 1962.

Kimball, G. Cook. "Leopold Hofmann." In *The Symphony 1720–1840*, B-7.

La France, Albert, and Jesse Read. "François Devienne." In *The Symphony 1720–1840*, D-10.

Landon, H. C. Robbins. *The Symphonies of Joseph Haydn*. London: Universal, 1955.

Münster, Robert, and Robert Machold. *Thematischer Katalog der Musikhandschriften der ehemaligen Klosterkirchen Weyarn, Tegernsee und Benediktbeuern. Kataloge bayrischer Musiksammlungen*, vol. I. Munich: Henle, 1971.

Murray, Sterling E. "Franz Ignaz von Beecke." In *The Symphony 1720–1840*, C-6.

The Music of Antonio Rosetti (Anton Rösler) ca. 1750–1792: A Thematic Catalog. Warren, MI: Harmonie Park, 1996.

"Paul Wineberger." In *The Symphony 1720–1840*, C-6.

Ottenberg, Hans-Günter. "Franz Anton Schubert." In *The Symphony 1720–1840*, C-10.

Parcell, Amzie D., Jr. "Giuseppe Maria Cambini." In *The Symphony 1720–1840*, D-5.

Poštolka, Milan. *Leopold Koželuh: Život a Dílo*. Prague: Státní hudební vydavatelství, 1964.

"Thematisches Verzeichnis der Sinfonien Pavel Vranickýs." *Miscellanea Musicologica* [Prague] 20 (1967): 101–28.

Powley, Harrison. "Georg Druschetzky." In *The Symphony 1720–1840*, B-14.

Répertoire international des sources musicales. Ser. A/I, *Einzeldrucke vor 1800*, 14 vols. Kassel: Bärenreiter, 1971–99.

Ser. A/II, *Music Manuscripts after 1600*. 8th edn. CD-ROM. Munich: Saur, 2000.

Ser. B/II, *Recueils imprimés XVIIIᵉ siècle*. Munich: Henle, 1964.

RISM Bibliothekssigel: Gesamtverzeichnis. Munich: Henle, 1999.

Riemann, Hugo. *Denkmäler Deutscher Tonkunst, Folge 2: Denkmäler der Tonkunst in Bayern*, Jg. 3/1. Leipzig: Breitkopf und Härtel, 1902.

Robins, Brian, ed. *The John Marsh Journals: The Life and Times of a Gentleman Composer (1752–1828)*. Stuyvesant, NY: Pendragon, 1998. Incl. work list based on Marsh's own catalogue, pp. 765–74.

Saceanu, Dan George. "François-Joseph Gossec." In *The Symphony 1720–1840*, D-3.

"Guillaume Navoigille." In *The Symphony 1720–1840*, D-1.

Shadko, Jacqueline A. "Francisco Javier Moreno." In *The Symphony 1720–1840*, F-4.

Sherman, Charles H., and T. Donley Thomas. *Johann Michael Haydn (1737–1806): A Chronological Thematic Catalogue of His Works.* Stuyvesant, NY: Pendragon, 1993.

The Symphony 1720–1840, see under Brook, p. 243 above.

Thouret, Georg. *Katalog der Musiksammlung auf der königlichen Hausbibliothek im Schlosse zu Berlin.* Leipzig: Breitkopf und Härtel, 1895.

van Boer, Bertil H., Jr. "Georg Joseph Vogler." In *The Symphony 1720–1840*, C-5.

"Johann Friedrich Grenser." In *The Symphony 1720–1840*, F-3.

Joseph Martin Kraus (1756–1792): A Systematic-Thematic Catalogue of His Musical Works and Source Study. Stuyvesant, NY: Pendragon, 1998.

Viano, Richard J. "Henri-Joseph Rigel." In *The Symphony 1720–1840*, D-2.

"Filippo Ruge." In *The Symphony 1720–1840*, D-2.

Warburton, Ernest. "Johann Christian Bach." In *The Symphony 1720–1840*, E-2.

Wolf, Eugene K. *The Symphonies of Johann Stamitz: A Study in the Formation of the Classic Style.* Utrecht and Antwerp: Bohn, Scheltema and Holkema, 1981.

Wolf, Jean K. "Christian Cannabich." In *The Symphony 1720–1840*, C-3.

Zakin, Anita. "Wenzel Pichl." In *The Symphony 1720–1840*, B-7.

Austria

A-Gd	Graz, Bibliothek des Bischöflichen Seckauer Ordinariats
A-GÖ	Göttweig, Benediktinerstift Göttweig, Musikarchiv
A-KR	Kremsmünster, Benediktiner-Stift Kremsmünster, Regenterei oder Musikarchiv
A-LA	Lambach, Benediktiner-Stift Lambach, Bibliothek
A-MB	Michaelbeuren, Benediktiner-Abtei Michaelbeuren, Bibliothek und Musikarchiv
A-Ssp	Salzburg, St. Peter, Musikarchiv
A-SEI	Seitenstetten, Stift
A-SL	St. Lambrecht, Benediktiner-Abtei, Bibliothek
A-ST	Stams, Zisterzienserstift, Bibliothek und Musikarchiv
A-VOR	Vorau, Stift
A-Wgm	Wien, Gesellschaft der Musikfreunde in Wien, Bibliothek

Belgium

B-Bc	Brussels, Conservatoire Royale de Musique, Bibliothèque

Croatia

HR-Zha	Zagreb, Zbirka Don Nikole Udina Algarotti; in Zagreb, Hrvatski glazbeni zavod, knjížnica

Czech Republic

CZ-Bm	Brno, Moravské zemské muzeum, oddělení dějin hudby
CZ-BRE	Březnice, kostel sv. Ignáce
CZ-KRa	Kroměříž, Arcibiskupsky zámek, hudební sbírka
CZ-Nlobkowicz	Nelahozeves, The Roudnice Lobkowicz Library, Nelahozeves Castle
CZ-Pnm	Prague, Národní muzeum-České muzeum hudby
CZ-Pr	Česky rozhlas, Ústřední notovy archiv
CZ-TRE	Třebon, Státní oblastní archiv

France

F-Pn	Paris, Bibliothèque nationale de France, Département de la Musique
F-V	Versailles, Bibliothèque municipale

Germany

D-Af	Augsburg, Fuggersche Domänenkanzlei, Bibliothek
D-BAR	Bartenstein, Fürst zu Hohenlohe-Bartensteinsches Archiv; in Neuenstein (Württemberg), Hohenlohe-Zentralarchiv
D-B	Berlin, Staatsbibliothek zu Berlin – Preußischer Kulturbesitz
D-BFb	Burgsteinfurt, Fürst zu Bentheimsche Musikaliensammlung Burgsteinfurt; in D-MÜu
D-Dl	Dresden, Sächsische Landesbibliothek – Staats- und Universitätsbibliothek Dresden, Musikabteilung
D-DO	Donaueschingen, Fürstlich Fürstenbergische Hofbibliothek
D-HR	Harburg (Schwaben), Fürstlich Öttingen-Wallerstein'sche Bibliothek, Schloß Harburg; in Augsburg, Universitätsbibliothek
D-LEm	Leipzig, Städtische Bibliotheken, Musikbibliothek
D-Mbs	Munich, Bayerische Staatsbibliothek, Musikabteilung
D-MÜu	Münster (Westfalen), Universitäts- und Landesbibliothek
D-OLBp	Olbersleben, Pfarrarchiv
D-RH	Rheda, Fürst zu Bentheim-Tecklenburgische Musikbibliothek Rheda; in D-MÜu
D-Rtt	Regensburg, Fürst Thurn und Taxis Hofbibliothek
D-RUh	Rudolstadt, Hofkapellarchiv; in Rudolstadt, Thüringisches Staatsarchiv
D-WD	Wiesentheid, Musiksammlung des Grafen von Schönborn-Wiesentheid
D-WEY	Weyarn, Pfarrkirche, Bibliothek; in Freising, Dombibliothek
D-WRtl	Weimar, Thüringische Landesbibliothek, Musiksammlung; in Weimar, Herzogin Anna Amalia Bibliothek

Hungary

H-Bn	Budapest, Országos Széchényi Könyvtár
H-KE	Keszthely, Helikon Kastélymúzeum Könyvtára

Italy

I-AN	Ancona, Biblioteca Comunale Luciano Benincasa
I-Bc	Bologna, Civico Museo Bibliografico Musicale G. B. Martini
I-Fc	Florence, Conservatorio di Musica Luigi Cherubini, Biblioteca
I-Gl	Genova, Conservatorio di Musica Niccolò Paganini, Biblioteca
I-MOe	Modena, Biblioteca Estense
I-Rc	Roma, Biblioteca Casanatense

Netherlands

NL-At	Amsterdam, Toonkunst-Bibliotheek

Slovakia

SK-BRnm	Bratislava, Slovenské národné múzeum, Hudobné múzeum
SK-KRE	Kremnica, Štátny okresny archív Žiar nad Hronom
SK-Mms	Martin, Matica slovenská

Sweden

S-L	Lund, Universitetsbiblioteket
S-Skma	Stockholm, Statens musikbibliotek
S-St	Stockholm, Kungl. teaterns bibliotek; in S-Skma

Switzerland

CH-BEl	Bern, Schweizerische Landesbibliothek
CH-E	Einsiedeln, Kloster Einsiedeln, Musikbibliothek
CH-EN	Engelberg, Kloster, Musikbibliothek
CH-FF	Frauenfeld, Thurgauische Kantonsbibliothek
CH-N	Neuchâtel, Bibliothèque publique et universitaire de Neuchâtel
CH-Zz	Zurich, Zentralbibliothek

United Kingdom

GB-Cu	Cambridge, University Library
GB-Lbl	London, The British Library

United States

US-Wc	Washington, DC, Library of Congress, Music Division
US-WS	Winston-Salem, NC, Moravian Music Foundation, Peter Memorial Library

Index of characteristic symphonies

Beecke, Ignaz von (1733–1803)

Pastorale sinfonie (Murray D2, 1787)
fl, 2 ob, bn, 2 hn, 2 vn, 2 va, vc, vlne, b

Un poco adagio – Allegro ma non troppo – Prima tempo –
Un poco più allegro –
Allegretto – Un poco più allegro – Un poco allegro
(all movements continuous)

Sinfonia di caccia (Murray F4, c. 1786)
2 fl, 2 ob, 2 cl, bn, 2 hn, 2 vn, va, vc, b

Un poco adagio – Allegro
Romance: Larghetto –
Menuetto: Fresco
Allegro

Comments: Additional ms. at D-BAR*

Boccherini, Luigi (1743–1805)

La casa del diavolo (Gérard 506, 1771)
2 ob, 2 hn, 2 vn, 2 va, 2 vc, b

Andante sostenuto – Allegro assai
Andantino con moto
Andante sostenuto – Allegro con molto: Chaconne qui représente
   L'enfer et qui a été faite à L'imitation de celle de M.ʳ Gluck dans le
   Festin de pierre

Editions: Milan: Suvini Zerboni, 1960 (Franco Gallini); Milan: Ricordi,
1963 (Pina Carmirelli); Vienna: Doblinger, 1991 (Antonio de Almeida,
Diletto musicale 606).

Brixi, František [Franz] Xaver (1732–71)

La Bataille de Torgau (prob. 1760–61; battle took place November 1760)
2 tpt, timp, 2 vn, va, b

Grave: Der preussische Trompeter fängt an zu blasen –
Presto: Der Feind greift an –
Largo: Der König und die Generales Lamentiren –
Allegro: Der Secours kommt von Weiten an – Der Secours kommt
   näher – Der König macht die Veranstaltung aufs neu –
Presto: Der König greift an – die Östreicher halten auf – der Feind ist
   geschlagen – der Feind retiret auf – der Feind ziehet ab –
Grave: Die Östreicher und Reiches Armée beziehen das Feindslager
(all movements continuous)

Ms: D-Rtt

Brunetti, Gaetano (1744–98)

Il maniatico (Jenkins 33, 1780)
solo vc, 2 ob, bn, 2 hn, 2 vn, va, b

Largo – Andantino –
Allegro
Quintetto – Minore: Allegretto
Allegro spiritoso – Andantino – Tempo I

Edition: Rome: Lorenzo del Turco, 1960 (Newell Jenkins, *Classici
italiani della musica*, vol. III).
Comments: On title page of autograph score (US-Wc): "Sinfonia, che
descrive per quanto si puote con l'uso de' soli Instrumenti, senza
l'aiuto delle parole, la fissazione di un delirante ad un oggetto, e
questa parte viene eseguita da un Violoncello solo, a cui si uniscono
gli altri instrumenti quasi amici impegnati a liberarlo dal suo deliro,
presentandogli una infinita varietà di idee nella varietà de' motivi.
Rimane il Maniatico per molto tempo fisso nel primo oggetto, finché
incontra un motivo allegro che lo persuade, e lo fa unire con gli altri,
dopo questo novamente ricade, ed in fine, trasportato dall'impulso
commune, termina cogli altri allegramente." Over first entrance of
solo vc: "Mania" (facsimile in *The Symphony 1720–1840*, A-5, xii).

Cambini, Giuseppe Maria (c. 1746 – c. 1825)

La Patriote (Parcell G6, 1794)
2 solo vn, 2 ob, 2 cl, 2 bn, 2 hn, tpt, 2 vn, va, vc, b

Allegro maestoso
Romance: Andante sostenuto – Andante moderato – Tempo I
Rondo: Allegretto spiritoso – Allegro

Edition: New York: Garland, 1983 (Amzie D. Parcell, Jr., *The Symphony
1720–1840*, D-5)

Camerloher, Placidus von (1718–82) or Joseph Anton (1710–43)

L'Amitié (Forsberg C31, c. 1740–50)
2 vn, va, b

Andante molto – Allegro – Andante – Allegro
Andante sempre piano
Allegro

Comments: Forsberg ascribes this work to Placidus on stylistic grounds.

Der Traum (Forsberg C34, c. 1730–43)
2 vn, va, b

Allegro
Andante molto
Presto

Comments: Forsberg ascribes this work to Joseph on stylistic grounds.

Croubelis, Simoni dall (c. 1727 – c. 1790)

Dans Le Goût asiatique (Hatting 1, c. 1780)
2 fl, 2 ob, 2 hn, 2 vn, va, b

Allegro con spirito
Andantino sotto voce
Presto

Edition: New York: Garland, 1983 (Carsten E. Hatting, Niels Krabbe, Nanna Schiødt, *The Symphony 1720–1840*, F-6)

Symphony in C (Hatting 7, c. 1780)
2 fl, 2 hn, 2 vn, va, vc, b

Allegro assai
Adagio
Minuetto
Allegro assai: Tempête

Simphonie chinoise (Hatting 10, c. 1780)
fl, 2 hn, 2 vn, va, b

Allegro
Andante
Allegro

Appendix 1

Dall'Oglio, Domenico (1700–64)

Sinfonia cossaca (no later than 1764)
2 hn, timp, 2 vn, b

Allegro
(Slow: no tempo indication)
(Fast: no tempo indication)

Ms: S-Skma
Comments: Advertised with title in Breitkopf 1767

Sinfonia russa (no later than 1764)
2 vn, va, b

Allegro
Adagio
Allegro

Ms: D-RH (without title)
Comments: Advertised with title in Breitkopf 1766

Devienne, François (1759–1803)

La Bataille de Gemmapp (La France 8, c. 1794)
fl/picc, 2 ob, 2 cl, 2 bn, 2 hn, 2 tpt, 3 tbn, timp, 2 vn, 2 va, b

On entend trois coups de canon
Rappel des trompettes
Moderato: Marche des Marseillais
Canons
Allegretto: Tocsin – La Générale –
Allegro assai: Rassemblement des troupes –
Lentement – Allegro: Le Général aux soldats –
Allegro assai: Départ des troupes – Départ de la cavalerie – Attaque –
  Feu de file – La charge –
Largo: [Plaintes et airs des blessés; title lacking in D1926, appears in
  D1927]
Allegro assai: Annonce et cris de la victoire –
Fanfare – La Carmagnole – Fanfare – La Carmagnole –
Ah ça ira

Comments: In addition to the orchestral parts listed in La France (Paris: Imbault, D1926 [D-MÜu]), the work was published in arrangements for keyboard trio (Paris: Imbault, D1927 [F-Pc]; London: Longman and Broderip, D1928) and solo keyboard (New York: Gilfert, D1929).

Dittersdorf, Carl Ditters von (1739–99)

Twelve Symphonies on Ovid's Metamorphoses

Comments: For dates of composition as well as the written descriptions by Dittersdorf (*Les Métamorphoses d'Ovide*) and Hermes (*Analyse*), see p. 32. Dittersdorf also authored prefaces in German and French to four-hand keyboard arrangements of *Jason qui enlève la toison d'or, Hercule changé en dieu,* and *Ajax et Ulisse qui se disputent les armes d'Achille* (autograph mss., CH-BEl). The German is reprinted in Krebs, Dittersdorfiana, 72–77. The French texts, given only for *Jason* and *Hercule,* include summaries of the myths but not, as in the German, descriptions of the individual movements. The Latin inscriptions below are from Hermes, *Analyse* (preserving his spelling and punctuation), which cites the same passages as Dittersdorf's pamphlet and the musical sources but frequently at greater length.

Les Quatre Ages du monde (Grave C17, prob. 1781)
fl, 2 ob, 2 bn, 2 hn, 2 tpt, timp, 2 vn, 2 va, vc, b

Larghetto: Aurea prima sata est (*Metamorphoses* 1: 89)
Allegro e vivace: Subiit argentea proles, auro deterior (1: 114–15)
Minuetto con garbo – Alternativo: Tertia post illam surrexit ahenea proles (1: 125)
Presto – Allegretto: De duro est ultima ferro (1: 127)

Editions: Leipzig: Reinecke, 1899/repr. New York: Da Capo, 1971 (Josef Liebeskind); Vienna: Doblinger, 1969 (Paul Angerer, *Diletto musicale* 117)
Comments: Described in Dittersdorf, *Les Métamorphoses d'Ovide,* and Hermes, *Analyse*

La Chute de Phaéton (Grave D1, prob. 1781)
fl, 2 ob, 2 bn, 2 hn, 2 tpt, timp, 2 vn, va, vc, b

Adagio non molto – Allegro: Regia Solis erat sublimibus alta columnis (2: 1)
Andante: Deposuit radios, propiusque accedere jussit (2: 41)
Tempo di Minuetto – Alternativo: Poenituit jurasse patrem (2: 49)
Vivace ma non troppo presto – Andantino: Intonat et dextra libratum fulmen ab aure misit in aurigam (2: 311–12)

Edition: Leipzig: Reinecke, 1899/repr. New York: Da Capo, 1971 (Josef Liebeskind)
Comments: Described in Dittersdorf, *Les Métamorphoses d'Ovide,* and Hermes, *Analyse*

Appendix 1

Actéon changé en cerf (Grave G15, prob. 1781)
fl, 2 ob, 2 hn, 2 vn, 2 va, vc, b

Allegro: Cum juvenis placido per devia lustra vagantes participes operum conpellat Hyantius ore (3: 146–47)
Adagio: Hic Dea sylvarum venatu fessa solebat virgineos artus liquido perfundere rore (3: 163–64)
Tempo di Minuetto – Alternativo: Ecce nepos Cadmi! (3: 174)
Vivace: Dilacerent falsi dominum sub imagine cervi! (3: 250)

Edition: Leipzig: Reinecke, 1899 / repr. New York: Da Capo, 1971 (Josef Liebeskind)
Comments: Described in Dittersdorf, *Les Métamorphoses d'Ovide*, and Hermes, *Analyse*

Andromède sauvée par Persée (Grave F3, prob. 1781)
2 ob, 2 hn, 2 vn, 2 va, vc, b

Adagio non molto: Caelo clarissimus alto Lucifer ortus erat (4: 664–65)
Presto: Motis talaribus aëra findit (4: 667)
Larghetto: Nisi quod levis aura capillos moverat, et tepido manabant lumina fletu marmoreum ratus esset opus (4: 673–75)
Vivace – Tempo di Minuetto: Unda insonuit, veniensque immenso belua ponto eminet . . . Ferrum curvo tenus abdidit hamo . . . Litora cum plausu, superasque deorum implevere domos, gaudent generumque salutant (4: 688–90, 720, 735–36)

Edition: Leipzig: Reinecke, 1899 / repr. New York: Da Capo, 1971 (Josef Liebeskind)
Comments: Described in Dittersdorf, *Les Métamorphoses d'Ovide*, and Hermes, *Analyse*

Phinée avec ses amis changés en rochers (Grave D34, prob. 1781)
fl, 2 ob, 2 bn, 2 hn, 2 tpt, timp, 2 vn, 2 va, vc, b

Andante più tosto allegretto: Nec coniugialia festa qui canat est clamor, sed qui fera nuntiet arma! (5: 3–4) –
Allegro assai: At ille jam moriens. . . (5: 70–71)
Andante molto: Qui pacis opus citharam cum voce moveres, jussus eras celebrare dapes festumque canendo (5: 112–13)
Vivace – Tempo di Minuetto: Renovataque proelia miscet. Gorgonis extulit ora (5: 156, 180)

Edition: Leipzig: Reinecke, 1899 / repr. New York: Da Capo, 1971 (Josef Liebeskind)
Comments: Described in Dittersdorf, *Les Métamorphoses d'Ovide*, and Hermes, *Analyse*

Index of characteristic symphonies

Les Paysans changés en grenouilles (Grave A9, prob. 1781–82)
2 fl, 2 bn, 2 hn, 2 vn, 2 va, vc, b

Allegretto non troppo presto: Agrestes illic fruticosa legebant vimina
cum iuncis, gratamque paludibus ulvam (6: 344–45)
Adagio ma non molto: Quem non blanda Deae potuissent verba
movere? (6: 360) –
Minuetto moderato – Alternativo: Hi tamen orantem perstant
prohibere (6: 361)
Adagio – Vivace ma moderato – Tempo I – Vivace: Vox quoque jam
rauca est (6: 377)

Edition: Leipzig: Reinecke, 1899/repr. New York: Da Capo, 1971 (Josef
Liebeskind)
Comments: Described in Dittersdorf, Les Métamorphoses d'Ovide, and
Hermes, Analyse

Jason qui enlève la toison d'or (prob. 1781–82)

Largo ma non troppo – Allegro: Adeunt regem, Phryxeaque vellera
poscunt (7: 7)
Andante: Concipit interea validos Aeetias ignes (7: 9)
Menuetto – Alternativo: Non magna relinquam, magna sequar (7:
55–56)
Ciaconna: Tetigit cum conjuge portus (7: 158)

Ms: CH-BEl (autograph arrangement for keyboard four hands)
Edition: Wellington: Artaria, 2000 (Allan Badley)
Comments: Described in Dittersdorf, preface to arrangement, and
Hermes, Analyse

La Siège de Mégare (prob. 1781–82)

Vivace: Praetemptatque sui vires Mavortis in urbe (8: 7)
Andante: Solita est . . . petere, exiguo resonantia saxa lapillo (8: 17–18)
Minuetto – Alternativo: Laudabat virgo junctam cum viribus artem
(8: 29)
Allegro assai – Andante – Andantino: Consumptis precibus
violentam transit in iram . . . in avem mutata vocatur Ciris (8: 106,
150–51)

Comments: No known sources. Described in Hermes, Analyse

Hercule changé en dieu (no later than 1786)

Appendix 1

Allegro e vivace: Actaque magni Herculis implerant terram
(9: 134–35)
Adagio non troppo: Flendoque dolorem diffudit miseranda suum
(9: 142–43)
Tempo di Minuetto allegro – Alternativo: Incursus animus varios
habet (9: 152)
Vivace – Adagio: Induiturque humeris Lernaeae virus Echidnae . . .
radiantibus intulit astris (9: 158, 272)

Ms: CH-BEl (autograph arrangment for keyboard four hands)
Edition: Wellington: Artaria, 2000 (Allan Badley)
Comments: Described in Dittersdorf, preface to arrangement, and
Hermes, *Analyse*

Orphée et Euridice (no later than 1786)

Larghetto: Quam satis ad superas postquam Rhodopeius auras
deflevit vates (10: 11–12)
Allegro moderato – Adagio – Tempo I: Talia dicentem – stupuit
Ixionis orbis (10: 40, 43)
Minuetto – Alternativo: Euridicen vocant . . . hanc simul et legem
Rhodopeius accipit heros (10: 48, 50)
Adagio – Vivace – Allegretto: Carpitur. . . trames . . . caligine densus
opaca . . . flexit amans oculos; et protinus illa relapsa est
(10: 53–54, 57)

Comments: No known sources. Described in Hermes, *Analyse*

Midas élu pour juge entre Pan et Apollon (no later than 1786)

Moderato: Et leve cerata modulatur arundine carmen (11: 154)
Largo: Quorum dulcedine captus Pana jubet Tmolus citharae
submittere cannas (11: 170–71)
Minuetto – Alternativo: Arguitur tamen, atque injusta vocatur unius
sermone Midae (11: 173–74)
Vivace: Induiturque aures lente gradientis aselli (11: 179)

Comments: No known sources. Described in Hermes, *Analyse*

Ajax et Ulisse qui se disputent les armes d'Achille (no later than 1786)

Allegro moderato: Et mecum confertur Ulisses! (13: 5–6)
Recitativo andantino – Arioso andantino: Meaque haec facundia . . .
invidia careat (13: 137, 139)
Menuetto – Alternativo: Fortisque viri tulit arma disertus (13: 383)

Index of characteristic symphonies

Allegro molto – Adagio non troppo: Invictumque virum vincit
dolor . . . in pectus . . . letalem condidit ensem. – Rubefactaque
sanguine tellus . . . genuit de caespite florem (13: 386, 392, 394, 395)

Ms: CH-BEl (autograph arrangment for keyboard four hands)
Edition: Wellington: Artaria, 2000 (Allan Badley)
Comments: Described in Dittersdorf, preface to arrangement, and
Hermes, *Analyse*

Il combattimento delle passioni umane (Grave D16, no later than 1771)
2 ob, 2 hn, 2 vn, va, b

Andante con majesta: Il Superbo
Andante: L'Umile
Menuetto poco allegro – Trio: Il Matto – Il Amante
Andante: Il Contento
Menuetto – Trio: Il Constante
Adagio: Il Malinconico
Allegro assai: Il Vivace

Edition: Leipzig: Reinecke, 1899/repr. New York: Da Capo, 1971 (Josef
Liebeskind); Wellington: Artaria, 1995 (Allan Badley)

Symphony in D (Grave D24, no later than 1772)
2 ob, 2 hn, 2 vn, va, b

Allegro
Andante
Allegro

Comments: Of four mss., one (CZ-Pnm) bears the title "Jupiter
Sinfonia" (see above, pp. 9–10)

Il ridotto or *Le carnaval* (Grave D32, after 1773)
2 fl, 2 ob, 2 cl, 2 bn, 2 hn, 2 tpt, timp, tr, cym, b.d., bell, 2 vn, va, vc, b

Menuetto – Trio I–III
Contradanza inglese: Allegro – Trio I–III
Concerto: Allegro e vivace
Ballo Straßburghese – Trio I–II
Polonese – Trio I–II
Ballo tedesco – Trio I–III
Kehraus: Presto

Edition: Leipzig: Reinecke, 1899/repr. New York: Da Capo, 1971 (Josef
Liebeskind)

Symphony in F (Grave F10, no later than 1781)
2 ob, 2 hn, 2 vn, va, vc, b

Appendix 1

Allegro
Andante
Menuetto – Trio: Allegro
Allegro

Comments: Of five mss., one (A-Ssp) bears the title "Sinfonie francese"

Sinfonia nazionale nel gusto di cinque nazioni (Grave A10, no later than 1766)
2 ob, 2 hn, 2 vn, va, b

Andantino: Tedesco
Allegro assai: Italiano
Allegretto: Inglese
Menuetto: Francese – Trio: Turco
Allegro assai

Editions: New York: Garland, 1985 (Eva Badura-Skoda, *The Symphony 1720–1840*, B-1); Wellington: Artaria, 1996 (Allan Badley)

Symphony in B♭ (Grave B♭2, nlt 1768)
2 ob, 2 hn, 2 vn, va, b

Presto assai
Andante
Menuetto – Trio
Presto

Editions: Mannheim: Mannheimer Musik-Verlag, 1956 (Eugen Bodart); Hamburg: Simrock, 1963 (Walter Höckner)
Comments: Of twelve mss., two bear titles related to the posthorn signal in the finale: D-Rtt ("Der Post-Zug") and HR-Zha* ("Il Postiglione"). The symphony was advertised without title in Breitkopf 1775.

Donninger, Ferdinand (1716–81)

Musikalische Vorstellung einer Seeschlacht (no later than 1781)
2 fl/picc, 2 ob, 2 cl, 2 bn, 2 hn, 4 tpt, 2 timp, 2 muskets, 2 cannons, 2 vn, va, b

Dieses musikalische Stück stellet vor eine Kriegsflotte, welche in dem Haven vor Anker liegt, und zum Auslaufen auf günstige Winde wartet.

[cannon shot]: 1. Den Anfang machet auf dem Admiralsschiffe ein Canonenschuß, welcher bey anbrechendem Tage das Signal giebt.

Reveil: 2. Gleich darauf schlägt der Tambour die Tageswacht.

Moderato: 3. Es wird auf dem Admiralsschiffe zur Bethstund geschlagen, und der Morgensegen geblasen. Kommt ein Aufzug mit Trompeten und Paucken.

Marsch: 4. Diesem folget der Seesoldaten Marsch.

Marsch. Maestoso: 5. Der Seeartilleristen Marsch.

Marsch: 6. Die Bootsknechte machen ihre Seemusik.

[cannon shot]: 7. Wird auf dem Admiralsschiffe das zweyte Signal gegeben.

Molto allegro: 8. Ein Trompeter bläst durch dreymaligen Ruf zum Absegeln.

Andante: 9. Ein *Allegro* [corrected to *Andante* in parts] stellet vor, wie die Flotte mit günstigen Winden in die offne See sticht.

Andante: 10. Ein *Andante* zeiget ein ganz stilles und ruhiges Meer an.

[cannon shots]: 11. Es werden von weitem etwelche Canonenschüsse gehört: einige ausgeschickte Brandwachten vermelden dem Admiral die nahe Gegenwart der Feinde.

[trumpet calls]: 12. Von einem feindlichen Schiffe wird ein dreymaliges Rufblasen vernommen.

Allegro: 13. Die Flotte stellet sich in Schlachtordnung, und mit beyderseitigem Canoniren nimmt das Seegefecht seinen Anfang. *Das Canonenfeuer wird durch eine Maschine vorgestellet. 14. Einige Schiffe kommen nahe zusammen, und geben mit Musqueten Feuer aufeinander. 15. Es wendet sich auf einmal der Wind. Ein Brausen erhebt sich, und die See wird nach und nach ungestümer. *Das Brausen der See wird durch eine Maschine vorgestellet. 16. Die feindliche Kriegsflotte läßt *Retirade* blasen, und nimmt die Flucht.

Allegro: 17. Auf der andern Flotte aber wird zum Zeichen des Sieges ein Aufzug mit Paucken und Trompeten gemacht.

Allegro: 18. Die Soldaten und Bootsknechte geben ihre Freude durch ein lustiges Stück zu erkennen.

Marsch. Maestoso: 19. Die siegende Flotte segelt unter beständiger Canonirung mit Trompeten- und Pauckenschall in den Haven.

Aufzug: 20. Und wird bey ihrer Ankunft mit Lösung der Canonen begrüsset.

Allegro molto: 21. Das Ende machet ein Victorie-*Allegro*.

Ms: D-Rtt (ms. parts and printed program in German and French)

Druschetzky, Georg [Družecky, Jiří] **(1745–1819)**

Sinfonia la pataglia (Powley C3, c. 1770s)
2 ob, 2 cl, 2 bn, 2 hn, s.d., b.d., 2 vn, va, b

Andante: Il riposo nella campagnia
March di cavalerie

Appendix 1

March di moschettiere
Allegro assai: La pataglia
Adagio: Lamentazione
Allegro molto: Victoria

Comments: CZ-Pnm, revised to become Powley C10

Sinfonia la pataglia (Powley C10, c. 1780s)
picc, fl, 2 ob, 2 cl, 2 bn, 2 hn, 2 tpt, timp, s.d., b.d., cym, 2 vn, va, b

Andante –
Allegro
Marcia di cavalliere
Marcia di regimento
Allegro: Pataglia
Marcia di regimento
Poco Adagio: Lamentazione
Allegro assai: Victoria –
Marcia di regimento
Fuoco fugara: Presto
Finale: Rondo a turgeso

Comments: H-Bn, revision of Powley C3

Sinfonia la pataglia (Powley C7, 1774–80)
Orch. 1: solo vn, solo vc, 2 ob, bn, 2 hn, 2 tpt, timp, b.d., 2 vn, va, b
Orch. 2: solo vn, fl, 2 ob, bn, 2 hn, timp, b.d., 2 vn, va, b

Andante poco adagio –
Allegro assai: [cavalry march] – La Pataglia –
March – [lamentations] –
Victoria – [march] – Ungaria – [lamentations]

Comments: A-Wgm, revised to become Powley C9. Written as
incidental music for Christoph Ludwig Seipp, *Adelheid von Ponthieu*,
and used at a 1780 performance in Linz; see Othmar Wessely, "Georg
Druschetzky: Der letzte Vertreter der 'heroischen' Paukerkunst in
Linz," *Heimatland: Wort und Bild aus Oberösterreich* 4 (1956), 30–31.
May also have been composed earlier; according to the edition in *Ein
Bändchen Theaterstückchen zu betrachten als eine Zugabe zu den
Hauptstücken der Ostermesse 1787* (Pressburg [Bratislava], 1787), the
play was premiered at Eszterháza in 1774.

Symphony in C (Powley C9, c. 1790s)
Orch. 1: solo vn, fl, ob, 2 tpt, timp, s.d., b.d., 2 vn, va, vc, b
Orch. 2: solo vn, fl, ob, bn, 2 hn, s.d., b.d., cym, 2 vn, va, b

Andante poco adagio –
Allegro assai: [cavalry march] – La Pataglia –
March –

260

Andante moderato: Lamentazione
Rondo: Presto

Comments: H-Bn, revision of Powley C7

Sinfonia la pataglia (Powley C13, c. 1790s)
2 ob, 2 cl, 2 bn, 2 hn, 2 tpt/posthn, timp, s.d., b.d., cym, 2 vn,
   va, vc, b

Version 1	*Version 2*
Andante –	
Allegro – Allegro recitativo	
Marcia di cavalerie	
Marcia di regimenti –	
Allegro – Recitativo –	
Marcia di cavalerie	
Andante con variazioni –	No. 1 Andante con variazioni
	(w/o 2nd var.) –
Marcia di cavalerie	Marcia di cavalerie
Marcia di regimenti –	Marcia di regimenti –
Allegro: Pataglia	Allegro: Pataglia
Marcia di regimenti –	Marcia di regimenti
Adagio: Lamentazione –	
Allegro	Allegro (new mvt. for four posthn) –
Allegretto –	
Recitativo	Recitativo
Marcia di regimenti	Marcia di regimenti
Intrada – Cadanz	
Allegro: [Victoria]	No. 2. Allegro [Victoria]
Intrada – Cadanz	
Marcia di regimenti	
Rondo: Allegro [Ungaria]	No. 3. Rondo: Allegro [Ungaria]

Comments: The two versions are indicated by cuts and paste-overs in
the sole source (H-Bn). A *fine* after the penultimate Allegro in some
parts indicates that some performances also omitted the concluding
Rondo. The movement titles "Victoria" and "Ungaria" appear in the
percussion parts only. There is no music in any part for the "Intrada –
Cadanz," which may have been improvised by the percussion or
trumpets.

Sinfonia turcia (Powley C4, c. 1770s)
picc, 2 fl, 2 cl, bn, 2 tpt, timp, b.d., cym, tr, 2 vn, va, vc, b

Allegro
Andante Echo
Menuetto
Allegro

Appendix 1

Edition: New York: Garland, 1985 (Harrison Powley, *The Symphony 1720–1840*, B-14)

Scherzando (Powley C5, c. 1770s)
2 ob, bn, 2 hn, 2 vn, va, b

Allegro assai
Andante: Ein Salzburger
Menuet
Allegro: Ein Jagd Stück

Sinfonia a la campagnia (Powley F1, c. 1770s)
2 ob, 2 cl, 2 bn, 2 hn, 2 vn, b

Allegro
Andante dolce
Menuetto
Allegro molto

Gassmann, Florian Leopold (1729–74)

Symphony in E♭ (Hill 26, 1765)
2 ob, 2 hn, 2 vn, va, b

Allegro assai
Un poco adagio
Menuetto – Trio alla greck
Allegro molto all'eclips

Edition: New York: Garland, 1981 (George R. Hill, *The Symphony 1720–1840*, B-10)

Gleissner, Franz Johannes (1759–1818)

Sinfonia Hamlet (1784)
2 ob, bn, 2 hn, 2 tpt, timp, 2 vn, 2 va, vc, b

[no tempo marking]
Andante moderato
Allegro assai

Ms: D-WEY (b only, with title page; other parts lost)
Comments: Probably composed for a 1784 performance of the play in Munich; title partially erased at a later date. See Münster, *Thematischer*

Index of characteristic symphonies

Katalog der Musikhandschriften der ehemaligen Klosterkirchen Weyarn, Tegernsee, und Benediktbeuern, 104.

Gossec, François-Joseph (1734–1829)

Symphony in E (Saceanu 23, c. 1758)
2 ob, 2 hn, 2 vn, va, b

Allegretto: Pastorella
Adagio
Minuetto – Trio con sordini
Presto

Symphony in D (Saceanu 27, 1761–62)
2 fl, 2 hn, 2 vn, va, b

Adagio lento – Allegro: Pastorella
Adagio
Minuetto – Trio
Allegro

Editions: Zurich: Kunzelmann, 1982 (Raimund Rüegge); New York: Garland, 1983 (ed. staff, *The Symphony 1720–1840*, D-3)

Sinfonia di caccia (Saceanu 62, c. 1773)
2 ob, 2 cl, 2 bn, 2 hn, 2 tpt, timp, 2 vn, va, b

Grave maestoso – Allegro
Allegretto poco allegro
Minuetto – Minuetto II
Tempo di Caccia

Edition: Charles Clauser, "François-Joseph Gossec: An Edition and Stylistic Study of Three Orchestral Works and Three Quartets" (Ph.D. diss., Univ. of Iowa, 1966).
Comments: Additional mss. at D-LEm* (shelf numbers III. 11. 37/1, III. 11. 37/2), and D-Rtt* (Gossec 14). Autograph score (F-Pc) identifies four hunting calls: [mvt. i.] Le Lancer – Hourvari – Volslé [mvt. ii.] Va l'eau.

Graf [Graaf], Christian Ernst (1723–1804)

Winter Sinfonia
2 fl, 2 hn, 4 bells, 2 vn, va, b

Allegro
Andante
Allegro

Ms: D-RUh
Comments: Andante, bell parts only: "Schütteln der Pferde"

Grenser, Johann Friedrich (1758–95)

Sinfonia alla posta (van Boer 1, 1783)
2 fl, 2 ob, 2 cl, 2 bn, 2 hn, posthn, 2 tpt, 2 vn, va, b

Allegro
Alla polacca
Allegro

Edition: New York: Garland, 1983 (Bertil H. van Boer, Jr., *The Symphony 1720–1840*, F-3)

Hauff, Ferdinand (d. 1812)

Grande Bataille à grand orchestre (1810)
picc, 2 fl, 2 cl, 2 bn, 2 hn, 2 tpt, timp, b.d., 2 vn, va, vc, cb

Adagio con expressione
Les Cors et trompettes donnent le signal deux fois
Canon
Air: Andante ["God Save the King"]
Cors et trompettes et timbales deux fois
Canon
Allegro assai: Allarme au camp –
Marche de bataille
Allegro moderato: La Cavallerie avance –
Recitativo –
Allegro moderato: Attaque et canonade –
Recitativo: Ordres du commandant –
Andante gratioso: Capitulation –
Rondo Allegretto alla Turka: Victoire

Print: Amsterdam: Hummel (H2358 [NL-At])

Haydn, (Johann) Michael (1737–1806)

Symphony in B♭ (Sherman 62, 1763)
2 ob, 2 bn, 2 hn, 2 vn, va, b

Index of characteristic symphonies

Allegro
Andante: La Confidenza
Allegro molto

Editions: New York: Garland, 1982 (Charles H. Sherman, *The Symphony 1720–1840*, B-8); Vienna: Doblinger, 1990 (Charles H. Sherman, *Diletto musicale* 353)

Hoffmeister, Franz Anton (1754–1812)

La Chasse (Hickman D6, 1784)
fl, 2 ob, 2 hn, 2 vn, va, vc, b

Allegro
Adagio
Menuetto – Trio
Allegro con brio

Edition: Bonn: Boosey and Hawkes, 1976 (Hermann Müller)

La primavera (Hickman F7, no later than 1792)
fl, 2 ob, bn, 2 hn, 2 vn, va, vc, b

Adagio – Allegro
Mezzo adagio
Menuetto – Trio
Allegro con brio

La festa della pace 1791 (Hickman G5, no later than 1792)
picc, fl, 2 ob, bn, 2 hn, 2 tpt, timp, b.d., cym, tr, campanelli, 2 vn, va, vc, b

Allegro
Poco Adagio
Menuetto: Allegretto
Allegro molto: Turcheso

Edition: New York: Garland, 1984 (Roger Hickman, *The Symphony 1720–1840*, B-5)

Holzbauer, Ignaz (1711–83)

Symphony in E♭ (Riemann E♭3, no later than 1769)
2 ob, 2 hn, 2 vn, va, b

Allegro non troppo
Andante grazioso (in London: Bremner, H6383 [D-Mbs]) or Adagio grazioso (in Paris: Bérault, H6375 [D-Mbs])
Minuetto – Trio

Appendix 1

La tempesta del mare

Editions: Leipzig: Breitkopf und Härtel, 1906 (Hugo Riemann, *Denkmäler der Tonkunst in Bayern* 7/2); London: Augener, 1939 (Adam Carse)

Kauer, Ferdinand (1751–1831)

Zinfonia militare (c. 1789–90)
2 ob, 2 cl, bn, 2 hn, 2 tpt, timp, 2 vn, va, b

Larghetto sostenuto
Allegro moderato
Allegro non troppo
Marcia: Allegro moderato
Largo

Ms: CH-N

Klöffler, Johann Friedrich (1725–90)

Bataille à deux orchestres (Götze 9, 1777)
Orch. 1: 2 fl, 2 ob, 2 hn, 2 tpt, timp, b.d., 2 vn, va, b
Orch. 2: 2 fl, 2 ob, 2 hn, 2 tpt, timp, b.d., 2 vn, va, b

1te Abteilung
Prologue de la bataille. Allegro molto, Andante, Presto Prestissimo: 1.
   Eine zweychörichte Overture, bestehend aus einem Allegro,
   Andante, und Presto, macht den Prolog zur Bataille; dann folgt:
Adagio grave: 2. Der Eingang, oder die ernsthafte und schreckbare
   Musik vor dem Marsch beyder Armeen.
Allegretto: 3. Die Avantgarde rückt vor, und die Husaren flankieren,
   man hört auch einige Musketen- und Kanonenschüsse.
Diverses marches: 4. Verschiedene Märsche der beyden Armeen,
   zwischen welchen einige Musketen, und Kanonenschüsse
   abwechseln.
Allegro molto: 5a. Die Bewegung der beyden Armeen zum
   Anmarschiren, begleitet von der Kanonade auf beyden Seiten. b.
   Das Pelotonfeuer der Infanterie von beyden Seiten. c. Der Sturm
   und Vernichtung der feindlichen Armee. d. Der lezte Angriff mit
   Musketenfeuer auf die erste feindliche Linie. e. Die Eroberung der
   Redoute.
Largo – Allegro tre molto: 6. Ein Ungewitter, welches beyden Armeen
   ein Stillstand macht.

Index of characteristic symphonies

2te Abteilung

Adagio con Recitatif: 7. Der Kriegsrat der einen Armee. Ein
begleitetes Recitativ, Violino solo.
March de la Cavallerie Coro 1mo: 8. Zeichen zum Angriff für die
Kavallerie.
Allegro moderato: 9. Der Angriff selbst. a. Der Trapp der Pferde. b.
Der Galopp. c. Geschrey der Kavallerie. d. Das Geräusch der
Waffen.
Allegro tre molto: 10. Die Flucht der Feinde.
Apell de la Cavallerie Coro 2do: 11. Die überwundene Armee blässt
zum Rückzuge und setzt sich wieder.
March de la Cavallerie Coro 1mo: 12. Zeichen zum abermaligen
Angriff für die Kavallerie der siegenden Armee.
Allegro moderato: 13a. Der Trapp der Pferde. b. Der Galopp. c.
Geschrey der Kavallerie. d. Unordentlicher Lärm beyder
Armeen.
Apell de la Cavallerie Coro 1mo: 14. Die siegende Armee blässt zum
Rückzuge, nachdem das feindliche Bataillon sich wohl vertheidigt
hat.
Allegretto: 15. Die Husaren flankiren noch, und man hört einige
Nachschüsse.
Largo: 16. Der Vorgang und die Einleitung zum Verbinden der
Verwundeten.
Andantino: 17. Die Empfindung vor der Verbindung.
Adagio grave: 18. Noch grössere Empfindung und Schmerzen.
Adagio Lamento: 19. Das Klagen und Seufzen der Verwundeten bey
der Verbindung.
Allegro moderato: 20. Viktoria, ein dreymal wiederholtes lebhaftes
Allegro, zwischen welchen ein Siegesfeuer von Musketen und
Artillerie gemacht wird.
Diverses Marches: 21. Verschiedene Märsche machen den Beschluss
der Bataille.
Sinphonia Finale: Largo – Allegro, Fuga a la breve

Comments: D-BFb preserves six autograph scores that reflect various
versions (for full descriptions see Götze): Klo 30¹ (as above), Klo 30^{1.1}
(arranged for one orchestra), Klo 30² (two orchestras, shortens or cuts
mvts. 2–7, 12–13, 15–18, 21, and Finale, includes programmatic
preface in French repr. in Götze, 100–01), Klo 30³ (one orchestra,
shortens or cuts mvts. 9, 15, 18, and 21), Klo 31 (one orchestra,
fragment of mvt. 1), and Klo 32 (fragments of mvts. 6, 7, & Fuga a la
breve); and two sets of partially autograph parts for two orchestras,
Klo 30⁴ (shortens or cuts mvts. 3–4, 9, 13, 15, 18–19) and Klo 30⁵ (full
version). In the musical sources, programmatic titles are given in a
mixture of German and French. The printed program, *Zergliederung
eines vom Kapelldirektor J.F. Kloeffler gesetzten Instrumental-Tonstücks,
eine Bataille vorstellend*, is repr. in Reichardt, *Musikalisches*

Appendix 1

Kunstmagazin 1 (1782): 52. A French version with different movement numbering appears at the beginning of Klo 31 (repr. in Götze, 112–13). Autograph parts also survive for seven symphonies comprising movements from the *Bataille* (arranged for one orchestra and often shortened) along with an additional March and Presto: *Simphonia l'orage o tempête* (Götze 15), *Simphonia tempête* (Götze 16), two works entitled *Sinfonia militaire* (Götze 10 and 11), and three entitled *Simphonia bravoura* (Götze 12–14).

Knecht, Justin Heinrich (1752–1817)

Le Portrait musical de la nature (Höhnen 1, 1785)
2 fl, 2 ob, 2 bn, 2 hn, 2 tpt, timp ad lib., 2 vn, va, b

Allegretto – Andante pastorale – Allegretto – Villanella grazioso, un poco adagio – Allegretto: 1. Une belle contrée ou le soleil luit, les doux zephirs voltigent, les ruisseaux traversent le vallon, les oiseaux gazouillent, un torrent tombe du haut en murmurant, le berger siffle, les moutons sautent et la bergère fait entendre sa douce voix.

Tempo medemo: 2. Le ciel commence à devenir soudain et sombre, tout le voisinage a de la peine de respirer et s'effraye, les nuages noirs montent, les vents se mettent à faire un bruit, le tonnerre gronde de loin et l'orage approche à pas lents.

Allegro molto: 3. L'orage accompagné des vents murmurans et des pluies battans gronde avec toute la force, les sommets des arbres font un murm[ure] et le torrent roule ses eaux avec un bruit épouvantable.

Tempo medemo: 4. L'orage s'appaise peu à peu, les nuages se dissipent, et le ciel devient clair.

L'inno con variazioni. Andantino – Coro Allegro con brio – Andantino: 5. La Nature transportée de la joie élève sa voix vers le ciel et rend au créateur les plus vives graces par des chants doux et agréables.

(nos. 2–5 are continuous)

Edition: New York: Garland, 1984 (Heinz Werner Höhnen, *The Symphony 1720–1840*, C-13)

Auf den Tod des Herzogs von Braunschweig (Höhnen 2, 1785)

Comments: No known sources. Knecht describes this work in the *Musikalische Realzeitung* (24 February 1790): cols. 59–60.

Erlebnisse des Don Quixote (Höhnen 3, 1787)

Comments: No known sources

Index of characteristic symphonies

Auf den Tod Kaiser Josephs des Zweiten (Höhnen 4, 1792)
Comments: No known sources

Kospoth, Otto Karl Endmann (1753–1817)

Composizioni sopra Il Pater noster consistenti in sette sonate caratteristiche con un' introduzione (1794)
2 ob, bn, 2 hn, 2 vn, va, b

Grave: Pater noster, qui es in coelis
Sonata I. Largo: Sanctificetur nomen tuum
Sonata II. Andante sostenuto maestoso: Adveniat regnum tuum
Sonata III. Largo: Fiat voluntas
Sonata IV. Adagio: Panem nostrum da nobis hodie
Sonata V. Adagio molto: Et remitte nobis debita nostra sicut
Sonata VI. Largo molto lento: Et ne nos inducas
Sonata VII. Largo con espressione: Sed libera nos a malo
Allegro spirituoso: Quia tuum est regnum et potentia et gloria in saecula saeculorum. Amen

Print: Darmstadt: Boßler (K1365 [D-Mbs])

Accampamento del Re di Prussia
2 ob, bn, 2 hn, 2 tpt, timp, 2 vn, 2 va, b

Largo maestoso: Preparamenti dei soldati per la marcia –
Marcia più allegro: Marciano al campo
Allegro moderato mezza voce: Gli soldati fanno l'esercizio – La cavalleria attacca l'infanteria – La retirata

Divertimenti dei soldati
Andantino: si portano alla taverna – si preparano a bere – bevano alla salute del Principe – s'ubriacono – L'evviva – fanno bavussa – si bastonano – fanno la pace –
Allegro: Si sente una musica da lontano, la Tarototella –
Tempo primo: Si preparano a ballare –
Menuetto moderato – Trio: Ballano
Allegro: Allemanda

Appendix 1

Altri divertimenti
Andante grazioso con variazioni: Si divertono al gioco della carte –
altri fumono tabacco – altri fanno l'amore – s'adormentano
Allegro: All'armi –
Allegro con molto: La bataglia
Largo: Lamento dei feriti
Allegro molto: La vittoria
Marcia
Menuetto – Trio
Contradanza
Larghetto con variazioni
Rondo finale. Allegro con molto: Si sente sonare le cinque ore di
notte – i virtuosi sono stanchi – sbadaglino – felice notte

Ms: CH-Zz

Kozeluch [Koželuh], Leopold (1747–1818)

Sinfonia francese (Poštolka I: 10, 1780–90?)
2 fl, 2 ob, 2 hn, 2 vn, va, b

Allegro molto
Poco adagio ma più andante
Menuetto – Trio
Presto con fuoco

L'Irrésolu (Poštolka I: 11, 1780–90?)
2 fl, 2 ob, 2 hn, 2 vn, 2 va, b

Allegro ma più presto – [recitative] - Adagio
Adagio
Menuetto vivace – Trio
Allegro molto poco presto – [recitative] – Adagio

Kraus, Joseph Martin (1756–92)

Symphonie funèbre or *Musik vid Konung Gustaf III:s Bisättning* (van Boer
148, 1792)
2 ob, 2 cl, 2 bn, 4 hn, 2 tpt, timp, 2 vn, va, vc, b

Andante mesto
Larghetto
Choral
Adagio

Editions: Stockholm: Riemers, 1979 (Jan Olof Rudén, *Monumenta
Musicae Svecicae* 9); Wiesbaden: Breitkopf und Härtel, 1956 (Walter
Lebermann)

Marsh, John (1752–1828)

Symphony in B♭ (1782)
2 ob, 2 hn, 2 vn, va, b

Allegro
Andante
Allegretto: La Chasse

Print: London: Preston (not in RISM; copy at GB-Cu)

La Chasse (1790)
fl, 2 ob or cl, 2 hn, 2 vn, va, vc

Andante: The Hunter's Call in the Morning and Gradually
    Assembling Together –
Allegretto: Setting out from Home (Trotting and Occasionally
    Cantering) – the Fox Discovered, etc. –
Allegro: Chasse
(all movements continuous)

Print: London: Preston (not in RISM; copy at GB-Cu)

Mašek, Vincenz [Václav] (1755–1831)

Symphonia militare (after 1780)
2 ob, 2 hn, bn, 2 vn, va, b

Allegro ma non tanto
Andante
Allegro molto

Mss: with title: CZ-BRE; without title: CZ-Pnm
Edition: New York: Garland, 1984 (Jitřenka Pešková, *The Symphony
1720–1840*, B-13)

Appendix 1

Massonneau, Louis (1766–1848)

La Tempête et le calme (1794)
2 fl, 2 ob, 2 bn, 2 hn, 2 vn, va, vc, b

Largo – Allegro con fuoco –
Andantino
Vivace assai

Print: Offenbach: André (M1332 [D-Mbs])

Moreno, Francisco Javier (1748–1836)

Sinfonia titolata le due opposti caratteri Superbia ed Umiltà (Shadko 2,
    c. 1801–05)
fl, 2 ob, bn, 2 hn, 2 vn, va, b

Introduzione: Maestoso –
Allegro

Edition: New York: Garland, 1981 (Jacqueline A. Shadko,
The Symphony 1720–1840, F-4)

Sinfonia titolata la sala di scherma (Shadko 3, c. 1801–05)
2 fl, 2 ob, 2 cl, 2 bn, 2 hn, 2 vn, va, vc, b

Introduzione: Adagio cantabile – Allegro
Supplemento. Minuetto: Vivace

Edition: New York: Garland, 1981 (Jacqueline A. Shadko,
The Symphony 1720–1840, F-4)

Mozart, Leopold (1719–87)

Jagd Parthia (Eisen D23, no later than 1768)
2 hn, cuculo obligato, 2 vn, va, b

Comments: No known sources

Sinfonia burlesca (Eisen G2)
bn, 2 va, 2 vc, b

[no title]
Menuet
Andante Il Signor Pantalone
Harlequino

Index of characteristic symphonies

Editions: Leipzig: Breitkopf und Härtel, 1908 (Max Seiffert, *Denkmäler der Tonkunst in Bayern* 9/2); Vienna: Doblinger, 1970 (Paul Angerer, *Diletto musicale* 83)
Comments: Ms. at D-HR also includes the second movement title "Menuet Hanswurst"

Sinfonia pastorale (Eisen G3, no later than 1751)
2 hn, corno pastoricio, 2 vn, va, b

Allegro
Andante
Presto

Editions: Zurich: Eulenburg, 1979 (Kurt Janetzky); missing 2 hn. Eisen, "Leopold Mozart Discoveries," *Mitteilungen der Internationalen Stiftung Mozarteum* 35 (1987): 1–10, notes errors in the edition and prints the authentic horn parts.

Jacht Sinfonia (Eisen G9)
2 hn, 2 vn, va, b

Allegro
Andante più tosto un poco allegretto a gusto d'un Echo
Menuet

Editions: Leipzig: Breitkopf und Härtel, 1908 (Max Seiffert, *Denkmäler der Tonkunst in Bayern* 9/2); Vienna: Universal, 1963 (Max Langer); Mainz: Schott, 1967 (Gabor Darvas); Zurich: Eulenburg, 1968 (Jürgen Braun); Vienna: Doblinger, 1970 (Helmut Riessberger, *Diletto musicale* 311)
Comments: On titles for this work see Eisen

Navoigille, Guillaume (c. 1745–1811)

Symphony in E♭ (Saceanu 11, no later than 1775)
2 vn, va, b

Allegro assai
Minuetto – Trio: Andante
Chasse

Neubauer, Franz Christoph (ca. 1760–95)

La Bataille (1789)
2 fl, 2 ob, bn, 2 hn, 2 tpt, timp, b.d., 2 vn, va, b

273

Adagio ma non tanto: Le Matin
Allegro: Allarme au camp
Andante: Harangue aux guerriers
Allegretto: Les Deux Armées se rangent en ordre de bataille
Allegro: La Bataille
Andante: Retour au camp
Allegro: Célébration de la victoire

Ms: D-Af (destroyed; according to a description preserved in the copy of N438 at D-Mbs, the ms. was entitled "La Bataille du Koburg" and included a program in German)
Prints: Offenbach: André (N437 & N438); Heilbronn: Amon (N485, arranged for keyboard with title "Bataille de Martinesti")
Edition: New York: Garland, 1985 (Elizabeth Wright, *The Symphony 1720–1820*, B-14)

Pichl, Václav [Pichel, Wenzel] **(1741–1805)**

Source information in Zakin is amplified and corrected, and dates of composition have been revised.

Terpsich[or]e (Zakin 1, no later than 1769)
2 fl, 2 bn, 2 hn, 2 vn, va, b

Allegro
Andante
Menuetto – Trio
Allegro poco presto

Mss: without title: CZ-Pnm XXVII B 68*, CZ-Pnm Doksy XXXIV E 70*
Comments: Advertised with title in Breitkopf 1769

Euterpe (Zakin 2, no later than 1769)
2 ob, 2 hn, 2 vn, va, b

Allegro assai
Andante
Menuetto – Trio
Finale

Mss: with title: I-MOe Mus. D. 332; without title: CZ-Pnm XXVII B 69*
Comments: Advertised with title in Breitkopf 1769

Uranie (Zakin 3, no later than 1769)
2 ob, 2 hn, 2 vn, va, b

Allegro moderato
Andante
Menuetto – Trio
Allegro assai

Mss: with title: CZ-Pnm Pachta XXII E 20* ("Uranie/Musa," dated 1769), CZ-Pnm Clam Gallas XLII E 99 ("Uranie"); without title: A-KR H 31/258*, A-VOR Sign. 956*, CZ-Pnm XXVII B 70*, CZ-Pnm Osek XXXII A 388*, CZ-Pnm Doksy XXXIV E 67*, CZ-Pnm Kuks XLIII C 311*, US-Wc
Comments: Advertised with title in Breitkopf 1769

Saturnus (Zakin 4, no later than 1772)
fl, 2 ob, 2 hn, 2 vn, va, b

Allegro assai
Andante
Menuetto – Trio
Presto

Mss: with title: A-SL [no call no.], CZ-Pnm Clam Gallas XLII E 100; without title: A-KR H 31/259*, CZ-Pnm Doksy XXXIV E 68*, SK-BRnm MUS XX 82*
Comments: Advertised without title in Breitkopf 1772

Pallas or *Alla francese* (Zakin 6, no later than 1773)
2 ob, 2 hn, 2 vn, va, b

Allegro
Andante rondo
Menuetto moderato – Trio
Allegro

275

Appendix 1

Mss: with title: D-Rtt Pichl 13/II ("Pallas/Alla francese"); with "alla francese" or variant only: A-GÖ 2870, A-SEI V 1048*, CZ-Pnm Clam Gallas XLII E 310*, I-MOe Mus. D. 660, CZ-Pr (in D, attributed to Vanhal); without title: A-Gd Bestand Aussee/Rottenmann, Ms. 215, A-KR H 30/240, A-ST K II 17, A-Wgm XIII 39996*, CH-E Th. 7,12 (Ms. 1728)*
Edition: Zurich: Kunzelmann, 1982 (Hermann Müller)
Comments: Advertised in Breitkopf 1773 as "Sinf. da PICHL al's DITTERS" (p. 483) and as a symphony without title by Dittersdorf (p. 485)

Flora (Zakin 7, 1765–70)
2 ob, 2 hn, 2 vn, va, b

Tempo di Minuetto
Andante
Minuetto – Trio
Allegro assai

Mss: with title: I-MOe Mus. D. 662; without title: A-GÖ 2872*, A-KR H 20/243*, A-LA
Comments: Dating based on similarity to other neoclassical symphonies

Clio (Zakin 8, no later than 1774)
2 ob, 2 hn, 2 vn, va, b

Allegro moderato
Andante in canone
Minuetto – Trio
Allegro

Mss: with title: CZ-Pnm Clam Gallas XLII E 96, I-MOe Mus. D. 326; without title: A-KR H 30/244, A-ST K II 16, CZ-Pnm XXVII B 67*, CZ-Pnm Doksy XXXIV E 71*
Edition: Wellington: Artaria, 1998 (Allan Badley)
Comments: Advertised without title in Breitkopf 1774. CZ-Pnm XXVII B 67 and CZ-Pnm Doksy XXXIV E 71 have a different slow movement, Andante.

Pallas (Zakin 9, no later than 1769)
2 ob, 2 hn, 2 tpt, timp, 2 vn, va, b

Allegro con garbo
Andante
Menuetto – Trio
Allegro

Mss: with title: CZ-Pnm Pachta XXII E 21 ("Pallas/Dea," dated 1769);
without title: A-KR 30/241, CZ-Bm (Tyn) A 6329, CZ-Pnm XIII F 137,
CZ-Pnm Osek XXXII A 170, CZ-Pnm Doksy XXXIV E 66, SK-BRnm
Kežmarok MUS IX 8, A-SF (attributed to Haydn), SK-Mms
(attributed to Vanhal)
Comments: Advertised without title in Breitkopf 1775

Polymnia (Zakin 10, no later than 1775)
2 ob, 2 hn, 2 vn, va, b

Allegro giusto
Rondo: Andante poco allegro
Menuetto – Trio
Presto

Mss: with title: CZ-Pnm Clam Gallas XLII E 98*; without title: S-L
Prints: Lyon: Guera and Paris: Boyer (H3095 and RISM B/II p. 381,
without title and lacking minuet)
Comments: Advertised without title in Breitkopf 1775. No mss. at
CZ-KRa, I-Bc; sources at GB-Cu, D-WD, F-V are H3095.

Calliope or *Polymnia* (Zakin 11, no later than 1769)
2 ob, 2 hn, 2 tpt, timp, 2 vn, va, b

Grave e Maestoso – Allegro
Andante
Minuetto – Trio
Allegro assai

Appendix 1

Mss: with title: CZ-Pnm Pachta XXII E 22* ("Polymnia/Musa," dated 1769), I-MOe Mus. D. 328 ("Calliope"); without title: CH-EN Ms A 563 (Ms. 5934)* (lacks tpt/timp), CZ-Pnm Doksy XXXIV E 69*
Edition: Wellington: Artaria, 1998 (Allan Badley)
Comments: Advertised without title in Breitkopf 1775. No ms. at CZ-TRE

Thalia (Zakin 12, no later than 1775)
2 ob, 2 hn, 2 vn, va, b

Allegro assai
Andante grazioso
Menuetto – Trio
Allegro

Mss: with title: I-Fc; without title: D-Rtt Pichl 7
Comments: Advertised without title in Breitkopf 1775. CZ-Pnm Clam Gallas XLII E 307 is Zakin 5.

Melpomene (Zakin 14, no later than 1775)
2 ob, 2 hn, 2 vn, va, b

Allegro con brio
Andante
Minuetto – Trio
Allegro

Mss: with title: I-MOe Mus. D. 327; without title: CZ-Pnm Doksy XXXIV E 72*, I-Fc D.5.87
Edition: Wellington: Artaria, 1998 (Allan Badley)
Comments: Advertised without title in Breitkopf 1775

Diana (Zakin 15, 1765–70)
2 ob, 2 hn, 2 vn, va, b

Cantabile Adagio – Presto assai

Menuetto – Trio I & II
Presto

Mss: with title: CZ-Pnm Clam Gallas XLII E 270; without title:
CZ-Pnm Doksy XXXIV C 169*
Comments: Dating based on similarity to other neoclassical
symphonies

Mars or *Diana* (Zakin 16, no later than 1775)
2 ob, 2 hn, 2 vn, va, b

Allegro troppo
Andante arioso
Minuetto – Trio
Presto

Mss: with title: CZ-Pnm Clam Gallas XLII E 271 ("Mars"), I-MOe
Mus. D. 329 ("Diana"); without title: A-ST K II 15, CZ-Pnm XXVII B
71*, D-OLBp Pfarrarchiv II B 18* (lacking 2hn), I-Fc D.5.87, SK-BRnm
Kežmarok MUS IX 7, SK-BRnm Pruské MUS XXVI 351* (lacking
winds), A-KR (attributed to Johann Stamitz)
Edition: Wellington: Artaria, 1998 (Allan Badley)
Comments: Advertised without title in Breitkopf 1775. No ms. at A-GÖ.

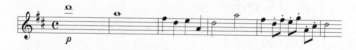

Sinfonia pastorella or *Polymnia* (Zakin 17, 1765–70)
fl, 2 ob, 2 hn, 2 vn, va, b

Allegro
Andante poco allegretto
Menuetto – Trio
Allegro

Mss: with title: D-Rtt Pichl 13/I ("Polymnia/Pastorella"); with
"pastorella" or variant only: A-GÖ 2871* (b only), A-KR H 30/242*
(lacking fl), A-SEI V 1070*, CH-FF UK 440*, CZ-Pnm Kuks XLIX E 61,
H-P P25*; without title: SK-BRnm Kežmarok MUS IX 6 (different
finale).
Comments: Dating based on similarity to other neoclassical
symphonies. CZ-Pnm Clam Gallas XLII E98 is Zakin 10.

Il Mars (Zakin 18, 1765–70)
fl, 2 ob, bn, 2 hn, 2 tpt, timp, 2 vn, va, b

Maestoso e poco adagio – Allegro assai
Andante
Menuetto in canone – Trio
Allegro con brio

Mss: with title: CZ-Pnm Clam Gallas XLII E 97, I-MOe Mus. D. 661;
without title: CZ-Pnm XXXI D 18*
Edition: New York: Garland, 1984 (Anita Zakin, *The Symphony 1720–1840*, B-7)
Comments: Dating based on similarity to other neoclassical symphonies

Apollo (sinfonia concertante) (Zakin 25, 1765–70)
fl, 2 ob, 2 bn, 2 hn, 2 tpt, timp, solo vn, solo vc, 2 vn, 2 va, vc, b

Adagio maestoso – Allegro assai
Adagio maestoso
Rondo: Allegro moderato

Mss: with title: D-Dl Mus. 3482-N-4, I-MOe Mus. D. 659; without title:
D-DO, D-Rtt Pichl 5*
Print: Berlin: Hummel (P2239, without title; see Figure 1.1, p. 42 above)
Edition: New York: Garland, 1984 (Anita Zakin, *The Symphony 1720–1840*, B-7)
Comments: Dating based on similarity to other neoclassical symphonies. No ms. at D-Mbs; US-WS is P2239.

Pugnani, Gaetano (1731–98)

Werther (c. 1795)
fl, 2 ob, eng hn, 2 cl, bn, 2 hn, 2 vn, va, vc, b

Parte Prima
Sinfonia: Allegro sostenuto – un poco più allegro – più presto –
Andante
Largo – Andante – Adagio – Tempo di prima –
Allegretto
Allegro moderato
Allegro
Inglese
Allegro assai – Più lento
Andantino
Largo – Andantino – Allegretto
Allegro

Parte Seconda
Andante
Andantino
Andante sostenuto – Allegro
Andantino
Lento – Un poco andante – Adagio (Recit.) – Allegro – Allegretto
Adagio – Andante – Allegro assai
Largo
Adagio sostenuto – Allegretto – Allegro – Adagio – Andantino –
    Andante – Adagio – Allegro – Adagio – Più presto – Andante –
    Allegro – Adagio – Allegro – Adagio – Recit.
Presto
Allegro assai – Largo assai – Presto – Allegro assai – Adagio
    sostenuto – Largo assai – Recit. – Allegro assai

Ms: A-Wgm
Edition: Milan: Suvini Zerboni, 1985 (Alberto Basso and Ruggero
Maghini, *Monumenti musicali italiani* 11)

Raimondi, Ignazio (c. 1735–1813)

Les Aventures de Télémaque dans l'isle de Calypso (1777)

Comments: No known sources. Program distributed at performance
of 15 January 1777 in Amsterdam, repr. *L'Esprit des journaux*
(March 1777): 301–04

Reichardt, Johann Friedrich (1752–1814)

Appendix 1

Overtura di vittoria (1814)
2 fl, 2 ob, 2 cl, 2 bn, 2 hn, 2 tpt, 3 tbn, timp, 2 vn, va, vc, vlne

Allegro di molto e maestoso

Ms: D-B

Schlacht-Symphonie (1814)
2 fl, 2 ob, 2 cl, 2 bn, 2 hn, 2 tpt, 3 tbn, timp, 2 vn, va, vc, vlne

Marcia: Molto moderato e maestoso –
Choral [Jesus meine Zuversicht] –
Allegro furioso – Più presto
Choral [Nun danket alle Gott]
Marcia: Vivace

Ms: D-B

Richter, Franz Xaver (1709–89)

La tempesta del mare (c. 1744–52)
2 vn, va, b

Allegro
Andante
Allegro: La Confusione

Ms: A-Gd (attributed to Camerloher)
Comments: On Richter's authorship see Suzanne Forsberg, "The Symphonies of Placidus von Camerloher (1718–82) and Joseph Camerloher (1710–43): An Investigation of Style and Authorship" (Ph.D. Diss., New York University, 1990), 226–33.

Ries, Ferdinand (1784–1838)

Symphony in D (Hill 1, 1809)
fl, 2 ob, 2 cl, 2 bn, 2 hn, 2 tpt, timp, 2 vn, va, vc, b

Adagio – Allegro molto vivace
Marche funèbre
Menuetto moderato
Allegro

Edition: New York: Garland, 1982 (Cecil Hill, *The Symphony 1720–1840*, C-12)

Romberg, Andreas Jakob (1767–1821)

Sinfonia alla turca (1798)
picc, fl, 2 ob, 2 cl, 2 bn, 2 hn, 2 tpt, cym, tr, b.d., timp, 2 vn, va, vc, b

Allegro
Menuetto: Vivace
Andante quasi Allegretto
Finale: Vivace

Prints: Leipzig: Peters (R2165 [A-Wgm]; R2166, arranged for keyboard four hands)

Romberg, Bernhard Heinrich (1767–1841)

Trauer-Symphonie, Dem Andenken der unvergeßlichen Hochseeligen Königin Louise von Preussen gewidmet (1810)
fl, 2 ob, 2 cl, 2 bn, 2 hn, timp, 2 vn, va, vc, cb

Andante lento maestoso – Allegro
Adagio non troppo – Allegro non troppo – Con più moto – Andante lento – Andante grazioso

Ms: D-B (score)
Prints: Leipzig: Kühnel (R2293; R2294, arranged for keyboard four hands); Dresden: Hilscher (R2295, arranged for keyboard)
Edition: New York: Garland, 1985 (Joshua Berrett, *The Symphony 1720–1840*, C-14)

Rosetti, Antonio [Rösler, Anton] (c. 1750–92)

Sinfonia pastoralis (Murray A15, no later than 1778)
2 fl, 2 ob, 2 hn, 2 vn, va, b

Grave – Allegro molto
Andante allegretto
Menuetto – Trio

Edition: Leipzig: Musikwissenschaftlicher Verlag, 1936 (Helmut Schultz)

Appendix 1

La Chasse (Murray A20, 1782)
2 fl, 2 ob, 2 cl, 2 bn, 2 hn, 2 tpt, timp, 2 vn, 2 va, vc, b

Vivace
Romance: Adagio non tanto
Menuetto majestoso – Trio
Allegro

Edition: Holzkirchen: Accolade, 1997 (Sterling E. Murray)

Calypso et Télémaque (1791?)

Comments: No known sources. Descriptions in *AmZ* 2 (1800), cols. 748–49, and *Journal générale de la littérature de France* 3 (1800), pp. 63, 189–91

Ruge, Filippo (c. 1725 – after 1767)

La nova tempesta (Viano 1, 1757)
2 hn, 2 vn, va, b

Con spirito
Andantino a mezza voce
Allegro ma non presto: La tempesta

Edition: Barry S. Brook, *La Symphonie française dans la seconde moitié du XVIIIe siècle*, vol. III.

Symphony in G (Viano 5, 1756)
2 hn, 2 vn, va, b

Allegro con spirito
Andantino quasi adagio
Spiritosetto: La tempesta

Edition: New York: Garland, 1984 (Michael Pilat and Richard J. Viano, *The Symphony 1720–1840*, D-2)

Symphony in F (Viano 7, 1755)
2 hn, 2 vn, va, b

Risoluto e spiritoso
Un andantino quasi adagio
A la cabriolet: Andante e non allegro

Edition: New York: Garland, 1984 (Richard J. Viano, *The Symphony 1720–1840*, D-2)

Sandel, Matthias (1740–1816)

L'imbroglio del matrimonio
fl, 2 ob, bn, 2 hn, 2 vn, va, vc, b

Allegro assai
Andante
Menuetto – Trio
Recitativo – Presto

Ms: D-Rtt

Schmitt, Joseph (1734–91)

Sinfonie pastorale (Dunning 8, c. 1790)
fl, 2 ob, 2 bn, 2 hn, 2 tpt, timp, 2 vn, 2 va, vc, b

Grave
Adagio – Poco andante – Allegro
Adagio – Andante pastorale – Un poco vivace – Andante [pastorale]
Adagio – Allegro molto – Lento – Allegro molto

Schmittbauer, Joseph Aloys (1718–1809)

Sinfonia hypochondrica
2 fl, 2 ob, 2 bn, 2 hn, tpt, 2 vn, va, b

Adagio molto – Allegro molto
Andante allegretto
Allegretto scherzoso tedesco in rondo

Ms: D-Rtt
Comments: Advertised with title in Breitkopf 1782–84

Stamitz, Carl (1745–1801)

Simphonie de chasse (Kaiser 31, 1772)
2 ob, 2 hn, 2 vn, 2 va, b

Grave – Allegro
Andante

Appendix 1

Allegro più moderato – Presto – Moderato – Presto – Moderato –
Presto

Comments: Advertised with title in Breitkopf 1779–80. Additional ms.
at CH-R*

Le Jour variable (Kaiser 32, 1772)
2 fl/picc, 2 ob, 2 hn, 2 tpt, 2 vn, 2 va, b

Andante moderato: Le Beau Matin. Pastorale –
Allegro con spirito: La Tempête
Andante moderato: La Nuit obscure –
Moderato un poco allegro – Allegro vivace – Moderato – Allegro
    vivace – Andante moderato – Moderato – Allegretto – Presto:
    La Chasse

Comments: Written at Versailles. Autograph parts (D-WRtl) titled as
above. According to Thouret, *Katalog der Musiksammlung auf der
königlichen Hausbibliothek im Schlosse zu Berlin*, 224, a source at D-B
(destroyed) was entitled "La Promenade royale," which is related to
Stamitz's description of the first movement in a letter of 12 April 1791
to Friedrich Wilhelm II of Prussia (repr. Kaiser, 55–56): "la Reine se
promenant le matin aux Environs des Campagnes, j'ai imitté une
Pastoralle."

Symphony in F (Kaiser 34, no later than 1773)
2 ob or cl, 2 hn, 2 vn, 2 va, b

Allegro assai
Andante
Allegro molto: La Chasse

God Save the King (Kaiser 49, 1792)
2 fl, 2 ob, 2 bn, 2 hn, 2 tpt, timp, 2 vn, 2 va, b

Grave ma andante moderato – Allegro assai, ma presto
Andante non troppo moderato. Grazioso
Rondo: Allegro assai

Stamitz, Johann (1717–57)

Sinfonia pastorale (Wolf D4, c. 1754–57)
2 ob, 2 hn, 2 vn, va, b

Presto
Larghetto
Menuè – Trio
Presto assai

Edition: Berlin: Vieweg, 1931 (Walter Upmeyer)

Sterkel, Johann Franz Xaver (1750–1817)

Sinfonia turca
2 fl, 2 ob, 2 bn, 2 hn, 2 tpt, timp, b.d., tri, 2 vn, 2 va, vc, b

Allegro – Andante – Allegro
March
Allegretto

Ms: CH-Zz

Süßmayr, Franz Xaver (1766–1803)

Sinfonia turchesa (c. 1790)
picc, 2 ob, 2 bn, 2 hn, tpt, tamburo tedesco, tamburo turcheso, s.d.,
  cym, tri, 2 vn, va, b

Allegro
Adagio
Menuetto – Trio
Finale

Ms: A-KR
Edition: New York: Garland, 1985 (Mary B. B. Innwood, *The Symphony
1720–1840*, B-14)

Vančura, Arnošt [Wanczura, Ernest] **(c. 1750–1802)**

*Trois Sinfonies nationales à grand orchestre arrangées de plusieurs chansons
  russes, ukrainiennes et polonoises* (1798)
2 fl, 2 cl, 2 bn, 2 hn, 2 tpt (in *Sinfonie I* only), 2 vn, va, b

Sinfonie I. Nationale ukrainienne
Allegro moderato (vn 1–2: Allegro non troppo)
Andante
Rondo

287

Sinfonie II. Nationale russe
Allegro moderato
Andante
Rondo

Sinfonie III. Nationale polonaise
Allegro assai à la masoure
Andante à la polonaise
Rondeau à la cosaque – Andante non troppo – Rondeau

Print: St. Petersburg: Sprewitz (W198 [GB-Lbl])
Edition: Kiev: Muzychna Ukraïna, 1983 (Margarita Pryashnikova; arranged for keyboard)

Vandenbroek, Othon Joseph (1758–1832)

La Prise de la Bastille (Brook 1, after 1795)
fl, 2 ob or 2 cl, 2 bn, 2 hn, b.d., 2 vn, va, b

Grave – Allegro assai
Adagio
Presto assai

Vanhal [Wanhal], Johann Baptist [Jan Křtitel] (1739–1813)

Sinfonia comista con per la sorta diversa (Bryan C11, 1775-78?)
2 ob, 2 bn, 2 hn, 2 tpt, timp, 2 vn, va, b

Allegro con brio: La speranza
Andante cantabile: Il sospirare e languire
Finale. Adagio più andante – Allegro: La lamentatione – L'allegrezza

Edition: New York: Garland, 1981 (facsimile of B-Bc, *The Symphony 1720–1840*, B-10)
Comments: Advertised without title in Breitkopf 1775. Of five mss., B-Bc (score) has all the titles, A-KR has "Speranza" and "Lamentatione," D-B has "Speranza" only, and A-MB and D-Rtt have no titles.

Index of characteristic symphonies

Symphony in E♭ (Bryan E♭1, 1763–65?)
2 ob, 2 hn, 2 vn, va, b

Allegro
Adagio
Menuetto – Trio
Allegro: La tempesta

Veichtner, Franz Adam (1741–1822)

Simphonie russienne (1771)
2 fl, 2 hn, 2 vn, va, b

Allegro assai
Allegretto
Menuetto – Trio
Presto

Prints: Riga: Hartknoch (V1094), Amsterdam: Hummel (V1095 [D-Rtt])

Vogler, Georg Joseph (1749–1814)

Bayrische nationale Sinfonie (van Boer 164, 1806)
2 picc, 2 fl, 2 ob, 2 cl, 2 bn, 4 hn, 2 tpt, timp, SATB, 2 vn, va, vc, b

Allegro
Choral: Exultet orbis gaudiis
Minuetto I–III
Presto

Comments: Revision (D-Mbs) of the Symphony in C (van Boer 164, 1799), adding title, chorus, choral text, and new second movement

Trauermusik auf Ludwig XVI (1793)
2 fl, 2 ob, 2 cl, 4 bn, 4 hn, 2 tpt, timp, 2 vn, va, b

Marche
Larghetto
Hymnus: Adagio
Fuga: Andante

Ms: S-St

Appendix 1

Volder, Pierre Jean de (1767–1841)

La Bataille d'Jena (1806)
picc, fl, 2 cl, 2 bn, 4 hn, 2 tpt, timp, s.d., b.d., tr, cym, 2 vn, va, b

Lento: Le Calme de la nuit –
Larghetto: Lever de l'aurore –
Lento: Le Canon – Tambour –
Vivace: Les Troupes prennent les armes
Mouvement de marche: Marche des troupes françaises infanterie
    legère
Trompette [cavalry signal] –
Allegretto: Départ de la cavalerie –
Maestoso: Arrivée de l'empereur –
Pas redouble: Marchons
Moderato: Ordres de l'empereur aux maréchaux – Discours de
    l'empereur aux soldats –
Allegro: Vive l'empereur
Allegro: La Générale –
Trompette –
Lento: Canon – Roulement –
Tres animé: La Bataille –
Plus lent – Canonade –
Pas redouble: L'Armée française debouche dans la plaine au pas
    redoublé – elle se mette en bataille
Vivace: Engagement général
Vite: La Charge –
Vivement: L'Ennemi est culbuté –
Allegretto: La Victoire est à nous –
Vivace: Vive l'Empereur – Fanfare
Lamentabile: Cris des blessées
Trompette – Tambour –
Vivace: Victoire
Pas redouble: L'Armée française marche sur Berlin

Ms: F-Pn (prob. autograph score)

Wineberger, Paul Anton (1758–1822)

Symphony in A (Murray A1, c. 1792)
2 fl, 2 cl, 2 hn, 2 vn, 2 va, vc, b

Larghetto – Allegro
Menuetto

290

Index of characteristic symphonies

Allegretto
Finale à la chasse: Allegro di molto

Winter [von Winter], Peter (1754–1825)

Schlacht-Sinfonie (Henderson 14, 1813)
2 picc, 2 fl, 2 ob, 2 cl, 2 bn, 6 hn, 4 tpt, 3 trbn, timp, b.d., s.d., SATB,
2 vn, va, vc, b

Grave –
Tempo di Marcia un poco Allegro – Adagio –
Allegro giusto –
Marcia l'istesso tempo – Tempo I –
Allegro molto – Schützenruf – Cavallerieruf – Russen –
Tempo di Marcia – Adagio – più Allegro – Tempo di Marcia
(all movements continuous)

Edition: New York: Garland, 1982 (Donald G. Henderson,
The Symphony 1720–1840, C-11)

Witt, Friedrich (1770–1836)

Sinfonie turque (Fisher 6, pub. 1808)
2 fl, 2 ob, 2 cl, 2 bn, 4 hn, 2 tpt, timp, b.d., s.d., tr, cym, 2 vn, va, b

Adagio – Allegro molto
Adagio
Minuetto: Allegretto – Trio
Finale: Allegro

Wranitzky, Anton [Vranický, Antonín] (1761–1820)

Aphrodite (Hennigová-Dubová C1, 1792)
2 fl, 2 ob, 2 bn, 2 hn, 2 tpt, timp, 2 vn, 2 va, vc, b

Adagio – Allegro con fuoco – Poco Adagio – Allegro: Das ruhige,
    sanfte Meer geräth plötzlich in eine brausende Gährung. Die
    Wogen thürmen sich, die Winde heulen, die See schäumt.
    Inzwischen heben die Seegötter ihre Häupter aus den Fluten
    empor, wundern sich der Ungestimme, und staunen der
    Erwartung großer Dinge entgegen. Aus dem Schaum steigt
    langsam Aphrodite herauf, vom Glanze himmlischer Schönheit
    umflossen. Entzüken der Seegötter.
Andante – Allegro: Nun eilt Zephir auf säuselnden Schwingen heran,
    legt sie mit flatternden Händen in eine weiche Seemuschel, und
    treibt sie sanft unter zarten Gefühlen nach Zypern an. Reichen Tanz
    der freudigen Horen und Grazien.
Adagio – Allegro: Aphrodite erscheint im Kreise der obernen
    Göttern. Sie staunen, und fühlen der Liebe Macht. Alle stimmen
    ein, der holden Schönen, den Nektar zu reichen, und sie in die

Appendix 1

Gesellschaft der Himmelbewohner aufzunehmen.
Triumphlied.

Symphony in D (Hennigová-Dubová D1, 1796)
2 fl, 2 ob, 2 cl, 2 bn, 2 hn, 4 tpt, timp, 2 vn, 2 va, vc, b

Allegro maestoso: Ausbruch einer lebhaften Freude
Andante: Sanfter Dankgefühl
Menuetto (Allegro): Munterer Ausbruch der Gegenliebe
Adagio sostenuto: Zärtliche Rührung
Finale (Allegro): Segenswünsche

Comments: Wranitzky mss. listed in Hennigová-Dubová as CZ-Pnm
(Lobkowicz) now at CZ-Nlobkowicz (The Roudnice Lobkowicz
Library, Nelahozeves Castle, Czech Republic).

Wranitzky, Paul [Vranický, Pavel] **(1756–1808)**

A' Magyar Nemzet Öröme (Poštolka 8, 1790)
2 fl, 2 ob, 2 bn, 2 hn, 2 tpt, timp, 2 vn, 2 va, vc, b

Adagio maestoso – Vivace assai: I. A' Nemzet' elsö vigassága, 's
ennek el terjesztése
Larghetto con moto. Affettuoso: II. A' Rendek' kellemetes
érzékenységei, és azok köztt vissza tértt Eggyesség
Finale. Allegro: III. A' Köszég Öröme a Szent Korona' vissza érkezése
alkalmatosságával

Edition: Budapest: Editio Musica, 1978 (Ferenc Bónis)
Comments: English trans. in Bónis: "Joy of the Hungarian Nation . . . I.
First joy of the nation and its diffusion. II. Pleasant sentiments of the
estates of the realm and the restored unity among them. III. Joy of the
community at the return of the holy crown."

Grande Sinfonie caractéristique pour la paix avec la République françoise
(Poštolka 12, 1797)
2 fl, 2 ob, 2 cl, 2 bn, 2 hn, 2 tpt, timp, s.d., b.d., 2 vn, va, vc, b

Andante maestoso – Allegro molto: La Révolution. Marche des
Anglois. Marches des Autrichiens et Prussiens
Adagio affettuoso – Marche funèbre: Le Sort et la mort de Louis XVI
Tempo di marcia movibile – Allegro: Marche des Anglois. Marche des
Alliés. Tumulte d'une bataille
Andante grazioso – Allegro vivace: Négociations de paix. Cris de joie
pour la paix restituée

La Chasse (Poštolka 25, 1793)
fl, 2 ob, 2 bn, 2 hn, timp, 2 vn, va, vc, b

Comments: Advertised without title in Breitkopf 1775. Two additional one-movement works (G, C, both Allegro) entitled "Sinfonia militare" at A-KR.

Pastoral symphonies and movements

See also the works by Beecke, Gossec, Leopold Mozart, Pichl, Rosetti, Schmitt, and Johann Stamitz in Appendix 1. Modern editions are listed in the notes.

composer	title	catalogue no. or sources	movements
Anonymous	*Pastorella* (A)	CH-FF	Allegro assai, Andante, Presto
Arrieta, Francesco	*Sinfonia con Pastorale* (D, 1791)	I-Rc (b only)	Allegro spiritoso, Larghetto, Allegro, Pastorale
Boccherini, Luigi	Symphony in C minor (1788)[1]	Gérard 519	Allegro vivo assai, Pastorale lentarello, Minuetto allegro, Allegro
Cannabich, Christian	*Pastorale* (D)	Wolf P1	Un poco andantino – Allegro
	Pastorale (D)	Wolf P2	Largo – Allegro pastorale
	Symphonia pastorale (F)	Wolf P3	Largo – Allegro
	Pastorella (C)	Wolf L2 (lost)	
Cherzelli, Francesco Saverio	*Pastorella* (D, no later than 1768)	lost, formerly A-GÖ	Allegro assai, other movements unknown

Composer	Title	Source	Movements
Dušek, František Xaver	Symphony in A[2]	Altner A1	Allegro assai, Andante alla pastorella, Menuetto, Presto
Falb, Remigius	Pastorellae Symphoniae (pub. 1755)	Augsburg; Lotter, F67 [D-DO]	
	A		Andante, Largo, Allegro ma non molto
	F		Andante, Largo, Allegro non molto
	D		Andante, Largo, Presto
	G		Andante, Largo, Allegro non molto
	C[3]		Andante, Largo, Allegro non molto
	Bb		Andante, Largo, Allegro non molto
Friebert, Joseph	Symphonia pastoralis (C, 1774)[4]	D-Po	Allegro, Pastorale: Adagio, Presto
Gherardeschi, Filippo	Sinfonia pastorale (D)	CH-N	Allegro, Larghetto pastorale, Andante comodo, Allegro
Graun, Johann Gottlieb	Overture in Bb	Bebbington Bb1	[unmarked] – Allegro – [unmarked], Pastorale, Loure
	Symphony in F	Bebbington F12	Allegro assai, Arietta e andantino, Pastorale, Presto
Haydn, Michael	Pastorello (C, 1766)	Sherman 83	Andante, Allegro
Hofmann, Leopold	Symphonia pastorella (prob. no later than 1766)	Kimball C12	Allegro molto, Andante, Presto assai
	Symphonia pastorella (no later than 1766)[5]	Kimball D1	Allegro molto, Andante, Presto
	Symphonia pastorella (prob. no later than 1766)	Kimball Bb4	Allegro molto, Andante ma non molto, Presto
	Sonata pastorella (prob. no later than 1766)	Kimball G4	Andante ma non molto – Allegro assai
[Lang, Johann Georg]	Pastoral Symphony	Davis G8?[6]	Allegro, Allegretto, Presto
Linek, Jiří Ignác	Symphonia pastoralis (C)[7]	CZ-Pnm	Allegro, Adagio, Presto

composer	title	catalogue no. or source	movements
Nappi, Emanuele	*Sinfonia pastorale* (D)	I-AN (vn 2 only)	Largo, Largo, Presto, Largo, Presto
Ott, Lorenz Justinian	*Sinfonia pastoritia* (F, no later than 1780)	D-WEY	Allegro molto alla pastorella – Andante – Allegro
	Sinfonia pastoritia (C, no later than 1784)	D-WEY	Presto non tanto, Andante, Menuetto, Presto ma non tanto
Partl	*Simphonia pastoralis* (D)	SK-BRnm	Allegro, Andante, Presto
Pelikan, Jozef	*Simphonia pastoralis* (C)	SK-BRnm	Allegro, Adagio, Presto
Pokorny, Franz Xaver	*Pastorella* (D, c. 1760)	Angerer D33	Andantino – Allegro moderato – Presto più
	Pastorella (D, no later than 1766)	Angerer D41	Andante – Allegro spiritoso – Presto
	Sinfonia pastorale (D, c. 1770)	Angerer D56	Adagio – Moderato – Andante – Presto[8]
	Sinfonia pastorale (D, c. 1770)	Angerer C15	Allegro, Larghetto, Presto
	Sinfonia pastorale (C, c. 1770)	Angerer C18	Allegro assai, Andantino, Menuet, Prestissimo
	Sinfonia pastorale (D, c. 1770)	Angerer D57	Adagio – Allegro assai, Andante, Menuet, Presto
Rigel, Henri-Joseph	*Sinfonia pastorale* (D, c. 1770)	Angerer D58	Allegro assai, Andante, Menuet, Presto
	Symphony in Bb (no later than 1786)	Viano 11	Pastorale andante, Allegretto, Adagio, Allegro
	Symphony in G minor (1783)	Viano 14	Allegro, Pastorale andante quasi adagio, Presto
Rößler, Greggor	*Sinfonia pastoritia* (F)	D-Dl	[fast], Andante, Allegro
Sandel, Matthias	*Pastoritia* (C)	D-DO	Allegro, Andante, Menuet, Presto
Schacht, Theodore von	*Sinfonia pastorale* (D, 1779)	Angerer D7	Allegro, Andante, Menuet, Allegro

Scheibe, Johann Adolf	*Sinfonia all'pastorale* (Bb, no later than 1766)	lost	[advertised in Breitkopf 1766]
Schubert, Franz Anton	*Pastorale* (D, 1803)	Ottenberg D6	Andantino affettuoso
	Pastorale (G, 1803)	Ottenberg G2	Andantino
	Pastorale (Bb, 1803)	Ottenberg Bb3	Andantino con espressione
	Pastorale (C, 1805)	Ottenberg C3	Andantino
	Pastorale (D, 1805)	Ottenberg D14	Andantino
	Pastorale (Eb, 1805)	Ottenberg Eb3	Andantino
	Pastorale (G, 1805)	Ottenberg G3	Andante
	Pastorale della Santa di Nattale (C, 1805)	Ottenberg C4	Andantino
	Pastorale della Notte Santa di Natale (Eb, 1806)	Ottenberg Eb4	Andantino affettuoso
	Pastorale della Notte Santa di Natale (Ab, 1806)	Ottenberg Ab2	Andantino affettuoso
	Pastorale per la Sant^{ma} Notte di Nattale (Bb, 1806)	Ottenberg Bb7	Andantino e cantabile
Schwindl, Friedrich	*La pastorale* (D, 1765)	Downs 16	Vivace, Andante, Minuetto, Presto
Stamitz, Johann	*Pastorella* (D)	D-Rtt	Andante poco adagio – Allegro
	Pastorella (G)	D-Rtt	Andante pastorella – Presto assai
Toeschi [Toesca da Castellamonte], Karl Theodore	*Sinfonie pastoral* (F, 1818)	D-Mbs, D-MÜu	Andante – Allegro moderato
Touchemoulin, Joseph	Symphony in F	Angerer 12	Allegro, Pastorale: Andante, Presto

composer	title	catalogue no. or sources	movements
Umstatt, Joseph	*Pastorella* (D, no later than 1768)	lost, formerly A-GÖ	Allegro, other movements unknown
Zach, Jan	*Sinfonia pastorella* (G)	Gottron C1	[fast], Andante, Menuet, Presto
	Sinfonia pastoral (C)	Gottron C5	Allegro, Andante, Menue, Presto assai
[Zechner, Johann Georg]	*Symphonia pastorella* (no later than 1756)	Freeman Q:D2 (lost)	Presto, other movements unknown
Zimmermann, Anton	*Sinfonia pastoritia* (G)	Biondi G3; additional mss. at H-KE*, SK-KRE*	Adagio – Presto, Andante, Presto

[1]Milan: Ricordi, 1956 (Pina Carmirelli); Vienna: Doblinger, 1988 (Antonio de Almeida; *Diletto musicale* 626)
[2]New York: Garland, 1984 (Vladimír Altner, *The Symphony 1720–1840*, B-12).
[3]Zurich: Kunzelmann, 1982 (Raimund Rüegge).
[4]Berlin: Vieweg, 1965 (Karlheinz Schultz-Hauser).
[5]New York: Garland, 1984 (G. Cook Kimball; *The Symphony 1720–1840*, B-7).
[6]Leipzig: Portius, n.d. (Walter Höckner). Location of original source unknown. Davis considers Lang's authorship uncertain; *The Symphony 1720–1840*, C-1, lxvi.
[7]Prague: Supraphon, 1976 (Vít Chlup).
[8]Moderato and Presto of Angerer D56 are revisions of the Allegro spiritoso and Presto of D41.

Symphonies and movements by subject

a Military and related

See also "Turkish" symphonies in Appendix 3d

Cambini, Giuseppe Maria	*La Patriote* (Parcell G6, 1794)
Haydn, Franz Joseph	Symphony No. 69, *Laudon* (mid-1770s)
	Symphony No. 100, *Military* (1793/94)
Klöffler, Johann Friedrich	*Sinfonia militaire* (2 exx., Götze 10–11, prob. 1770s)
	Sinfonia bravoura (3 exx., Götze 12–14, prob. 1770s)
Mašek, Vincenz	*Symphonia militare* (after 1780)
Pichl, Václav	*Il Mars* (Zakin 18, 1765–70)
Reichardt, Johann Friedrich	*Overtura di vittoria* (1814)
Stamitz, Carl	*God Save the King* (Kaiser 49, 1792)
Zimmermann, Anton	*Sinfonia militare* (Biondi C2, c. 1770)
	Sinfonia militare (2 exx., n.d.)

b Hunts

Asterisks indicate symphonies with hunting music in the finale only.

Beecke, Ignaz von	*Sinfonia di caccia* (Murray F4, c. 1786)
Druschetzky, Georg	*Scherzando* (Powley C5, c. 1770s)*
Gossec, François-Joseph	*Sinfonia di caccia* (Saceanu 62, c. 1773)
Haydn, Joseph	Symphony No. 73, *La Chasse* (no later than 1782)*
Hoffmeister, Franz Anton	*La Chasse* (Hickman D6, 1784)
Marsh, John	Symphony in B♭ (1782)*
	La Chasse (1790)
Mozart, Leopold	*Jagd Parthia* (Eisen D23, no later than 1768; no known sources)
	Jacht Sinfonia (Eisen G9)
Navoigille, Guillaume	Symphony in E♭ (Saceanu 11, no later than 1775)*
Rosetti, Antonio	*La Chasse* (Murray A20, 1782)*
Stamitz, Carl	*Simphonie de chasse* (Kaiser 31, 1772)
	Symphony in F (Kaiser 34, no later than 1773)*

Appendix 3

Wineberger, Paul   Symphony in A (Murray A1, c. 1792)*
Wranitzky, Paul   La Chasse (Poštolka 25, 1793)*

c Storms

*Asterisks indicate symphonies with storm finales but no other characterizing texts,
except for Haydn's Symphony No. 8 which also bears the work title Le Soir. In Ruge's
La nova tempesta and Richter's La tempesta del mare, the finale subject was adopted
as a work title.*

Croubelis, Simoni dall   Symphony in C (Hatting 7, c. 1780)*
Haydn, Joseph   Symphony No. 8, *Le Soir* (1761)*
Holzbauer, Ignaz   Symphony in E♭ (Riemann E♭3, no later than
                                     1769)*
Klöffler, Johann Friedrich   *Simphonia tempête* (2 exx., Götze 15–16, prob.
                                     1770s)
Richter, Franz Xaver   *La tempesta del mare* (c. 1744–52)*
Ruge, Filippo   Symphony in G (Viano 5, 1756)*
                                   La nova tempesta (Viano 1, 1757)*
Vanhal, Johann Baptist   Symphony in E♭ (Bryan E♭1, 1763–65?)*
Wranitzky, Paul   Symphony in Dm (Poštolka 30, n.d.)*

d National and regional styles and dances

Bach, Johann Christian   Symphony in F (Warburton MS.F3, n.d.)
                                     (ii: Alla polacca)
Beecke, Ignaz von   Symphony in Dm (Murray Dm1, 1783)
                                     (iv: Allegro vivace al'Inglese)
Croubelis, Simoni dall   *Dans Le Goût asiatique* (Hatting 1, c. 1780)
                                   Simphonie chinoise (Hatting 10, c. 1780)
Dall'Oglio, Domenico   *Sinfonia cossaca* (no later than 1764)
                                   Sinfonia russa (no later than 1764)
Dittersdorf, Carl Ditters von   *Il ridotto* or *Le carnaval* (Grave D32,
                                     after 1773) (ii: Contradanza inglese;
                                     iii: Ballo Straßburghese; iv: Polonese;
                                     v: Ballo tedesco)
                                   Sinfonia nazionale nel gusto di cinque nazioni
                                     (Grave A10, no later than 1766)
Druschetzky, Georg   *Sinfonia turcia* (Powley C4, c. 1770s)
                                   Scherzando (Powley C5, c. 1770s)
                                     (ii: Ein Salzburger)
Gassmann, Florian Leopold   Symphony in E♭ (Hill 26, 1765)
                                     (iii: Trio alla greck)
Grenser, Johann Friedrich   *Sinfonia alla posta* (van Boer 1, 1783)
                                     (ii: Alla polacca)
Hoffmeister, Franz Anton   *La festa della pace 1791* (Hickman
                                     G5, no later than 1792) (iv: Turcheso)

300

Kammel, Antonín

Symphony in G (no later than 1766)
(ii: Andante alla francese; iii: Allegro
representa Bürkheim-Pfaltz)
Symphony in D (n.d.) (ii: Adagio
representa Auerhann-Pfaltz)

Kozeluch, Leopold — *Sinfonia francese* (Poštolka I: 10, 1780–90?)

Ordonez, Carlo d' — Symphony in C (Brown C5, no later
than c. 1775) (ii: Andante alla
francesa)

Pichl, Václav — *Sinfonia alla francese* (Zakin 6, no later
than 1773)

Romberg, Andreas Jakob — *Sinfonia alla turca* (1798)

Schmittbauer, Joseph Aloys — *Sinfonia hypochondrica* (n.d.)
(iii: Allegretto scherzoso tedesco in
rondo)

Stamitz, Carl — *Ouverture du bal* (Kaiser 33, 1781)
(ii: Polonaise)

Sterkel, Johann Ferdinand Xaver — *Sinfonia turca* (n.d.)

Süßmayr, Franz Xaver — *Sinfonia turchesa* (c. 1790)

Vančura, Arnošt — *Sinfonie nationale russe* (1798)
Sinfonie nationale ukrainienne (1798)
Sinfonie nationale polonaise (1798)

Veichtner, Franz Adam — *Simphonie russienne* (1771)

Vogler, Georg Joseph — *Bayrische nationale Sinfonie* (van Boer 164,
1806)

Witt, Friedrich — *Sinfonie turque* (Fisher 6, pub. 1808)

Wranitzky, Paul — *A' Magyar Nemzet Öröme* (Poštolka
8, 1790)
Symphony in D (Poštolka 18, c. 1799)
(ii: Russe; iii: Polonese)

e Battles

Beethoven, Ludwig van — *Wellingtons Sieg* (1813)

Brixi, František Xaver — *La Bataille de Torgau* (prob. 1760–61)

Devienne, François — *La Bataille de Gemmapp* (La France 8,
c. 1794)

Donninger, Ferdinand — *Musikalische Vorstellung einer Seeschlacht*
(no later than 1781)

Druschetzky, Georg — *Sinfonia la pataglia* (Powley C3/C10,
c. 1770s–80s)
Sinfonia la pataglia (Powley C7/C9,
1774–80/c. 1790s)
Sinfonia la pataglia (Powley C13, c. 1790s)

Hauff, Ferdinand — *Grande Bataille à grand orchestre* (1810)

Kauer, Ferdinand — *Zinfonia militare* (c. 1789–90)

Klöffler, Johann Friedrich — *Bataille à deux orchestres* (Götze 9, 1777)

Kospoth, Otto Karl Endmann	*Accampamento del Re di Prussia* (n.d.)
Neubauer, Franz Christoph	*La Bataille* (1789)
Reichardt, Johann Friedrich	*Schlacht-Symphonie* (1814)
Vandenbroek, Othon Joseph	*La Prise de la Bastille* (Brook 1, after 1795)
Volder, Pierre Jean de	*La Bataille d'Jena* (1806)
Winter, Peter von	*Schlacht-Sinfonie* (Henderson 14, 1813)

f Symphonies based on literature, biblical texts, or extended original scenarios

Beethoven, Ludwig van	*Pastoral* Symphony (1808)
Brunetti, Gaetano	*Il maniatico* (Jenkins 33, 1780)
Dittersdorf, Carl Ditters von	*Les Quatre Ages du monde* (Grave C17, prob. 1781)
	La Chute de Phaéton (Grave D1, prob. 1781)
	Actéon changé en cerf (Grave G15, prob. 1781)
	Andromède sauvée par Persée (Grave F3, prob. 1781)
	Phinée avec ses amis changés en rochers (Grave D34, prob. 1781)
	Les Paysans changés en grenouilles (Grave A9, prob. 1781–82)
	Jason qui enlève la toison d'or (prob. 1781–82)
	Le Siège de Mégare (prob. 1781–82, no known sources)
	Hercule changé en dieu (no later than 1786)
	Orphée et Euridice (no later than 1786, no known sources)
	Midas élu pour juge entre Pan et Apollon (no later than 1786; no known sources)
	Ajax et Ulisse qui se disputent les armes d'Achille (no later than 1786)
Gleissner, Franz Johannes	*Sinfonia Hamlet* (1784)
Haydn, Joseph	Symphony No. 60 in C, *Il distratto* (no later than 1774)
	The Seven Last Words of our Savior on the Cross (1787)
Knecht, Justin Heinrich	*Le Portrait musical de la nature* (Höhnen 1, 1785)
	Auf den Tod des Herzogs von Braunschweig (Höhnen 2, 1785; no known sources)
	Erlebnisse des Don Quixote (Höhnen 3, 1787; no known sources)
Kospoth, Otto Karl Endmann	*Composizione sopra Il Pater noster consistenti in sette sonate caratteristiche con un' introduzione* (1794)
Massonneau, Louis	*La Tempête et le calme* (1794)
Pugnani, Gaetano	*Werther* (c. 1795)

Raimondi, Ignazio	*Les Aventures de Télémaque dans l'isle de Calypso* (1777, no known sources)
Rosetti, Antonio	*Calypso et Télémaque* (1791?; no known sources)
Stamitz, Carl	*Le Jour variable* (Kaiser 32, 1772)
Wranitzky, Anton	*Aphrodite* (Hennigová-Dubová C1, 1792)
	Symphony in D (Hennigová-Dubová D1, 1796; see movement titles in Appendix 1)
Wranitzky, Paul	*Grande Sinfonie caractéristique pour la paix avec la République françoise* (Poštolka 12, 1797)

g Emotions and "moral characters"

Camerloher, Placidus or Joseph	*L'Amitié* (Forsberg C31, c. 1740–50)
Dittersdorf, Carl Ditters von	*Il combattimento delle passioni umane* (Grave D16, no later than 1771)
Haydn, Michael	Symphony in B♭ (Sherman 62, 1763) (ii: La Confidenza)
Kozeluch, Leopold	*L'Irrésolu* (Poštolka I: 11, 1780–90?)
Moreno, Francisco Javier	*Sinfonia titolata le due opposti caratteri Superbia ed Umiltà* (Shadko 2, c. 1801–05)
Schmittbauer, Joseph Aloys	*Sinfonia hypochondrica* (n.d.)
Vanhal, Johann Baptist	*Sinfonia comista con per la sorta diversa* (Bryan C11, 1775–78?) (i: La speranza; ii: Il sospirare e languire; iii: La lamentatione – L'allegrezza)

h Mourning

Includes funeral marches. See also lamenting movements in battle symphonies, Appendix 3e.

Beethoven, Ludwig van	*Eroica* Symphony (1803) (ii: Marcia funebre)
Haydn, Joseph	Symphony No. 26, *Lamentatione* (no later than 1770)
Kraus, Joseph Martin	*Symphonie funèbre* (van Boer 148, 1792)
Mozart, Wolfgang Amadeus	*Mauerische Trauermusik* (1785)
Ries, Ferdinand	Symphony in D (Hill 1, 1809) (ii: Marche funèbre)
Romberg, Bernhard Heinrich	*Trauer-Symphonie* (1810)
Vogler, Georg Joseph	*Trauermusik auf Ludwig XVI* (1793)
Wranitzky, Paul	*Grande Sinfonie caractéristique pour la paix avec la République françoise* (Poštolka 12, 1797) (ii: Le Sort et la mort de Louis XVI. Marche funèbre)

BIBLIOGRAPHY

Ackermann, Peter. "Struktur, Ausdruck, Programm: Gedanken zu Joseph Haydns Instrumentalmusik über *Die Sieben letzten Worte unseres Erlösers am Kreuze.*" In Anke Bingmann, Klaus Hortschansky, and Winfried Kirsch, eds., *Studien zur Instrumentalmusik: Lothar Hoffmann-Erbrecht zum 60. Geburtstag*, 253–60. Tutzing: Schneider, 1988.

Algarotti, Francesco. *Saggio sopra l'opera in musica*. Livorno, 1755.

Allanbrook, Wye Jamison. *Rhythmic Gesture in Mozart: "Le nozze di Figaro" and "Don Giovanni."* Chicago: University of Chicago Press, 1983.

Allgemeine musikalische Zeitung. Leipzig, 1798–1848.

Anderson, Benedict. *Imagined Communities: Reflections on the Origin and Spread of Nationalism*. 2nd rev. edn. London: Verso, 1991.

Augsburger musikalischer Merkur auf das Jahr 1795. Augsburg, 1795.

Avison, Charles. *An Essay on Musical Expression*. 2nd edn. London, 1753.

Baker, Nancy Kovaleff and Thomas Christensen, eds. *Aesthetics and the Art of Musical Composition in the German Enlightenment: Selected Writings of Johann Georg Sulzer and Heinrich Christoph Koch*. Cambridge: Cambridge University Press, 1995.

Bakhtin, Mikhail. *The Dialogic Imagination: Four Essays*. Trans. Michael Holquist and Caryl Emerson, ed. Holquist. Austin: University of Texas Press, 1981.

Barbour, J. Murray. *Trumpets, Horns and Music*. Lansing, MI: Michigan State University Press, 1964.

Barth, Karl. *Protestant Theology in the Nineteenth Century: Its Background and History*. Trans. Brian Cozens and John Bowden. London: SCM Press, 1972.

Bartha, Dénes. "A 'Sieben Worte' változatainak keletkezése az Esterházy-gyüjtemény kéziratainak tükrében." *Zenetudományi tanulmányok* 8 (1960): 107–86.

Bartlitz, Eveline, ed. *Die Beethoven-Sammlung in der Musikabteilung der Deutschen Staatsbibliothek*. Berlin: Deutsche Staatsbibliothek, 1970.

Batteux, Charles. *Les Beaux-arts réduits à un même principe*. Paris, 1746.

Beales, Derek. *Joseph II*. Vol. I, *In the Shadow of Maria Theresa 1741–1780*. Cambridge: Cambridge University Press, 1987.

Ludwig van Beethoven: Briefwechsel Gesamtausgabe. 7 vols. Ed. Sieghard Brandenburg. Munich: Henle, 1996–98.

Beethoven, Ludwig van. *Ein Skizzenbuch zur Chorfantasie op. 80 und zu anderen Werken*. Ed. Dagmar Weise. Bonn: Beethovenhaus, 1957.

Ein Skizzenbuch zur Pastoralsymphonie op. 68 und zu den Trios op. 71, 1 und 2. 2 vols. Ed. Dagmar Weise. Bonn, Beethovenhaus, 1961.

Bent, Ian, ed. *Music Analysis in the Nineteenth Century*. 2 vols. Cambridge: Cambridge University Press, 1994.

Bérenger, Jean. "The Austrian Church." In William J. Callahan and David Higgs, eds., *Church and Society in Catholic Europe of the Eighteenth Century*, 88–105. Cambridge: Cambridge University Press, 1979.

Berg, Darrell L. "C. P. E. Bach's Character Pieces and his Friendship Circle." In Stephen L. Clark, ed., *C. P. E. Bach Studies*, 1–32. Oxford: Clarendon Press, 1988.

Berlinische musikalische Zeitung. Ed. Johann Friedrich Reichardt. Berlin, 1805–06.

Berlioz, Hector. *A travers chants*. 3rd edn. Paris, 1880.

Bernstein, Leonard. *The Unanswered Question*. Cambridge, MA: Harvard University Press, 1976.

Beutner, Eduard. "Aufklärung versus Absolutismus? Zur Strategie der Ambivalenz in der Herrschersatire der österreichischen Literatur des Josephinischen Jahrzehnts." In Gerhard Ammerer and Hanns Haas, eds., *Ambivalenzen der Aufklärung: Festschrift für Ernst Wangermann*, 241–52. Vienna: Verlag für Geschichte und Politik; Munich: Oldenbourg, 1997.

Biba, Otto, ed. *"Eben komme ich von Haydn...": Georg August Griesingers Korrespondenz mit Joseph Haydns Verleger Breitkopf & Härtel 1799–1819*. Zurich: Atlantis, 1987.

Biba, Otto, and David Wyn Jones, eds. *Studies in Music History Presented to H. C. Robbins Landon on his Seventieth Birthday*. London: Thames and Hudson, 1996.

Blackbourn, David. *The Long Nineteenth Century: A History of Germany, 1780–1918*. Oxford: Oxford University Press, 1998.

Blangini, Felice. *Souvenirs de F. Blangini (1797–1834) dédiés à ses élèves, et publiés par son ami Maxime de Villemarest*. Paris, 1834.

Bockholdt, Rudolf. *Beethoven: VI. Symphonie F-dur op. 68 Pastorale*. Meisterwerke der Musik 23. Munich: Fink, 1981.

Bockmaier, Claus. *Entfesselte Natur in der Musik des achtzehnten Jahrhunderts*. Tutzing: Schneider, 1992.

Bodi, Leslie. *Tauwetter in Wien: Zur Prosa der österreichischen Aufklärung 1781–1795*. Frankfurt am Main: S. Fischer, 1977.

Bonds, Mark Evan. "Haydn, Laurence Sterne, and the Origins of Musical Irony." *Journal of the American Musicological Society* 44 (1991), 57–91.

"Idealism and the Aesthetics of Instrumental Music at the Turn of the Nineteenth Century." *Journal of the American Musicological Society* 50 (1997): 387–420.

"The Symphony as Pindaric Ode." In Sisman, ed., *Haydn and His World*, 131–53.

Wordless Rhetoric: Musical Form and the Metaphor of the Oration. Cambridge, MA: Harvard University Press, 1991.

Böschenstein, Renate. *Idylle*. Stuttgart: Metzler, 1968.

Botstein, Leon. "The Demise of Philosophical Listening: Haydn in the 19th Century." In Sisman, ed., *Haydn and His World*, 255–85.

Boyle, Nicholas. *Goethe: The Poet and the Age*. Vol. I, *The Poetry of Desire*. Oxford: Oxford University Press, 1992.

Brandenburg, Sieghard. "Die Stichvorlage zur Erstausgabe von Beethovens Pastoralsymphonie op. 68: Eine neuaufgefundene Primärquelle." In

Festschrift Rudolf Elvers zum 60. Geburtstag, ed. Ernst Hettrich and Hans Schneider, 49–61. Tutzing: Schneider, 1985.

"Once Again: On the Question of the Repeat of the Scherzo and Trio in Beethoven's Fifth Symphony." In Lewis Lockwood and Phyllis Benjamin, eds., *Beethoven Essays in Honor of Elliot Forbes,* 146–98. Cambridge, MA: Harvard University Press, 1984.

Braunbehrens, Volkmar. *Mozart in Vienna 1781–1791.* Trans. Timothy Bell. New York: Grove Weidenfeld, 1986.

Brauneis, Walther. "Die Familie Ditters in Wien und Umgebung." In Hubert Unverricht, ed., *Carl Ditters von Dittersdorf: Leben, Umwelt, Werk,* 39–60. Tutzing: Schneider, 1997.

Breitkopf, Johann Gottlob Immanuel. *The Breitkopf Thematic Catalogue: The Six Parts and Sixteen Supplements 1762–1787,* ed. Barry S. Brook. New York: Dover, 1966.

Brinkmann, Reinhold. "In the Time of the *Eroica.*" In Scott Burnham and Michael P. Steinberg, eds., *Beethoven and His World,* 1–26. Princeton: Princeton University Press, 2000.

Brown, A. Peter. "The Sublime, The Beautiful, and the Ornamental: English Aesthetic Currents and Haydn's London Symphonies." In Biba and Jones, eds., *Studies in Music History Presented to H.C. Robbins Landon,* 44–71.

Brown, Bruce Alan. *Gluck and the French Theatre in Vienna.* Oxford: Clarendon Press, 1991.

Brown, Clive. *A New Appraisal of the Sources of Beethoven's Fifth Symphony.* Wiesbaden: Breitkopf und Härtel, 1996.

Broyles, Michael. *Beethoven: The Emergence and Evolution of Beethoven's Heroic Style.* New York: Excelsior, 1987.

Burke, Edmund. *A Philosophical Enquiry into the Origin of our Ideas of the Sublime and Beautiful.* London, 1757.

Burnham, Scott. *Beethoven Hero.* Princeton: Princeton University Press, 1995.

"Mozart's *felix culpa: Così fan tutte* and the Irony of Beauty." *Musical Quarterly* 78 (1994): 77–98.

Chabanon, Michel Paul Gui de. *Observations sur la musique.* Paris, 1779.

Chew, Geoffrey. "The Austrian Pastorella and the *stylus rusticanus*: Comic and Pastoral Elements in Austrian Music, 1750–1800." In Jones, ed., *Music in Eighteenth-Century Austria,* 133–93.

"Haydn's Pastorellas: Genre, Dating, and Transmission in the Early Church Works." In Biba and Jones, eds., *Studies in Music History Presented to H.C. Robbins Landon,* 21–43.

"The Night-Watchman's Song Quoted by Haydn and its Implications." *Haydn-Studien* 3 (1973–74): 106–24.

Chua, Daniel K. L. *Absolute Music and the Construction of Meaning.* Cambridge: Cambridge University Press, 1999.

Clark, Christopher. "The Wars of Liberation in Prussian Memory: Reflections on the Memorialization of War in Early Nineteenth-Century Germany." *Journal of Modern History* 68 (1996): 550–76.

Clausewitz, Carl von. *On War.* Trans. and ed. Michael Howard and Peter Paret. Princeton: Princeton University Press, 1976.

Cole, Malcolm. "Momigny's Analysis of Haydn's Symphony No. 103." *Music Review* 30 (1969): 261–84.

Comini, Alessandra. *The Changing Image of Beethoven: A Study in Mythmaking.* New York: Rizzoli, 1987.

Compan, Charles. *Dictionnaire de danse.* Paris, 1787.

Connerton, Paul. *How Societies Remember.* Cambridge: Cambridge University Press, 1989.

Cooper, Barry. "Schindler and the *Pastoral* Symphony." *Beethoven Newsletter* 8/1 (1993): 2–6.

Dahlhaus, Carl. *Beethoven: Approaches to his Music.* Trans. Mary Whittall. Oxford: Clarendon Press, 1991.

———. *Esthetics of Music.* Trans. William Austin. Cambridge: Cambridge University Press, 1982.

———. "E. T. A. Hoffmanns Beethoven-Kritik und die Ästhetik des Erhabenen." *Archiv für Musikwissenschaft* 38 (1981): 80–92.

———. "Ethos und Pathos in Glucks *Iphigenie auf Tauris.*" *Die Musikforschung* 27 (1974): 289–300.

———. *The Idea of Absolute Music.* Trans. Roger Lustig. Chicago: University of Chicago Press, 1989.

———. "Thesen über Programmusik." In Dahlhaus, ed., *Beiträge zur musikalischen Hermeneutik,* 187–204. Regensburg: Bosse, 1975.

Danckwardt, Marianne. "Zu zwei Haydnschen Sinfoniesätzen mit liturgischer Melodien (Sinfonien Nr. 30, 1. Satz und Nr. 26, 2. Satz)." In Norbert Dubowy and Sören Meyer-Eller, eds., *Festschrift Rudolf Bockholdt zum 60. Geburtstag,* 193–99. Pfaffenhofen: Ludwig, 1990.

Dannreuther, Edward. *Oxford History of Music.* Vol. VI, *The Romantic Period.* Oxford: Clarendon Press, 1905.

Diderot, Denis. *Entretiens sur le Fils naturel.* Paris, 1757. Trans. in *Selected Writings on Art and Literature,* ed. Geoffrey Bremner. London: Penguin, 1994.

Dies, Albert Christoph. *Biographische Nachrichten von Joseph Haydn nach mündlichen Erzählungen desselben entworfen und herausgegeben.* Vienna, 1810.

Dittersdorf, Carl Ditters von. *Lebensbeschreibung, seinem Sohne in die Feder diktiert.* Ed. Karl Spazier. Leipzig, 1801. Modern edn. by Norbert Miller, Munich: Kösel, 1967.

———. *Les Métamorphoses d'Ovide mises en musique par Mr. Charles Ditters noble de Dittersdorf.* Vienna, 1786.

Donakowski, Conrad L. *A Muse for the Masses: Ritual and Music in an Age of Democratic Revolution 1770–1870.* Chicago: University of Chicago Press, 1972.

Drury, Jonathan Daniels. "Haydn's 'Seven Last Words': An Historical and Critical Study." Ph.D. diss., University of Illinois, 1976.

DuBos, Jean-Baptiste. *Réflexions critiques sur la poësie, la peinture et la musique.* Paris, 1719.

Edge, Dexter. "Review Article: Mary Sue Morrow, *Concert Life in Haydn's Vienna.*" *Haydn Yearbook* 17 (1992): 108–66.

Eggebrecht, Hans Heinrich. *Zur Geschichte der Beethoven-Rezeption: Beethoven 1970.* Mainz: Akademie der Wissenschaften und der Literatur, 1972.

Bibliography

Eisen, Cliff. "Leopold Mozart Discoveries." *Mitteilungen der Internationalen Stiftung Mozarteum* 35 (1987): 1–10.

Engel, Johann Jakob. *Über die musikalische Malerei.* Berlin, 1780. Reprint. *J. J. Engel's Schriften*, vol. IV, 299–342. Berlin, 1802.

Feder, Georg. "Haydns Korrekturen zum Klavierauszug der 'Jahreszeiten.'" In Thomas Kohlhase and Volker Scherliess, eds., *Festschrift Georg von Dadelsen zum 60. Geburtstag*, 101–12. Neuhausen-Stuttgart: Hänssler, 1978.

Fétis, François-Joseph. "Deux Symphonies pastorales." *Revue et gazette musicale de Paris* (28 October 1866): 337–38.

Fischer, Kurt von. *Die Beziehungen von Form und Motiv in Beethovens Instrumentalwerken.* 2nd edn. Baden-Baden: Koerner, 1972.

Flora. Ed. Carl Friedrich Cramer. Hamburg, 1787.

Floros, Constantin. *Beethovens Eroica und Prometheus-Musik: Sujet-Studien.* Wilhelmshaven: Heinrichshofen, 1978.

"Das 'Programm' in Mozarts Meisterouvertüren." *Studien zur Musikwissenschaft* 26 (1964): 140–86.

Forkel, Johann Nikolaus. *Allgemeine Geschichte der Musik.* 2 vols. Leipzig, 1788 and 1801.

Forsberg, Suzanne. "The Symphonies of Placidus von Camerloher (1718–82) and Joseph Camerloher (1710–43): An Investigation of Style and Authorship." Ph.D. diss., New York University, 1990.

Foster, Susan Leigh. *Choreography & Narrative: Ballet's Staging of Story and Desire.* Bloomington and Indianapolis: Indiana University Press, 1996.

Fried, Michael. *Absorption and Theatricality: Painting and Beholder in the Age of Diderot.* Berkeley: University of California Press, 1980.

Frogley, Alain. "Beethoven's Struggle for Simplicity in the Sketches for the Third Movement of the Pastoral Symphony." *Beethoven Forum* 4 (1995): 99–134.

Fubini, Enrico. *Music and Culture in Eighteenth-Century Europe: A Source Book.* Trans. Wolfgang Freis, Lisa Gasbarrone, and Michael Louis Leone. Ed. Bonnie Blackburn. Chicago: University of Chicago Press, 1994.

Fuller, David. "Of Portraits, 'Sapho' and Couperin: Titles and Characters in French Instrumental Music of the High Baroque." *Music & Letters* 78 (1997): 149–74.

Geck, Martin, and Peter Schleuning. *"Geschrieben auf Bonaparte." Beethovens "Eroica": Revolution, Reaktion, Rezeption.* Reinbek bei Hamburg: Rowohlt, 1989.

Gerber, Ernst Ludwig. *Historisch-biographisches Lexikon der Tonkünstler.* 2 vols. Leipzig, 1790–92.

Germer, Mark. "The Austro-Bohemian Pastorella and Pastoral Mass to c1780." Ph.D. diss., New York University, 1989.

Gerstenberg, Heinrich Wilhelm von. "Schlechte Einrichtung des Italienischen Singgedichts. Warum ahmen Deutsche sie nach?" *Briefe über Merkwürdigkeiten der Litteratur* 1 (1766): 116–36.

Ghircoiaşiu, Romeo. "Das Musikleben in Großwardein (Oradea) im 18. Jahrhundert." *Haydn Yearbook* 10 (1978): 45–55.

Gillespy, Edward. *The Military Instructor, or, New System of European Exercise and Drill as Now Practised by the British Army According to General Dundas.* Boston, 1809.

Gillis, John R. "Memory and Identity: The History of a Relationship." In Gillis, ed., *Commemorations: The Politics of National Identity*, 3–24. Princeton: Princeton University Press, 1994.

Goldstein, Laurence. *Ruins and Empire: The Evolution of a Theme in Augustan and Romantic Literature*. Pittsburgh: University of Pittsburgh Press, 1977.

Göllner, Theodor. *"Die Sieben Worte am Kreuz" bei Schütz und Haydn*. Munich: Bayrische Akademie der Wissenschaften, 1986.

Gossett, Philip. "Beethoven's Sixth Symphony: Sketches for the First Movement." *Journal of the American Musicological Society* 27 (1974): 248–84.

Götze, Ursula. "Johann Friedrich Klöffler." Diss., University of Münster, 1965.

Grace, Harvey. *Ludwig van Beethoven*. London: Kegan Paul, Trench and Trubner, J. Curwen: 1927.

Grave, Floyd K. and Margaret G. Grave. *In Praise of Harmony: The Teachings of Abbé Georg Joseph Vogler*. Lincoln: University of Nebraska Press, 1987.

Griesinger, Georg August. *Biographische Notizen über Joseph Haydn*. Leipzig, 1810.

Grove, George. *Beethoven and His Nine Symphonies*. 3rd edn. London, 1898. Reprint. New York: Dover, 1962.

"The Birds in the Pastoral Symphony." *The Musical Times* 33 (15 December 1892): 14–15.

Guest, Ivor Forbes. *The Ballet of the Enlightenment: The Establishment of the Ballet d'action in France 1770–1793*. London: Dance Books, 1996.

Halbwachs, Maurice. *On Collective Memory*. Trans. and ed. Lewis A. Coser. Chicago: University of Chicago Press, 1992.

Halm, August. *Von zwei Kulturen der Musik*. 3rd edn. Stuttgart: Ernst Klett, 1947.

Hanslick, Eduard. *Concerte, Componisten und Virtuosen der letzten fünfzehn Jahre, 1870–85*. Berlin: Allgemeiner Verein für Deutsche Literatur, 1886.

Geschichte des Concertwesens in Wien. 2 vols. Vienna: Wilhelm Braumüller, 1869–70.

Harris, James. *Three Treatises Concerning Art*. London, 1744.

Harrison, Bernard. *Haydn: Paris Symphonies*. Cambridge Music Handbook. Cambridge: Cambridge University Press, 1998.

Haydn: Gesammelte Briefe und Aufzeichnungen: Unter Benützung der Quellensammlung von H. C. Robbins Landon herausgegeben und erläutert von Dénes Bartha. Kassel: Bärenreiter, 1965.

Heartz, Daniel. *Haydn, Mozart, and the Viennese School, 1740–1780*. New York: Norton, 1995.

"The Hunting Chorus in Haydn's *Jahreszeiten* and the 'Airs de Chasse' in the *Encyclopédie*." *Eighteenth-Century Studies* 9 (1975–76): 523–39.

Mozart's Operas. Ed. with contributing essays by Thomas Bauman. Berkeley and Los Angeles: University of California Press, 1990.

Heinz, Günther. "Veränderungen in der religiösen Malerei des 18. Jahrhunderts mit besonderer Berücksichtigung Österreichs." In Kovács, ed., *Katholische Aufklärung und Josephinismus*, 349–70.

Helm, Eugene. "The 'Hamlet' Fantasy and the Literary Element in C. P. E. Bach's Music." *Musical Quarterly* 58 (1972): 277–96.

Hepokoski, James. "Fiery-Pulsed Libertine or Domestic Hero? Strauss's *Don Juan* Reinvestigated." In Bryan Gilliam, ed., *Richard Strauss: New Perspectives on the Composer and His Work*, 135–75. Durham and London: Duke University Press, 1992.

"Genre and Content in Mid-Century Verdi: 'Addio, del passato' (*La traviata*, Act III)." *Cambridge Opera Journal* 1 (1989): 249–76.

Hermes, Johann Timotheus. *Analyse de XII Métamorphoses tirées d'Ovide, et mises en musique par Mr. Charles Ditters de Dittersdorf*. Breslau, 1786. Repr. in Krebs, *Dittersdorfiana*, 167–82.

Herzog, Urs. *Geistliche Wohlredenheit: Die katholische Barockpredigt*. Munich: Beck, 1991.

Hilton, Wendy. *Dance of Court and Theater: The French Noble Style 1690–1725*. Princeton: Princeton Book Publishers, 1981. Repr. in *Dance and Music of Court and Theater: Selected Writings of Wendy Hilton*. Stuyvesant, NY: Pendragon, 1997.

E. T. A. Hoffmanns Briefwechsel. 3 vols. Ed. Hans von Müller and Friedrich Schnapp. Munich: Winkler, 1967–69.

E. T. A. Hoffmann's Musical Writings: Kreisleriana, The Poet and the Composer, Music Criticism. Ed. David Charlton. Trans. Martyn Clarke. Cambridge: Cambridge University Press, 1989.

Holmström, Kirsten Gram. *Monodrama, Attitudes, Tableaux vivants: Studies on Some Trends of Theatrical Fashion 1770–1815*. Stockholm, Almqvist & Wiksell, 1967.

Holschneider, Andreas. "C. Ph. E. Bachs Kantate *Auferstehung und Himmelfahrt Jesu* und Mozarts Aufführung des Jahres 1788." *Mozart-Jahrbuch* (1968–70): 264–80.

Hopkins, David. "Dryden and Ovid's 'Wit out of Season.'" In Charles Martindale, ed., *Ovid Renewed: Ovidian Influences on Literature and Art from the Middle Ages to the Twentieth Century*, 167–90. Cambridge: Cambridge University Press, 1988.

Hoppe, Bernhard M. *Predigtkritik im Josephinismus: Die "Wöchentlichen Wahrheiten für und über die Prediger in Wien" (1782–1784)*. St. Ottilien: EOS Verlag, 1989.

Hosler, Bellamy. *Changing Aesthetic Views of Instrumental Music in 18th-Century Germany*. Ann Arbor: UMI Research Press, 1981.

Huray, Peter le and James Day, eds. *Music and Aesthetics in the Eighteenth and Early-Nineteenth Centuries*. Cambridge: Cambridge University Press, 1981.

Hyatt-King, Alexander. "Mountains, Music, and Musicians." *Musical Quarterly* 31 (1945): 395–419.

Ingrao, Charles. *The Habsburg Monarchy 1618–1815*. Cambridge: Cambridge University Press, 1994.

Irwin, David. "Sentiment and Antiquity: European Tombs 1750–1830." In Joachim Whaley, ed. *Mirrors of Mortality: Studies in the Social History of Death*, 131–53. London: Europa, 1981.

Jahn, Otto. *Gesammelte Aufsätze über Musik*. Leipzig: Breitkopf und Härtel, 1866.

Jam, Jean-Louis. "Marie-Joseph Chénier and François-Joseph Gossec: Two Artists in the Service of Revolutionary Propaganda." In Malcolm Boyd, ed., *Music and the French Revolution*, 221–35. Cambridge: Cambridge University Press, 1992.

Jander, Owen. "The Prophetic Conversation in Beethoven's 'Scene by the Brook.'" *Musical Quarterly* 77 (1993): 508–59.

Johnson, James H. *Listening in Paris: A Cultural History*. Berkeley and Los Angeles: University of California Press, 1995.

Jones, David Wyn. *Beethoven: "Pastoral Symphony."* Cambridge Music Handbook. Cambridge: Cambridge University Press, 1995.

Jones, David Wyn, ed. *Music in Eighteenth-Century Austria*. Cambridge: Cambridge University Press, 1996.

Jung, Hermann. "Antiker Mythos im symphonischen Gewand der Wiener Klassik: Karl Ditters von Dittersdorfs Symphonien nach Ovids Metamorphosen (1785)." In Petr Macek, ed., *Das internationale musikwissenschaftliche Kolloquium "Wenn es nicht Österreich gegeben hätte...,"* *30.9.–2.10.1996*, 162–69. Brno: Filozofická fakulta Masarykovy univerzity Brno, 1997.

Die Pastorale: Studien zur Geschichte eines musikalischen Topos. Bern: Francke, 1980.

"Zwischen *Malerey* und *Ausdruck der Empfindung*: Zu den historischen und ästhetischen Voraussetzungen von Justin Heinrich Knechts *Le Portrait musical de la Nature* (1785)." In Annegrit Laubenthal, ed., *Studien zur Musikgeschichte: Eine Festschrift für Ludwig Finscher*, 417–31. Kassel: Bärenreiter, 1995.

Junker, Carl Friedrich. *Tonkunst*. Bern, 1777.

Betrachtungen über Mahlerey, Ton- und Bildhauerkunst. Basel, 1778.

Kallberg, Jeffrey. *Chopin at the Boundaries: Sex, History, and Musical Genre*. Cambridge, MA: Harvard University Press, 1996.

Kinsky, Georg, ed. *Versteigerung von Musiker-Autographen aus dem Nachlaß des Herrn Kommerzienrates Wilhelm Heyer in Köln*, Pt. 1. Berlin: Henrici & Liepmannssohn, 1926.

Kirby, F. E. "Beethoven's Pastoral Symphony as a *Sinfonia caracteristica*." *Musical Quarterly* 56 (1970): 605–23.

"The Germanic Symphony in the Eighteenth Century: Bridge to the Romantic Era." *Journal of Musicological Research* 5 (1984): 51–84; 6 (1986): 357–62.

Klauwell, Otto. *Geschichte der Programmusik von ihren Anfängen bis zur Gegenwart*. Leipzig: Breitkopf und Härtel, 1910.

Koch, Heinrich Christoph. *Musikalisches Lexikon*. Frankfurt am Main, 1802.

Versuch einer Anleitung zur Composition. 3 vols. Leipzig, 1782–93.

Kollmann, Augustus Frederic Christopher. *An Essay on Practical Musical Composition, According to the Nature of That Science and the Principles of the Greatest Musical Authors*. London, 1799.

König, Ingeborg. *Studien zum Libretto des "Tod Jesu" von Karl Wilhelm Ramler und Karl Heinrich Graun*. Munich: Katzbichler, 1972.

Körner, Christian Gottfried. "Über Charakterdarstellung in der Musik." *Die Horen* 5 (1795): 97–121. Repr. in Seifert, *Christian Gottfried Körner*, 147–58. Trans. in Riggs, "'On the Representation of Character in Music,'" 612–25.

Koukal, Petr. "Die letzten Jahre: Dittersdorf in Sudböhmen." In Hubert

Unverricht, ed., *Carl Ditters von Dittersdorf 1739–1799: Sein Wirken in Österreichisch-Schlesien und seine letzten Jahre in Böhmen*, 21–24. Würzburg: Korn, 1993.

Kovács, Elisabeth, ed. *Katholische Aufklärung und Josephinismus*. Munich: Oldenbourg, 1979.

Kramer, Richard. "The New Modulation of the 1770s: C. P. E. Bach in Theory, Criticism, and Practice." *Journal of the American Musicological Society* 38 (1995): 551–92.

Kraus, Joseph Martin. *Etwas von und über Musik fürs Jahr 1777*. Frankfurt am Main, 1778. Facsimile reprint. Ed. Friedrich W. Riedel. Munich: Katzbichler, 1977.

Krause, Christian Gottfried. *Von der musikalischen Poesie*. Berlin, 1752.

Krebs, Carl. *Dittersdorfiana*. Berlin, 1900. Reprint. New York: Da Capo, 1972.

Krones, Hartmut. "'Meine Sprache verstehet man durch die ganze Welt': Das 'redende Prinzip' in Joseph Haydns Instrumentalmusik." In Krones, ed., *Wort und Ton im Europäischen Raum: Gedenkschrift für Robert Schollum*, 79–108. Vienna: Böhlau, 1989.

Kunze, Stefan, ed. *Ludwig van Beethoven: Die Werke im Spiegel seiner Zeit. Gesammelte Konzertberichte und Rezensionen bis 1830*. Laaber: Laaber-Verlag, 1987.

Lacépède, Bernard Germain Etienne Médard de la Ville-sur-Illon. *La Poétique de la musique*. Paris, 1785.

Landon, H. C. Robbins. *Haydn: Chronicle and Works*. 5 vols. London: Thames and Hudson, 1976–80.

The Mozart Essays. London: Thames and Hudson, 1995.

Langrock, Klaus. *Die Sieben Worte Jesu am Kreuz: Ein Beitrag zur Geschichte der Passionskomposition*. Essen: Blaue Eule, 1987.

LaRue, Jan. *A Catalogue of Eighteenth-Century Symphonies*. Vol. I, *Thematic Identifier*. Bloomington: Indiana University Press, 1988.

Lichtenthal, Pietro (Peter). *Dizionario e bibliografia della musica*. 2nd edn. 4 vols. Milan, 1836.

Lippman, Edward A. *A History of Western Musical Aesthetics*. Lincoln: University of Nebraska Press, 1992.

Lippman, Edward A., ed. *Musical Aesthetics: A Historical Reader*. 3 vols. New York: Pendragon Press, 1986–90.

Lessing, Gotthold Ephraim. *Laokoon: oder über die Grenzen der Malerei und Poesie*. Berlin, 1766. Trans. Edward Allen McCormick. Indianapolis: Bobbs Merrill, 1962.

MacIntyre, Bruce C. *The Viennese Concerted Mass of the Early Classic Period*. Ann Arbor: UMI Research Press, 1986.

Magazin der Musik. Ed. Carl Friedrich Cramer. Hamburg, 1783–87.

Marpurg, Friedrich Wilhelm, ed. *Der Critische Musikus an der Spree*. Berlin, 1749–50.

Marx, Adolf Bernhard. *Ludwig van Beethoven: Leben und Schaffen*. 2 vols. Berlin: Otto Janke, 1859.

Musical Form in the Age of Beethoven: Selected Writings on Theory and Method. Trans. and ed. Scott Burnham. Cambridge: Cambridge University Press, 1997.

Marx-Weber, Magda. "'Musiche per le tre ore di agonia de N.S.G.C.': Eine italienische Karfreitagsandacht im späten 18. und frühen 19. Jahrhundert." *Die Musikforschung* 33 (1980): 136–60.

Massow, Albrecht von. "Programmusik." In Hans Heinrich Eggebrecht and Albrecht Riethmüller, eds., *Handwörterbuch der musikalischen Terminologie*. Stuttgart: Steiner, 1992.

McNeill, William H. *Keeping Together in Time: Dance and Drill in Human History*. Cambridge, MA: Harvard University Press, 1995.

McVeigh, Simon. *Concert Life in London from Mozart to Haydn*. Cambridge: Cambridge University Press, 1993.

Melton, James Van Horn. *Absolutism and the Eighteenth-Century Origins of Compulsory Schooling in Prussia and Austria*. Cambridge: Cambridge University Press, 1988.

Millen, Ronald Forsyth and Robert Erich Wolf. *Heroic Deeds and Mystic Figures: A New Reading of Rubens' "Life of Maria de' Medici."* Princeton: Princeton University Press, 1989.

Momigny, Jérôme-Joseph de. *Cours complet d'harmonie et de composition, d'après une théorie nouvelle et générale de la musique*. 3 vols. Paris, 1803–05.

Mongrédien, Jean. *French Music from the Enlightenment to Romanticism 1789–1830*. Trans. Sylvain Frémaux. Portland: Amadeus, 1996.

Morrow, Mary Sue. *Concert Life in Haydn's Vienna: Aspects of a Developing Musical and Social Institution*. Stuyvesant, NY: Pendragon, 1989.

German Music Criticism in the Late Eighteenth Century: Aesthetic Issues in Instrumental Music. Cambridge: Cambridge University Press, 1997.

Mozart: Briefe und Aufzeichnungen. *Gesamtausgabe*. 7 vols. Ed. W. A. Bauer, O. E. Deutsch, and J. H. Eibl. Kassel: Bärenreiter, 1962–75.

Musikalische Realzeitung. Ed. Heinrich Philipp Boßler and Johann Friedrich Christmann. Speyer, 1788–90. Continued as *Musikalische Korrespondenz der Teutschen Filharmonischen Gesellschaft*. Speyer, 1790–92.

Musikalischer Almanach für Deutschland. Ed. Johann Nikolaus Forkel. Leipzig, 1782–89.

Musikalisches Kunstmagazin. Ed. Johann Friedrich Reichardt. Berlin, 1782 and 1791.

Musikalisches Taschenbuch. Ed. J. Werden [J. G. Winzer], A. Werden [F. T. Mann], and W. Schneider. Penig, 1803 and 1805.

Neubauer, John. *The Emancipation of Music from Language: Departure from Mimesis in Eighteenth-Century Aesthetics*. New Haven: Yale University Press, 1986.

Newman, Ernest. "Programme Music." In *Musical Studies*, 2nd edn., 103–86. London: Lane, 1910.

Niecks, Frederick. *Programme Music in the Last Four Centuries: A Contribution to the History of Musical Expression*. London: Novello, 1906.

Nisbet, H. B., ed. *German Aesthetic and Literary Criticism: Winckelmann, Lessing, Hamann, Herder, Schiller, Goethe*. Cambridge: Cambridge University Press, 1985.

Norton, Robert E. *The Beautiful Soul: Aesthetic Morality in the Eighteenth Century*. Ithaca: Cornell University Press, 1995.

Bibliography

Nottebohm, Gustav. *Beethoveniana*. Leipzig: C. F. Peters, 1872.

Ludwig van Beethoven: Thematisches Verzeichnis von Gustav Nottebohm nebst der Bibliotheca Beethoveniana von Emerich Kastner, ergänzt von Theodor Frimmel. Wiesbaden: Sändig, 1969.

Zweite Beethoveniana. Leipzig, 1887.

Noverre, Jean-Georges. *Lettres sur la danse, et sur les ballets*. Stuttgart, 1760.

Ozouf, Mona. *Festivals and the French Revolution*. Trans. Alan Sheridan. Cambridge, MA: Harvard University Press, 1988.

Palisca, Claude V. "French Revolutionary Models for Beethoven's *Eroica* Funeral March." In Anne Dhu Shapiro, ed., *Music and Context: Essays for John M. Ward*, 198–209. Cambridge, MA: Harvard University Department of Music, 1985.

Palm, Albert. "Mozarts Streichquartett D-moll, KV 421, in der Interpretation Momignys." *Mozart-Jahrbuch* (1962–63), 256–79.

"Unbekannte Haydn-Analysen." *Haydn Yearbook* 4 (1968): 169–94.

Pauly, Reinhard. "The Reforms of Church Music under Joseph II." *Musical Quarterly* 43 (1957): 372–82.

Poggioli, Renato. *The Oaten Flute: Essays on Pastoral Poetry and the Pastoral Ideal*. Cambridge, MA: Harvard University Press, 1975.

Pohl, Carl Ferdinand. *Joseph Haydn*. 2 vols. Leipzig: Breitkopf und Härtel, 1878–82.

Prendergast, Christopher. *Napoleon and History Painting: Antoine-Jean Gros's "La Bataille d'Eylau."* Oxford: Clarendon Press, 1997.

Prod'homme, J.-G. *Les Symphonies de Beethoven*. 4th edn. Paris: Delagrave, 1906.

Rambach, Johann Jacob. *Betrachtungen über die sieben letzten Worte des gecreuzigten Jesu*. Halle, 1726.

Ratner, Leonard. *Classic Music: Expression, Form, and Style*. New York: Schirmer, 1980.

Reichart, Sarah Bennett. "The Influence of Eighteenth-Century Social Dance on the Viennese Classical Style." Ph.D. diss., City University of New York, 1984.

Rice, John. "New Light on Dittersdorf's Ovid Symphonies." *Studi musicali* 29 (2000): 453–98.

Richter, Jean Paul. *Vorschule der Aesthetik*. Hamburg, 1804. Trans. Margaret Hale as *Horn of Oberon: Jean Paul Richter's School for Aesthetics*. Detroit: Wayne State University Press, 1973.

Richter, Simon. "Sculpture, Music, Text: Winckelmann, Herder, and Gluck's *Iphigénie en Tauride*." *Goethe Yearbook* 8 (1996): 157–71.

Riedel, Friedrich W. "Die Trauerkompositionen von Joseph Martin Kraus: Ihre geistes- und musikgeschichtliche Stellung." In Riedel, ed., *Joseph Martin Kraus in seiner Zeit*, 154–69. Munich: Katzbichler, 1982.

Riepel, Joseph. *Anfangsgründe zur musikalischen Setzkunst*. Vol. II, *Grundregeln zur Tonordnung insgemein*. Frankfurt and Leipzig, 1755.

Ries, Ferdinand, and Franz Gerhard Wegeler. *Biographische Notizen über Ludwig van Beethoven*. Coblenz: K. Bädeker, 1838.

Riethmüller, Albrecht. "*Wellingtons Sieg* op. 91." In *Beethoven: Interpretationen seiner Werke*, II: 34–45.

Riethmüller, Albrecht, Carl Dahlhaus, and Alexander L. Ringer, eds. *Beethoven: Interpretationen seiner Werke*. 2 vols. Laaber: Laaber-Verlag, 1994.

Riggs, Robert. " 'On the Representation of Character in Music': Christian Gottfried Körner's Aesthetics of Instrumental Music." *Musical Quarterly* 81 (1997): 599–631.

Ringer, Alexander L. *The "Chasse": Historical and Analytical Bibliography of a Musical Genre*. Ph.D. diss., Columbia University, 1955.

Röder, Thomas. "Beethovens Sieg über die Schlachtenmusik: Opus 91 und die Tradition der Battaglia." In Helga Lühning and Sieghard Brandenburg, eds., *Beethoven zwischen Revolution und Restauration*, 229–58. Bonn: Beethoven-Haus, 1989.

Rosen, Charles. *Sonata Forms*. Rev. edn. New York: Norton, 1988.

Ruiter, Jacob de. *Der Charakterbegriff in der Musik. Studien zur deutschen Ästhetik der Instrumentalmusik 1740–1850*. Beihefte zum Archiv für Musikwissenschaft 29. Stuttgart: Steiner, 1989.

Russell, Gillian. *The Theatres of War: Performance, Politics, and Society, 1793–1815*. Oxford: Clarendon Press, 1995.

Sandberger, Adolf. *Ausgewählte Aufsätze zur Musikgeschichte*. 2 vols. Munich: Drei Masken, 1921–24.

Schachter, Carl. "The Triad as Place and Action." *Music Theory Spectrum* 17 (1995), 149–69.

Schauffler, Robert Haven. *Beethoven: The Man Who Freed Music*. 2 vols. Garden City, NJ, and New York: Doubleday, 1929.

Schenker, Heinrich. *The Masterwork in Music: A Yearbook*. Vol. III (1930). Trans. Ian Bent, Alfred Clayton, and Derrick Puffett, ed. William Drabkin. Cambridge: Cambridge University Press, 1997.

Schering, Arnold. *Musikgeschichte Leipzigs*. Vol. III, *Johann Sebastian Bach und das Musikleben Leipzigs im 18. Jahrhundert*. Leipzig: Fr. Kistner & C. F. W. Siegel, 1941.

Schindler, Anton. *Biographie von Ludwig van Beethoven*. 3rd edn. Münster: Aschendorff, 1860.

Schmenner, Roland. *Die Pastorale: Beethoven, das Gewitter und der Blitzableiter*. Kassel: Bärenreiter, 1998.

Schmidt, Hans. "Die Beethovenhandschriften des Beethovenhauses in Bonn." *Beethoven-Jahrbuch* 7 (1969/70): 1–443.

Schnaus, Peter. *E. T. A. Hoffmann als Beethoven-Rezensent der Allgemeinen musikalischen Zeitung*. Munich: Katzbichler, 1977.

Schneider, Hans. *Der Musikverleger Heinrich Philipp Boßler 1744–1812*. Tutzing: Schneider, 1985.

Schroeder, David P. *Haydn and the Enlightenment: The Late Symphonies and their Audience*. Oxford: Clarendon Press, 1990.

Schulin, Karin. *Musikalische Schlachtengemälde in der Zeit von 1756 bis 1815*. Tutzing: Schneider, 1986.

Schwartz, Judith L. "Periodicity and Passion in the First Movement of Haydn's 'Farewell' Symphony." In Eugene K. Wolf and Edward H. Roesner, eds., *Studies in Musical Sources and Style: Essays in Honor of Jan LaRue*, 293–338. Madison: A-R Editions, 1990.

Seifert, Wolfgang. *Christian Gottfried Körner, ein Musikästhetiker der deutschen Klassik*. Regensburg: Bosse, 1960.

Semmel, Stuart. "Reading the Tangible Past: British Tourism, Collecting, and Memory after Waterloo." *Representations* 29 (2000): 9–37.

Shaw's Music: The Complete Musical Criticism of Bernard Shaw. 2nd rev. edn. 3 vols. Ed. Dan H. Laurence. London: Bodley Head, 1989.

Simms, Brendan. *The Struggle for Mastery in Germany, 1779–1850*. New York: St. Martin's, 1998.

Sipe, Thomas. *Beethoven: "Eroica Symphony."* Cambridge Music Handbook. Cambridge: Cambridge University Press, 1998.

Sisman, Elaine R. "Haydn's Theater Symphonies." *Journal of the American Musicological Society* 43 (1990): 292–352.

Mozart: The "Jupiter" Symphony No. 41 in C major, K. 551. Cambridge Music Handbook. Cambridge: Cambridge University Press, 1993.

Sisman, Elaine R., ed. *Haydn and His World*. Princeton: Princeton University Press, 1997.

Smither, Howard E. *A History of the Oratorio*. Vol. III, *The Oratorio in the Classical Era*. Chapel Hill: University of North Carolina Press, 1987.

Solomon, Maynard. *Beethoven*. 2nd rev. edn. New York: Schirmer, 1998.

Spitzer, John. "Metaphors of the Orchestra – The Orchestra as a Metaphor." *Musical Quarterly* 80 (1996): 234–64.

Statham, H. Heathcote. *My Thoughts on Music and Musicians*. London: Chapman and Hall, 1892.

Steinbeck, Wolfram. "6. Symphonie F-Dur Pastorale op. 68." In *Beethoven: Interpretationen seiner Werke*, I: 503–15.

Stevenson, Robert. "Haydn's Iberian World Connections." *Inter-American Music Review* 4/2 (1982): 3–30.

Studien für Tonkünstler und Musikfreunde. Ed. Johann Friedrich Reichardt and Friedrich Ludwig Aemilius Kunzen. Berlin, 1793.

Sulzer, Johann Georg. *Allgemeine Theorie der schönen Künste*. 2nd expanded edn. 4 vols. Leipzig, 1792–94.

Szabo, Frank A. J. *Kaunitz and Enlightened Absolutism 1753–1780*. Cambridge: Cambridge University Press, 1994.

Thayer, Alexander Wheelock. *Thayer's Life of Beethoven*. Rev. edn. 2 vols. Ed. Elliot Forbes. Princeton: Princeton University Press, 1967.

Thomas, Downing A. *Music and the Origins of Language: Theories from the French Enlightenment*. Cambridge: Cambridge University Press, 1995.

Tovey, Donald Francis. *Beethoven*. London: Oxford University Press, 1945.

Essays in Musical Analysis, 6 vols. London: Oxford University Press, 1935–39.

Essays and Lectures on Music. London: Oxford University Press, 1949.

Musical Articles from the Encyclopaedia Britannica. London: Oxford University Press, 1944.

Treitler, Leo, gen. ed. *Source Readings in Music History*. Rev. edn. New York: Norton, 1998.

Türk, Daniel Gottlob. *Klavierschule*. Leipzig and Halle, 1789.

Von den wichtigsten Pflichten eines Organisten. Halle, 1787.

van Boer, Bertil H., Jr. *Dramatic Cohesion in the Music of Joseph Martin Kraus: From Sacred Music to Symphonic Form*. Lewiston, Lampeter, and Queenston: Edwin Mellen, 1989.

Vogler, Georg Joseph, ed. *Betrachtungen der Mannheimer Tonschule.* 3 vols. Mannheim, 1778–81.

Wackenroder, Wilhelm Heinrich. *Sämtliche Werke und Briefe.* Ed. Silvio Vietta and Richard Littlejohns. 2 vols. Heidelberg: Carl Winter Universitätsverlag, 1991.

Wilhelm Heinrich Wackenroder's Confessions and Fantasies. Trans. Mary Hurst Schubert. University Park: Pennsylvania State University Press, 1971.

Waldvogel, Nicolas Henri. "The Eighteenth-Century Esthetics of the Sublime and the Valuation of the Symphony." Ph.D. diss., Yale University, 1992.

Wallace, Robin. *Beethoven's Critics: Aesthetic Dilemmas and Resolutions During the Composer's Lifetime.* Cambridge: Cambridge University Press, 1986.

Wallace, William. "The Scope of Programme Music." *Proceedings of the Royal Musical Association,* Session 25 (1898–99): 139–56.

Walter, Horst. "Über Haydns 'charakteristische' Sinfonien." In Gerhard J. Winkler, ed., *Das symphonische Werk Joseph Haydns,* 65–78. Eisenstadt: Burgenländisches Landesmuseum, 2000.

Wangermann, Ernst. "Josephinismus and katholischer Glaube." In Kovács, ed., *Katholische Aufklärung und Josephinismus,* 332–41.

"Reform Catholicism and Political Radicalism in the Austrian Enlightenment." In Roy Porter and Mikulás Teich, eds., *The Enlightenment in National Context,* 127–40. Cambridge: Cambridge University Press, 1981.

Weber, William. "Did People Listen in the 18th Century?" *Early Music* 25 (1997): 678–91.

Webster, James. *Haydn's "Farewell" Symphony and the Idea of Classical Style.* Cambridge: Cambridge University Press, 1991.

Weiss, Piero, and Richard Taruskin, eds. *Music in the Western World: A History in Documents.* New York: Schirmer, 1984.

Wieland, Christoph Martin. "Versuch über das Deutsche Singspiel und einige dahin einschlagende Gegenstände." *Der Teutsche Merkur* (1775). Reprint. *Sämmtliche Werke,* vol. XXVI, 299–342. Leipzig, 1796.

Will, Richard. "Programmatic Symphonies of the Classical Period." Ph.D. diss., Cornell University, 1994.

"Time, Morality, and Humanity in Beethoven's *Pastoral* Symphony." *Journal of the American Musicological Society* 50 (1997): 271–329.

"When God Met the Sinner, and Other Dramatic Confrontations in Eighteenth-Century Instrumental Music." *Music & Letters* 78 (1997): 175–209.

Winckelmann, Johann. *Gedancken über die Nachahmung der Griechischen Wercke in der Mahlerey und Bildhauer-Kunst.* Friedrichstadt, 1755. Repr. in Helmut Pfotenhauer, Markus Bernauer, and Norbert Miller, eds., *Frühklassizismus: Position und Opposition: Winckelmann, Mengs, Heinse.* Frankfurt am Main: Deutscher Klassiker Verlag, 1995.

Winn, James Anderson. *Unsuspected Eloquence: A History of the Relations between Poetry and Music.* New Haven: Yale University Press, 1981.

Winter, Eduard. *Der Josefinismus: Die Geschichte des österreichischen Reformkatholizismus 1740–1848.* Berlin: Rütten & Loening, 1962.

Bibliography

Wiora, Walter. *Das musikalische Kunstwerk*. Tutzing: Schneider, 1983.

Wolf, Ernst Wilhelm. *Musikalischer Unterricht für Liebhaber und diejenigen, welche die Musik treiben und lehren wollen*. 2 vols. Dresden, 1788.

Wolf, Eugene K. "The Mannheim Court." In Neal Zaslaw, ed., *The Classical Era: From the 1740s to the End of the 18th Century*, 213–39. London: Macmillan, 1989.

The Symphonies of Johann Stamitz: A Study in the Formation of the Classic Style. Utrecht and Antwerp: Bohn, Scheltema and Holkema, 1981.

Wolfsgruber, Cölestin. *Christoph Anton Kardinal Migazzi, Fürsterzbischof von Wien*. Saulgau: Kitz, 1890.

Zaslaw, Neal. "Mozart, Haydn, and the *Sinfonia da chiesa*." *Journal of Musicology* 1 (1982): 95–124.

Mozart's Symphonies: Context, Performance Practice, Reception. Oxford: Clarendon Press, 1989.

INDEX

affect, *see* character; expression of emotion

Angiolini, Gasparo, 53

Arietta, Francesco, 294

Artaria (publisher), 54

associative listening, *see* listening, associative

Austrian empire, 2–3
  political reform in, 30, 79–82
  religious reform in, *see* Reform Catholicism
  wars of, 5–6, 79–80, 82, 190–91, 200–01, 205–07, 230, 237–39
  see also Franz III; Joseph II; Maria Theresa

Aventures de Télémaque, Les, see Raimondi, Ignazio

Avison, Charles, 131, 132, 134

Bach, Carl Philipp Emanuel
  reception of, 11, 14–15
  WORKS
  Die Auferstehung und Himmelfahrt Jesu, 116
  character pieces for keyboard, 4, 62
  Heilig, 116–17

Bach, Johann Christian, 300

Bach, Johann Sebastian, 99, 109

Bakhtin, Mikhail, 175

ballet
  and associative listening, 11
  ballet d'action, 7, 52–54, 65
  use of programs in, 7, 138 n. 24
  see also dance rhythms; Gluck; *Metamorphoses* Symphonies; Noverre

Banier, L'Abbé, 33, 78

Barth, Karl, 118

Batteux, Charles, 130

battle pieces, 1, 6, 59, 149, 190–91
  in Dittersdorf's *Metamorphoses*, 67–68, 76–78
  see also battle symphonies; march rhythms; military music

battle symphonies, 1, 2, 9, 17, 24, 26–27, 190–209, 229–33, 237–39
  celebration in, 229–33, 237–39
  and commemoration, 26–27, 188–90, 229, 238–39
  dances in, 193–94, 230–33
  form of, **192**, 198–99
  historical accuracy of, 191, 205–06
  index of, 301–02
  and nationalism, 237–39
  performance of, 191, 196, 199–200, 216, 237–38
  physical effort in, 199–200
  mourning in, 200, 205
  representation of community in, 193–94, 229–33, 237–39
  representation of individual in, 200–09
  songs in, 193–94, 199, 230–31, 237–38
  and the sublime, 197–99
  volume of, 196–97

Bavarian Succession, War of the, 79–80

Beecke, Ignaz von, 167, 249, 294, 300
  Sinfonia di caccia, 58–59, 167, 249, 299

Beethoven, Ludwig van
  Egmont Overture, 239
  Der glorreiche Augenblick, 238
  Leonore Overture No. 1, 6
  Prometheus, 165
  Sonata, op. 81a, "Les Adieux," 6
  Symphonies
    No. 3, *see Eroica* Symphony
    No. 5, 156, 186
    No. 6, *see Pastoral* Symphony
    No. 9, 211
  Wellington's Victory, 1, 196, 200, 210, 215, 237, 301
    form of, **192**
    reception of, 230–31, 239
    "Schlacht," **194–96, 197–98**
    "Sieges–Sinfonie," **230–31**

Benda, Georg
  Ariadne auf Naxos, 6

Index

Index

Index

325

Index

Index

Index

Wineberger, Paul
  Symphony in A (Murray A1, with
    hunt), 58, 290–91, 300
Winter, Peter
  Schlacht-Sinfonie, 193, 196, 199, 230, 237,
    238, 239, 291, 302
Witt, Friedrich, 191 n. 10, 291, 301
*Wöchentliche Wahrheiten für und über die
  Prediger in Wien*, 99, 110
Wordsworth, William, 26
  "Michael," 176–77
Wranitzky, Anton, 291–92
  Aphrodite, 30, 75, 157, **158–60**, 161,
    166, 169, 170, 175, 291–92,
    303
  Symphony in D, 170, 292, 303

Wranitzky, Paul, 292–93, 300, 301
  *Grande Sinfonie caractéristique pour la paix
    avec la République françoise*, 5–6, 9
    n. 29, 30, 157, 166 n. 19, 169, 170,
    205–09, 292, 303
  and Beethoven's *Eroica*, 210, 211, 213,
    215
  text of, 206
  first movement, **207–09**
  second movement, 225
  finale, 230, 232–35, 236

Zach, Jan, 298
Zechner, Johann Georg, 298
Zelter, Carl Friedrich, 145–49, 150
Zimmermann, Anton, 293, 298, 299

329